CHINESE AND GLOBAL FINANCIAL INTEGRATION THROUGH STOCK CONNECT

This significant and timely book explores a novel market mechanism, Stock Connect, which gives mutual market access to Chinese and international investors, and provides original analyses and fresh insights. This mechanism could become the new normal in future global financial integration.

By examining this cross-border scheme from a regulatory perspective via a three-tiered analytical framework (investors, issuers and regulators), this book unearths the profound implications of Stock Connect to local and global financial markets and the legal impediments to its implementation. It covers a broad range of topics in this cross-boundary investment channel, including an overview of four existing connectivity arrangements (Shanghai–Hong Kong, Shenzhen–Hong Kong, Shanghai–London and China–Switzerland), the uniqueness of these connectivity arrangements, investor protection, regulations of connect issuers, regulatory cooperation and enforcement, the impacts on local and global financial markets, the implications for the world market connectivity as well as the challenges and future of Stock Connect.

This pioneering study will appeal to a broad range of readers who are interested in the ongoing reshaping of international financial systems and China's emerging influence in the international financial order.

Hart Studies in Commercial and Financial Law: Volume 11

Hart Studies in Commercial and Financial Law
Series Editors: John Linarelli and Teresa Rodríguez de las Heras Ballell

This series offers a venue for publishing works on commercial law as well as on the regulation of banking and finance and the law on insolvency and bankruptcy. It publishes works on the law on secured credit, the regulatory and transactional aspects of banking and finance, the transactional and regulatory institutions for financial markets, legal and policy aspects associated with access to commercial and consumer credit, new generation subjects having to do with the institutional architecture associated with innovation and the digital economy including works on blockchain technology, work on the relationship of law to economic growth, the harmonisation or unification of commercial law, transnational commercial law, and the global financial order. The series promotes interdisciplinary work. It publishes research on the law using the methods of empirical legal studies, behavioural economics, political economy, normative welfare economics, law and society inquiry, socio-legal studies, political theory, and historical methods. Its coverage includes international and comparative investigations of areas of law within its remit.

Volume 1: The Financialisation of the Citizen: Social and Financial Inclusion through European Private Law
Guido Comparato

Volume 2: MiFID II and Private Law: Enforcing EU Conduct of Business Rules
Federico Della Negra

Volume 3: Reforming Corporate Retail Investor Protection: Regulating to Avert Mis-Selling
Diane Bugeja

Volume 4: The Future of Commercial Law: Ways Forward for Change and Reform
Edited by Orkun Akseli and John Linarelli

Volume 5: The Cape Town Convention: A Documentary History
Anton Didenko

Volume 6: Regulating the Crypto Economy: Business Transformations and Financialisation
Iris H-Y Chiu

Volume 7: The Future of High-Cost Credit: Rethinking Payday Lending
Jodi Gardner

Volume 8: The Enforcement of EU Financial Law
Edited by Jan Crijns, Matthias Haentjens and Rijnhard Haentjens

Volume 9: International Bank Crisis Management: A Transatlantic Perspective
Marco Bodellini

Volume 10: Creditor Priority in European Bank Insolvency Law: Financial Stability and the Hierarchy of Claims
Sjur Swensen Ellingsæter

Volume 11: Chinese and Global Financial Integration through Stock Connect: A Legal Analysis
Flora Huang

Chinese and Global Financial Integration through Stock Connect

A Legal Analysis

Flora Huang

• HART •
OXFORD • LONDON • NEW YORK • NEW DELHI • SYDNEY

HART PUBLISHING

Bloomsbury Publishing Plc

Kemp House, Chawley Park, Cumnor Hill, Oxford, OX2 9PH, UK

1385 Broadway, New York, NY 10018, USA

29 Earlsfort Terrace, Dublin 2, Ireland

First published in Great Britain 2023

A catalogue record for this book is available from the British Library.

A catalogue record for this book is available from the Library of Congress.

Library of Congress Control Number: 2023940031

ISBN: HB: 978-1-50994-928-1
ePDF: 978-1-50994-930-4
ePub: 978-1-50994-929-8

Typeset by Compuscript Ltd, Shannon

PREFACE AND ACKNOWLEDGEMENTS

This book is based on the findings of my project entitled 'Stock Connect: A New Model of Financial Market Integration', which was funded by the British Academy Mid-Career Fellowship (2019–20, project ref.: MD19\190017). With the generous financial support of the funder, I visited the Shanghai Stock Exchange, the Shenzhen Stock Exchange, the Hong Kong Stock Exchange, Tsinghua University, Renmin University of China, China University of Political Science and Law, and DeHeng Law Firm (Shenzhen).

The book explores a novel market connectivity mechanism, Stock Connect, which gives mutual market access to Chinese and international investors, with original analyses and fresh insights. Such mechanism could become the new normal in future global financial integration. By examining this cross-border scheme from a regulatory perspective via a three-tiered analytical framework (investors, issuers and regulators), this book unearths the profound implications of Stock Connect for local and global financial markets and the legal impediments to its implementation. It covers a broad range of topics in this cross-boundary investment channel, including a comparison of four existing connectivity arrangements (Shanghai–Hong Kong, Shenzhen–Hong Kong, Shanghai–London and China–Switzerland), the uniqueness of these connectivity arrangements, investor protection, regulation of corporate issuers, regulatory cooperation and enforcement, the impacts on local and global financial markets, the implications for the world market connectivity, as well as the potential challenges and future of Stock Connect.

Valuable feedback and insights were obtained from esteemed academics, judges, legal and financial professionals, and securities regulators. In particular, the book benefited from discussion with Prof Peter Muchlinski, SOAS, University of London; Prof Ping He, Tsinghua University; Prof Junhai Liu, Renmin University; Assoc Prof Horace Yeung, Leicester University; Xian Tang, judge of the Supreme People's Court of China; Ping Lu and Zhou Chen from the Shanghai Stock Exchange; Peixian Sun and Zongyang Lu from the Shenzhen Stock Exchange; and lawyers such as Youchen LV, Qiyun Su and Jiangli Tu from DeHeng Law Firm.

I would also like to acknowledge the support of my previous and current home institutions, the Universities of Essex and Derby, especially for their generous academic study leave policy which allowed me to spend precious time in completing this project. Additionally, I would like to thank my colleagues and friends for their feedback on various parts of this book through different meetings, seminars, and conferences. Lastly, I am grateful to the team at Hart, particularly Roberta Bassi, Verity Stuart and Rosie Mearns for guiding me through various stages of the book production process.

The views and opinions expressed in this book are my own and do not reflect the positions of my home institutions, hosts in China, funders, or publisher. Any errors in the work remain my responsibility.

Flora Huang
February 2023

CONTENTS

LIST OF ABBREVIATIONS

ACMF	ASEAN Capital Markets Forum
AfCFTA	African Continental Free Trade Area
ASBE	Accounting Standard of the People's Republic of China for Business Enterprises
ASEA	African Securities Exchanges Association
ASEAN	Association of Southeast Asian Nations
AUM	Assets Under Management
BHB	Bahrain Bourse
BSE	Beijing Stock Exchange
CA	Companies Act
Cap	Chapter
CBIRC	China Banking and Insurance Regulatory Commission
CCASS	Central Clearing and Settlement System
CDR	Chinese Depository Receipt
CEPA	Closer Economic Partnership Arrangement
CFTC	Commodity Futures Trading Commission
CHF	Swiss Francs
CIBM	China Interbank Bond Market
CIS	Collective Investment Scheme
CO	Companies Ordinance
CSRC	China Securities Regulatory Commission
CT	Consolidated Tape
C(WUMP)O	Companies (Winding Up and Miscellaneous Provisions) Ordinance
DCS	Dual Class Shares

DR	Depository Receipt
DSM	Doha Securities Market
DTR	Disclosure Guidance and Transparency Rules
EAC	East African Community
EC	European Commission
ECOWAS	Economic Community of West African States
ESMA	European Securities and Markets Authority
ETF	Exchange-traded Fund
EU	European Union
FCA	Financial Conduct Authority
FCIL	Foreign Capital Investment Law
FinIA	Financial Institutions Act
FINMA	Swiss Financial Markets Supervisory Authority
FinMIA	Financial Market Infrastructure Act
FinSA	Financial Services Act
FinSO	Swiss Financial Services Ordinance
FS	Financial Secretary
FSA	Financial Services Authority
FSDC	Financial Services Development Council
FSMA	Financial Services and Markets Act
FTSE	Financial Times Stock Exchange
GBP	British Pound Sterling
GCC	Gulf Cooperation Council
GDP	Gross Domestic Product
GDR	Global Depository Receipt
GEM	Growth Enterprise Market
HKCC	HKFE Clearing Corporation Limited
HKD	Hong Kong Dollar
HKEX	Hong Kong Exchanges and Clearing Limited

HKFE	Hong Kong Futures Exchange Limited
HKLR	Hong Kong Listing Rules
HKMA	Hong Kong Monetary Authority
HKSCC	Hong Kong Securities Clearing Company Limited
HSLI	Hang Seng Composite LargeCap Index
HSMI	Hang Seng Composite MidCap Index
HSSI	Hang Seng Composite SmallCap Index
IA	Insurance Authority of Hong Kong
IMF	International Monetary Fund
IOSCO	International Organization of Securities Commissions
IPO	Initial Public Offering
KSE	Kuwait Stock Exchange
LR	Listing Rule(s)
LSE	London Stock Exchange
MAR	Market Abuse Regulation
MENA	Middle East and North Africa
MiFID	Markets in Financial Instruments Directive
MMoU	Multilateral Memorandum of Understanding
MOF	Ministry of Finance
MORC	Memorandum of Regulatory Co-operation
MoU	Memorandum of Understanding
MPFA	Mandatory Provident Fund Schemes Authority of Hong Kong
MSCI	Morgan Stanley Capital International
MTF	Multilateral Trade Facilities
NBBO	National Best Bid and Offer
NCA	National Competent Authority
NEEQ	National Equities Exchange and Quotation System
NMS	National Market System
NYSE	New York Stock Exchange

OECD	Organisation for Economic Co-operation and Development
OTC	Over-the-counter
OTF	Organised Trading Facility
PACOB	Public Company Accounting Oversight Board
PBOC	People's Bank of China
PRA	Prudential Regulation Authority
PRD	Pearl River Delta
QDII	Qualified Domestic Institutional Investor
QFI	Qualified Foreign Investor
QFII	Qualified Foreign Institutional Investor
Reg NMS	Regulation National Market System
RQDII	RMB Qualified Domestic Institutional Investor
RQFII	RMB Qualified Foreign Institutional Investor
RM	Regulated Market
RMB	Renminbi
SAFE	State Administration of Foreign Exchange
SAR	Special Administrative Region
SCSC	State Council Securities Committee of China
SEC	Securities and Exchange Commission
SEOCH	SEHK Options Clearing House Limited
SEHK	Stock Exchange of Hong Kong
SFC	Securities and Futures Commission
SFCO	Swiss Federal Code of Obligations
SFO	Securities and Futures Ordinance
SIP	Securities Information Processors
SME	Small and Medium-sized Enterprises
SMLR	Securities and Futures (Stock Market Listing) Rules
SOE	State-owned Enterprise
SPC	Supreme People's Court

SRC	Securities Review Committee
SSE	Shanghai Stock Exchange
SSLR	SIX Swiss Listing Rules
STAR	Science and Technology Innovation Board
SZSE	Shenzhen Stock Exchange
UAE	United Arab Emirates
UKLA	UK Listing Authority
UKLR	UK Listing Rules
USD	United States Dollar
WACMIC	West African Capital Markets Integration Council
WFOE	Wholly Foreign Owned Enterprise
WVR	Weighted Voting Right

LIST OF TABLES AND FIGURES

LIST OF CASES

Cases and Administrative Sanctions

United Kingdom

China and Hong Kong

LIST OF LAWS AND LEGAL INSTRUMENTS

EU

Hong Kong

Kuwait

New Zealand

Oman

Qatar

Saudi Arabia

Switzerland

UAE

United Kingdom

United States

Bilateral or International Agreements

Mainland China–Hong Kong

1

Introduction

As the world's second largest economy, China has gradually established and developed its financial markets to become more liberalised. On 10 April 2014, the China Securities Regulatory Commission (CSRC, the regulator on the Mainland side) and the Securities and Futures Commission (SFC, the regulator on the Hong Kong side) approved the development of a pilot programme to establish mutual market access between Mainland China's exchanges and Hong Kong Exchanges and Clearing Limited (HKEX).[1] As a result, Shanghai–Hong Kong Stock Connect and Shenzhen–Hong Kong Stock Connect were officially launched on 17 November 2014 and 5 December 2016 respectively. Later, Stock Connect was expanded to include Shanghai–London Stock Connect in June 2019 and China–Switzerland Stock Connect in July 2022.

Stock Connect represents Beijing's most recent opening-up effort and has quickly become the dominant cross-boundary investment channel connecting Chinese and international markets. It is a mutual market access programme that allows investors from Mainland China and international markets to trade eligible stocks listed on each other's stock exchanges through a cross-border trading link. Under Stock Connect, investors can buy and sell shares in designated companies listed on the participant stock exchanges. The programme also enables foreign investors to trade Chinese A-shares, which are stocks of Mainland China-based companies traded on the Shanghai and Shenzhen stock exchanges.

Stock Connect is a unique mechanism in China that has introduced a number of 'firsts'. It is the first time that foreign companies are effectively allowed to list in China, and the first time for Chinese and international investors to invest directly in designated securities listed in each other's market. On the one hand, it is viewed as an important landmark for China's financial liberalisation process and the internationalisation of the Chinese currency, Renminbi (RMB). While pre-existing schemes in China, such as the Qualified Foreign Institutional Investor (QFII) and Qualified Domestic Institutional Investor (QDII) schemes, focus on one-way flows, Stock Connect relaxes restrictions on capital flows in both directions and promotes RMB investment and settlement in foreign exchange transactions. On the other hand, Stock Connect provides international investors with greater access to Chinese stocks, which can help diversify their portfolios and provide exposure to one of the world's fastest-growing economies. Prior to the Stock Connect

[1] In this book, China or Mainland China refers to the People's Republic of China, as opposed to the Hong Kong Special Administrative Region (SAR).

programme, investing in Chinese stocks could be complicated and difficult for international investors. Stock Connect simplifies the process by allowing investors to trade eligible stocks listed on each other's stock exchanges through a cross-border trading link.

This introductory chapter sets out the objectives of the book, and examines the theoretical foundations on stock market integration and the mechanisms for such integration. Afterwards, it provides a chapter-by-chapter outline to flesh out the structure of whole book.

1.1. Objectives of the Book

Despite the frequent featuring of Stock Connect in newspapers and exchange reports, this scheme has not been adequately understood and studied, especially from a legal perspective. Most of the literature focuses on the economic analysis of Stock Connect while very little relates to the legal issues arising from such an emerging viable cross-border investment channel.[2] In particular, there have been significant legal and regulatory changes as well as developments since the launch of Stock Connect, for instance, the new Chinese Securities Law 2019,[3] the amended Stock Connect Rules, the new expansion of Stock Connect and many initiatives in regulatory cooperation and enforcement between China and other regulators. This timely and significant book fills in the literature gap by exploring the legal issues in Stock Connect and makes practical contributions to the existing analysis by appraising the successes and failures of this scheme as well as its implications for the local and global financial markets. It will be the first comprehensive research study and law monograph focused on Stock Connect.

The book thus aims to investigate to what extent Stock Connect promotes financial market integration and its consequences in light of the three-tiered regulation of investors, issuers and regulators, and discuss the barriers to its implementation as well as the implications to the global financial markets. The following research questions will be asked:

1. What differences exist between the four existing Connect links, and what is the uniqueness of Stock Connect compared to pre-existing Chinese

[2] Eg for price disparity, see MK Chan and S Kwok, 'Connecting the Markets? Recent Evidence on China's Capital Account Liberalisation' (2018) 70 *Economic Modelling* 417; for daily price co-movements, see S Li and Q Chen, 'Do the Shanghai–Hong Kong & Shenzhen–Hong Kong Stock Connect programs enhance co-movement between the Mainland Chinese, Hong Kong, and U.S. stock markets?' (2020) 26 *International Journal of Financial & Economics* 2871; for market liquidity, see Y Bai et al, 'Shanghai-Hong Kong Stock Connect: An Analysis of Chinese Partial Stock Market Liberalisation Impact on the Local and Foreign Markets' (2017) 50 *Journal of International Financial Markets, Institutions & Money* 182.

[3] The Chinese Securities Law was enacted on 29 December 1998, and then amended a few times in 2004, 2013, 2014, 2019. The current version was adopted on 28 December 2019 and came into effect on 1 March 2020.

liberalisation schemes and other market connectivity models in the rest of the world?
2. Does Stock Connect stimulate the reconciliation and integration of the financial regulations of four relevant jurisdictions (Mainland China, Hong Kong, the UK and Switzerland), and if so how?
3. How will cross-border investors and corporate issuers be regulated under Stock Connect? And how will cross-border enforcement issues or regulatory co-operation be dealt with between their regulators and the stock exchanges?
4. What are the impacts of Stock Connect on the local and global financial markets?

1.2. Theoretical Foundations of Stock Market Integration

According to Robson, 'Integration is taken to denote a state of affairs or a process involving attempts to combine separate national economies into larger economic regions'.[4] Integration as a means of stimulating trade and capital as well as improving the division of labour amongst countries has been recommended by many economists, from Ricardo on.[5] Traditionally, global financial markets were thought to be segmented owing to factors like regulatory barriers, taxes and information constraints.[6] The increasing process of economic globalisation and financial liberalisation makes international financial markets more interconnected than ever before. There also exists a heated debate in literature on the costs and benefits of financial market liberalisation. Many have argued that financial market openness can increase liquidity,[7] optimise capital allocation,[8] increase international financial linkage and increase the depth of stock markets.[9] However, others doubt the beneficial consequences of financial market openness as they believe it will cause high volatility and lead to increasing financial fragility and crises.[10]

[4] P Robson, *The Economics of International Integration* (London, Allen and Unwin, 1980), 1.

[5] U Koester, 'Market Integration: How it Works' in A Burrell and A Oskam (eds), *Agricultural Policy and Enlargement of the European Union* (Wageningen, Wageningen Pers, 2000). David Ricardo, economist (1772–1823).

[6] SR Foerster and GA Karolyi, 'The Effects of Market Segmentation and Investor Recognition on Asset Prices: Evidence from Foreign Stocks Listing in the United States' (1999) 54(3) *Journal of Finance* 981.

[7] HR Stoll, 'Future of Securities Markets: Consolidation or Competition?' (2008) 64(6) *Financial Analysts Journal* 15, 16.

[8] J Wurgler, 'Financial Markets and the Allocation of Capital' (2000) 58 *Journal of Financial Economics* 187, 189.

[9] Eg G Bekaert and CR Harvey, 'Emerging Equity Market Volatility' (1997) 43(1) *Journal of Financial Economics* 29.

[10] JE Stiglitz, 'Capital Market Liberalization, Economic Growth, and Instability' (2000) 28 *World Development* 1075; J Furman et al, 'Economic Crises: Evidence and Insights from East Asia' (1998) 29(2) *Brookings Papers on Economic Activity* 1.

Stock market integration is mainly based on the efficient market hypothesis, which suggests that markets incorporate all available information and adjust stock prices accordingly.[11] Other theoretical foundations include portfolio diversification,[12] which reduces risk by investing in multiple markets, and globalisation, which has led to increased cross-border capital flows and the emergence of global financial networks. The gravity model is also used to explain the degree of integration between markets, with factors such as economic size, distance, and trade playing a role.[13] The model is based on the principle that the flow of capital between two countries is proportional to their economic size and the distance between them. In other words, the greater the economic size of the two countries and the closer they are geographically, the more likely they are to engage in capital flows.

Stock markets can be linked in various ways such as cross-listing, international funds, or direct connection between trade-matching platforms.[14] Among these, the simplest way is cross-listing, that is, the listing of securities on an exchange outside of the issuer's home jurisdiction. Cross-listing can provide companies with access to larger pools of capital and more diverse investor bases, as well as increased visibility and improved corporate governance.[15] However, it can also increase regulatory burdens and compliance risks, as well as lead to market fragmentation and additional costs.[16] Another channel for linking markets is international funds whose unit-/share-holders are located in one jurisdiction but investing in securities listed on the other exchange(s). Investment funds can create multilateral linkages through the parent fund itself, or indirectly through subsidiary fund companies located in the respective jurisdictions where the investments are made. A third way of linking markets is direct market connectivity to provide access to, or replicate relevant parts of market mechanisms across jurisdictions. Direct market connectivity can be achieved by creating a single national securities market, in the case of the United States (US); or supranational treaty area, in the case of the European Union (EU); or providing mutual market access between bourses, in the case of China's Stock Connect.[17] The relative merits of different methods of linkage should be evaluated on the basis of the jurisdiction's stage of

[11] E Fama, 'Efficient Capital Markets: A Review of Theory and Empirical Work' (1970) 25(2) *Journal of Finance* 383.

[12] A Chari and PB Henry, 'Risk Sharing and Asset Prices: Evidence from a Natural Experiment' (2002) 59 *Journal of Finance* 1295.

[13] AD Rose and MM Spiegel, 'A Gravity Model of Sovereign Lending: Trade, Default, and Credit' (2004) *IMF Staff Papers, special issue vol 51.*

[14] DC Donald, 'Bridging Finance Without Fragmentation: A Comparative Look at Market Connectivity in the US, Europe and Asia' (2015) 16 *European Business Organisation Law Review* 173, 177–81.

[15] MR King and D Segal, 'The Long-Term Effects of Cross-Listing, Investor Recognition, and Ownership Structure on Valuation' (2009) 22(6) *Review of Financial Studies* 2393.

[16] For the regulatory competition debate, see J Coffee, 'Racing Towards the Top? The Impact of Cross-Listing and Stock Market Competition on International Corporate Governance' (2002) 102 *Columbia Law Review* 1757; and AN Licht, 'Cross-Listing and Corporate Governance: Bonding or Avoiding?' (2003) 4(1) *Chicago Journal of International Law* 141.

[17] T Boskovia, C Cerruti and M Noel, 'Comparing European and US Securities Regulations: MiFID versus Corresponding US Regulations' (2009), *World Bank Working Paper No 184*; and Donald (2015), see n 14 above.

technological development, market liquidity, efficiency and fairness to the constituencies using the markets.[18]

Apart from integrating world markets, there is an increasing tendency to create new regional integration schemes. The EU is one of the most prominent examples. In contrast to international trade, there is no single international organisation to provide governance for international capital markets. In part, this is because there are many different kinds of capital (and capital markets); thus, a central organisation would make little sense. However, just as important is the fact that the boundary between domestic and international capital markets has become so blurred that centralised international governance would require substantial transfers of sovereignty.

Harmonisation of investment services and activities has been a prominent topic since the US introduced its Regulation National Market System (Reg NMS) in 2004, and in the same year the EU introduced its Markets in Financial Instruments Directive (MiFID I), which was later revised by MiFID II in 2014. Financial markets in the US and Europe have evolved from fragmented structures comprising several independent exchanges and numerous trading systems to largely consolidated structures comprising the primary listing venues, regional exchanges and the over-the-counter (OTC) markets. These changes have been fuelled by an increase in computational capabilities, improvements in networking technologies and several regulatory initiatives like the Reg NMS in the US and the MiFID in the EU.[19] The change in market structure enables the entry of new players to attract trading volume from incumbent exchanges. This competition for order flows among various trading venues makes the market increasingly complex.

In contrast to these laws with a focus on how securities are offered and traded in fragmented markets – within the EU passport system or the US national marketplaces – China's Stock Connect aims to provide cross-border investors with direct access to trading on a real-time basis. Historically, there was very little interaction between onshore and offshore investors in China, with both of them restricted to their respective markets. Stock Connect has created a direct linkage between Chinese and other international exchanges in this regard. Whilst Stock Connect links up Chinese investors with international markets such as Hong Kong, the UK and Switzerland, there are considerable differences in terms of their transaction rules, laws and regulations, and regulatory systems.[20]

Coinciding with these changes in the competitive environment, a large body of academic literature debates whether trading is best consolidated into a single setting or dispersed across multiple venues.[21] Theoretical works arguing in favour

[18] DC Donald, 'Networked Securities Markets: From Cross-listing to Direct Connection' in DW Warner et al (eds), *Research Handbook on Asian Financial Law* (Cheltenham, Edward Elgar, 2020), 86.

[19] P Gomber et al, 'Competition between Equity Markets: A Review of the Consolidation versus Fragmentation Debate' (2016) 31(3) *Journal of Economic Surveys* 792, 792–93.

[20] F Huang, 'Stock Connect: Integration, Internationalisation and Implementation' (2021) 7 *Journal of Business Law* 558.

[21] For a review of the consolidation versus fragmentation debates, see Gomber et al (2016), see n 19 above.

of consolidation are based on the idea that exchanges are often viewed as natural monopolies due to the presence of network externalities and economies of scale.[22] On the supply side, a consolidated market enjoys economies of scale in processing transactions. Therefore, a dominant exchange has lower average costs than a satellite competitor using the same technology with a lower market share. On the demand side, as markets function like networks, the attractiveness of a market depends on the number of traders participating. The higher the number of traders, the higher is the probability of finding a counterparty. Consequently, network externalities will lead to 'first-mover advantages' so as to protect the market share of incumbent exchanges.[23]

As suggested by Petrella, a fragmented market will naturally consolidate when the two conditions are met: information about trades and quotes for each trading venue is available quickly and cheaply; and traders always seek the best conditions for executing their orders.[24] The first condition ensures that the resulting market prices quickly incorporate all available information, regardless of the venue where the last trade was executed. The second condition implies that, because of the order flow externality, a pool of liquidity will form in the most efficient trading venue. Pre-trade (ie quote-related) and post-trade (ie trade-related) transparency requirements set forth by regulation address the first condition, while the best execution provisions address the second one.

But consolidation has negative effects as well. In other words, fragmentation of order flow has also positive effects. As Stoll points out, 'The term fragmentation has a harmful connotation, but, in fact, fragmentation is just another word for competition'.[25] Competition across markets is positive because it fosters innovation. The key incentive to innovate is the profits from market power resulting from delivering a superior product or service to that of rivals. These profits are required to offset the costs of innovation.[26] The second positive effect of fragmentation is associated with heterogeneity in traders' preferences because no single venue seems to serve the interests of all investors.[27] This is because investors differ both with respect to their motivations to trade and the magnitude of their trading interests.

[22] Eg A Madhavan, 'Consolidation, Fragmentation, and the Disclosure of Trading Information' (1995) 8(3) *Review of Financial Studies* 579.

[23] G Petrella, 'MiFID, Reg NMS and Competition across Trading Venues in Europe and the USA' (2010) 18(3) *Journal of Financial Regulation and Compliance* 257, 259.

[24] ibid.

[25] H Stoll, 'Market Microstructure' in G Constantinides et al (eds), *Handbook of the Economics of Finance*, Vol 1A (Amsterdam, Elsevier, 2003).

[26] For the theoretical insights on competition and innovation, see the UK government, 'Competition and Innovation in Digital Markets' (2021), *BEIS Research Paper Number: 2021/040*, 12, available at: assets.publishing.service.gov.uk/government/uploads/system/uploads/attachment_data/file/1003985/uae-ccp-report__1_.pdf.

[27] LE Harris, 'Consolidation, Fragmentation, Segmentation, and Regulation' (1993) 48(3) *Journal of Finance* 1092; and B Biais and T Foucault, 'HFT and Market Quality' (2014) 128 *Bankers, Markets & Investors* 5.

Despite the theoretical debates, the empirical evidence is mixed regarding whether market quality is higher in a fragmented or consolidated market. Market quality, defined as liquidity and price efficiency, is positively associated with the ease of risk-sharing and the allocative efficiency of resources in the economy.[28] Thus high liquidity and high price efficiency are features of good markets. On the one hand, Bennett and Wei find that overall execution costs fall when the stocks move from trading on the fragmented Nasdaq market to the more consolidated New York Stock Exchange (NYSE).[29] Gajewski and Gresse show that trading costs in Europe are lower in a centralised order book than when orders are split between an order book and competing dealers.[30] On the other hand, some results confirm that fragmentation significantly improves market quality both in the US and Europe, with lower transaction costs and faster execution speed.[31] Liquidity, measured by depth, increased when trading expanded, supporting the notion that fragmentation of order flow can enhance the liquidity supply, but the specific effects of this fragmentation differ across firm sizes and listing venues.[32]

In summary, there has been an increasing number of studies globally on stock market integration and the debates between market fragmentation and consolidation. As observed by Raju and Pavto, the concept of stock market integration was initially popular among developed economies such as the US, the UK, the EU, and Australia.[33] However, following the Asian financial crisis in 1997 and the subprime global financial crisis in 2008, researchers shifted their focus towards emerging markets, especially those in Asia.[34] The research activities have mainly concentrated on identifying the degree of linkage among the markets but not the implications of those links.[35] Therefore, further research is necessary in this area to explore the factors that may affect the degree of integration among stock markets and the implications of stock market integration at the international level.

The increasing link between emerging markets and developed markets as a major channel of foreign investment will challenge and change the regulatory

[28] Gomber et al (2017), see n 19 above, 794.

[29] P Bennett and L Wei, 'Market Structure, Fragmentation, and Market Quality' (2006) 9(1) *Journal of Financial Markets* 49.

[30] JF Gajewski and C Gresse, 'Centralised Order Books versus Hybrid Order Books: A Paired Comparison of Trading Costs on NSC (Euronext Paris) and SETS (London Stock Exchange)' (2007) 31(9) *Journal of Banking & Finance* 2906.

[31] M Aitken et al, 'The Impact of Fragmentation, Exchange Fees and Liquidity Provision on Market Quality' (2017) 41 *Journal of Empirical Finance* 140; T Foucault and AJ Menkveld, 'Competition for order flow and smart order routing systems' (2008) 63(1) *Journal of Finance* 119.

[32] M O'Hara and M Ye, 'Is Market Fragmentation Harming Market Quality?' (2011) 100 *Journal of Financial Economics* 459.

[33] GA Raju and VS Pavto, 'Stock Market Integration: A Review of Literature from a Global Perspective' (2019) 25 (3) *Journal of Applied Finance* 66.

[34] Eg RW Click and MG Plummer, 'Stock Market Integration in ASEAN After the Asian Financial Crisis' (2005) 16(1) *Journal of Asian Economics* 5; L Wang, 'Who Moves East Asian Stock Markets? The Role of the 2007–2009 Global Financial Crisis' (2014) 28 *International Financial Markets, Institutions and Money* 182.

[35] A Sharma and N Seth, 'Literature Review of Stock Market Integration: A Global Perspective' (2012) 4(1) *Qualitative Research in Financial Markets* 84, 114.

landscape, given the inherent limitations in domestic regulations for unilaterally regulating transnational investments. Global and regional financial integration in the EU, Latin America, and Southeast Asia has been observed.[36] Although numerous studies have been conducted on Chinese financial liberalisation, there has been little investigation into the whole scheme of Stock Connect and its related implementation issues. This book aims to enrich the existing literature by adding a new link to connect the Eastern and Western financial markets, discussing the legal and enforcement issues involved in this cross-border investment channel, and exploring its implications for the global financial markets.

1.3. Chapter Outline

After the introductory Chapter one, Chapter two will provide an overview of the different stages of capital market development in China. Stock Connect is a part of the Chinese government's efforts to liberalise its capital markets and to connect them more closely with the rest of the world. Currently, Stock Connect consists of four different links: Shanghai–Hong Kong, Shenzhen–Hong Kong, Shanghai–London and China–Switzerland Stock Connect. Each Connect link shares some similarities but at the same time has its own characteristics. As such, this chapter will also cover the evolution and structure of these four Stock Connect links, as well as the differences between them and the uniqueness of Stock Connect as distinguished from pre-existing Chinese liberalisation schemes.

Chapters three to five will examine the three tiers of regulation of Stock Connect in relation to investors, issuers, and regulators, but with a clear understanding that these three tiers are not completely distinct from each other. Chapter three focuses on Connect investors. It starts by reviewing the literature on investor protection, including notable scholars such as La Porta and colleagues, who have long stressed the interplay between investor protection and the size of financial markets, despite its contentious nature.[37] As per the fundamental principle of Stock Connect – 'home market rules' – the applicable securities law and the rules of the home market shall apply to investors in such securities. In the scenario of international investors purchasing Chinese shares via Stock Connect, China is the home market and thus those investors should observe Chinese securities law

[36] Eg T Jappelli and M Pagano, 'Financial market Integration under EMU' (March 2008) *European Commission Economic Papers 312*; PR Lane et al, 'International Financial Integration in the Aftermath of the Global Financial Crisis' (2017), *IMF Working Paper WP/17/115*.

[37] The theory of 'law and finance' originated from a series of papers by R La Porta et al, 'Law and Finance' (1998) 106(6) *Journal of Political Economy* 1113; R La Porta et al, 'The New Comparative Economics' (2003) 31 *Journal of Comparative Economics* 595; R La Porta et al, 'The Economic Consequences of Legal Origins' (2008) 46 *Journal of Economic Literature* 285. For its counter arguments, see K Pistor, 'Rethinking the "Law and Finance" Paradigm' [2009] *BYU Law Review* 1647; and D Katelouzous and M Siems, 'Disappearing Paradigms in Shareholder Protection: Leximetric Evidence for 30 Countries, 1990–2013' (2015) 15 *Journal of Corporate Law Studies* 127.

and listing rules. Yet certain host market laws and rules may simultaneously apply. Conversely, Chinese investors who trade securities via the Hong Kong or London/Switzerland links are subject to the latter's laws. Thus, the protection of Connect investors covered by four different legal regimes, at a securities law level, will be thoroughly examined.

Chapter four moves on to the regulation of issuers under Stock Connect. Similarly to the preceding chapter, it examines the applicable legal regimes under the four different Connect links. The biggest difference between them lies in their market operation mechanisms (hence leading to legal differences). Under Shanghai/Shenzhen–Hong Kong Stock Connects, the investors on both sides directly buy and sell stocks in the market on the other side, with the investors crossing borders but the products still remaining local. Therefore, the fundamental principle of 'home market rules' is to apply in a direct sense, ie only the regulation of the home country (company law, securities law, listing rules and so on) applies. In contrast, under Shanghai–London Stock Connect and China–Switzerland Stock Connect, depository receipts converted from the stocks in the opposite market are listed and traded in the local market, with the products crossing the border but the investors still remaining local. Hence Chinese and British/Swiss issuers under this link are not only regulated by their home country's securities law, but also subject to the host country's listing rules, owing to the need to issue depository receipts in the host market. In summary, the necessity of regulation of issuers, and the similarities and differences between the four Connect links, at a company law and listing rules level, will be identified and discussed in this chapter.

Chapter five will start from discussing cross-border regulatory cooperation, which is of critical significance for effective oversight in transnational securities transactions. As the four participant jurisdictions are members of the International Organization of Securities Commissions (IOSCO), their regulators are subject to a widely used Multilateral Memorandum of Understanding (MMoU) for sharing information and mutual assistance. In addition, a few MoUs have been signed between China–Hong Kong and China–UK. But all these memoranda constitute more an expression of a desire to cooperate than a binding agreement. Considering their divergent jurisdictions, cross-border enforcement remains a thorny issue. Stock Connect, with an attempt to deepen and strengthen connectivity between China and other markets, may bring their regulators closer. This chapter discusses the patterns of their regulatory cooperation before and after Stock Connect. Empirical data such as enforcement-related requests for regulatory cooperation and selected securities cases (eg *Tang Hanbo vs the Securities and Futures Commission of Hong Kong*, the first Connect case) will also be brought in and analysed to highlight the enforcement difficulties arising from the complexity of this scheme.

Chapter six will evaluate the economic and regulatory impacts of Stock Connect in the context of four existing Connect markets and the global financial markets, drawn from quantitative and qualitative assessments. The Stock Connect scheme creates a single Chinese stock market that ranks the second biggest in the world (behind the US) in terms of market capitalisation and daily trading turnover. It not only helps diversify the portfolios of Chinese and international investors, but also increases the likelihood of further integrating China into the international financial system. Looking forward and more broadly, the underlying (both financial and legal) mechanisms can indeed be replicated by non-Chinese markets. The size and scale of the Stock Connect scheme (in both nominal and relative senses), and the related regulatory implications for the financial systems at both national and international levels will be a focus in this chapter.

Chapter seven will offer an analytical schema for understanding existing mechanisms for linking securities markets in the world (such as the US, EU, Asia, Africa and the Middle East), in addition to Stock Connect. The chapter will examine the different methods employed in the US National Market System (Reg NMS) and EU Market in Financial Instruments Directive (MiFID) projects, the Association of Southeast Asian Nations (ASEAN) Trading Link, the Intra-African Trade and Investment Union as well as Gulf Cooperation Council. It will also provide a comparative analysis of these market connectivity mechanisms to find out which is the best model for linking securities markets.

Chapter eight is the conclusion chapter that draws on all the important findings in previous chapters and makes a concluding assessment of the future of Stock Connect; for example, the extension of Connect to other securities and commodities, and to/between other foreign markets such as the US, Japan and Singapore, etc. It also takes into account the potential challenges from the geopolitics and tensions between China and the West over Stock Connect.

2

Chinese Capital Market Development and Stock Connect

This chapter will cover the liberalisation process of Chinese capital markets, examine the evolution of Stock Connect, and make a comparison between the four Stock Connect links. It will also highlight the uniqueness of Stock Connect in comparison to pre-existing Chinese liberalisation schemes.

2.1. Chinese Capital Market Development

China's economic reforms since the late 1970s gave birth to the emergence and development of domestic capital markets. Over several decades, China's capital markets have rapidly developed from the originally small and regional markets into a marketplace whose legal systems, trading rules and regulatory framework are increasingly aligned with international developed markets. The development of Chinese capital markets can be divided into four stages as follows.

2.1.1. Emergence of China's Capital Markets (1978–91)

Prior to 1978, China was in its planned socialist economy comprising of mostly state-owned enterprises (SOEs). Funds and capital were typically centrally administered and allocated to enterprises. However, due to inadequate capital resources, inferior management techniques and outmoded technology and equipment, these SOEs began experiencing financial difficulties.[1] In response, from early 1978 to 1992, China initiated full-scale economic reform and opening-up policies, transforming China's socialist economy into a market economy and simultaneously encouraging foreign equity investment into China.

Like China's economic opening-up policy, the liberalisation of China's capital markets is being undertaken in a gradual way. The opening-up of Chinese capital markets includes two aspects: allowing Chinese companies to join global capital markets, and allowing foreign investors to enter Chinese capital markets.

[1] P Torbert, 'Broadening the Scope of Investment' (1994) 21 *China Business Review* 48.

But the authorities seem more cautious about opening China's capital markets to foreign investors than about lifting the restrictions on Chinese companies going abroad.[2] This has protected its financial sector from the risk of investment rushes and 'capital flight'.

A series of programmes were broken into three stages and first tested in 'special economic zones' such as Shanghai and Guangdong.[3] First, foreign investors were permitted to set up 'limited liability companies' by means of joint ventures with domestic entities. Second, companies were allowed to be wholly owned by foreign investors (wholly foreign-owned enterprise or 'WFOE'). Third, Beijing, Guangzhou and Shanghai selected a few large and medium-sized enterprises to experiment with a shareholding system. In 1986 the State Commission for Restructuring the Economy listed the emergence of a shareholding system as one of the major theoretical issues facing the country's reform process.[4] Such shareholding system was then extended to a national strategy to encourage SOEs to issue shares publicly or semi-publicly, leading to the creation and expansion of the securities industry.

As the volume of securities issued increased and the number of investors grew, there was a pressing demand for securities brokerages and trading. China's stock market officially started from 1990 with the establishment of two domestic exchanges: Shanghai Stock Exchange (SSE) and Shenzhen Stock Exchange (SZSE). Located in the Pudong New Area of Shanghai, the SSE is the largest stock market in Mainland China in terms of total market capitalisation and trading volume. The SZSE is in the coastal city of Shenzhen, one of the designated Special Economic Zones intended to foster the opening of China's economy in the 1980s. The SZSE adopts a similar trading mechanism to the SSE, but what distinguishes the SZSE from the SSE is the support for small enterprises.

The original purpose in developing China's stock market was to provide SOEs with a new financing channel in addition to bank loans, and to promote a so-called socialist economy.[5] This move would extricate the Chinese government from substantial budgetary burdens caused by SOEs' losses. In addition, it was hoped that exposing companies to the rigours of the capital market would improve internal management and raise productivity.[6] The stock market could be a tool providing a direct measure of management effectiveness. Permission for all this was embedded in the Preamble of the 1982 Constitution Law.[7] Against this backdrop, it was not surprising that almost all the listed companies were transformed

[2] Y Zhen, *China's Capital Markets* (Oxford, Chandos Publishing, 2013), 239.

[3] S Huo, 'The Company Law of the People's Republic of China' (1995) 13 *Pacific Basin Law Journal* 373, 375.

[4] OK Tam, 'Capital Market Development in China' (1991) 19(5) *World Development* 511, 511.

[5] F Huang and H Yeung, *Chinese Companies and the Hong Kong Stock Market* (Abingdon, Routledge, 2014), 33.

[6] For more details on the impacts of stock market on SOEs, see CH Chen and HT Shih, *The Evolution of The Stock Market in China's Transnational Economy* (Cheltenham, Edward Elgar, 2002), 77–79.

[7] The 1982 Constitution Law of China, the fourth constitution in China, was adopted by the fifth National People's Congress on 4 December 1982 with further revisions approximately every five years. The Constitution Law was most recently amended in 2018.

from SOEs, but they remained under the government's control and influence, rather than being governed by market discipline.

However, during that time, certain stocks offered more generous dividends than bank deposits, and with few joint stock enterprises selling shares to the public – initial public offerings (IPOs) – demand exceeded supply. This led to investors flocking to Shenzhen and Shanghai to purchase shares. Municipal governments tried to cool the market, but the limited number of subscription forms, market irregularities, and malpractice led to the 'August 10 Incident', where investors protested against the irregularities. Additionally, the central government established annual stock issuance and provincial quotas, which were often under pressure from banks and other government bodies that relied on public deposits and debt issuance, fearing potential crowding out. In addition to the objective requirements necessary for a company to issue stocks, many domestic market participants placed great importance on political decision-making in the selection process.[8] Access to IPOs was also limited and had been a significant factor in corruption scandals.[9] These market irregularities sparked many socio-economic and legal debates in China because people were concerned that the shareholding reform by restructuring SOEs into shareholding companies and then listing them on a stock exchange would change their socialist nature and cause the loss of state assets.[10] Some even questioned whether the establishment of capital markets could co-exist with socialist China.

2.1.2. Reform and Opening-up of Chinese Capital Markets (1992–98)

The speech made by Deng Xiaoping during his southern tour of China in early 1992 ushered in a new era of reform and opening-up. While visiting Shenzhen, Deng Xiaoping made the following remarks on securities markets: 'Securities, stock markets, are they good or evil? Are they dangerous or safe? Are they unique to capitalism or also applicable to socialism? Let's try and see.'[11] In that same year, China defined its key economic reform objective as the 'construction of a socialist market economy', pursuant to the resolution passed at the 14th National Congress. The key strategy was to transform the SOEs into joint stock companies and allow them to raise funds through the stock market. In the following year, the stock issuance piloted in Shanghai and Shenzhen was further extended nationwide, turning a new page in the history of China's capital markets.

[8] Objective requirements were the following: a minimum capitalisation of over five million RMB; 25 per cent sale to the public; over 500 shareholders, with any shareholder holding over five per cent being registered and approved; and the company must have shown a profit for the last two years.

[9] M Hasenstab, 'Financial System Reform and Implications' in R Garnart and LG Song (eds), *China: Twenty Years of Economic Reform* (Canberra, Australian National University E Press, 2012), 139.

[10] J Chen, 'Securitization of State-owned Enterprises and the Ownership Controversy in the PRC' (1993) 15 *Sydney Law Review* 59, 60.

[11] XP, Deng, *Selected Words by Deng Xiaping* (Beijing, People's Publishing House, 1993), Vol III, 373.

2.1.2.1. First Chinese Company Law

Along with the regulations of the China Securities Regulatory Commission (CSRC), China's first Company Law 1993,[12] which was enacted on 29 December 1993 and came into force on 1 July 1994, set out specific provisions for the conditions of setting up a company, share issuance and transfer, corporate bonds, liquidation procedures and legal liabilities. The Company Law 1993 was the blending of western corporate principles with traditional concepts in Chinese law such as the 'legal representative', an individual who had the authority to bind a legal entity and who was personally liable for misconduct.[13] In addition, workers played a role in determining corporate policy and profit allocation for workers' welfare. Finally, the Law relied primarily on administrative sanctions rather than on derivative actions to deter and publicise misconduct by managers.

Despite the noticeable progress in the regulatory system, the government closely controlled both the issuing and listing of securities. With regard to issuing of stocks, the requirement of minimum actually paid-in registered capital of Renminbi (RMB) 10 million,[14] or net assets of RMB 30 million in case of corporate debenture issuing,[15] effectively precluded almost all private enterprises from having access to securities markets. Moreover, the purpose of any proposed issuing had to be in line with the state industrial policy[16] and supported by governmental authorities at both local and central levels. Further, any issuing was subject to the state annual quota. For example, Article 164 of the Company Law 1993 stated that the annual volume of corporate debenture issuing shall be determined by the State Council. The actual issuing approved by the securities authority may not exceed the limit set by the State Council. In 1993, the State Council Securities Committee (SCSC) even ordered the suspension of any new issuing of stocks until the state treasury bonds of that year were fully subscribed.[17] Furthermore, the state examination of any issuing application was a substantive scrutiny of the issuer's various records, such as the profit and lawful operation history. Last but not least, an issuing was also subject to many other state regulations. For instance, an SOE must be approved by the state authority concerned for its corporation[18] and its asset appraisal must be approved by the State Access Administration Bureau.[19]

[12] China's Company Law 1993 has been amended several times since its promulgation. The most current version of the Law took effect in 2018.

[13] R Art and MK Gu, 'China Incorporated: The First Corporation Law of the People's Republic of China' (1995) 20 *Yale Journal of International Law* 273, 275.

[14] Chinese Company Law 1993, art 78.

[15] ibid, art 161.

[16] ibid, art 161(4) (describing corporate debenture issuing) and also the Interim Regulations on Stock Issuing and Trading of 1993, art 8 (describing stock issuing).

[17] Item 2 of the Notice of the SCSC Concerning Stock Issuing and Subscription for the Year of 1993 on 18 August 1993.

[18] See, eg The Interim Provisions on Macro-administration Measures over Enterprise Incorporation on a Trial Basis, jointly issued by the State Planning Commission and the State Commission of Economic System Reform on 15 June 1992.

[19] See, eg Chapter 6 of Implementation Rules of Incorporation of State-Owned Asset Appraisal Measures Issued by the State Asset Administration Bureau on 18 July 1992.

2.1.2.2. *First Chinese Securities Law*

The Chinese securities market had developed rapidly since the establishment of two stock exchanges. By the end of 1998, about 850 companies were listed on two exchanges with a market value of RMB 1.96 trillion.[20] Along with the rapid market development, the legal infrastructure had also been constructed at a swift pace. According to Professor Li, the head of the drafting group, before the adoption of the Securities Law 1998, 251 pieces of legislation were promulgated.[21] They formed a solid basis for the unified national legislation. The first long-awaited Chinese Securities Law was adopted by the Standing Committee of the National People's Congress on 29 December 1998 and entered into force on 1 July 1999, ending the eight-year history of operating securities markets in China without formal national legislation.

The passage of the Securities Law represented the nation's firm commitment to further develop the young market in an orderly way. With 214 articles in 12 chapters, the Securities Law 1998 intended to regulate the issuance and subsequent trading of stock, while penalising fraud and helping investors make well-informed investment decisions in a fair, equal and open stock market. When drafted, this legislation could be expected to reflect the strong influence of US securities law. China accepted an offer from the US Securities Exchange Commission (SEC) to provide technical advice, and the overall intent was to meet international standards of securities regulation in order to attract more foreign investment.[22]

Nevertheless, an imported model of regulation would produce different results when it was superimposed on China's unique economic system and ideology. A key element delineating the scope of securities regulation was the definition of 'securities'. In China, only shares, corporate bonds and such other securities recognised by the State Council were regarded as securities. The Company Law was left to deal with any remaining securities which were not included within these narrow groups. This narrow interpretation was far less inclusive than the US interpretation, which included puts, calls, options, and such vague and encompassing concepts as 'investment contracts' and 'participation in any profit-sharing agreement'.[23] China's extremely cautious approach to defining the area of regulation reflected the fact that its securities law was still at an early stage.

2.1.2.3. *Changes of Regulatory Structures*

Prior to 1998, the function of securities supervision in China was allocated to three different institutions under the State Council. The Securities Supervision

[20] SW Sun, 'Securities Law Giving overwhelming Approval' (*China Daily*, 30 December 1998).

[21] XC Zhang, 'The Old Problems, The New Law, and the Developing market – A Preliminary Examination of the First Securities Law of the People's Republic of China' (1999) 33(4) *The International Lawyer* 983, 984.

[22] MK Gu and R Art, 'Securitisation of State Ownership: Chinese Securities Law' (1996) 18 *Michigan Journal of International Law* 115, 117.

[23] See the definition of security provided by the US Securities Exchange Act of 1934, sec. 3(10).

Office of People's Bank of China (PBOC), established in May 1992, was the first institution exercising supervision over China's securities companies. In October of the same year, two authorities were established by the State Council: the SCSC and the CSRC. The SCSC was set up for administration of the market at the macro-level with the powers to promulgate decrees and provisions, to formulate policies and development plans, and to coordinate markets of different regions. On the lower tier is the CSRC, which was formed of officials and securities experts as the executive branch of the SCSC to carry out concrete supervision and regulation of the market as well as securities firms.

In November 1997, the supervision of securities companies which had been carried out the PBOC was transferred to the CSRC. In April 1998, the SCSC also merged with the CSRC. Since then, the CSRC has become the sole regulator supervising nationwide securities and futures markets by consolidating the supervisory functions of the SCSC and the PBOC. Article 167 of the Chinese Securities Law 1998 provides that the CSRC should perform the following duties with regard to the supervision and regulation of the securities market:

- Formulating rules and regulations related to the supervision and regulation of the securities market;
- Supervising and regulating the offering, listing, trading, registration, custody and clearing of securities, pursuant to applicable laws;
- Supervising and regulating securities-related business activities of issuers, listed companies, securities firms, securities investment fund management companies, securities service providers, securities exchange and securities depository and clearing agencies;
- Formulating qualification criteria and codes of conduct for practitioners in the securities industry and supervising their implementation;
- Supervising and inspecting information disclosures in connection with securities offering, listing and trading;
- Providing guidance on and supervising the activities of the securities industry associations;
- Investigating and punishing violations of securities market laws and administrative regulations;
- Other duties as provided by applicable laws and administrative regulations.

During this stage, the CSRC formulated a number of rules and regulations for the securities markets since its inception, including the following:

- The 'Provisional Regulation on the Issuing and Trading of Shares' was promulgated in April 1993 to regulate share issuance and trading as well as the acquisition of listed companies.
- The 'Implementation Rules on Information Disclosures of Companies Issuing Public Shares', issued in June 1993, set up standards for required information disclosures of listed companies.

- The 'Provisional Measures on Prohibiting Fraudulent Conducts Relating to Securities' and the 'Circular on Prohibiting Securities Market Manipulation', promulgated in August 1993 and October 1996, respectively, specified the criteria for defining illegal trading activities and related supervisory sanctions.
- The 'Administrative Procedures for Securities Brokerage Institutions' Equity Underwriting Businesses and Proprietary Trading Businesses' was issued in November 1997 to supervise the activities of financial intermediaries.

Article 180 of the Chinese Securities Law 1998 also empowered the CSRC to take regulatory actions such as conducting on-site inspections on securities market participants and restricting the securities trading of the parties concerned. Moreover, the CSRC developed a regional supervision system by absorbing the provincial securities regulatory offices. The CSRC headquarters is in charge of formulating, amending and improving regulations and rules governing the securities and future markets; granting approvals in connection with major issues; organising investigations into and imposing sanctions for major violations as well as guiding, overseeing and coordinating supervisory efforts nationwide.[24] The regional offices are responsible for front-line supervisory tasks within the provincial-level jurisdictions. With a total of 36 regional offices across the nation, a centralised supervisory framework was established.

It is worth noting that the CSRC is a quasi-governmental organisation under the State Council, in contrast to independent agencies such as the US SEC and the UK's Financial Conduct Authority (FCA). On paper, the CSRC is the national regulator with responsibilities for enforcing rules, maintaining order and generally protecting investors. Meanwhile, the regulator is also a government agency, operating under Party direction, and as such it has also been mandated to support the government's industrial policy.[25] This primarily involved supporting SOEs via the quota and approval systems to allow funds to be channelled towards SOEs (more discussion in sections 2.1.3 and 2.1.4 below).[26]

2.1.3. Further Liberalisation and Development of the Capital Markets (1999–2007)

From 1999 onwards, with the promulgation of the Securities Law, the legal framework of China's capital market was formalised and strengthened. The Securities Law codified the regulatory practices that China had implemented in the past to

[24] CSRC, 'CSRC Annual Report 2012', 13, available at: www.csrc.gov.cn/csrc_en/c102063/c1372580/1372580/files/P020130716403852654782.pdf (accessed on 4 June 2022).

[25] S Green, *China's Stockmarket: A Guide to its Progress, Players and Prospects* (London, Profile Books, 2003), 168.

[26] The quota system operated in 1993 to create a governance structure that aimed to protect a 'pre-mature market', see F Huang, 'In Defence of China's Public Enforcement in Equity Market' (2010) 21(10) *International Company and Commercial Law Review* 327, 328.

regulate its emerging securities market. It also incorporated China's accumulated experience so far, and took into account the lessons learned from the Asian financial crisis of 1997. However, there was no legal provision regarding the trading of state-owned shares, nor any provision regarding investment funds. This implied that Chinese legislators still struggled with certain fundamental socialist ideological issues and were cautious about new market practices.[27] Consequently, rules and regulations have been constantly amended, developed, and implemented, as exemplified by the amendments to the Company Law and Securities Law in 2005. These revisions resulted in profound changes in China's capital markets.

2.1.3.1. Non-tradable Share Reform

The Chinese capital market has distinct characteristics that set it apart from other jurisdictions. Unlike Russia and Eastern Europe, where the privatisation of enterprises has transferred control from the state to private hands, China introduced a special mechanism to prevent the loss of state control when companies went public. From the very beginning, the Chinese stock market was divided into state shares, legal person shares held by state-owned firms, and individual shares, creating an irrational division according to ownership (see Table 2.1). The split-share structure, which consists of both tradable and non-tradable shares, is unique to China's stock market. State shares and legal person shares carried significant constraints on tradability, as they were generally state-owned or state-controlled. Additionally, the law prohibited any transfer of state shares without the approval of the state authorities concerned.[28]

On the other hand, tradable shares are usually divided into different categories: A-shares are listed in Mainland China and traded in RMB for Chinese investors; B-shares are listed in Mainland China for foreign investors; H-shares are Chinese companies that are listed in Hong Kong and traded in Hong Kong dollars (HKD) for a broader range of investors. Domestic investors were restricted to the A-share markets where multiple classes of shares were issued. Tradable A-shares, which made up a minimum of 25 per cent of total shares at the time of the IPO but rarely made up a controlling stake, were the only class of shares that could be traded.[29] In the early 1990s, China faced a great shortage of foreign currencies and thus took very tight control of foreign exchange. To help SOEs solve the shortage of foreign currencies and attract foreign investment sources under a closed capital account regime, China allowed the issue of B-shares, namely RMB-dominated shares exclusively to foreigners. But they were subscribed and traded in USD and HKD. In November 1991, Shanghai Vacuum Electron Device Corporation Limited was issued RMB 1 million B-shares at par value of RMB 100 to overseas

[27] Huang and Yeung (2014), see n 5 above, 36.

[28] The Interim Regulations on Stock Issuing and Trading of 1993, art 36 (further stating that transfer of state shares shall not harm the rights and interests of the state).

[29] Hasenstab (2012), see n 9 above, 139.

investors. This was the first B-share market in China's stock market. Foreigners can also invest in Chinese companies through H-shares and Red Chip stocks listed in Hong Kong, and in overseas listed companies in New York (N-shares), Singapore (S-shares) and other exchanges.

Table 2.1 China's Share Categories

	Category	**Definition**
Non-tradable	State Shares	Shares that are held by the department or institution authorised by the State Council, or held by the department or institution authorised by the local people's government during the process in which the state-owned enterprise are converted into a joint stock company. The ultimate owner of state shares is the State Council. But after reforms in 2005, the state shares became tradable.
	Legal Person (LP) Shares	Shares that are sold to institutional shareholders (eg securities companies and other SOEs) during the corporatisation process. These cannot be traded on the stock market.
	Employee Shares	Shares sold to companies' employees during the same process.
Tradable	A-Shares	Shares issued by Chinese companies that are listed and traded in the Shanghai or Shenzhen Stock Exchange; these shares are sold to and held by Chinese investors.
	B-Shares	Shares issued by Chinese companies that are listed and traded on both SSE and SZSE exclusively to foreign investors. Since 19 February 2001, however, this market was opened to domestic individual investors. On the SSE, prices are denominated in US dollars (USD) while on the SZSE prices are denominated in Hong Kong dollars (HKD).
	H-Shares	These are the shares of companies incorporated in Mainland China but listed and traded on the Hong Kong Stock Exchange and Clearing Limited (HKEX). The shares which were dually issued on the HKEX and the SSE/SZSE are called A+H shares. Like other securities trading on the HKEX, there are no restrictions on who can trade H shares.
	Red Chip	A company is incorporated outside the People's Republic of China (PRC) that trades on the HKEX and is substantially owned, directly or indirectly, by Mainland China state entities with the majority of its revenue or assets derived from Mainland China.

Source: F Huang, 'Modernising the Chinese Capital Market: Old Problems and New Legal Reponses' (2010) 1 *International Company and Commercial Law Review* 26, 30.

At the beginning of 2005, approximately two-thirds of the Chinese stock market comprised non-tradable shares. Regulatory authorities soon recognised the issues associated with the predominance of non-tradable shares.[30] First, holders of tradable shares were typically minority shareholders with limited power to affect management decisions. Thus, the split-share structure hindered the functioning of an active market for corporate control. Second, the split-share structure made major shareholders relatively indifferent to stock price movements because they were unable to sell their shares. Third, the limited free float[31] made the Chinese domestic market extremely illiquid and volatile. The inefficiency of the domestic market induced many valuable Chinese companies to list overseas, with Hong Kong being one of the preferred destinations. This adversely affected domestic investors, who were prevented from investing in the best companies and were stuck with holdings of lesser-performing local companies.

Attempts to reform the non-tradable shares were made to meet the needs of SOEs for funds, liquidity, better governance, and reorganisation from 1999 to 2001.[32] In the first attempt, two companies were selected to sell their state shares to floating shareholders. However, the experiment did not meet investors' expectations, and within 15 days of the announcement of the transfer programme, the share price of the two companies had fallen by about 40 per cent. The second attempt failed in 2001 because the proposal envisaged equal pricing for tradable and non-tradable shares. Due to the gap between market expectations of the value of non-tradable shares and their actual realisation, the pilot programme was soon suspended.

On 31 January 2004, the State Council announced its intention to 'actively address the problem of split-share structure'. On 29 April 2005, with the approval of the State Council, the CSRC issued the 'Circular on Publicising the Measures for the Administration of the Share-trading Reform of Listed Companies', representing the commencement of the split-share structure reform. As compensation for the renegotiation of the implicit contract, the reform forces the holders of non-tradable shares to pay holders of tradable shares in exchange for the possibility to sell their shares in the future. Through terms negotiated with the owners of tradable shares, the non-tradable shares were gradually converted into tradable shares. The reform of the split-share structure of listed companies is a process of eliminating the institutional differences in share transfers within the A-share market through the negotiation mechanism of interest balance between tradable and non-tradable shareholders. Since then, the Chinese government has reduced state ownership in most SOEs and shifted them toward a more market-driven environment.

[30] A Beltratti et al, 'The Stock Market Reaction to the 2005 Non-Tradable Share Reform in China' (2011) *European Central Bank Working Paper Series No 1339*, 11.

[31] Meaning the shares of a company that can be publicly traded. Otherwise known as 'public float'.

[32] GX Hu et al, 'Chinese Capital Market: An Empirical Overview' (2018) *NBER Working Papers 24346*, 10–11.

2.1.3.2. (R)QFII and (R)QDII

By 2001, the Chinese securities market had already developed into one of the largest and the most vibrant securities markets in the Asia-Pacific. However, because the proportion of institutional investors in the Chinese securities market was far behind that of developed markets at that time – which seriously restricted the development of the capital market in China – Chinese regulators introduced the Qualified Foreign Institutional Investor (QFII) and the Qualified Domestic Institutional Investor (QDII) programmes in 2002 and 2006 to expand market-based channels for capital inflow and outflow, respectively. The QFII programme sought to improve the quality of China's forex holdings by attracting valuable medium- and long-term foreign capital while deterring short-term speculative inflows ('hot money'). With a complementary objective, the QDII programme sought to improve the returns on and diversity of China's forex holdings by permitting broader channels for capital outflow into offshore markets.

Under the QFII programme, overseas institutional investors can invest in China's equities and bonds markets without having to incorporate a local entity in China. Prior to this, foreign investors were only allowed to invest through the B-share market. On 5 November 2002, CSRC and PBOC jointly promulgated 'Interim Measures on Domestic Securities Investment by Qualified Foreign Institutional Investor' (QFII Interim Measures), which formed the regulatory foundation for the QFII operation. But the QFII Interim Measures was soon replaced by 'Measures on Administration of Domestic Securities Investment of Qualified Foreign Institutional Investors' (QFII Measures) issued on 24 August 2006.[33] The QFII Measures regulated the operation of QFIIs in various aspects regarding qualification, approval procedure, custody, registration and accounting, investment, capital management and supervision. To qualify as a QFII, a foreign fund management institution, insurance company, securities company, or other asset management institution, should (1) meet certain eligibility conditions; (2) have approval from the CSRC to invest in securities in China; and (3) have an investment quota from the State Administration of Foreign Exchange (SAFE).[34]

Subsequently in 2011, the RMB Qualified Foreign Institutional Investor (RQFII) scheme was introduced as part of an effort to internationalise RMB. The RQFII scheme is a modified version of the QFII scheme that facilitates the use of RMB held outside Mainland China for investing in those markets. The key difference between the QFII scheme and the RQFII scheme is that QFIIs remit foreign currency, which is then converted into RMB, whereas RQFIIs use offshore RMB.

While it is desirable for China to have an influx of capital into the country, it is equally important to allow capital outflows to support the desire of domestic

[33] The 2006 QFII Measures were abolished by the new QFI rules 'Administrative Measures for Securities and Futures Investment Made in China by Qualified Foreign Institutional Investors and RMB Qualified Foreign Institutional Investors' (issued on 25 September 2020 and effective on 1 November 2020).

[34] The 2002 QFII Interim Measures, arts 2, 7 and 8.

investors to have a legal channel through which to diversify their investments abroad. Whilst the (R)QFII schemes allow for influx of international capital into Chinese domestic financial markets, the QDII programme introduced in April 2006 permits qualified domestic institutional investors to make limited investments in foreign capital markets.

The CSRC promulgated the 'Trial Measures for the Administration of Securities Investment Outside the Territory of China by Qualified Domestic Institutional Investors' (QDII Trial Measures) in June 2007 and issued the 'Notice by the CSRC on the Issues Concerning the Implementation of the Pilot Rules on the Administration of Overseas Securities Investment by Qualified Domestic Institutional Investors' (QDII Notice). These regulations officially permitted five types of Chinese entities to invest abroad – banks, trust companies, fund houses, securities firms and insurance companies. These entities can make investments in fixed income products, equities and derivatives in approved overseas markets, both for themselves and on behalf of retail or other clients. To be an eligible QDII, those entities must (1) satisfy certain financial requirements; (2) have the CSRC's approval to raise capital in China; (3) use such capital to invest in foreign securities markets.[35] Fresh quotas were granted by the SAFE every year.

However, the regulations, particularly the QDII Notice, provide very detailed requirements and restrictions, reflecting the government's wariness of foreign markets and its desire to limit the exposure of domestic investors to disproportionate risks. For example, the QDII Notice imposes investment caps on excessively risky investment activities. QDIIs' funds/pooled plans in aggregate may not invest more than specified percentages of their net values in a single entity, in illiquid assets, or in foreign jurisdictions that have not signed MOUs with the CSRC.[36] Furthermore, a fund or pooled plan may not be a controlling shareholder in an overseas entity (eg, a single fund or pooled plan may not hold more than 10 per cent of the total outstanding voting shares of any single company).[37]

Later in 2014, a modified version of QDII, namely RMB Qualified Domestic Institutional Investors (RQDII), was launched to allow domestic financial institutions to invest in RMB-denominated products. However, at first, the RQDII programme did not attract much market attention or interest because traditional RMB-denominated products were relatively limited in scope and size in the international market. Unlike the QDII regime, RQDIIs are generally not subject to approval from the SAFE to obtain any foreign exchange quota. RQDIIs may invest as much RMB funds as they are able to raise from domestic investors, provided that the funds are within the maximum amount reported to or approved by the regulatory authorities. Nevertheless, regulators feared capital outflow as rapid fundraising and investment activities by banks and securities firms increased.

[35] QDII Trial Measures, art 7.
[36] QDII Notice, art 4.
[37] ibid.

Therefore, the RQDII regime was suspended in December 2015 and then resumed in May 2018.[38]

2.1.4. Establishment of Multi-tier Capital Markets (2008–Present)

Several recent developments which have contributed to the development of a more mature equities environment in China include the amended Securities Law 2019, the launch of mutual market access schemes, and the merger of QFII and RQFII, as well as the new establishment of the third exchange – Beijing Stock Exchange.

2.1.4.1. New Chinese Securities Law 2019

The newly revised Securities Law 2019 came into effect on 1 March 2020, marking an important step in China's ongoing efforts to liberalise its capital markets. The revised Law includes over 100 changes, including the addition of two new chapters on information disclosure and investor protection. Most significantly, the Law implements a registration-based system for all IPOs. Under the registration-based IPO system, the requirement for a company to qualify for a new listing has been eased from 'capable of continuous profitability' to 'capable of continuous operation'. The goal is to move away from the government's involvement in closely vetting IPOs for listings, and instead to allow initial offer prices to be set by the market while companies fully disclose material information to investors.

Previously, IPOs in China were subject to regulatory approvals by the CSRC. Under the new Securities Law, the approval system is abolished and a more market-oriented registration system is implemented (Article 9). At the same time, considering that the registration-based system reform is a gradual process, this revision also authorises the State Council to stipulate the specific scope and implementation steps of the securities registration system, leaving the necessary gaps for the step-by-step implementation of the registration system for particular sectors and securities types. Under the new registration system, applications for the issuance of securities have to be registered with the CSRC or other agencies authorised by the State Council. Stock exchanges will review whether issuers comply with the issuance conditions and information disclosure requirements (Article 21).

The registration-based IPO system has already been adopted by SSE's Science and Technology Innovation Board, SZSE's ChiNext board, and the Beijing Stock Exchange. Now, it is to be expanded to the main boards in Shanghai and Shenzhen,

[38] X Yu, 'China Resumes Outbound Investment Scheme but With Tighter Controls' (*South China Morning Post*, 3 May 2018), available at: www.scmp.com/business/global-economy/article/2144575/china-resumes-outbound-investment-scheme-tighter-controls (accessed on 4 August 2021).

according to the CSRC's announcement on 17 February 2023.[39] Under the new system, stock exchanges will be responsible for vetting IPOs with a focus on information disclosure, while the CSRC will only ensure that listings align with national industrial policy. The IPO reforms represent a major overhaul of China's IPO mechanism and are expected to facilitate and encourage more companies, especially large blue-chip companies, to list on Mainland China stock exchanges.

The new Securities Law also contains stricter rules for information disclosure and considerably heavier penalties for market violators. It provides that if new securities are publicly issued and traded in China and overseas simultaneously, any information disclosed overseas must also be disclosed domestically (Article 78). The penalty for fraudulent listings under the revised Law is a fine of up to 20 million RMB or the entire proceeds from the IPO (Article 181). The penalty for similar violations under the previous Law was a fine of up to RMB 600,000 or five per cent of the proceeds (Article 189). Breaching information disclosure rules is punishable by a fine of up to RMB 10 million under the revised Law (Article 197), an increase from the maximum of RMB 600,000 under the old Law.

2.1.4.2. Stock Connect and Bond Connect

Two mutual market access schemes, Stock Connect and Bond Connect were established, giving offshore investors licence-free (at the individual investor level) and quota-free access to Chinese assets, while also providing outbound investment channels for Chinese institutions and residents.

The Stock Connect programme was first launched between Shanghai and Hong Kong in 2014. It was a result of the increased economic integration between Hong Kong and Mainland China, which was formalised through the Closer Economic Partnership Arrangement (CEPA). The CEPA is the first free trade agreement between Hong Kong and Mainland China that was signed in 2003. For Hong Kong, CEPA provides a window of opportunity for Hong Kong businesses to gain greater access to the Mainland market. CEPA also benefits the Mainland as Hong Kong serves as a perfect 'springboard' for Mainland enterprises to reach out to the global market and accelerate the Mainland's full integration with the world economy.[40] Stock Connect builds on the principles of CEPA and aims to create a more seamless, convenient and cost-effective way for investors to access the Chinese stock market. Stock Connect clearly links Mainland China and international infrastructure: exchange to exchange, clearing house to clearing house, depository to depository. Currently, Stock Connect consists of four links

[39] The 'Measures on Full Implementation of the Registration-based System for Initial Public Offerings' was issued by the CSRC on 17 February 2023, available at: www.csrc.gov.cn/csrc/c100028/c7123213/content.shtml (accessed on 23 February 2023).

[40] Trade and Industry Department of Hong Kong, 'Mainland and Hong Kong Closer Economic Partnership Arrangement', available at: www.tid.gov.hk/english/cepa/cepa_overview.html (accessed on 3 December 2022).

between Mainland China and Hong Kong/London/Switzerland (see more details in section 2.2).

Another connectivity scheme, Bond Connect, was launched in July 2017 to allow investors from Mainland China and overseas to trade in each other's bond markets, which would widen the pool of investors in each territory, with greater demand boosting assets. Bond Connect, by virtue of the fact that most bonds offshore are traded over the counter, does not have the same links. There is no exchange link and no clearing house either, since China's interbank bond market doesn't have central clearing, so it is just depositories that are linked.

In addition, Bond Connect currently only handles Northbound trading, ie overseas investors buying and selling bonds on markets in Mainland China. The opening of the Southbound channel will depend very much on China's attitude to capital flight. By contrast, Stock Connect is open to both Southbound and Northbound trading. There are two routes for international investors to gain access to China's bond market: the first one is known as China Interbank Bond Market (CIBM), by which route foreign central banks, international financial organisations and sovereign wealth funds can purchase bonds and engage in bond lending, bond forwards, interest rate swaps, forward rate agreements and bond repos; the second route is known as Bond Connect, which is a mutual market access scheme that allows foreign investors to trade bonds in the CIBM through an international electronic platform (ie Tradeweb or Bloomberg) outside China. Both routes are regarded as supplementary to the QFII and RQFII schemes.

The main difference between Bond Connect and CIBM Direct is that, under Bond Connect, account opening, trading and settlement can be conducted in the offshore market, whereas under CIBM Direct, the whole process is completed in the onshore market. Additionally, unlike CIBM Direct, which requires foreign institutions to complete the necessary filing and account opening procedures, offshore investors under the Bond Connect scheme are permitted to make use of their existing accounts in Hong Kong to directly access Mainland China's bond market. This avoids the need to deal with Chinese authorities for market entry, trading qualifications, foreign exchange settlement and other issues.

2.1.4.3. QFI as the Merger of QFII and RQFII

Both the (R)QFII schemes have undergone various reforms over the years. The key reforms regarding the process of Chinese financial liberalisation are summarised in Table 2.2. In particular, the reforms have centred around an increasing relaxation of the restrictions on eligibility, quotas, investment options and the remittance of funds.

The total investment quotas were USD 4 billion for QFII and USD 20 billion for RQFII initially, increasing to USD 80 billion for each scheme in 2012 and reaching USD 150 billion respectively in 2018. The quotas were granted by China's SAFE, and the quotas could be adjusted at any time in response to the country's economic and financial conditions. In an effort to attract more foreign investment, the SAFE announced its decision to abolish the quota restrictions for (R)QFII in September 2019.[41]

Following the landmark removal of the investment quota for (R)QFII, Chinese regulators released official regulations to combine these two current parallel regimes into a single 'Qualified Foreign Investor' (QFI) regime. The People's Bank of China, the CSRC and the SAFE jointly released two QFI Rules: the *Measures for the Administration of Domestic Securities and Futures Investment by (R)QFII* (the Measures) on 25 September 2020, together with the *Provisions on Implementing QFI Rules* (the Provisions) which became effective on 1 November 2020.[42]

Table 2.2 Chinese Liberalisation Schemes at a Glance

B-Shares	(R)QFII	(R)QDII	Stock Connect	Bond Connect	QFI
1992	2002 and 2011	2006 and 2014	2014, 2016, 2019 and 2022	2017	2020
Introducing B-shares allowing investments from foreign investors in Chinese companies	QFII (2002): Allowing foreign institutional investors who meet certain qualifications to invest in equities and bonds in China. RQFII (2011): Allowing foreign institutional investors using RMB held outside Mainland China to invest in China's capital markets.	QDII (2006): Allowing Chinese institutional investors who meet certain qualifications to invest in equities and bonds outside of China. RQDII (2014): permitting qualified institutional investors to invest in overseas RMB denominated products using their own RMB funds or RMB funds raised from the PRC institutional or individual investors.	Allowing mutual market access between Shanghai–Hong Kong (2014); Shenzhen–Hong Kong (2016); Shanghai–London (2019); China–Switzerland (2022).	Allowing foreign investors to access the fixed income markets in Mainland China via Hong Kong.	Merging both QFII and RQFII into a single QFI regime

[41] SAFE, 'Abolish Restrictions on the Investment Quota of Qualified Foreign Investors (QFII/ RQFII) and Further Expand the Opening up of Financial Markets', 10 September 2019, available at: www.safe.gov.cn/en/2019/0910/1552.html (accessed on 3 August 2021).

[42] Full text of the Measures and the Provisions on the CSRC's website, 'CSRC, PBOC and SAFE Release the Measures for the Administration of Domestic Securities and Futures Investment by

The QFI Rules aim to consolidate the previous separate regulatory regimes applicable to QFIIs and RQFIIs, representing China's latest step to open up key areas of the onshore financial markets to international investors. The key reforms under the QFI Rules are summarised below.

First, relaxation of qualification requirements is applied to QFIs. QFIs are no longer treated differently according to the currencies they use for investment. They now are subject to the same qualification requirements. Although the QFI Rules have maintained the minimum qualification requirements which were previously applicable to QFIIs and RQFIIs (such as stable financial status, good creditworthiness, sound corporate governance and no disciplinary penalty record, etc.), some of the more stringent criteria (eg the minimum operation period requirement and asset management quantity requirement, etc) have been removed. The relaxation of the qualification requirements will definitely attract more small- to medium-sized overseas institutional investors to invest in the Chinese financial markets.

Second, under the QFI Rules, the application process is simplified. The QFI applicant only needs to complete the online forms on the website designated by CSRC, while a PRC custodian bank that has been engaged will submit the application pack to CSRC on behalf of the QFI applicant. The requisite application materials have also been simplified. For example, the investment plan book, fund-source explanation and financial sheets are no longer required. In addition, CSRC's approval timeline has also been shortened from 20 working days (for QFIIs) and 60 days (for RQFIIs) to 10 working days (for all QFIs).

Third, the QFI Rules greatly expand the investment scope of QFIs by including more investment products on the stock exchange market, China inter-bank bond market and exchange-traded derivative market.

Having removed regulatory obstacles and simplified the investment process, the QFI Rules have become a new regulatory landmark to attract foreign institutional investments in the Chinese financial markets.

2.1.4.4. New Beijing Stock Exchange (BSE)

In addition to the two existing national stock exchanges in Shanghai and Shenzhen, Chinese President Xi Jinping announced the launch of a new stock exchange in Beijing for small and medium-sized enterprises (SMEs), in an online speech given for the opening of the China International Fair for Trade in Services on 2 September 2021.[43] The BSE was established based on the select tier (NEEQ Select), which is the highest tier of the National Equities Exchange and Quotation

Qualified Foreign Institutional Investors and RMB Qualified Foreign Institutional Investors', available at: www.csrc.gov.cn/pub/csrc_en/newsfacts/release/202009/t20200925_383652.html (accessed on 3 August 2021).

[43] Xinhua News Agency, 'Full text of Chinese President Xi Jinping's remarks at Global Trade in Services Summit of 2021 China International Fair for Trade in Services' (*China Daily*, 2 September 2021), available at: www.chinadaily.com.cn/a/202109/02/WS6130dc6ea310efa1bd66cfc1.html (accessed on 31 December 2021).

System (NEEQ, commonly known as the New Third Board). The NEEQ is an entry level and over-the-counter market for trading of stocks in smaller companies before listing on a stock exchange, either in mainland China or abroad.[44] The previous NEEQ, founded in 2012, was unsuccessful in raising sufficient capital for SMEs. Thus, this is the starting point for the BSE in its transformation from the NEEQ Select into a stock exchange, and to convert non-listed public companies on the NEEQ into exchange listed companies.

SMEs play an essential role in the Chinese economy, contributing to over 50 per cent of tax revenue, 60 per cent of gross domestic product (GDP), 70 per cent of technological innovations, and more than 80 per cent of national employment and 90 per cent of the number of companies in China.[45] However, Chinese SMEs have been facing financing difficulties for a long time, due to the country's state-dominated banking system resulting in the less efficient allocation of financial resources.[46] To resolve the SME financing dilemma, the BSE focuses on innovation-oriented companies as a way of boosting strategic emerging and high-tech industries, and to provide an injection of capital in SMEs. The creation of the BSE is also much needed by Chinese entrepreneurs amidst the current geopolitical tension between China and the US when stock markets in New York are closing their doors to Chinese businesses. China Mobile and some other Chinese SOEs have been asked by the NYSE to delist their shares due to the US investment ban on foreign corporations that might pose a national security threat.[47] Besides, China's ride-hailing giant Didi Global planned to withdraw from the NYSE and pursue a Hong Kong listing, as the Chinese authorities have increased regulatory scrutiny over the country's overseas listed technology groups due to the data safety concern.[48]

The BSE is expected to play a different role from the Shanghai and Shenzhen exchanges and to better serve the development of innovation-oriented SMEs. However, the question is whether the BSE overlaps with the existing exchanges because the SSE's Science and Technology Innovation Board (STAR) Market and the SZSE's ChiNext board have similar functions to the BSE with a focus on SMEs.

[44] The NEEQ includes three tiers: base tier, innovation tier and select tier. Although the number and total share capital of these companies are far smaller than those in the base and innovation tiers, the liquidity of the shares of the companies on the NEEQ Select is significantly higher than that of the companies in other NEEQ tiers.

[45] Chinese Government, 'We Will Give Policy Support to Small and Medium-sized Enterprises' (1 April 2021), available at: www.gov.cn/zhengce/2020-04/01/content_5497938.htm (accessed on 6 January 2022).

[46] L Lu, *Private Lending in China: Practice, Law and Regulation of Shadow Banking and Alternative Finance* (Abingdon, Routledge, 2019), 24.

[47] CK Ping and A Osipovich, 'NYSE to Delist Chinese Telecom Carriers After Rejecting Appeals' (*Wall Street Journal*, 7 May 2021), available at: www.wsj.com/articles/nyse-to-delist-chinese-telecoms-carriers-afterrejecting-appeals-11620394719 (accessed on 5 January 2022).

[48] R McMorrow et al, 'China's Didi to delist from New York and switch to Hong Kong' (*Financial Times*, 3 December 2021), available at: www.ft.com/content/c30cf911-51da-4b40-a969-161351de6f04 (accessed on 5 January 2022).

Established on the SZSE in October 2009, ChiNext was set up to list companies in high-growth sectors such as technology and pharmaceuticals. ChiNext is considered an important capital market instrument to broaden China's industrial structure and promote economic reform, especially given the difficulties that some start-ups still face in securing bank financing. As of 7 February 2023, 1,233 companies had successfully listed on ChiNext, with a total market capitalisation (total value of shares on the market – 'total market cap') of RMB 12,463 billion.[49] Thus the SZSE has the framework of a multi-tiered capital market comprising the Main Board, SME Board, and the ChiNext market.

The STAR Market, opening in summer 2019 on the SSE, has been touted as Shanghai's equivalent to the US's Nasdaq, its purpose being to support sci-tech and innovative enterprises that align with national strategies and to support Shanghai's bid to become an international financial centre and science and innovation hub. As of 7 February 2023, 504 companies had been listed on the SSE STAR Market with a total market cap of RMB 3,191 billion.[50]

The BSE has some things in common with SSE's STAR Market and SZSE's ChiNext board. They all serve the same purpose to support SMEs. But compared with the others, the enterprises the BSE serves are even smaller and newer. In the CSRC's press release dated 3 September 2021, the BSE positions itself as serving innovative SMEs and playing the role of transferring companies to list on other markets.[51] The new BSE provides an extra financing channel for the so-called 'Zhuan, Jing, Te, Xin' SMEs which stands for those companies with the special characteristics of 'specialisation, refinement, differentiation, and innovation' that are the robust mainstay of the Chinese economy. In addition, the BSE fully implements a US-style registration-based IPO system that is reliant on adequate information disclosure instead of substantial regulatory checks by the CSRC. This is in line with the practices of the STAR Market and the ChiNext board, as the BSE aims to build a bespoke IPO system for SMEs.

Apart from their similarities, the BSE, STAR Market and ChiNext board are divergent in their listing standards, continuous regulation requirements and investor suitability (as shown in Table 2.3). First, the minimum market cap standard for a profitable company seeking a listing on the BSE is RMB 200 million.[52] If the predicted market cap of a company exceeds RMB 1.5 billion, it will not need to make any profits – a standard much lower than that of Star Market and ChiNext.

According to the Listing Rules of Beijing Stock Exchange (Trial), the BSE allows companies to list with dual class share structures (DCS) with differentiated

[49] SZSE, 'Market Overview', available at: www.szse.cn/market/overview/index.html (accessed on 7 February 2023).

[50] SSE, 'STAR Market', available at: english.sse.com.cn/aboutsse/overview/ (accessed on 7 February 2023).

[51] Press release by the CSRC (3 September 2021), available at: www.csrc.gov.cn/csrc/c100029/cb7acea9e3b6c4c94bef46eb0ff3e5525/content.shtml (accessed on 20 August 2021).

[52] Listing Rules of Beijing Stock Exchange 2021 (Trial), section 2.1.3.

voting rights.[53] For a long time, the use of DCS structures in listed companies was a corporate governance taboo. A corporate governance risk commonly associated with DCS structures was the risk of management entrenchment and 'tunnelling' – the extraction of private benefits of control by controlling shareholders by various means.[54] Recently, however, the permissibility of DCS listings has become an increasingly important matter of competitiveness for capital markets globally.[55] Moreover, The listing rules have no restrictions on red-chip companies[56] and variable interest entities,[57] which has sent out a positive message that the BSE is open to the financial and corporate innovations happening across the world.

Second, the validity period of financial statements quoted in the prospectus for initial public offering remains unchanged at six months in the BSE's Listing Rules, but the allowable period for extension in special circumstances can be adjusted from one month to three months. This means that the validity period of financial reports will be extended from 6+1 months to 6+3.[58] Furthermore, the new Listing Rules of BSE have provided a more speedy and streamlined process for the listing entities, as the time for reviewing the application documents has been shortened from three to two months.[59] Thus, it only takes approximately six to eight months for a company meeting the formalities and pre-set standards of the BSE to float their shares. This is welcomed by many SMEs who are in urgent need of funding and prefer a fast financing conduit comparable to bank loans and private equity funds.

Third, qualified individual investors on the BSE must have more than two years of stock trading experience and hold more than RMB 500,000 on average in securities assets for 20 trading days.[60] There is no requirement for institutional investors.

Fourth, the BSE has no restriction on share price movement on the first trading day, while the daily limit will be 30 per cent for the subsequent trading sessions, compared with the 20 per cent limit for the STAR Market and ChiNext

[53] ibid, section 4.4.1.

[54] See for instance S Johnson et al, 'Tunnelling' (2000) 90(2) *American Economy Review* 22, and RJ Gilson and JN Gordon, 'Controlling Controlling Shareholders' (2003) 152(2) *University of Pennsylvania Law Review* 785, 787.

[55] F Huang, 'Dual Class Shares around the Top Financial Centres' [2017] *Journal of Business Law* 137.

[56] A red chip is a company incorporated outside of Mainland China that trades on the Hong Kong Stock Exchange.

[57] The term 'variable interest entity', as used by the US Financial Accounting Standards Board in its Accounting Standards Codification 810-10, generally refers to an entity in which a public company has a variable interest that is not based on having the majority of voting rights. But most Chinese overseas listings which are incorporated in offshore tax havens adopt the VIE structure to circumvent China's foreign ownership restrictions, creating complications for investigation and enforcement. See F Huang, 'Stock Connect: Integration, Internationalisation and Implementation' [2021] *Journal of Business Law* 558, 567–68.

[58] Rules for Review Offering Shares to Non-Specific Qualified Investors of Beijing Stock Exchange 2021 (Trial), art 43.

[59] ibid, art 38.

[60] Rules of Investors Suitability of Beijing Stock Exchange 2021 (Trial), art 5.

and 10 per cent for the main boards of the SSE and SZSE.[61] This apparently will encourage more investors to trade on the BSE, supplying more capital and liquidity to the nascent market. However, it also comes with greater risks, such that investors need to behave in a vigilant manner when investing in SMEs.

The high-profile launch of the BSE and the promulgation of targeted rules for tech companies and SMEs indicate that the Chinese authorities have shown a clear determination to address the financing difficulties of smaller businesses. Learning from the existing standards and leading market practices of the NEEQ select tier, ChiNext and the STAR Market, the BSE adheres to the principal rules with adjustment to suit the economic reality and financing demands of innovative SMEs. As such, China has been hosting three major bourses located in the North (BSE), Middle (SSE), and South (SZSE) of the country, which form an institutionally sound, multi-tier, and nationally connected capital market financing system. With their differentiated focuses, they can meet the diverse demands of different kinds of enterprises.

Table 2.3 Comparison between BSE, SSE's STAR Market and SZSE's ChiNext Market

	BSE	**STAR Market (SSE)**	**ChiNext (SZSE)**
Supported industries	Innovative SMEs in advanced manufacturing and modern service industries	Information technology, high-end equipment, new materials, new energy sources, biomedicine etc	Growing innovative and entrepreneurial enterprises
Minimum Market Capitalisation	For profitable company, Market Cap≥ RMB 200 million For non-profitable company, Market Cap≥ RMB 1.5 billion	For profitable company, Market Cap ≥RMB 1 billion For non-profitable company, Market Cap ≥ RMB 4 billion	For profitable company, Market Cap ≥RMB 1 billion For non-profitable company, Market Cap ≥RMB 5 billion
Investor suitability	Individual investors with at least 2 years' trading experience≥ RMB 500,000 for 20 trading days No restrictions for institutional investors	same as BSE	Individual investors ≥ RMB 100,000 No restrictions for institutional investors
Price Fluctuation Limit	30%	20%	20%

(continued)

[61] Trading Rules of Beijing Stock Exchange 2021 (Trial), section 3.3.11.

Table 2.3 ***(Continued)***

	BSE	STAR Market (SSE)	ChiNext (SZSE)
Prospectus Regime	Valid time of financial statements: 6+3 months Time to process IPO documents: 2 months	Valid time of financial statements: 6+3 months Time to process IPO documents: 3 months	Valid time of financial statements: 6+3 months Time to process IPO documents: 3 months

2.2. Establishment and Operation of Stock Connect

Since the announcement of China's Third Plenum of the 18th Party Congress on 12 November 2013, a series of financial reforms have been initiated in China.[62] These include liberalising the interest rate regime, reforming the country's state-owned banking system, internationalising China's RMB and opening the country's capital markets to more international investment. This last objective is where the Mutual Market Access Pilot Programme for the establishment of Stock Connect is targeted.

Previously, foreign participation in Chinese stock markets had been limited mainly to the QFII and RQFII schemes, and foreign retail investors could only participate through investment funds offered by QFIIs and RQFIIs. Similarly, the QDII and RQDII schemes had been the only official channels for Mainland participation in overseas stock markets. Stock Connect represents a milestone in the opening of Mainland China's capital account. With a daily quota and a closed loop of cross-border flow of funds, it allows for orderly cross-border capital investment activities with close monitoring, thereby reducing the potential impact of financial risk on the Mainland domestic stock market. The programme is scalable in size, scope, and market segments to match the pace of the Mainland market's further development.

As shown in Table 2.4, Stock Connect, also known as the 'Through Train', currently consists of four different links: Shanghai–Hong Kong Stock Connect, Shenzhen–Hong Kong Stock Connect, Shanghai–London Stock Connect, and China–Switzerland Stock Connect. Each link has its own characteristics while sharing some similarities. This section will outline the details of each link and the differences between them.

[62] China's Government, 'Decision of the Central Committee of the Communist Party of China on Some Major Issues Concerning Comprehensively Deepening the Reform' is available at: www.china.org.cn/china/third_plenary_session/2014-01/16/content_31212602.htm (accessed on 6 August 2021).

Table 2.4 Stock Connect 'Operational Directions'

Shanghai–Hong Kong Stock Connect (Shanghai Connect)	Shenzhen–Hong Kong Stock Connect (Shenzhen Connect)	Shanghai–London Stock Connect (London Connect)	China–Switzerland Stock Connect (Switzerland Connect)
Northbound Shanghai Trading Link	Northbound Shenzhen Trading Link	Eastbound Shanghai Business Link	Eastbound Chinese Business Link
Southbound Hong Kong Trading Link	Southbound Hong Kong Trading Link	Westbound London Business Link	Westbound Swiss Business Link

- *Northbound trading*: Hong Kong and international investors can trade in selected equities on the Shanghai (SSE) and Shenzhen (SZSE) Stock Exchanges, routed through Hong Kong brokers.
- *Southbound trading*: Investors in Mainland China can trade selected equities on the Hong Kong Stock Exchange through brokers in Mainland China.
- *Eastbound business*: Eligible companies listed on London Stock Exchange (LSE) or SIX Swiss Exchange (SIX) can issue Chinese Depository Receipts (CDRs) in Mainland China and apply for their listing on the SSE and SZSE.
- *Westbound business*: Eligible companies listed on the SSE or SZSE can issue Global Depository Receipts (GDRs) and apply for their listing on the Main Markets of the LSE and SIX.

2.2.1. Shanghai–Hong Kong Stock Connect (Shanghai Connect)

On 10 April 2014, the CSRC and the Hong Kong Securities and Futures Commission (SFC) announced that they had approved in principle the development of a pilot programme for establishing mutual stock market access between Mainland China and Hong Kong.[63] Later, on 4 September 2014, the Stock Exchange of Hong Kong (SEHK) and Hong Kong Securities Clearing Company Limited (HKSCC), wholly-owned subsidiaries of Hong Kong Exchanges and Clearing Limited (HKEX),[64] signed a four-party agreement with the SSE and China Securities Depository and Clearing Corporation Limited (ChinaClear) for the establishment of Shanghai Connect.[65] With this agreement, a basic framework has built up for Shanghai Connect that clarifies the rights and responsibilities of the four related parties

[63] The joint announcement of the CSRC and the SFC is available at: apps.sfc.hk/edistributionWeb/gateway/EN/news-and-announcements/news/doc?refNo=14PR41 (accessed on 27 November 2020).

[64] The HKEX is the holding company of the SEHK and the Hong Kong Futures Exchange Limited (HKFE). It owns three clearing houses, namely HKSCC, HKFE Clearing Corporation Limited (HKCC) and the SEHK Options Clearing House Limited (SEOCH), and operates two clearing and settlement systems.

[65] HKEX, 'Four-Party Agreement for Shanghai-Hong Kong Stock Connect Signed' is available at: www.HKEX.com.hk/News/News-Release/2014/1409042news?sc_lang=en (accessed on 22 November 2020).

in terms of trading, clearing, custody and market surveillance. It is viewed as a milestone indicating that the two exchanges and the two clearing houses have had consensus about the market mechanism and business arrangement. The HKEX subsequently published a number of approved amendments to its rules to clarify certain key aspects of Shanghai Connect.[66] These documents provide market participants with welcome clarifications in a number of key areas.

After a few months' market preparation and system testing, Shanghai Connect was formally launched on 17 November 2014. It is an unprecedented mechanism to allow investors in Shanghai and Hong Kong to directly purchase shares in each other's markets, albeit within a confined scope. Shanghai Connect is designed as a bi-directional channel connecting China through Hong Kong to the rest of the world. As seen in Table 2.4, a 'Northbound' link allows non-Chinese investors to buy and sell Chinese stocks via the more accessible SEHK. The counterpart 'Southbound' link allows Chinese investors to buy and sell international stock through Hong Kong.

2.2.1.1. *Eligible Securities*

The theme of Shanghai Connect is to enable Hong Kong and overseas investors to trade SSE-listed securities on the Mainland market (Shanghai Northbound Trading) and Mainland investors to trade SEHK-listed securities in the Hong Kong market (Shanghai Southbound Trading), within the eligible scope of the programme. Among the different types of Chinese securities, only A-shares were initially included in Shanghai and Shenzhen Connect. The joint announcement dated 16 August 2016 provided that the CSRC and the SFC had reached consensus to include exchange-traded funds (ETFs) as eligible securities under the mutual market access programme.[67] In addition to shares of listed companies, ETFs were included as eligible securities to be traded under Shanghai Connect and Shenzhen Connect on 4 July 2022.[68] The inclusion of ETFs was a significant step in opening-up the Chinese markets to international investors, as ETFs are a popular investment vehicle that is widely used by investors globally. Therefore, under current Shanghai and Shenzhen Connect, securities that are eligible for trading by Hong Kong and overseas investors include eligible A-shares, A–H-shares and eligible SSE/SZSE-listed ETFs.[69] Other product types such as B-shares, bonds, and other securities are not included.

[66] The full text of 'Shanghai-Hong Kong Stock Connect FAQ for Market Participants' is available at: www.charltonslaw.com/newsletters/hong-kong-law/en/2014/264/Shanghai-hong-kong-stock-connect-information-faq-for-market-participants.pdf (accessed on 27 November 2020).

[67] See n 73 below.

[68] HKEX, 'HKEX to Include ETFs in Stock Connect on 4 July' (28 June 2022), available at: www.hkex.com.hk/News/News-Release/2022/220628news?sc_lang=en (28 December 2022).

[69] HKEX, 'Information Book for Investors' (4 July 2022), section 2 'Investor and participant Eligibility', available at: www.hkex.com.hk/-/media/HKEX-Market/Mutual-Market/Stock-Connect/Getting-Started/Information-Booklet-and-FAQ/Information-Book-for-Investors/Investor_Book_En.pdf (accessed on 2 January 2023).

On 19 December 2022, China's CSRC and Hong Kong's SFC jointly announced their plan to further expand the scope of eligible stocks under Shanghai and Shenzhen Connect, as shown in Table 2.5.[70]

Southbound trading: The scope of eligible stocks will be expanded to include stocks of international companies that are primary-listed in Hong Kong, and are 1) constituent stocks of the Hang Seng Composite LargeCap Index (HSLI) or Hang Seng Composite MidCap Index (HSMI), or 2) constituent stocks of the Hang Seng Composite SmallCap Index (HSSI) with a market capitalisation of HKD 5 billion or above. In addition, the scope of eligible stocks for Southbound trading under Shanghai–Hong Kong Stock Connect will be expanded to include constituents of the HSSI with a market capitalisation of HKD 5 billion or above, which will align with the existing scope of eligible stocks for southbound trading under the Shenzhen–Hong Kong Stock Connect.

Northbound trading: The scope of eligible stocks for Northbound trading under Stock Connect will be changed to 1) constituent stocks of the SSE A-Share Index and the SZSE Composite Index which have a market capitalisation of RMB 5 billion or above and meet certain requirements such as liquidity criteria; and 2) SSE/SZSE-listed stocks of companies which have issued both A-shares and H-shares. The move will boost the number of Mainland stocks eligible for trading via the Northbound link to about 2,516, up from the previous 1,458.[71]

Prior to the expansion, among the Northbound stocks under Shanghai Connect, the SSE 180 Index constituents are the most representative 180 A-shares on the SSE while the SSE 380 Index constituents are the 380 stocks with modest scale, representing the segment of emerging blue-chips outside the 180 Index on the SSE. The Northbound stocks in the SSE 180 Index are therefore considered 'large-cap' stocks in parallel with the Southbound HSLI stocks and the Northbound stocks in SSE 380 Index are considered 'mid-cap' stocks in parallel with the Southbound HSMI stocks.

After the expansion, the scope of Northbound stocks under Shanghai Connect covers constituent stocks of the SSE A-Share Index which have a market capitalisation of RMB 5 billion or above. The relevant requirements on companies that have issued both A-shares and H-shares will remain unchanged. After this adjustment, more diversified stocks will be included, so Stock Connect can better meet investors' investment needs and further enhance the influence of the A-share market. For the Southbound stocks, the list of eligible securities will be widened to include both securities of foreign corporations that are primarily listed in Hong Kong and the HSSI constituents with a market capitalisation of at least HKD 5 billion, aligning it with the current list of eligible stocks for Southbound trading under Shenzhen Connect.

[70] HKEX, 'HKEX Welcomes Further Expansion of Stock Connect' (19 December 2022), available at: www.hkex.com.hk/News/News-Release/2022/2212192news?sc_lang=en (accessed on 2 January 2023).

[71] C Leng, 'Hong Kong and Mainland China to Expand Stock Connect Scheme' (*Financial Times*, 20 December 2022), available at: www.ft.com/content/8983e7fe-3e88-4fc1-9e13-46add87ff9c2 (accessed on 2 January 2023).

Table 2.5 The Expansion of Shanghai–Hong Kong Stock Connect

Stocks Eligible for Trading via Shanghai–Hong Kong Stock Connect				
	Prior to the Expansion		**After the Expansion**	
	Northbound Trading	**Southbound Trading**	**Northbound Trading**	**Southbound Trading**
Eligible Stocks	Constituents of the SSE 180 Index and SSE 380 Index A-shares of SSE–SEHK A+H	Constituents of the Hang Seng Composite LargeCap or MidCap Index; H-shares of SSE–SEHK A+H	SSE A Share Index which have a market capitalisation of RMB 5 billion or above; A-shares of SSE–SEHK A+H	Stocks of international companies that are primary-listed in Hong Kong; Constituents of the Hang Seng Composite LargeCap or MidCap Index; Constituent stocks of the Hang Seng Composite SmallCap Index with a market capitalisation of HKD 5 billion or above; H-shares of SSE–SEHK A+H
Ineligible Stocks	SSE-listed shares which are not traded in RMB; SSE-listed shares which are under risk alert	Local shares that are not traded in HKD; H-shares with correspondent A-shares tradable on SZSE; H-shares which have corresponding A-shares put under risk alert	Same as pre-expansion	Same as pre-expansion

In addition to the stocks, SSE-listed ETFs that satisfy all of the following criteria at any regular review will be accepted as eligible ETFs for Northbound trading:

- The ETF must be traded in RMB and have a daily average assets under management (AUM) in the last six months of not less than RMB 1.5 billion;
- The ETF must be listed for at least six months;
- The benchmark index must be launched for at least one year;
- The total weighting of SSE-listed and SZSE-listed A-shares in the benchmark index must not be less than 90 per cent and the total weighting of Stock

Connect Northbound eligible constituents in the benchmark index must not be less than 80 per cent; and
- The benchmark index or the index methodology of the benchmark index must fulfil the criteria of broad-based indices.

On the Hong Kong side, ETFs primarily regulated by the SFC and listed on the SEHK that satisfy all of the following criteria at any regular review will be accepted as eligible ETFs for Southbound trading under Shanghai Connect:

- The ETF must be traded in HKD and have a daily average AUM in the last six months of not less than HKD 1.7 billion;
- The ETF must be listed for at least six months;
- The benchmark index must be launched for at least one year;
- The ETF must not be synthetic ETFs or Leveraged and Inverse Products;
- The total weighting of SEHK-listed stocks in the benchmark index must not be less than 90 per cent;
- The total weighting of Stock Connect Southbound eligible constituents in the Hang Seng Index (HSI), the Hang Seng China Enterprises Index (HSCEI), the Hang Seng TECH Index (HSTECH) and the Hang Seng Hong Kong-Listed Biotech Index (HSHKBIO) must not be less than 70 per cent and the total weighting of Stock Connect Southbound eligible constituents in other benchmark indices must not be less than 80 per cent; and
- The benchmark index or the index methodology of the benchmark index must fulfil the criteria of broad-based indices.

2.2.1.2. Eligible Participants

In Hong Kong, except STAR stocks of the SSE which are limited to institutional professional investors, there is no restriction imposed on Hong Kong and overseas investors participating in Shanghai and Shenzhen Connect. In China, Mainland institutional investors and those individual investors who satisfy the eligibility criteria (ie individual investors who hold an aggregate balance of not less than RMB 500,000 in their securities and cash accounts) will be accepted to trade SEHK securities in Southbound trading, which is a threshold that excludes most retail investors.[72]

In Northbound trading, investors in Hong Kong will trade through Hong Kong brokers, and trades are executed on the SSE platform. In Southbound trading, Mainland investors will trade through Mainland brokers, and trades are executed on the HKEX platform. Northbound trading and Southbound trading follow the market practices of their respective trade execution platforms.

[72] HKEX, 'Information Book for Investors', see n 69 above.

Shanghai and Shenzhen Connect is also open to all exchange participants including SSE members, SZSE members and SEHK members, and to clearing participants such as HKSCC's Clearing participants, and ChinaClear participants, providing that they meet certain information technology capability, risk management and other requirements as may be specified by the relevant exchange and/or clearing house.

2.2.1.3. Quota

Both Northbound Trading and Southbound Trading under Stock Connect would be subject to an aggregate quota that caps the absolute amount of cross-boundary flow of funds, together with a daily quota that limits the maximum daily net purchase value of cross-boundary trades, which will be monitored in real time on a 'first come, first served' basis. Initially, Southbound trading was subject to a daily quota of RMB 10.5 billion and an aggregate quota of RMB 250 billion, while Northbound trading was subject to a daily quota of RMB 13 billion and an aggregate quota of RMB 300 billion. Once that daily quota is reached, investors cannot buy, but can only sell, for the remainder of the day.

This aggregate quota was subsequently abolished on the announcement date (16 August 2016) of Shenzhen Connect while the daily quota is still applicable.[73] From 1 May 2018, the Northbound daily quota has been increased from RMB 13 billion to 52 billion for each of Shanghai and Shenzhen Connect and the Southbound daily quota has been increased from RMB 10.5 billion to 42 billion for each of Shanghai and Shenzhen Connect.[74] The change was made in anticipation of increased overseas interest in the Chinese stock market following the inclusion of A-shares in the Emerging Market Index of the US finance company MSCI in June 2017, accounting for about 28 per cent of the Index.[75]

2.2.1.4. Clearing and Settlement

For Shanghai Connect, the HKSCC and ChinaClear have established Clearing Links, whereby the two clearing houses have become a participant of each other, and have agreed to undertake the settlement obligations in respect of Northbound and Southbound trades executed through the relevant HKEX subsidiary and

[73] The CSRC and SFC, 'Joint Announcement of the China Securities Regulatory Commission and the Securities and Futures Commission' (16 August 2016), available at: apps.sfc.hk/edistributionWeb/gateway/EN/news-and-announcements/news/doc?refNo=16PR80> (accessed on 2 December 2020).

[74] HKEX, 'HKEX Comments on Stock Connect Daily Quota Expansion' (11 April 2018), available at: www.HKEX.com.hk/News/News-Release/2018/180411news?sc_lang=en (accessed on 2 December 2020).

[75] W Zhen, 'Emerging Markets Since China A Shares' Inclusion' (5 December 2019), available on the MSCI's website: www.msci.com/www/blog-posts/emerging-markets-since-china-a/01662775315 (accessed on 2 December 2020).

the SSE subsidiary respectively. HKSCC settles Northbound trades with CCASS participants in RMB. HKSCC also settles the same with ChinaClear in RMB.

For Northbound trades, ChinaClear acts as the host central counterparty (CCP) and HKSCC is a participant of ChinaClear. HKSCC takes up settlement obligations of the central clearing and settlement system (CCASS) participants in respect of Northbound trades and settles the trades directly with ChinaClear on the Mainland. Vice versa for Southbound trades, HKSCC is the host CCP and ChinaClear is its clearing agency participant. ChinaClear takes up settlement obligations of its clearing participants in respect of Southbound trades and settles the trades with HKSCC in Hong Kong.

Northbound trades executed under Shanghai and Shenzhen Connect will follow the settlement cycles of the Shanghai and Shenzhen markets. Both markets adopt the same settlement cycle – stock settlement on T day (trade day), and money settlement on T+1 day. For securities settlement ChinaClear will debit or credit its participants' (including HKSCC as clearing participant) stock accounts before 6:00pm on T day to settle their trades in the Connect markets. To facilitate the settlement cycles of Connect securities, HKSCC will conduct securities settlement on Northbound trades for its CCASS participants via four rounds of Batch Settlement Runs at around 4:45pm, 5:30pm, 6:15pm and 7:00pm on T day for each Connect market. Money settlement for Northbound trades will be effected by around noon on T+1 day on a net money position of SSE securities and SZSE securities.

2.2.2. Shenzhen–Hong Kong Stock Connect (Shenzhen Connect)

On 16 August 2016, the CSRC and the SFC jointly announced the establishment of Shenzhen Connect – the mutual stock market access between Shenzhen and Hong Kong, as an extended version of Shanghai Connect. Shenzhen has become known for the range and depth of the mid and smaller capitalised companies listed on its exchange. It is sometimes referred to as 'the Nasdaq of China'. Most of these are companies that are owner-managed; they have been more involved in fast-growth businesses, such as technology or leisure, services or manufacturing and other modern industries.

Following the joint announcement by both China and Hong Kong's regulators, the SZSE formally released eight sets of rules governing Shenzhen Connect on 30 September 2016. These rules include the 'Measures for the Implementation of Shenzhen–Hong Kong Stock Connect Programme', the 'Guidelines on the Management of Investor Suitability for Shenzhen–Hong Kong Connect', the 'Mandatory Provisions for the Risk Disclosure Statement for Shenzhen–Hong Kong Connect Trading', the 'Mandatory Provisions for the Client Agreement for Shenzhen–Hong Kong Connect', the 'Circular on Information Disclosure by Listed Companies and Relevant Issues under Shenzhen–Hong Kong Stock Connect', the 'Guidelines on the Implementation of HKSCC Participation in Online Voting', and the revised 'Detailed Implementation Rules on Online Voting at Shareholders' General Meetings and SZSE Trading Rules'.[76] These rules set out the basic model, trading and settlement mechanism as well as regulatory requirements for Shenzhen Connect. They are largely consistent with those for Shanghai Connect but with stricter requirements for investor education on risk awareness because vulnerable investors may be exposed to higher risks caused by the expanding scope of investment.

As the eligible shares for Shenzhen Connect include part of the constituents of the HSSI, which generally are small in size with unstable performance and volatile stock prices, the 'Mandatory Provisions for the Risk Disclosure Statement for Shenzhen–Hong Kong Connect Trading' place special emphasis on the following risks:

- first, in consideration of the expansion of the scope of eligible shares, investors are requested to note the risk that there may be significant fluctuations in the fundamentals and share prices of some small- and mid-cap companies (section 3);
- second, given the existing differences in both rules and systems between the Hong Kong and Shenzhen stock markets, the provisions note that due to a lack of delisting risk alerts and pre-delisting arrangements in the Hong Kong market, there is a risk that shares may be suspended from trading for long periods or delisted directly, and nominee services are likely to be restricted for delisted shares (sections 6–8);
- third, the provisions summarise the characteristics of the so-called 'cheating shares' ('*Laoqiangu*' in Chinese, meaning refinancing instruments like deeply discounted rights issues and share consolidations), which have caught market attention lately, and draw investors' attention to the risks that investors' interests may be damaged as a result of deeply discounted rights issues, placements, and frequent share splits and consolidations by some poor performing, low-priced listed companies (section 4).

Apart from that, the aggregate quota was not applicable to Shenzhen Connect; at the same time, the aggregate quota for Shanghai Connect had been removed with effect from 17 August 2016.

2.2.2.1. *Eligible Equities*

As seen in Table 2.6, after the expansion in 2022, the constituent stocks of the SZSE Composite Index that have a market capitalisation of RMB 5 billion or above and

[76] SZSE, 'SZSE Releases Rules on Shenzhen-Hong Kong Stock Connect Programme' (12 October 2016), available at: www.szse.cn/enSzhk/introduction/news/t20161013_558113.html (accessed on 30 November 2020).

Table 2.6 The Expansion of Shenzhen–Hong Kong Stock Connect

Stocks Eligible for Trading via Shenzhen–Hong Kong Stock Connect				
	Prior to the Expansion		After the Expansion	
	Northbound Trading	Southbound Trading	Northbound Trading	Southbound Trading
Eligible Stocks	Constituents of the SZSE Component Index, and SZSE Small/ Mid Cap Innovation Index (with a market capitalisation of at least RMB 6 billion); A-shares of SZSE–SEHK A+H	Constituents of Hang Seng Component LargeCap or MidCap Index; Constituent stocks of the Hang Seng Composite SmallCap Index (with market capitalisation HKD 5 billion) or above; H-shares of SZSE–SEHK A+H	Constituents of the SZSE Composite Index which have a market capitalisation of RMB 5 billion or above; A-shares of SZSE–SEHK A+H	Stocks of international companies that are primary-listed in Hong Kong; Constituents of the Hang Seng Composite LargeCap or MidCap Index; Constituent stocks of the Hang Seng Composite SmallCap Index with a market capitalisation of HKD 5 billion or above; H-shares of SZSE–SEHK A+H
Ineligible Stocks	SZSE-listed shares which are not traded in RMB; SZSE-listed shares which are under risk alert	Local shares that are not traded in HKD; H-shares which have corresponding shares listed and traded on any exchange in Mainland China other than SSE/SZSE H-shares which have corresponding A-shares put under risk alert or delisting arrangement	Same as pre-expansion	Same as pre-expansion

meet certain liquidity criteria will be selected to replace the constituent stocks of the Shenzhen Index and the SZSE Small/Mid Cap Innovation Index that have a market capitalisation of RMB 6 billion or above under Shenzhen Connect. The relevant requirements on companies that have issued both A-shares and H-shares will remain unchanged. The scope of underlying stocks eligible for Southbound trading under Shenzhen Connect will be expanded on its current basis to include the stocks of foreign companies primarily listed in Hong Kong which meet relevant criteria, while the existing scope of other underlying stocks eligible for the same will remain unchanged. The specific criterion is that such foreign companies primarily listed in Hong Kong shall be the constituents of the HSLI or HSMI, or those of the SmallCap Index (HSSI) with a market capitalisation of HKD 5 billion or above. Likewise, ETFs are also included in Shenzhen Connect (refer to section 2.2.1 above for the scope of ETFs).

2.2.2.2. *Eligible Participants*

While Mainland eligible investors for Southbound trading under Shenzhen Connect are the same as those under Shanghai Connect, eligible investors for Northbound trading of shares listed on the ChiNext board of SZSE are confined, at the initial stage, to institutional professional investors as defined in the 'Securities and Future (Professional Investors) Rules' of Hong Kong.[77]

2.2.2.3. *Quota*

The same daily quota as for Shanghai Connect is applied to Shenzhen Connect and the aggregate quota is no longer applicable.

2.2.2.4. *Clearing and Settlement*

The same clearing and settlement procedure is applied to both Shanghai and Shenzhen Connect.

2.2.3. Shanghai–London Stock Connect (London Connect)

In September 2015, the UK former Chancellor of the Exchequer George Osborne announced a 'landmark feasibility study' into the idea of linking the Chinese and British stock exchanges together, when he attended the 7th China–UK Economic and Financial Dialogue.[78] 'I want to see our stock markets in London and Shanghai formally connected, with UK firms raising funds from Chinese savers, and Chinese firms listing in London', the Chancellor said when he visited the SSE.[79] His trip came ahead of a state visit to the UK by Chinese President Xi Jinping

[77] See the definition of 'Institutional Professional Investor' in the Securities and Futures (Professional Investor) Rules under the Securities and Future Ordinance of Hong Kong, Cap. 571, section 391(1): www.elegislation.gov.hk/hk/cap571D.

[78] *BBC*, 'UK–China Stocks Link Plan Unveiled' (22 September 2015), available at: www.bbc.co.uk/news/business-34322446 (accessed on 11 April 2023).

[79] The UK Government website, 'Chancellor: "Let's Create a Golden Decade for the UK–China Relationship"' (22 September 2015), available at: www.gov.uk/government/speeches/chancellor-lets-create-a-golden-decade-for-the-uk-china-relationship (accessed on 21 June 2021).

in October 2015. In December 2017, London and Beijing restated their commitment to defend global free trade when the then Chancellor, Philip Hammond, attended the 9th China–UK Economic and Financial Dialogue in Beijing. The Chancellor stated, 'we have agreed to accelerate the final preparations for the London–Shanghai Stock Connect initiative and we have agreed to commence feasibility studies for a UK-China bond connect and for mutual recognition of funds between the two jurisdictions'.[80]

Since then, the Chinese and British regulators have been working on the long-awaited launch of London Connect and have issued applicable rules and regulations for this connectivity mechanism. On China's side, the State Council issued 'Several Opinions on Launching the Pilot Programme for Innovative Enterprises Domestically Issuing Stocks or Depository Receipts'[81] on 22 March 2018, which built up a platform of rules for issuing depository receipts domestically by Chinese companies, especially for those high-tech innovative enterprises listed overseas. On 6 June in the same year, the CSRC issued the 'Administrative Measures for the Issuance and Trading of Depository Receipts (for Trial Implementation)'[82] together with eight corresponding regulations and guidelines. They clarify the requirements for the issuance, trading and information disclosure of Chinese Depository Receipt (CDR) and break through the legal systems which forbid foreign companies from listing in Mainland China. Together, the opinions, measures and supporting documents mark the launch of a significant new approach to capitalising a select group of Chinese technology companies through CDRs, representing a further opening-up of the Chinese capital market.

On 12 October 2018, the CSRC issued the 'Provisions on the Supervision and Administration of Depository Receipts under the Stock Connect Scheme between Shanghai Stock Exchange and London Stock Exchange (for Trial Implementation)' (No 30 [2018] of CSRC),[83] providing a legal and institutional basis for the connectivity of the two markets and issuance of depository receipts. On the same day, the SSE simultaneously published its consultation on the relevant systems of London Connect. On 2 November, the SSE promulgated seven regulations to set forth specific provisions on the listing process, cross-border conversion and the market-making system for depository receipts, such as the 'Notice on Issuing

[80] *South China Morning Post*, 'Britain and China Promise to Speed Up Work on London–Shanghai Stock Connect' (16 December 2017), available at: www.scmp.com/news/china/diplomacy/article/2124601/britain-and-china-promise-speed-work-london-shanghai-stock (accessed on 21 June 2021).

[81] No 21 [2018] of State Council, the full text in Chinese is available at: http://www.gov.cn/zhengce/content/2018-03/30/content_5278689.htm (accessed on 1 December 2020).

[82] No 143 [2018] of CSRC, the full text in Chinese is available at: www.csrc.gov.cn/xiamen/xxfw/gfxwj/201806/t20180611_339645.htm (accessed on 1 December 2020). English version at: www.lawinfochina.com/display.aspx?id=28709&lib=law&SearchKeyword=&SearchCKeyword=.

[83] The Trial Implementation was repealed by the CSRC's 'Provisions on the Supervision and Administration of Depository Receipts under the Stock Connect Scheme between Domestic and Overseas Stock Exchanges' (No 28 [2022] of CSRC) on 11 February 2022.

the Guidelines for the Pre-Listing Review of Chinese Depository Receipts under the Stock Connect Scheme between Shanghai Stock Exchange and London Stock Exchange' and 'Notice on Issuing the Guidelines for the Cross-Border Conversion of Depository Receipts under the Stock Connect Scheme between Shanghai Stock Exchange and London Stock Exchange'.[84]

On the UK side, the London Stock Exchange (LSE) announced the 'Consultation on Amendments to the Admission and Disclosure Standards' on 10 July 2018, soliciting advice on the addition of the Shanghai–London Stock Connect Segment and other associated revisions. On 17 September, the LSE issued the amended 'Admission and Disclosure Standards',[85] adding the Shanghai–London Stock Connect segment to the main market and corresponding issuance and disclosure requirements. The standards came into effect on 1 October 2018.

In addition to complying with the above-mentioned rules, an SSE-listed company issuing Global Depository Receipts (GDR) is still subject to the related requirements of the Securities Law and Special Regulations of the State Council Concerning Floating and Listing of Shares Overseas by Companies Limited by Shares, and the relevant rules of GDR issuance promulgated by the UK securities regulatory authorities, such as the 'Prospectus Regulation Rules' promulgated by the FCA.

Although the depository receipt market is already well-established in the UK, there are some nuances specific to London Connect, including the different lengths for settlement cycles in Shanghai and London, the different currencies in each market, as well as time zone differences between the two. Obtaining a London GDR listing pursuant to Stock Connect involves a two-part process that requires both: (i) an application to the FCA for the admission of the Chinese company's GDRs to the official list maintained by the UK FCA; and (ii) an application to the London Stock Exchange for the GDRs to be admitted to the Shanghai–London Stock Connect segment (Shanghai Segment) of the LSE's Main Market.

2.2.3.1. Eligible Securities

Depository receipts (DRs) are securities certificates issued by depository banks to represent a company's publicly traded securities which can be listed and traded independently from the underlying shares. Chinese companies would be the ones issuing GDRs on the LSE and Swiss stock exchange. On the other hand, international companies would be issuing CDRs on China's markets. These GDRs permit the indirect exercise of the membership and property rights attached to the deposited equity securities, by depositing the underlying shares with a depository. The relationship between the company and the depository is governed by a

[84] All seven regulations in English are available on the SSE's website: english.sse.com.cn/start/rules/related/slsc/ (accessed on 1 December 2020).

[85] The full text is available on the LSE's website: docs.londonstockexchange.com/sites/default/files/documents/admission-and-disclosure-standards-new2018.pdf (accessed on 1 December 2021).

depository agreement, which regulates, inter alia, how membership and property rights attached to the deposited underlying shares may be exercised.

2.2.3.2. Eligible Participants

London Connect can be divided into two sub-programmes: Eastbound and Westbound, which provide the cross-border conversion of depository receipts for those listed companies which plan to obtain a second listing in the counterpart market (see Table 2.4 'Operational Directions' above). With respect to issuers under the Westbound London business link, initially only high-quality Chinese companies with a market capitalisation of over RMB 20 billion, already listed on the SSE were able to issue GDRs. The issuers also should comply with 25 per cent free float requirements for their GDR listing. In addition, companies must further be approved by China's CSRC to issue a GDR as well as produce a full English-language approved prospectus for the UK Listing Authority (UKLA). GDRs could be listed in USD and other currencies while CDRs are listed in RMB.[86] But according to the modified Listing Rules (LR) of LSE, all securities to be listed on the Main Market must have the expected aggregate market value at least GBP 30 million (LR 2.2.7R), a 10 per cent minimum free float (LR 14.2.2R), and audited historical financial information for three years or such shorter period for which the issuer has been in operation (depending on the applicable LR Annexes). In this regard, it could be implied that the capital eligibility criteria for Chinese GDRs in London has been decreased from RMB 20 billion (approximately USD 2.9 billion) to GBP 30 million (approximately USD 38.4 million, around 1.3 per cent of the previous capital requirement).

Conversely, in order to list CDRs in China under the Eastbound Shanghai business link, issuers must have a market capitalisation of over RMB 20 billion; already have been listed on the LSE for at least three years (one year premium listed); issue a minimum of 50 million units of CDRs representing RMB 500 million worth of underlying shares; and hold or acquire sufficient underlying shares.[87] Companies will also be approved by CSRC and SSE/SZSE to take part in Stock Connect.

Both institutional and individual investors can participate in London Connect. But Chinese individual investors wishing to trade CDRs have to meet a number of requirements including: having no less than RMB 500,000 (previously 3 million) in cash and securities in their accounts over the previous 20 trading days; have been trading securities for 24 months; have no serious adverse entry in their integrity

[86] For the listing and trading requirements, see LSE, 'Shanghai-London Stock Connect', available at: www.londonstockexchange.com/discover/china/shanghai-london-stock-connect (accessed on 22 December 2022).

[87] SSE, 'Notice on Issuing the Interim Measures for the Listing and Trading of Depository Receipts under the Stock Connect Scheme between Shanghai Stock Exchange and Overseas Stock Exchanges' (No 37 [2022] of the SSE) (25 March 2022), art 6, available at: english.sse.com.cn/start/sserules/icbb/slsc/c/5700286.pdf (accessed on 3 January 2023).

record; and not be prohibited from trading securities under any circumstance by Chinese law.[88] But there is no such requirement for the UK investors.

2.2.3.3. Quota

There is no quota limit for either the trading of GDRs in London or CDRs in China. But quotas apply to the creation of new CDRs and GDRs. For example, in order to list CDRs in Shanghai, the UK issuers must issue a minimum of 50 million units of CDRs, representing RMB 500 million worth of underlying shares. GDR issuers also must comply with 25 per cent free float requirements for their listing.

2.2.3.4. Clearing and Settlement

Regarding Westbound issuance of depository receipts for listed companies, Chinese A-share companies wishing to be traded in the LSE will proceed through the issuance of GDRs. Meanwhile, Eastbound issuance means that UK-listed companies will have the opportunity to list on the SSE directly by issuing CDRs. In theory, depository receipts are not shares but they represent equity interests in foreign companies through an off shore custodian bank.

In terms of the cross-border conversion mechanism, the clearing and settlement service for CDR issuers will be provided by ChinaClear, and the clearing service for GDR issuers will be provided by London Clearing House and the settlement will be executed via Euroclear Bank.

Designated brokers (also referred to as 'cross-border conversion institutions' in the SSE and CSRC rules) will consist of securities companies that obtain a special licence to conduct business on selling and purchasing CDRs and GDRs on behalf of their clients. For trading GDRs on the LSE, designated brokers can create and redeem the GDRs through buying and selling the underlying shares in China, with the underlying shares being held by the depository bank. However, in line with the CSRC rules, the buy-back of GDRs within 120 days is not allowed, in order to prohibit opportunistic GDR issuers from selling GDRs at a higher price and repurchasing such securities at a lower price immediately (speculative arbitrage).[89] However, no restrictions exist on the buy-back of CDRs. Home market rules apply when trading the underlying A-shares, meaning pre-funding and pre-delivery are required in China. To address the differences in settlement cycle, designated brokers will be able to hold cash and underlying shares as inventory to manage risk. Therefore, on a normal settlement cycle, GDR creation settles on T+2, while redemption takes T+3 days (this can be shortened to T+2 using inventory).

For trading CDRs on the SSE, designated brokers are able to create and redeem the CDRs through buying and selling the underlying shares in London.

[88] ibid, art 48.
[89] Art 38 of the CSRC's Provisions on the Supervision and Administration of Depository Receipts under the Stock Connect Scheme between Domestic and Overseas Stock Exchanges 2022.

Home market rules apply when trading the underlying securities, meaning securities settle on T+2. To address the differences in settlement cycle, designated brokers will be able to hold cash and underlying shares as inventory to manage risk. Furthermore, they are able to participate in the securities borrowing and lending market in London, trade over-the-counter securities and manage risk through various hedging tools. On a normal settlement cycle, CDR creation settles on T+3. This can be streamlined to T+1 using borrowed stocks and over-the-counter trading, while redemption is on T+3.

The SSE will be responsible for managing the procedure of how to become a cross-border designated broker which will be the principal market-makers for CDR transactions. For an LSE member broker who wishes to become a GDR cross-border designated broker, it must appoint an SSE member broker to help it to submit the relevant application and supporting documents as required, whereas the SSE and CSRC will directly designate certain member securities companies to become CDR cross-border conversion institutions. To become GDR cross-border designated brokers, securities brokers have to satisfy the following standards:[90]

- have a full membership of the LSE;
- be qualified as QFIs, or be a subsidiary wholly owned by QFIs; and
- comply with the regulatory requirements and rules set by the SSE.

CDR cross-border designated brokers will have to meet extra requirements imposed by the SSE/SZSE and CSRC, including:[91]

- be approved by the SSE or SZSE;
- be approved and rated by the CSRC;
- be able to carry out market-making services, initial liquidity, and bilateral quotation;
- be qualified to be involved in proprietary trading of securities;
- be classified as a BBB-level securities company or above in the most recent two years; and
- have more than three years' history in trading overseas securities.

[90] The qualifications of CDR and GDR designated brokers are listed on the LSE's website, 'Trading through Shanghai-London Stock Connect' available at: www.lseg.com/markets-products-and-services/our-markets/shanghai-london-stock-connect/trading-through-shanghai-london-stock-connect (accessed on 21 June 2022).

[91] Art 6 of the SSE's 'Notice on Issuing the Guidelines No. 1 for Depository Receipts under the Stock Connect Scheme of Shanghai Stock Exchange – Cross-Border Conversion of Depository Receipts' (No 38 [2022] of the SSE) issued on 25 March 2022, available at: english.sse.com.cn/start/sserules/icbb/slsc/c/5700287.pdf and art 6 of the SZSE's 'Notice on Issuing the Guidelines No. 1 for Depository Receipts under the Stock Connect Scheme of Shenzhen Stock Exchange – Cross-Border Conversion of Depository Receipts' (No 300 [2022] of the SZSE) issued on 25 March 2022, available at dr.szse.cn/rules/t20220325_592078.html (accessed on 12 December 2022).

2.2.4. China–Switzerland Stock Connect (Switzerland Connect)

Whilst London is possibly still perceived as somewhat scattered due to the implications of Brexit, China is looking for more connects with other countries, to gain access to a broad international investor base, thereby achieving a high level of brand awareness and visibility even beyond China. Following London Connect, China's connectivity programme has expanded to link with Switzerland and soon Germany.

On 28 July 2022 the CSRC and the Swiss Federal Department of Finance jointly announced the official launch of China–Switzerland Stock Connect, opening a new chapter in the capital market cooperation between the two countries.[92] The background to all this was the revision by the CSRC of the Stock Connect Rules on 11 February 2022, to now include, amongst others, the SZSE and the SIX Swiss Exchange. Thereafter, on 25 July 2022, the Swiss Financial Market Supervisory Authority (FINMA) approved a relevant revision of the SIX Listing Rules (LR) and the introduction of a new designated GDR trading segment on the SIX. This all paved the way for the signing of supplementary Memoranda of Understanding (MoUs) between the three exchanges involved – the SSE, SZSE and SIX Swiss Exchange – and for the quadruple GDRs listings on 28 July 2022, underpinning not only the longstanding close relationship between China and Switzerland overall, but also the friendly and fruitful collaboration between the Chinese stock exchanges and SIX dating back to 2015, where initial MoUs were signed, as renewed in 2019. On the same launch day, the first four Chinese companies (namely, Gem, Gotion High-Tech, Keda Industrial Group and Ningbo Shanshan) listed GDRs on the SIX Swiss Exchange (SIX), thereby successfully raising around USD 1.6 billion in total. Until now, there have been nine Chinese companies choose the SIX to issue GDRs. But unfortunately no Swiss companies have listed CDRs in China thus far.

Meanwhile, the CSRC revised the 'Provisions on the Supervision and Administration of Depository Receipts under the Stock Connect Scheme between Domestic and Overseas Stock Exchanges' (CSRC Announcement [2022] No 28) on 11 February 2022.[93] The revision focuses on expanding the scope of the original Provisions for London Connect, allowing for financing through CDR offerings, and optimising ongoing supervision. Major elements of the revision include:[94]

- Expanding the scope of application by including SZSE, Switzerland, Germany, and potentially other international markets;
- Allowing overseas issuers to raise new capital in Chinese domestic markets through CDR offerings;

[92] CSRC, 'China-Switzerland Stock Connect Officially Launched' (28 July 2022), available at: www.csrc.gov.cn/csrc_en/c102030/c4885446/content.shtml (12 December 2022).

[93] The full text of the Provisions is available on the CSRC's website, www.csrc.gov.cn/csrc_en/c102034/c1885832/content.shtml (accessed on 3 January 2023).

[94] CSRC, 'Revision Notes on the Provisions on the Supervision and Administration of Depository Receipts under the Stock Connect between Domestic and Overseas Stock Exchanges' (11 February 2022) www.csrc.gov.cn/csrc_en/c102034/c1885832/content.shtml (accessed on 3 January 2023).

- Simplifying disclosure requirements on financial information and internal control of overseas issuers. An overseas issuer that adopts equivalent accounting standards does not need to make additional disclosure of the differences between the accounting standards it adopts and the Chinese Accounting Standards for Business Enterprises; nor does it need to disclose the information on difference adjustment according to the Chinese accounting standards.

2.2.4.1. Eligible Securities

Switzerland Connect employs the same model as London Connect by trading depository receipts representing shares cross-border. Article 90 of the SIX Exchange Listing Rules (LR) defines GDRs as tradable certificates which are issued to represent deposited equity securities, ie underlying shares. These GDRs permit the indirect exercise of the membership and property rights attached to the deposited equity securities, by depositing the underlying shares with a depository. The relationship between the company and the depository is governed by a depository agreement, which regulates, inter alia, how membership and property rights attached to the deposited underlying shares may be exercised. On the other hand, similarly to London Connect, SIX-listed companies would be issuing CDRs on China's SSE or SZSE.

2.2.4.2. Eligible Participants

The requirements to be fulfilled by issuers of GDRs remain unchanged and are the same as for the main market segment in the LR. These requirements include the rules on the required minimum equity capital of at least CHF 25 million (approximately USD 27 million) (Article 15 LR), a company track record of three years, application of the recognised account standards and compliance with the rules regarding auditors and audit reports (Articles 12–14). Companies listing GDRs are subject to similar transparency requirements to the other primary listed equity securities, such as ad hoc publicity obligations, financial reporting and disclosure of management transactions, yet GDRs are not deemed to be mainly listed in the sense of the Financial Market Infrastructure Ordinance (FinMIO). As far as the accepted accounting standards in respect to Chinese GDRs are concerned, SIX accepts the Accounting Standards of the People's Republic of China for Business Enterprises (ASBE) as an accounting standard.

But Swiss issuers that apply for the listing of CDRs on the SSE or SZSE for the first time have to meet the same requirements as those under London Connect, including an average market capitalisation of at least RMB 20 billion over the 120 trading days prior to the offering application date and a trading history of three years, as well as other requirements prescribed by Chinese law.[95]

[95] SSE, 'Notice on Issuing the Interim Measures for the Listing and Trading of Depository Receipts under the Stock Connect Scheme between Shanghai Stock Exchange and Overseas Stock Exchanges' 2022, see n 87 above, art 6.

With respect to qualified investors, the eligibility requirements are also the same for all Chinese GDR investors participating in London and Switzerland Connects (either institutional investors or individual investors must hold an aggregate balance of not less than RMB 500,000 in their securities and cash accounts), whereas there are no such requirements for Swiss investors.

2.2.4.3. Quota

Similarly to London Connect, the Swiss-listed companies issuing CDRs in China must issue a minimum of 50 million units of CDRs representing RMB 500 million worth of underlying shares. Chinese GDR issuers also must comply with 20 per cent free float requirements for their listing (Article 19 LR).

2.2.4.4. Clearing and Settlement

The clearing and settlement of GDRs are the same as for any other equity security listed on SIX Swiss Exchange. The depository (Article 92 LR) must fulfil at least one of the following criteria:

- a Swiss bank (as per the Swiss Banking Act) or a Swiss securities firm (as per the Financial Institutions Act);
- a depository must be subject to an equivalent foreign supervision;
- the Regulatory Board may require that suitable documents be presented as evidence of the depository's regulatory status.

In addition, a depository applying to the SSE or SZSE to become a Chinese cross-border conversion institution should abide by the CSRC and the two exchanges' rules as discussed above in section 2.2.3 'London Connect'.

2.3. What Makes Stock Connect Special?

Stock Connect brings together one of the world's largest domestic capital market with the world's leading international markets. This programme represents a number of firsts: the first time any foreign companies are able to list in Mainland China and the first time SSE/SZSE-listed companies are able to raise capital abroad through instruments fungible with their domestic shares; the first time Chinese investors are able to access international stocks from within China without being subject to domestic capital controls; the first time international investors are able to access China A-shares from outside Greater China and through international trading and settlement practices. This section distinguishes Stock Connect from Chinese existing liberalisation schemes.

2.3.1. Comparison of Four Stock Connect Links

2.3.1.1. Shanghai Connect vs. Shenzhen Connect

Shenzhen Connect was launched two years after Shanghai Connect. It draws on the successful experience of Shanghai Connect by following its basic framework and model with all the main operational mechanisms and institutional arrangements such as trade settlement, quota control, investor suitability, market surveillance and self-regulation.

Previously, the scope of investment securities under Shenzhen Connect was much wider than that of Shanghai Connect. Compared to Shanghai Connect, Shenzhen Connect extended its eligible investment for Northbound investors by adding ChiNext-listed shares and constituents of the SZSE Small/Mid Cap Innovation Index with market capitalisation of above RMB 6 billion. The Southbound channel also broadened the scope for Chinese investors from the HSLI/HSMI to the HSSI with market capitalisation above HKD 5 billion.

However, in December 2022, the scope of eligible stocks for Southbound trading under Shanghai Connect was expanded to include constituents of the HSSI with a market capitalisation of HKD 5 billion or above, which brings it in line with the existing scope of eligible stocks for Southbound trading under Shenzhen–Hong Kong Stock Connect. The expansion for Northbound trading also adopts unified rules for both Connects. Therefore, the current scopes of eligible equities, including stocks and ETFs, are the same for Northbound trading under both Shanghai and Shenzhen Connect. Similarly, the Southbound trading links of both Connects also have the same scope of eligible equities. Hence, despite being two different links, Shanghai Connect and Shenzhen Connect have the same business operation models, clearing and settlement procedures, daily quota, as well as suitability guidelines for investors and investment products.

2.3.1.2. China–Hong Kong Stock Connect (Hong Kong Connect) vs. China–London/Switzerland Stock Connect (London/Switzerland Connect)

London/Switzerland Connect is a mechanism under which listed companies in China and London/Switzerland, satisfying certain conditions, can issue their depository receipts in the market on the other side. Trading and settlement of the depository receipts is similar to that for stocks. In addition, with reference to international practices, the depository receipts and the underlying stocks can be converted into each other. With the mutual conversion mechanism between the underlying stocks and the depository receipts, the trading in the two markets will be connected, and as such achieve cross-border fungibility. However, both Connects differ significantly in several ways as follows.

2.3.1.2.1. Market Mechanism

Hong Kong Connect, ie, Shanghai/Shenzhen Connect is a secondary market trading scheme. Investors in one market can purchase shares of listed companies in the counterpart's market through Stock Connect. But it does not support primary market activities such as Initial Public Offerings (IPOs).

By contrast, London/Switzerland Connect is a scheme that covers both primary and secondary markets. Investors can trade the depository receipts in the secondary market. For Westbound business, SSE/SZSE listed Companies can use newly-issued shares for the issue of GDRs to achieve primary market security issuance.

2.3.1.2.2. Eligibility Criteria

Generally speaking, the eligibility criteria for issuers and investors under London/Switzerland Connect were much higher than those of Shanghai/Shenzhen Connect. Regarding issuers, LSE/SIX-listed companies with a minimum market capitalisation of RMB 20 billion (approximately USD 2.9 billion) are permitted to issue CDRs in Chinese markets, while Hong Kong companies with a market capitalisation of HKD 5 billion or above (approximately USD 0.64 billion, less than one-fourth of CDR issuers) can participate in Southbound trading of Shanghai/Shenzhen Connect.

Regarding investors, previously CDRs under London Connect were only available to Chinese investors with more than RMB 3 million in financial assets, which was six times higher than the eligibility criteria for Chinese investors under Shanghai/Shenzhen Connect (RMB 500,000). However, in 2022, the CSRC lowered the asset entry standard for Chinese CDR investors to RMB 500,000, which aligns with the eligibility criteria for investors under Hong Kong Connect and Switzerland Connect.

2.3.1.2.3. Scope of Investment

Stocks and ETFs are eligible securities under Shanghai/Shenzhen Connect, while depository receipts are eligible securities under London/Switzerland Connect. Eligible stocks can be traded automatically under Shanghai/Shenzhen Connect, without the companies having to apply for inclusion in the system. In contrast, the scope of the underlying shares of companies listed in the counterpart's stock exchange is taken into account for the purpose of issuing the corresponding depository receipts, but those eligible shares do not automatically enter the trading system of London/Switzerland Connect. The issuance and listing of depository receipts are subject to the voluntary applications of eligible companies and the approval of regulatory bodies in China and London/Switzerland.

In essence, with the Shanghai/Shenzhen Connect programme, investors on both sides can directly trade stocks in the market on the other side, and the traded products remain local. Conversely, with the London/Switzerland Connect programme, depository receipts created by converting stocks from the opposite market are listed and traded in the local market, with the traded products crossing borders, but the investors remaining local.

2.3.2. Comparison between Stock Connect and Other Chinese Liberalisation Schemes

Prior to Stock Connect, foreign investors had limited access to Chinese stock markets due to the different classes of Chinese shares, as mentioned above. Chinese financial authorities had mostly restricted international investment in the country's stock markets to foreign currency-denominated shares, known as B-shares, which were traded in foreign currency on two Chinese exchanges. However, B-shares were hampered by low trading volumes and concerns over the quality of listed companies. An alternative channel for foreign investors to enter China's capital markets was the QFII and RQFII schemes, which provided access to Chinese stock markets but only to selected and government-approved institutional investors. On 1 November 2020, the QFII and RQFII were merged into a single QFI regime. In the opposite direction, the QDII and RQDII schemes had been the only official channels for Mainland participation in overseas stock markets.

The differences between Stock Connect and (R)QFII, QFI, and (R)QDII have been summarised in Table 2.7. Among these, a few key differences are highlighted as follows.

- First, Stock Connect provides direct mutual market access for Chinese and international investors to trade directly on each other's exchanges, while QFI and QDII are one-way investment channels that require investors to go through licensed intermediaries or custodians to make investments. Stock Connect allows for two-way trading, where both Chinese and foreign investors can buy and sell equities across the participating markets without prior approval. In contrast, QFI is an inbound investment channel for international institutional investors, while QDII is an outbound investment channel for Chinese institutional investors.
- Second, they have different scopes of eligible investments. Initially, only A-shares were covered in Stock Connect, excluding B-shares, ETFs, bonds, and other securities. The products were later expanded to include ETFs in 2016 and depository receipts in 2019. On the other hand, (R)QFII and (R) QDII have a much broader range of investments, including stocks, bonds, investment funds, and other products such as warrants and index futures.

In addition to the traditional categories of investment products of QFII and QDII, QFI has significantly expanded the categories of products by including over-the-counter securities, derivatives on the China Interbank Bond Market, commodity futures contracts and options, and private investment funds.

- Third, the scope of investors in the pre-existing schemes is narrower than those of Stock Connect. QFII and QDII are limited to institutional investors with eligibility requirements regarding minimum business experience, capital and assets under management. Particularly, QFII is only available to qualified institutions domiciled in a country that is party to a memorandum of understanding (MoU) with China. Likewise, RQFII is only available to qualified institutions in the approved RQFII jurisdictions. By contrast, trading in securities under Stock Connect is open to all Hong Kong and overseas investors including institutional and individual investors, which are free from any approval and eligibility requirements. Even investors located in jurisdictions that do not qualify for QFII or RQFII can have access to A-shares via Stock Connect. The only exception to Stock Connect is ChiNext stocks of the SZSE and STAR Market stocks of the SSE which are only traded by institutional professional investors. Apart from that, Hong Kong and overseas investors are allowed to trade any Connect securities through Stock Connect.
- Four, QFII or RQFII used to involve an approval process for a certain associated quota, and the holder was responsible for trading within the limits and disclosing all required information. However, their quota limits were recently removed on 7 May 2020, while a registration process is in place to monitor qualified foreign investors to transfer capital into and out of China. It is a gesture to further open Chinese capital markets to the world, despite the criticism that it will make very little difference because foreign investors have been relying more heavily on other cross-border channels with better arrangements such as Stock Connect to allow easier access to trade in China. But the quota for (R)QDII is still applied and reviewed by the SAFE every year.

  By contrast, the aggregate quota of RMB 300 billion for Shanghai Connect has been abolished since 16 August 2016 and no aggregate quota has been established for Shenzhen Connect. Instead, trading under Stock Connect is subject to a daily quota for the total market level, with no additional approval or separate quota allocation at the investor level. And no quota system for depository receipts is applied to London/Switzerland Connect.

In summary, the key differences between Stock Connect and other pre-existing Chinese liberalisation schemes are that Stock Connect provides two-way mutual market access while others focus on one-way investment. Additionally, both individual and institutional investors can participate in Stock Connect without regulatory approval and licensed quota, whereas other schemes are limited to qualified institutional investors, despite the limited selection of investable securities available under Stock Connect.

Table 2.7 Comparison between Stock Connect and Other Liberalisation Schemes

	Stock Connect	**(R)QFII (Replaced by QFI in 2020)**	**QFI**	**(R)QDII**
Approval	None	Apply to CSRC for licence/permit and register with SAFE	Apply to CSRC for licence/permit and register with SAFE, but simpler application process with electronic filing enabled.	Apply to CSRC for licence/permit and register with SAFE
Eligible Investors	Institutional and individual investors	Institutional investors with (R)QFII licences*	Institutional investors with QFI licences (expanding to future companies, sovereign funds and international organisations)	Five types of institutional investors: insurance companies, banks, trust companies, funds, and securities firms
Currency	Transactions in RMB in Mainland China and Hong Kong --------------- GDRs in GBP, CHF, USD or other currencies in London or Switzerland	QFII: Transactions in USD and other currencies ---------------- RQFII: Transactions in RMB	Free to choose the currency remitted inwards	QDII: Transactions in USD and other currencies ---------------- RQDII: Transactions in RMB
Quota	Market-level daily quota for China-Hong Kong Stock Connect -------------- No quota for London/ Switzerland Connect	QFII: Allocated to each institutional investor (removed in May 2020) --------------- RQFII: Allocated to offshore regions (removed in May 2020)	No quota	Quota granted and reviewed by SAFE

(continued)

Table 2.7 ***(Continued)***

	Stock Connect	(R)QFII (Replaced by QFI in 2020)	QFI	(R)QDII
Eligible Products	Selected A-shares and H-shares, ETFs and DRs	RMB denominated products approved by CSRC ***	More listed investment products, China Inter-bank Bond Market products, and exchange-traded derivatives	Overseas market products, fixed-income products, DRs, and certain equity products.
Regulation of Funds	Funds must return to origin; no lock-up period	Funds were subject to a lock-up period of a year which was then reduced to three months in 2009. The lock-up requirement was removed in 2018.	No lock-up period	No lock-up period
Investor's Rights	Subject to limitations****	No limitations	No limitations	No limitations

* Only asset managers, banks, insurance companies, securities companies and other types of FIIs such as pension funds, charitable funds, endowment funds, trust companies, government investment management institutions, with a certain amount of assets under management and number of years of operations were eligible to apply for a QFII or RQFII licence.

** Market wide quota of RMB 52 billion for SSE and SZSE, RMB 42 billion for SEHK.

*** Stocks, bonds, warrants, funds, index futures fixed income products in interbank-market; primary market activities such as IPO, convertible bond issuance, additional shares issuance and seasoned equity offerings.

**** Shares acquired as entitlements can only be sold if they are not one of the eligible stocks of Stock Connect but are SSE/SZSE-listed, and cannot be bought or sold using the Stock Connect scheme if they are not SSE/SZSE-listed.

2.4. Concluding Remarks

The capital market in China has undergone significant growth and development in recent decades, becoming an important source of financing for businesses and a key driver of economic growth. At the same time, China has been gradually liberalising its capital markets to open up to foreign investment and integrate more fully with global financial markets. The launch of Stock Connect was part of China's efforts to liberalise its capital market and attract international investment into the country. By connecting with international financial centres such as Hong Kong,

London, Switzerland, and soon Germany, China aims to make its capital market more accessible and transparent to international investors and increase the international profile of its stock exchanges.

While all financial liberalisation schemes in China are designed to facilitate investment flows between China and overseas financial markets, the most significant differences between Stock Connect and others lie in market access, investor suitability, types of investment, and regulatory restrictions. Compared to other schemes, Stock Connect offers investors and market participants a range of benefits, including a wider range of participants such as institutional and individual investors, reduced regulatory barriers, and enhanced market integration.

In the existing four Connect links, China expanded the investment scope for Shanghai and Shenzhen Connects and consolidated the measures for the listing and trading of depository receipts under London and Switzerland Connects in 2022. With the expansion, Shanghai and Shenzhen Connects are becoming more consistent in terms of investment products, participant eligibility, daily quota, clearing, and settlement. Additionally, the expansion of the investment scope will give international investors more choice in A-shares and enhance Hong Kong's position as a gateway to Mainland China. For the latter, while the same Chinese rules apply to all CDR issuers participating in the listing and trading of depository receipts under Stock Connect in China, GDR issuers listed in London or Switzerland are subject to different rules set by their respective exchanges. Despite the same depository receipts and clearing and settlement arrangements, Switzerland sets much lower liquidity criteria for Chinese CDRs than London. In addition, the similarities and differences in regulating investor protection and company issuers in different Connect markets will be discussed in later chapters.

3

Investor Protection under Stock Connect

In the previous chapter, the development of Chinese capital market and its commitment to internationalisation through different initiatives have been discussed. One such initiative, also the focus of this book, is Stock Connect. As explained before, from a legal and regulatory perspective, the headline principle of 'home market rules' means that the laws, rules and regulations of the listed companies' domicile should apply.[1] Does it mean that the source of investor protection will come from one country/jurisdiction only? It is important to decipher this principle through the lens of different layers of rules and regulations. When a company (Company A) is incorporated and registered in a country (Country A), this company is, without any doubt, subject to the company law of Country A. When this company is then listed and admitted to the exchange in its home market, the listing rules and other trading arrangements of Country A will also apply. This part of the regulatory landscape will be the focus of the next chapter. However, when Company A's shares can be traded in a foreign market (Country B), the situation will get more complicated, especially with respect to the applicable securities law. It may actually be more appropriately described as a case of co-regulation, as opposed to the simple 'home market rules', depending on the exact trading arrangement of the Stock Connect scheme. Sometimes, it will be direct trading (as in the case of China/Hong Kong Connect). Sometimes, it will be through the issuance of depository receipts (as in the case of China/Foreign Countries Connect). In the former case, the 'home market rules' will apply in principle. In the latter case, the depository receipts are indeed a form of security issued in Country B, therefore casting doubt on the 'home market rules' principle. In fact, even in the former case, investors in Country B may still enjoy a degree of protection offered by their country's securities law.[2] In this chapter, I will examine

[1] Investor and Financial Education Council of Hong Kong, 'Understand Stock Connect', available at: www.ifec.org.hk/web/en/investment/investment-products/stock/stockconnect/understand-stock-connect.page (accessed on 1 February 2023); F Huang, 'Stock Connect: Integration, Internationalisation and Implementation' [2021] *Journal of Business Law* 558, 569.

[2] Using the China/Hong Kong Connect as an example, since 1 January 2020, the Investor Compensation Fund of Hong Kong has extended its coverage to the Shanghai and Shenzhen A-shares traded under the Stock Connect (Northbound trades of A-shares). Meanwhile, the fund does not cover southbound trading of Hong Kong shares by China-based investors. Part XII of the Securities and Futures Ordinance of Hong Kong established the Fund and defines the scope and procedures of its use.

the scope of investor protection under the securities law in four jurisdictions – namely, China, Hong Kong, the UK and Switzerland – all of which are involved in various Stock Connect schemes. In the next section, I will first explain the role of securities law in investor protection and set out the framework of analysis in the subsequent four sections (each for one jurisdiction). The final part will conclude by reconciling how the potential difference(s) in the four jurisdictions may affect the perceived level of investor protection for Stock Connect participants.

3.1. Significance and Strategies of Investor Protection under Securities Law

According to the International Organization of Securities Commissions (IOSCO) 'Objectives and Principles of Securities Regulation', three principal objectives of securities regulation are: (1) protecting investors; (2) ensuring that markets are fair, efficient and transparent; and (3) reducing systemic risk.[3] With respect to the first objective, the term 'investor' is intended to cover 'customers or other consumers'[4] of financial services. 'Customer protection' is important because of the presence of problems like information asymmetry and agency problems. Information asymmetry describes a situation where an investor may not always receive adequate information to make an informed investment decision. To address the problem, one legal solution is to require mandatory disclosures from securities issuers and listed companies.[5] The agency problem is a concern too. In this situation, corporate insiders, notably top managers and controlling shareholders, are predicted to have the tendency to expropriate the legal interests of outsiders, notably minority shareholders and creditors. According to Kraakman and colleagues, a set of legal strategies is in place to mitigate the vulnerability of the outsiders to the opportunism of the corporate insiders.[6] This chapter, together with the next one, seeks to explore precisely the question of how securities law will function together with company law and listing rules to form an effective regulatory package to address all these problems, but with a clear understanding that the two spheres (and therefore the two chapters) are not mutually exclusive and there may be an overlap in certain areas.

The theoretical foundation of modern securities market regulation has often started with the Efficient Market Hypothesis.[7] Under the Hypothesis, securities prices should fully reflect all available information. There are three possible forms: weak, semi-strong and strong. In a nutshell, the weak form has readily reflected

[3] IOSCO, 'Objectives and Principles of Securities Regulation' (May 2017), available at: www.iosco.org/library/pubdocs/pdf/IOSCOPD561.pdf (accessed on 1 February 2023).

[4] ibid.

[5] J Armour et al, *Principles of Financial Regulation* (Oxford, OUP, 2016) 62.

[6] R Kraakman et al, *Anatomy of Corporate Law* (Oxford, OUP, 2017) 31.

[7] See R Gilson, 'The Mechanisms of Market Efficiency' (1984) 70 *Virginia Law Review* 549; E Fama, 'Efficient Capital Markets: A Review of Theory and Empirical Work' (1970) 25 *Journal of Finance* 383.

all past information; the semi-strong form would take account of all public announcements as well; the strong form would entail all information (both public and undisclosed, ie inside information). The reason why the understanding of this is important in the context of this chapter (and also the next one) is that this theoretical foundation has justified the existence of a mandatory disclosure regime in corporate and securities law.[8] The regime serves as an affiliation strategy, that is intended to address the information asymmetry problem between insiders and outsiders by compelling companies to disclose information (in terms of initial, periodic and ad hoc disclosures), and seeks to make sure that investors are adequately informed before they make an investment decision.[9] For example, Easterbrook and Fischel argued that there are two basic components of US securities law: a prohibition against fraud, and requirements of disclosure at the time when securities are issued and periodically thereafter.[10] The mandatory disclosure system has been used as a tool to 'combat manager/shareholder agency problems'.[11] In the view of Ferrell, various transnational empirical studies have pointed to the positive effects of more demanding mandatory disclosure regimes, which were shown to be correlated with higher levels of financial development.[12] Crucially, there must be appropriate remedies and enforcement mechanisms in place to address false/misleading/omitted disclosures.[13]

Meanwhile, preserving market integrity is another major goal of securities regulation. In the absence of regulation, there can be widespread market misconduct at the expense of investor interests. Three major forms of market misconduct are insider trading, market manipulation, and short selling.[14] Take insider trading as an example. It is indeed a contentious issue in financial regulation. In a general sense, insider trading, sometimes known as insider dealing, means 'taking advantage of specific unpublished price-sensitive information to deal in securities to make a profit or avoid a loss'.[15] Some argue that we should not prohibit it because it can be advantageous to the market. Prominent supporters of deregulation, such as Manne and Carlton and Fischel, have asserted that insider trading fosters efficient capital markets by improving the accuracy of stock prices.[16] Some say that insider

[8] Armour et al (2016), see n 5 above, 104.

[9] L Gullifer and J Payne, *Corporate Finance Law* (Oxford, Hart, 2020) 543; Kraakman et al (2017), see n 6 above, 245.

[10] F Easterbrook and D Fischel, 'Mandatory Disclosure and the Protection of Investors' (1984) 70 *Virginia Law Review* 669, 669.

[11] P Mahoney, 'Mandatory Disclosure as a Solution to Agency Problems' (1995) 62 *The University of Chicago Law Review* 1047, 1111.

[12] A Ferrell, 'The Case for Mandatory Disclosure in Securities Regulation around the World' (2007) 2 *Brooklyn Journal of Corporate, Financial & Commercial Law* 81, 124.

[13] Armour et al (2016), see n 5 above, 178.

[14] ibid, 181.

[15] J Law and E Martin, *A Dictionary of Law* (Oxford, OUP, 2014), available at: www.oxfordreference.com/view/10.1093/acref/9780199551248.001.0001/acref-9780199551248-e-1984?rskey=Q7MJOc&result=2081? (accessed on 22 June 2021).

[16] H Manne, *Insider Trading and the Stock Market* (New York, The Free Press, 1966); D Carlton and D Fischel, 'The Regulation of Insider Trading' (1983) 35 *Stanford Law Review* 857. Meanwhile, McVea believed that proposers of deregulation like Manne and Carlton and Fischel focused too much on

trading is immoral and also constitutes a violation of trust, because from the perspective of broader legal principles, company officers owe a fiduciary duty to the company, and certain professionals may owe the same duty to their clients. All these entities indeed have a high risk of being accused of insider trading. Strudler and Orts believe that it is theoretically sound to accept insider trading as a type of fraud.[17] Mervyn King, ex-Governor of the Bank of England, and his colleague likewise went far enough to liken insider trading to theft.[18] Despite a debatable theoretical foundation for the regulation of insider trading, an inconvenient truth to the supporters of deregulation is that it is virtually certain that there will be some form of insider trading regulation, wherever public trading of shares is possible.[19] The form of regulation can differ; for example, in the US it is based on one general anti-fraud provision and then supplemented by the common law, and elsewhere statutes are normally present to explicitly define different essential elements of the illegal conduct.[20]

As stated at the beginning of this section, one last principal objective of regulation is to reduce systemic risks. To put it simply, the aim is to protect all participants in the market from a systemic collapse. The focus has been on the regulation of banks and other financial institutions.[21] Despite the fact that there are banks and other financial institutions involved in Stock Connect via an intermediary role and/or as listed companies, the chapter/book will not try to cover this regulatory objective directly and in detail because of its specialist nature.

One more important element of regulation is enforcement. As stated in the IOSCO Principles, a well-designed regulatory system 'should ensure an effective and credible use of inspection, investigation, surveillance and enforcement powers and implementation of an effective compliance program.'[22] Enforcement can be

economic efficiency, which risks ignoring other important non-economic values as well as the most important question of 'whether society is best served by rules which prohibit or promote the practice.' See H McVea, 'What's Wrong with Insider Dealing' (1995) 15 *Legal Studies* 390, 392.

[17] Strudler and Orts asserted that 'A moral understanding of insider trading as a particular kind of fraud provides a rational framework for judges, legislators, and administrators to deal with [insider trading] cases.' A Strudler and E Orts, 'Moral Principle in the Law of Insider Trading' (1999–2000) 78 *Texas Law Review* 375, 377.

[18] M King and A Roell, 'Insider Trading' (1988) 6 *Economic Policy* 165.

[19] U Bhattacharya and H Daouk, 'The World Price of Insider Trading' (2022) 57 *Journal of Finance* 75, 88.

[20] In the US, insider trading is largely regulated by the Securities Exchange Act of 1934. However, some commentators argue that SEC Rule 10b-5, implementing section 10(b) of the 1934 Act, does not expressly prohibit insider trading. Across the Atlantic in the EU, insider trading has been regulated much more recently than in the US. The EU legal framework in this regard were introduced by Directive 89/592/EEC coordinating regulations on insider dealing, then the Market Abuse Directive 2003/6/EC, and more recently the Market Abuse Regulation (Regulation (EU) No 596/2014 on market abuse). Commenting on the differences in regulatory approach between the US and the EU, Ventoruzzo opined that the US legal framework was 'complex and sometimes contradictory', whereas the EU had 'a more clear, systematic and probably straightforward approach.' M Ventoruzzo, 'Comparing Insider Trading in the United States and in the European Union: History and Recent Developments' (2014) 11 *European Company and Financial Law Review* 554.

[21] Gullifer and Payne (2020), see n 9 above, 26.

[22] International Organization of Securities Commissions (2017), see n 3 above, 6.

broadly classified into two categories: (i) a public enforcement mechanism where the law gives the regulator the responsibility to gather information and prosecute the offence; (ii) a private enforcement mechanism which serves as the means for the private parties to sue and recoup losses in court. The two forms of enforcement are complementary to each other. In addition to the functions fulfilled by public enforcement, ie justice and deterrence, civil remedies can compensate the wronged. For public enforcement, a quantifiable approach to measuring enforcement is to focus on inputs and outputs. Jackson and Roe have measured the intensity of public enforcement based on budgetary resources and staffing levels.[23] A higher budget and greater staffing allow the regulator to conduct more activities, for instance, investigation of wrongdoing, market surveillance and drafting rules. At the output level, enforcement can be measured either in terms of the number of actions brought or the aggregate financial sanctions levied. Nonetheless, a high number of these is not necessarily an indicator of an effective regulator. As asserted by Coffee, a regulator may opt for an advisory and consulting relationship with the regulated entities, but others may adopts a 'deterrent' approach by emphasising enforcement actions and the imposition of sanctions as the principal means by which to cause regulated entities to comply.[24] Meanwhile, the empirical results shown in La Porta and colleagues' article in 2006 pointed to the significance of the role of private enforcement in securities laws.[25] Both extensive disclosure requirements and standards of liability facilitating investor recovery of losses are associated with larger stock markets. However, the problem with their argument is that private enforcement in some leading markets, for example the UK, is not entirely efficient or widely utilised.[26] The relative value of public and private enforcement is a key issue, not yet fully understood, underpinning how financial markets deepen and broaden.

In the subsequent four sections, I will discuss the scope of securities regulation in the four countries/jurisdictions (China, Hong Kong, the UK, and Switzerland), using the analytical framework developed above. First, I will start by giving a quick overview of their regulatory development, and then will pinpoint three specific aspects of regulation, namely information regulation, regulation of market misconduct, and enforcement.

3.2. Protection in China

China's stock market was established at a rather late stage in the 1990s (at least when compared to the other three markets examined later), as part of their

[23] H Jackson and M Roe, 'Public and Private Enforcement of Securities Laws: Resource-based Evidence' (2009) 93 *Journal of Financial Economics* 207.

[24] J Coffee, 'Law and the Market: The Impact of Enforcement' (2007) 156 *University of Pennsylvania Law Review* 229, 261–62.

[25] R La Porta et al, 'What Works in Securities Laws?' (2006) 61 *Journal of Finance* 1.

[26] For example, ss 90 and 90A of the Financial Services and Markets Act (FSMA) 2000 give the shareholders significant potential claims, although these remedies are rarely used in practice.

national integrated economic reform initiated towards the end of the 1970s. The Shanghai Stock Exchange was founded on 26 November 1990 and opened for its first trading day on 19 December 1990. The Shenzhen Stock Exchange was founded in the same year, on 1 December, and formally opened for trading on 3 July 1991. After around three decades of development, these two exchanges are now among the largest in the world.[27] Before that, arguably, there had not been a strong demand for a comprehensive set of securities laws. Before the first Securities Law was introduced in 1998, the domestic market had been regulated by the 'Provisional Regulations on the Administration of Share Issuance and Trading', which, according to Zhu, just managed to provide basic protection for investors.[28] Chapter VI (Articles 57–67) of the Provisional Regulations outlined the requirements for corporate disclosures. The Provisional Regulations also provided the basis of public enforcement[29] and private enforcement[30] of the law, in relation to market misconduct.

The introduction of the first Company Law in China on 1 July 1994 was a milestone in developing a formal framework regulating corporate activities.[31] Before the enactment of the first Securities Law in 1998, the first Company Law had for a period of time carried the dual functions of governing the activities of both companies and the market. For example, there were provisions regarding the requirements for the listing, delisting and suspension of securities.[32] The first Securities Law came into effect in July 1999.[33] It was a result of strong influence from foreign jurisdictions, especially the US.[34] China has accepted technical advice from the US Securities Exchange Commission (SEC) since 1994, when the SEC signed a Memorandum of Understanding with its Chinese counterpart.

[27] As of the end of 2022, the Shanghai Stock Exchange was the third largest exchange in the world, just behind the New York Stock Exchange and NASDAQ. The Shenzhen Stock Exchange was the sixth largest, just behind the 'big three', Euronext and the Tokyo Stock Exchange. Data from the World Federation of Exchanges.

[28] The Provisional Regulations were promulgated by Decree No 112 of the State Council of the People's Republic of China on 22 April 1993 and effective as of the same date. One problem was that the Provisional Regulations remained silent about the civil liability and civil compensation when dealing with securities frauds. See S Zhu, 'Civil Litigation Arising from False Statements on China's Securities Market' (2005) 31 *North Carolina Journal of International Law & Commercial Regulation* 377, 380.

[29] Provisional Regulations on the Administration of Share Issuance and Trading 1993, arts 74–76.

[30] ibid, art 77.

[31] The Chinese Company Law was adopted by the Standing Committee of the National People's Congress on 29 December 1993, effective as of 1 July 1994, revised on 25 December 1999 and 27 October 2005; and then amended in 2013 and in 2018; the current version became effective as of 26 October 2018.

[32] See Chapter IV, section 3 of the Company Law 1993.

[33] The Chinese Securities Law was adopted by the Standing Committee of the National People's Congress on 29 December 1998, effective as of 1 July 1999, amended on 28 August 2004 and revised on 27 October 2005; and then amended in 2013 and 2014; last revised in 2019; the current version became effective as of 1 March 2020.

[34] According to Tang, the Securities Law 1998 imitated the US disclosure principle and numerous substantive provisions. See X Tang, 'Protecting Minority Shareholders in China: A Task for Both Legislation and Enforcement' in H Kanda et al (eds), *Transforming Corporate Governance in East Asia* (London, Taylor & Francis, 2008) 141.

Furthermore, during the work of drafting the first Securities Law, international symposia were held with foreign experts from Hong Kong, the US, the UK and other countries.[35]

According to Zhou, there were notable flaws in the first Securities Law.[36] For example, there were contradictory provisions.[37] In both 2005 and 2019, there were extensive revisions to the law. Some key changes included introducing a registration-based system for issuers (as opposed to an approval-based system),[38] enhanced disclosures, strengthened investor protection, increased powers to the regulator, and heavier penalties for market misconduct.[39]

One noteworthy change in the context of this book is that depository receipts are now formally recognised as a type of security by the new Securities Law.[40] Previously only shares and bonds were recognised.[41] But the Securities Law itself does not try to distinguish much between depository receipts and other types of securities defined by the law, when the former is only mentioned once more in the law.[42] The substantive regulation of them is largely left to the 'Administrative Measures for the Offering and Trading of Depository Receipts (Trial Implementation)'.[43] In general, the *Trial Administrative Measures* regularly refer back to the Securities Law, suggesting that the provisions applicable to shares should largely apply. Article 56 stipulates the 'home market rules', namely that domestic Chinese issuers issuing depository receipts in a foreign market are subject to Chinese law. Meanwhile, for the opposite flow, the 'Trial Administrative Measures' also stipulate the requirements for overseas issuers which seek to issue depository receipts in China. The level of investor protection given by the foreign regime is expected to be not lower than the Chinese equivalent.[44]

As said before, the theoretical underpinning of modern securities law has been information regulation, so as to foster an 'efficient market'. The legal strategy employed is a mandatory disclosure regime. A typical listed company will be

[35] J Fu and J Yuan, *PRC Company & Security Laws: A Practical Guide* (Singapore, CCH Asia, 2006) 24.

[36] Y Zhou, *Zhengjuanfa Xinlun (New Study on Securities Law)* (Beijing, Law Press China, 2020) 31.

[37] Ibid. One example was the liability of the auditor profession. Article 161 seemed to impose civil liability on the auditors; but Article 202 only sought to impose civil liability on the firm they were representing.

[38] An initial public offering in China used to require a CSRC approval. See the Chinese Securities Law 2005, art 10. Contrast the change in wordings in Securities Law 2019, art 9.

[39] A good summary of the most recent changes was given by Lu. See L Lu, 'PRC Securities Law 2020: Promoting More Efficient and Transparent Capital Markets in China' (2021) 36 *Journal of International Banking and Financial Law* 237.

[40] Securities Law 2019, art 2.

[41] See eg Securities Law 2005, art 2.

[42] Securities Law 2019, art 12.

[43] 'Administrative Measures for the Issuance and Trading of Depository Receipts (Trial Implementation)' were issued by the CSRC on 6 June 2018. Furthermore, the 'Provisions on the Supervision and Administration of Depository Receipts under the Stock Connect Scheme between Domestic and Overseas Stock Exchanges', issued on 11 February 2022, provided further clarification on issues in light of the addition of new Stock Connect schemes, as well as changes in securities law.

[44] Trial Administrative Measures, art 3.

expected to make both initial and ongoing disclosures.[45] For the former, in addition to the Securities Law, other relevant regulations include the 'Administrative Measures on the Initial Public Offerings and Listing of Stocks', which outline the substantive requirements of a company listing. The actual content and format of an IPO prospectus are prescribed by the 'Standards for the Content and Format of Information Disclosure by Companies Offering Securities to the Public, No 1 – Prospectus'.[46] In relation to ongoing disclosures, again in addition to the Securities Law, other relevant regulations include the 'Administrative Measures on Information Disclosure of Listed Companies', as well as 'Standards for the Content and Format of Information Disclosure by Companies Offering Securities to the Public, No 2 – Content and Format of Annual Reports', which prescribes the contents and format of an annual report.[47] There are also other regulations governing half-yearly and quarterly reports.[48] Ad hoc disclosures are governed by Article 80 of the Securities Law. The Law prescribes 12 types of material events requiring ad hoc disclosures. Although the laws applicable in other markets are to be introduced in the later parts of this chapter, it is safe to say at this point that the information requirements in China are broadly similar and comparable to other markets.

The Securities Law outlines four types of market misconduct, namely insider trading, market manipulation, misrepresentation, and other prohibited conduct.[49] Insider trading was first regulated by the 'Provisional Regulation on the Administration of Share Issuance and Trading' 1993. Insider trading was prohibited and related administrative penalties outlined by Article 72 of the Provisional Regulations. The meaning of 'insider' and 'inside information' was also defined in the Provisional Regulations.[50] The Provisional Regulations were supplemented by the 'Provisional Regulations on the Prevention of Securities Frauds' (repealed) which set out a list of examples of 'insider trading behaviour', 'insiders', and 'insider information'.[51] In 1997, the Criminal Code recognised insider trading as a new type of crime.[52] When the first Securities Law was introduced in 1999, insider trading was again expressly prohibited, with provisions trying to define 'insider' and 'insider information' respectively.[53] In the subsequent revision of the Securities Law, one important reform was to introduce a civil remedy.[54] To further

[45] Securities Law 2019, arts 20, 79 and 80.
[46] The Standards No 1, issued by the CSRC, were last revised in 2015.
[47] The Standards No 2, issued by the CSRC, were last revised in 2021.
[48] Zhou (2020), see n 36 above, 346–47.
[49] See Securities Law 2019, Chapter III section 3.
[50] Provisional Regulations, art 72.
[51] Provisional Regulations on the Prevention of Securities Frauds (repealed), arts 4–6. The Provisional Regulations on the Prevention of Securities Frauds were issued by the State Council Securities Committee on 2 September 1993.
[52] Art 180 of Criminal Code. The maximum penalty can be 10 years of imprisonment and fines of five times the illegal proceeds.
[53] Securities Law 1998, arts 67–69.
[54] Securities Law 2005, art 76. The offence of insider trading was covered by arts 73–76.

fill the gaps in this area of regulation, the China Securities Regulatory Commission (CSRC) issued the '(Provisional) Guide for the Recognition and Confirmation of Insider Trading Behaviour in the Securities Markets' in 2007. However, in a critical account of this 2007 *Guide*, Howson argued that the document was 'legally defective'.[55] In 2010, the CSRC and other related authorities jointly issued the 'Opinions on Legally Suppressing, Preventing and Controlling Insider Trading on Capital Markets' to clarify the key elements of insider trading. In 2012, the Supreme People's Court and the Supreme People's Procuratorate jointly issued the 'Interpretation on Several Issues Concerning the Specific Application of Law in the Handling of Criminal Cases of Engaging in Insider Trading or Leaking Insider Information' to assist courts at all levels to apply the law. Finally, the current version of the Securities Law further broadens the scope of the law.[56]

After the Securities Law's last major revision in 2019, there is now a dedicated chapter, Chapter V (Articles 78–87) on information disclosures. The requirements stipulated are relatively basic, which therefore must be supplemented by other legislation (such as the Company Law), as well as administrative rules issued by regulators such as the CSRC and the stock exchanges. Amongst which, the most important one is the 'Administrative Measures on Information Disclosure of Listed Companies'.[57] The Administrative Measures outline more prescriptive ongoing disclosure requirements (including both periodic and ad hoc disclosure) for listed companies. The information requirements for initial public offerings are, on the other hand, regulated by the 'Administrative Measures on the Initial Public Offering and Listing of Stocks'.[58]

Article 78 of the Securities Law 2019 stipulates the general principles of information disclosure: 'Information disclosed by the parties under disclosure obligation shall be truthful, accurate, complete, concise and clear, easy to understand, and shall not contain any false record, misleading representation or major omission.' The civil liability for falling short of the required standard is covered by Article 56 of the Law.[59] The relevant administrative penalty is covered by Article 193 of the Law. There can also be criminal consequences as provided by Article 181 of the Chinese Criminal Code. The Supreme People's Court (SPC) of China specifies three types of misrepresentation: false disclosure, misleading statement, and material omission.[60] This was built on the general information requirement in

[55] N Howson, 'Enforcement without Foundation? – Insider Trading and China's Administrative Law Crisis' (2012) 60(4) *American Journal of Comparative Law* 955, 963.

[56] Securities Law 2019, arts 50–53.

[57] The Administrative Measures were adopted by the CSRC on 13 December 2006 and came into force on 30 January 2007. The most recent version was adopted on 4 March 2021 and came into force, as amended, on 1 May 2021.

[58] The Administrative Measures were first adopted by the CSRC on 17 May 2006, revised in 2015, and then revised again in 2022.

[59] Art 63 of the Securities Law 1998 and art 69 of the Securities Law 2005.

[60] 'Several Regulations Concerning the Adjudication of Civil Compensation Securities Cases Based upon Misrepresentation', issued by the SPC on 9 January 2003. These were revised by the SPC on 30 December 2021 and came into force, as revised, on 22 January 2022. See art 4 of the Regulations as revised.

the Securities Law that any disclosed information must be 'truthful, accurate and complete'.[61] Similar to the US approach, the Chinese law has placed a focus on the materiality of information to determine instance(s) of misrepresentation.[62] One yardstick to determine materiality is whether the information will affect investors' 'value judgment and investment decision'.[63] Another yardstick is whether there will be 'a significant impact on the trading prices of the shares of a listed company'.[64]

For both offences, insider trading and misrepresentation, the law has sought to keep the scope of liability reasonably broad as to the question of who can be made liable. The early law in China seemingly adopted a narrow approach. The Provisional Regulations defined 'insider' (*neimu renyuan*) as:

> [Any person] who comes into contact with or can obtain inside information by way of holding shares of an issuer or serving as director, supervisor or senior managing personnel of the issuer or an enterprise which has close relations with the issuer or by taking advantage of its membership, managerial post, supervisory job or professional position or as an employee or by performing the duty as a professional advisor.[65]

The later Securities Laws then expanded the scope of this definition by replacing 'insider' with the term 'persons with knowledge of inside information' (*zhiqingren*).[66] The first Securities Law set out seven groups of persons who would be deemed 'persons with knowledge of inside information'.[67] The list is now expanded to nine groups of persons under the current Securities Law.[68] In the view of Huang, the law arguably seeks to 'cast a very wide net and provide a clear legal basis for pursuing insider liability'.[69] Similarly, a wide range of people can be made liable for misrepresentation.

On the face of it, the company itself is the primary entity responsible for timely, accurate and complete disclosures.[70] Although the Securities Law has not been explicit about it, the duty to ensure these disclosures are duly made in general falls on the directors, supervisors and senior managers.[71] The law has particularly

[61] Securities Law 2019, art 19; Securities Law 2005, art 63.

[62] Zhou (2020), see n 36 above, 331; Gullifer and Payne (2020), see n 9 above, 641.

[63] Securities Law 2019, art 19; 'Administrative Measures on Information Disclosure of Listed Companies', art 12.

[64] Securities Law 2019, art 80.

[65] Provisional Regulations, art 81.

[66] Art 51 of Securities Law 2019. The first Securities Law in 1998 once used the term '*zhiqing renyuan*'. In the view of Li, the problem of using *zhiqing renyuan* was that this might cover natural persons only but exclude companies. But *zhiqingren* can cover both. See D Li, *Zhengquan Jianguan Falun* (*Securities Regulation Law Theory*) (Beijing, Peking University Press, 2019) 656.

[67] Securities Law 1998, art 68.

[68] Securities Law 2019, art 51. These include, for example, the issuer and its directors, supervisors, and officers; a shareholder holding 5 per cent of shares or more; relevant persons of a securities trading venue, securities firms, securities depository and clearing institutions, securities service institutions, or regulatory agencies.

[69] H Huang, 'The Regulation of Insider Trading in China: Law and Enforcement' in S Bainbridge (ed), *Research Handbook on Insider Trading* (Cheltenham, Edward Elgar, 2013) 309.

[70] Securities Law 2019, arts 78 and 79.

[71] *Administrative Measures for Information Disclosure of Listed Company*, as amended, art 4.

highlighted four types of officers who should bear the 'main responsibility'.[72] They are the chairman of the board of directors, its secretary, the general manager (more commonly known as the CEO), and the finance manager (commonly known as the CFO). Furthermore, the law has also imposed duties on other groups of stakeholders which should be responsible. One notable example will be the controlling shareholders and/or the de facto controllers. They have the duty to notify the company, as well as cooperating with it in relation to discharging certain information disclosure obligations, especially regarding 'material events'.[73] The duty of shareholders to disclose will normally be triggered when an individual shareholder holds, or he/she jointly holds with others, five per cent of shares or more.[74] Another notable example will be a securities service provider, such as sponsors, lawyers, accountants, and credit-rating agencies. They may bear joint and several liabilities together with company in the case of misrepresentation.

There are also laws curbing market manipulation.[75] The law specifies eight types of market manipulation.[76] Furthermore, the CSRC has issued guidelines to help identify market manipulation conduct.[77] For brevity, this section will not go into all of these in details. However, it is worth noting that China has not explicitly prohibited short selling and instead uses the regulatory framework for market manipulation to regulate short selling activities.[78]

As regards enforcement, the CSRC is the competent authority supervising the securities markets in China.[79] It formulates the relevant rules and regulations on the supervision and administration of the securities market.[80] It also carries out supervision on the issuance, listing and trading of securities.[81] Issuers, listed companies, stock exchanges, organisations in the securities industry such as securities companies, clearing houses and stockbrokers as well as professionals such as auditors and lawyers are all under the supervision of the CSRC.[82] It is empowered by law to investigate and deal with violations of the laws and regulations.[83] The CSRC's supervision of listed companies covers information disclosure, corporate governance, related parties transactions, and mergers and acquisitions.

Chen and colleagues documented the CSRC enforcement actions around two decades ago, over the five-year period of 1999–2003, revealing that about

[72] ibid, art 51.

[73] An exhaustive list of 'material events' is given by art 80 of Securities Law 2019 (art 67 of Securities Law 2005).

[74] Securities Law 2019, art 63 (art 86 of Securities Law 2005).

[75] Securities Law 2019, art 55; Criminal Code, art 182; and *Several Regulations Concerning the Adjudication of Criminal Cases of Market Manipulation in the Securities and Futures Markets*. The *Several Regulations* were jointly issued by the Supreme People's Court and the Supreme People's Procuratorate in 2018.

[76] Securities Law 2019, art 55.

[77] The Guideline was issued by the CSRC on 27 March 2007.

[78] S Yang and Q Shi, 'Eyi Zuokong de Shengcheng Luoji Falu Guizhi' ('The Logic and Regulation of "Malicious" Short Selling') [2017] *Jingji Fa Yanjiu (Studies on Economic Law)* 68.

[79] Securities Law 2019, art 168.

[80] ibid, art 169(1).

[81] ibid, art 169(2).

[82] ibid, arts 169(3) and 169(4).

[83] ibid art 169(9).

12 per cent of listed firms were subjected to CSRC investigations that resulted in enforcement actions.[84] While many of these cases involved problems with published financial statements, the majority related to irregular or one-off reports or events (such as IPO prospectuses). Failure to disclose information was the major type of violation identified, although false statements and delays in disclosing information were also quite common. In relation to insider trading, Weng surveyed all relevant sanctions issued by the CSRC since 1994 and identified 48 sanctioning decisions.[85] He discovered that the definition of 'insider' in China was getting broader and broader, but enforcement targets remained managers and executives, which might not fit well with the concentrated ownership pattern there, where controlling shareholders and bureaucrats should be an equally if not more powerful group within a company. Huang conducted two empirical studies of China's insider trading cases to provide insights into public and private enforcement of the law.[86] In the first study, he examined all insider trading cases reported nationwide til the end of May 2011, covering a period of about 20 years from the establishment of the two stock exchanges in China in the early 1990s.[87] He discovered a rising number of insider trading cases over the years, with a growing tendency to use criminal sanctions. He attributed this to China's commitment that the country had 'vowed to strengthen their efforts to crack down on insider trading, as it is essential for China, now the world's second-largest economy, to have a reliable and competitive securities market.'[88] In the second study, he updated and extended the cases he surveyed to mid-2017.[89] In this time he identified a total of 268 insider trading cases handled by the CSRC and criminal courts. Again, cases have been on the rise throughout the years. In a further comparison with six other jurisdictions, he alleged that 'China had the highest level of enforcement intensity.'[90]

Generally, it is observed that China has been stepping up its public enforcement efforts over the years, thereby enabling the possibility of private enforcement.[91] Some scholars notice a pattern of regulatory favouritism by the CSRC. For example, Xu and Xu observe that the CSRC sanctions will reduce external debt financing

[84] G Chen et al, 'Is China's Securities Regulatory Agency a Toothless Tiger? Evidence from Enforcement Actions' (2005) 24 *Journal of Accounting and Public Policy* 452.

[85] C Weng, 'Who is an Insider? A Case Study on Chinese Insider Trading Enforcement Principles' (2014) 22 *Asia Pacific Law Review* 85. The actual period covered is not clear from the article. But by estimation it was from 1994 to around 2014 when the article was then published.

[86] H Huang, 'Insider Trading and the Regulation on China's Securities Market: Where are We Now and Where do We Go from Here?' (2012) 5 *Journal of Business Law* 379; H Huang, 'Enforcement of Chinese Insider Trading Law: An Empirical and Comparative Perspective' (2020) 68(3) *American Journal of Comparative Law* 517.

[87] ibid.

[88] Huang (2012), see n 86 above, 380.

[89] Huang (2020), see n 86 above.

[90] Huang (2020), see n 86 above, 572.

[91] B Ke and X Zhang, 'Does Public Enforcement Work in Weak Investor Protection Countries? Evidence from China' (2021) 38 *Contemporary Accounting Research* 1231; C Xi, 'CSRC Enforcement of Securities Laws: Preliminary Empirical Findings' in S Griffith et al (eds), *Research Handbook on Representative Shareholder Litigation* (Cheltenham, Edward Elgar, 2018); and F Huang, 'In Defence of China's Public Enforcement in Equity Market' (2010) 21 *International Company and Commercial Law Review* 327. Also, there has been a shift from an initial focus on violations of disclosure rules to targeting a much wider spectrum of wrongdoing, such as insider trading and investment advisor violations.

capacity of sanctioned companies and the CSRC is less likely to sanction larger companies.[92] Zhou shares a similar view that the CSRC took more enforcement actions and imposed heavier fines against private background listed companies than against listed SOEs.[93]

As regards private enforcement, Hutchens provided a detailed account of the rules enabling private securities litigation in China but at the same time highlighting the Chinese state's 'broad discretion to intervene in commercial affairs' and the consequential weak role of the courts.[94] On this particular topic, Huang completed two important studies. In the first study, he identified 65 securities civil enforcement cases during the 10-year period of 2002 to 2011, of which over 90 per cent of them were successful.[95] In the subsequent study, he explored the relationship between public and private enforcement, and highlighted the procedural prerequisite for a securities civil suit, that there must be a prior criminal judgment or administrative sanction by the relevant regulators.[96] During the aforementioned 10-year period, only around one-fourth of the public enforcement cases would eventually lead to a civil case.[97] One recent strategy in China to encourage private enforcement is enabling a securities class action. Although a class action was permitted as early as 1991 by China's Civil Procedure Law, it has not been enabled for securities litigation until the recent revision to the Securities Law.[98] The first case came in late 2021 against Kangmei Pharmaceutical in Guangzhou.[99]

3.3. Protection in Hong Kong

Trading of shares in Hong Kong can be traced back to about 1860.[100] In 1891 the Association of Stockbrokers in Hong Kong was formed, changing its name to the

[92] W Xu and G Xu, 'Understanding Public Enforcement of Securities Law in China: An Empirical Analysis of the Enforcement Actions of the CSRC and its Regional Offices against Informational Misconduct' (2020) 61 *International Review of Law and Economics* 1; W Xu, J Chen, and G Xu, 'An Empirical Analysis of the Public Enforcement of Securities Law in China: Finding the Missing Piece of the Puzzle' (2017) 18 *European Business Organization Law Review* 367.

[93] T Zhou, 'Is the CSRC Protecting a "Level Playing Field" in China's Capital Markets: Public Enforcement, Fragmented Authoritarianism and Corporatism' (2015) 15 *Journal of Corporate Law Studies* 377, 387.

[94] W Hutchens, 'Private Securities Litigation in China: Material Disclosure about China's Legal System' (2003) 24 *University of Pennsylvania Journal of International Economic Law* 599, 673.

[95] H Huang, 'Private Enforcement of Securities Law in China: A Ten-Year Retrospective and Empirical Assessment' (2013) 61 *American Journal of Comparative Law* 757.

[96] H Huang, 'Rethinking the Relationship between Public Regulation and Private Litigation: Evidence from Securities Class Action in China' (2018) 19 *Theoretical Inquiries in Law* 333.

[97] ibid, 343.

[98] Securities Law 2019, art 95.

[99] See eg F Chen, 'Special Representative Litigation System; The Chinese-style Securities Class Action Mechanism for Investor Protection: Context, Content, Comparison and Consequence' (2022) 30 *Asia Pacific Law Review* 287.

[100] Securities and Futures Commission, *Securities Regulation in Hong Kong* (Hong Kong, Securities and Futures Commission, 2002) 3, available at: https://www.sfc.hk/sfc/doc/EN/speeches/public/others/speechbook/fullversion.pdf.

Hong Kong Stock Exchange in 1914. Until the 1930s, Shanghai dominated international finance in East Asia. The political and economic chaos that plagued China through the 1930s and 1940s, however, dislodged Shanghai from its dominant position and Hong Kong soon replaced it as the regional financial centre.[101] In the 1970s, the Hong Kong financial sector started as a local commercial banking community only to emerge as one of the largest financial centres in the world.[102] In 1969, 32 new banks and branches were opened in Hong Kong, bringing the total to 86 licensed banks with 142 branches.[103] In addition to the original Hong Kong Stock Exchange, established in 1891, the Far East Exchange opened its doors at the end of 1969. The next to start trading, the Kam Ngan Stock Exchange, opened its doors on 15 March 1971. The Kowloon Stock Exchange, the fourth exchange, opened on 5 January 1972. Altogether, these exchanges generated a turnover of HKD 49,000 million in 1973, almost 25 times the level in 1969 before the advent of the Far East Exchange. With the advent of China's open door policy, Hong Kong has re-emerged as a premier trading centre, serving not only China but indeed the entire Asia Pacific region. The role of Hong Kong in the process has been pivotal and can be summarised into four main functions: financier, trading partner, middleman, and facilitator.[104] With particular respect to finance, Hong Kong is the predominant source of foreign finance in China. Hong Kong has contributed to foreign loans made to China in terms of: (1) direct lending; (2) loan syndication and (3) lending from Hong Kong banks to non-bank customers in China. After 1990, a new dimension of Hong Kong's role as a financier has been to provide a fund-raising platform for Chinese companies. In 2007 and 2008, China-related shares accounted for over half of the Hong Kong Stock Exchange's market capitalisation.[105]

The development of Hong Kong's corporate and financial law regime has a close connection with its historical status as a colony of the British Empire. The genesis of the current framework is the Companies Ordinance (CO) of 1865 that mirrored the English Companies Act of 1862, which in turn incorporated both the Joint Stock Companies Registration and Regulation Act of 1844 and the Limited Liability Act of 1855.[106] Likewise, the Companies Act of 1908 in the UK was followed by the CO of 1911 in Hong Kong. The CO was designated as Chapter (Cap) 32 in 1933 and no further significant legislative initiative in company law was introduced until 1984, which reflected the Companies Act of 1948.[107]

[101] C Schenk, 'Banks and the Emergence of Hong Kong as an International Financial Centre' (2002) 12 *Journal of International Financial Markets, Institutions and Money* 321, 323.

[102] Securities and Futures Commission (2002), see n 100 above, 7.

[103] ibid, 4.

[104] ibid, 17.

[105] Data from the Hong Kong Stock Exchange.

[106] M Gu, *Understanding Chinese Company Law* (Hong Kong, Hong Kong University Press, 2006) 9.

[107] J Farrar, 'Developing Corporate Governance in Greater China' (2002) 25 *UNSW Law Journal* 474. The Companies Law Revision Committee was established in the early 1960s to review the company law in Hong Kong. It was subsequently replaced by the Standing Committee on Company Reform, which started the drafting work of the Companies (Amendment) Ordinance 1984.

Since then, the law has constantly been revised. The first major rewrite of Hong Kong company law in more than a century came into effect in 2014 when the CO was re-designated as Cap 622.

Regarding securities law, formal regulation started in 1974 when the market crash attracted government attention and led to the introduction of legislation. In the same year, the Securities Ordinance and the Protection of Investors Ordinance became effective. They required the registration of all stockbrokers, dealers, and investment advisors. However, in the view of Gunningham, the government regulation of the stock market at this point was more apparent than real.[108] First, the government was still committed to laissez-faire and non-intervention. Second, the regulator was in fact starved of resources by the colonial government, which had little understanding of the complexities of financial market regulation. As a result, the Securities Commission took a passive and reactive role instead of actively monitoring markets and brokers. In 1987, when the world's securities markets braced themselves for another crash, the Hong Kong government started to realise the need to strengthen its systems and regulatory arrangements to maintain its position as the primary capital market in the Asian region. The crash of 1987 led to the appointment of the Securities Review Committee. The Securities and Futures Commission Ordinance, which passed its final reading in 1989, marked the beginning of a strong single regulator. In 1991, the Securities (Disclosure of Interests) Ordinance and Securities (Insider Dealing) Ordinance came into force. In 2003, the Securities and Futures Ordinance (SFO) consolidated and modernised all these previous ordinances regulating the securities and futures markets in Hong Kong.[109]

In Hong Kong, the requirements to make initial and periodic disclosures of information are contained in the Listing Rules, despite some disclosure requirements in Part XV of the SFO. Specific requirements for the information in a prospectus are set out in Chapter 11 and Appendix 1 of the Hong Kong Listing Rules. Meanwhile, the requirements stipulated in the CO must also be taken into account.[110] All these requirements under the Listing Rules and the CO are not mutually exclusive and they overlap as to the content required. In general, information about the issuer and its management, the securities for which listing is sought, the issuer's financial position, the intended use of proceeds, business activities and its advisors is required.

A statement included in a prospectus is deemed to be untrue if it is misleading in the form and context in which it is included.[111] This also includes a material omission from the prospectus.[112] An untrue statement can give rise to a range of potential liabilities involving administrative, civil and criminal sanctions.

[108] N Gunningham, 'Moving the Goalposts: Financial Market Regulation in Hong Kong and the Crash of October 1987' (1990) 15 *Law and Social Inquiry* 1, 20.

[109] SFO (Cap 571, Ordinance No. 5 of 2002).

[110] Companies (Winding Up and Miscellaneous Provisions) Ordinance (C(WUMP)O) (Cap 32) s 38.

[111] C(WUMP)O (Cap 32) s 41A.

[112] C(WUMP)O (Cap 32) s 41A(2) and s 343 (2A).

The Listing Rules provide that each of the directors of the company is required to accept responsibility for the information contained in the listing document and that a statement to that effect is to be included in the listing document.[113] Failure to comply with the prospectus requirements can render the company and any responsible entities liable for a fine.[114] Under the CO, civil liability is imposed on certain categories of persons to pay compensation to investors who apply for securities on the faith of the prospectus and suffer loss because of an untrue or misleading statement in the prospectus.[115] Furthermore, under the SFO, a person who makes a fraudulent, reckless or negligent misrepresentation in a prospectus can be liable to pay compensation where a person has invested in reliance on such misrepresentation and suffers a pecuniary loss as a result.[116] Criminal liability can also be imposed on any person who authorises the issue of a prospectus containing an untrue statement or a material omission.[117] The deliberate or reckless making of a false statement of a material fact with intent to defraud can even constitute the criminal offence of fraud.[118]

As for their ongoing disclosure obligations, listed companies are generally required to disclose their financial and operating conditions to the public. In Hong Kong, apart from the regulation of prospectuses, listed companies are required under the CO to maintain proper accounting records, prepare them in a specified form, ensure that they present a true and fair view of the state of affairs of the company and present them to their members.[119] This form of information disclosure is generally in the format of annual reports and accounts as well as interim reports. Specific content requirements are set out in Appendix 16 of the Listing Rules regarding the annual reports and accounts. The Listing Rules also contain a number of provisions obliging companies to keep shareholders and the wider market informed.[120] Certain transactions undertaken or proposed to be undertaken by a company – notably notifiable transactions and connected

[113] Hong Kong Listing Rules (HKLR) 11.12.

[114] C(WUMP)O (Cap 32) s 38.

[115] C(WUMP)O (Cap 32) s 40. The following persons are potentially liable: (1) every director of the company at the time of the issue of the prospectus; (2) a promoter of the company (being any person who was a party to the preparation of the prospectus); (3) every person who authorised the issue of the prospectus. Possible defences include, but are not limited to: (1) the prospectus was issued without their consent; (2) they had reasonable grounds to believe, and did believe, that the statement was true.

[116] SFO (Cap 571) s 108. Liability may also arise out of contract or tort law. As a general principle, all those involved in the preparation and issue of material used in connection with the offering may be liable for negligence if they fail to exercise due care in the preparation of the material and investors relying on the material suffer losses.

[117] C(WUMP)O (Cap 32) s 40A. Such person will be liable to imprisonment for up to three years and a fine of up to HKD 700,000. Under the SFO, a person who makes a fraudulent or reckless misrepresentation in a prospectus may be liable to imprisonment of up to seven years and a fine of up to HKD 1 million, see SFO (Cap 571) s 107.

[118] Theft Ordinance (Cap 210) s 16A.

[119] Companies Ordinance (Cap 622) ss 379–380.

[120] HKLR 13.03. There are two general principles: (1) price-sensitive information should be disclosed immediately; and (2) any information which is necessary to enable the market to appraise the position of the company, or which might affect market activity or assist in establishing a false market should be disclosed as soon as reasonably practicable. See also HKLR 13.05 and 13.09.

transactions – must be disclosed to shareholders or the prior approval of shareholders should be sought. The civil and criminal liabilities for misrepresentation are covered by the SFO accordingly.[121]

To combat financial market crimes, there are six types of market misconduct specified: insider dealing; false trading; price rigging; the disclosure of information about prohibited transactions; the disclosure of false and misleading information inducing transactions; and stock market manipulation.[122] These six forms of market misconduct are all subject to civil remedies, and wrongdoing can be punishable as a criminal offence.[123] As regards short selling, it was first regulated in 1994, and is now covered by the SFO.[124]

The SFC was established as an autonomous statutory body and is responsible for regulating the securities and futures markets in Hong Kong.[125] Its regulatory objectives, duties, functions and powers are stipulated in the SFO.[126] Similarly to other seasoned regulators in the world, the SFC has employed a spectrum of remedies including administrative, civil and criminal sanctions to deter wrongdoing and protect the market and investors. Under sections 194 and 196 of the SFO, the SFC can impose a fine either on its own or together with other disciplinary sanctions. The SFC regards a fine as a more severe sanction than a reprimand, and a public reprimand as more severe than a private reprimand. For more serious offences, the SFC will either refer civil cases to the Market Misconduct Tribunal or criminal cases to the court. The Tribunal has the jurisdiction to enquire into and punish all forms of market misconduct stipulated in Parts XIII and XIV of the SFO.[127] The types of orders made by the Tribunal include disgorgement orders, disqualification orders, government costs orders and disciplinary referral actions against wrong-doers by the relevant professional body. Freshfields Bruckhaus Deringer, a Magic Circle law firm has undertaken a review of SFC's enforcement in the six-year period of 2016–21; it concluded that the regulator has been focusing its resources on fewer investigations than before, and that has resulted in fewer investigations concluded and fewer enforcement outcomes.[128] Instead, the SFC has focused on larger/more significant cases, which have generally resulted in larger total financial penalties. Freshfields Bruckhaus Deringer referred to the SFC's shift as a 'less is more' enforcement approach.[129]

[121] SFO (Cap 571) ss 384 and 391.

[122] Parts XIII and XIV of the SFO (Cap 571).

[123] See Part XIII of the SFO (Cap 571) for civil liability and Part XIV for criminal liability. In the civil route, the standard of proof is 'on the balance of probabilities'. The criminal route is likely to be used when the government considers it has sufficient evidence to prove that a person is guilty of market misconduct 'beyond all reasonable doubt'.

[124] SFO (Cap 571) ss 170–172.

[125] SFO (Cap 571) s 3. The SFC was indeed established on 1 May 1989 under the Securities and Futures Commission Ordinance (repealed in 2002).

[126] SFO (Cap 571) ss 4–7.

[127] SFO (Cap 571) ss 252–254.

[128] Freshfields Bruckhaus Deringer, 'Enforcement Trends – 2021 Year in Review and Looking Ahead' (4 March 2022), available at: www.freshfields.com/en-gb/our-thinking/knowledge/briefing/2022/03/hong-kong-regulatory-enforcement-trends/ (accessed on 1 February 2023).

[129] ibid.

As Coffee has suggested, the more satisfactory approach to measuring enforcement is to focus on both inputs and outputs.[130] In the investigation by Jackson and Roe, the Hong Kong market had the highest staffing and budget in 2006.[131] The direct ratio of staff per million of population in Hong Kong was 59.59.[132] The figure for the US, a country where the enforcement intensity is perceived as high, was 23.75. Concerning budgets, Hong Kong had a budget of around USD 320,000 per billion GDP, whereas in markets such as the US and UK, the figures were around USD 80,000.[133] All this, to a large extent, illustrates the disproportionately large role of the financial market in Hong Kong. The government is committed to preserving the integrity and efficiency of the market. The SFC has clearly possessed and spent adequate financial resources to enable its enforcement actions.[134] Between 2005 and 2015, the SFC reported annual expenditures more than trebling from HKD 497 million in 2005 to about HKD 1.7 billion in 2015. It can be seen that the public enforcement of securities regulation in Hong Kong has been comparable with, if not one of the best among, the world's renowned markets. However, private enforcement is relatively weak. As indicated by Donald and Cheuk, the data on judicial actions taken pursuant to corporate and securities laws clearly show that such enforcement in Hong Kong is primarily public.[135] This sharply contrasts to jurisdictions like the US where private actions play a leading role. Such a disinclination to litigate can partly be attributed to the reluctance of ordinary Chinese to seek justice through the courts, in order to preserve harmony. After all, even though Hong Kong was under British rule for over 100 years, local people still retain a traditional Chinese mentality. However, it is notable that the private enforcement of shareholder rights in the UK has equally been rare.[136]

3.4. Protection in the UK

The historical root of finance in the UK is undoubtedly stronger than in the other two markets. The London Stock Exchange is one of the world's oldest stock exchanges and can trace its history back more than 300 years.[137] In 1801, the first ever 'regulated exchange' was born, in a sense that it did not only provide a market for securities but also incorporated regulations on how business was to

[130] Coffee (2007), see n 24 above.

[131] H Jackson and M Roe, 'Public and Private Enforcement of Securities Laws: Resource-based Evidence' (2009) 93 *Journal of Financial Economics* 207, 214–15.

[132] ibid.

[133] ibid.

[134] D Donald and P Cheuk, 'Hong Kong's Public Enforcement Model of Investor Protection' (2017) 4 *Asian Journal of Law and Society* 349.

[135] ibid.

[136] J Armour et al, 'Private Enforcement of Corporate Law: An Empirical Comparison of the US and UK' (2009) 6 *Journal of Empirical Legal Studies* 687.

[137] The Exchange was formally established in 1773 by a group of stockbrokers who had been trading in the area's coffee houses. For more about its early history, see C Smith, 'The Early History of the London Stock Exchange' (1929) 19 *American Economic Review* 206.

be conducted.[138] Adherence to these rules and regulations was monitored and adjudicated by a committee, including full-time administrative staff, and any non-compliance could lead to expulsion from the market. In the view of Michie, from around the 1850s to the onset of the First World War, the Exchange firmly established itself as the biggest and most important of its kind in the world.[139] As of today, despite being leapfrogged by other emerging market exchanges, it is still one of the most prestigious, and the City, together with New York, remains one of the most recognised international financial centres.[140]

In terms of the rules and regulations, on the face of it, the Financial Services and Markets Act (FSMA) 2000 is the principal piece of securities law. But indeed, under the influence of the EU law (despite Brexit), the likes of the Prospectus Regulation Rules, the Market Abuse Regulation as well as the Disclosure Guidance and Transparency Rules may actually play a more notable role in their specialist area of regulation. In the view of Knauss, during the early days, in the UK, like other European markets, there was not a sharp distinction between corporate law and securities law, in contrast to the US.[141] For example, the Companies Act of 1948 contained restrictions on the public offer of securities, and licensing of securities brokers and antifraud provisions were found in separate legislation, the Prevention of Fraud Act 1958.[142] The prospectus requirements of the US Securities Act of 1933 were modelled on the English Companies Act.[143]

Under the Prospectus Regulation, a prospectus should contain the necessary information which is material to an investor for making an informed assessment of different aspects of their securities, and should be written and presented in an easily analysable, concise and comprehensible form.[144] On the face of it, it is not different from the other two markets discussed above. FSMA 2000 provides a statutory liability regime for a defective prospectus,[145] under which any person responsible for the prospectus is liable to pay compensation to an investor who acquired the relevant securities and suffered loss by reason of any misrepresentation in the prospectus. The liable parties can include the issuer, the directors of the issuer, and professionals such as accountants.[146] On top of private enforcement,

[138] R Michie, *The London Stock Exchange: A History* (Oxford, OUP, 2001) 35–36.

[139] For example, in 1914 the London Stock Exchange was 10 times larger than the New York Stock Exchange. See ibid, 70.

[140] According to the most recent data from the World Federation of Exchanges, the London Stock Exchange is just the tenth largest stock exchange in the World, smaller than its developing market counterparts like Shanghai and Shenzhen Stock Exchanges, Hong Kong Stock Exchange, as well as the National Stock Exchange of India. But it remains perceived as a leading market in the world, second only to New York, for example, according to the Global Financial Centres Index.

[141] R Knauss, 'Securities Regulation in the United Kingdom: A Comparison with United States Practice' (1974) 5 *Vanderbilt Law Review* 47.

[142] ibid.

[143] S Gleeson and H Bloomenthal, 'The Public Offer of Securities in the United Kingdom' (1999) 27 *Denver Journal International Law and Policy*, 359, 359.

[144] Prospectus Regulation (Regulation (EU) 2017/1129), art 6(1) and (2).

[145] FSMA 2000 s 90.

[146] Gullifer and Payne (2020), see n 9 above, 529.

there are also criminal and administrative sanctions under public enforcement. Under section 85 of FSMA 2000, it is unlawful to offer shares to the public unless there is an approved prospectus. The offender may receive a prison term of up to two years and/or a fine. As regards administrative sanctions, there is a range of powers at the disposal of the Financial Conduct Authority (FCA). The regulator will have the power to suspend, restrict or prohibit a listing and the offer of shares to the public.[147] The regulator will also have the option to issue a public censure to the issuer.[148]

On top of initial disclosures, listed companies will be expected to provide periodic disclosures as well. This is covered by the Disclosure Guidance and Transparency Rules (DTR),[149] as well as the Companies Act (CA) 2006. The directors of companies are expected to produce annual reports and accounts and these should present 'a true and fair view of the assets, liabilities, financial position and profit or loss' of the company.[150] The DTR impose a stricter time limit for listed companies to lay their accounts before the general meeting and then file them with the registrar.[151] The DTR also prescribe the requirement for a half-yearly report.[152] A quarterly report can be given on a voluntary basis. Meanwhile, there are requirements to make ad hoc disclosures, such as inside information, major shareholdings, significant transactions and connected transactions.[153] FSMA 2000 stipulates the civil liability for any misrepresentation in the course of these ongoing disclosures.[154] Meanwhile, public enforcement is also possible.[155]

In the UK, as a former part of the EU, the legal framework in tackling market misconduct has been heavily influenced by the EU legislation.[156] Insider trading was first made an offence through the Companies Act 1980, and the law is now contained in the Criminal Justice Act 1993, and the UK Market Abuse Regulation (MAR), as amended by the Market Abuse (Amendment) (EU Exit) Regulations 2019.[157] One headline feature, common to both the UK and EU framework, is to

[147] FSMA 2000 ss 87K and 87L.
[148] FSMA 2000 s 87M.
[149] Disclosure Guidance and Transparency Rules (DTR): www.handbook.fca.org.uk/handbook/DTR.pdf.
[150] CA 2006, s 393.
[151] DTR 4.1.3.
[152] DTR 4.2.
[153] Gullifer and Payne (2020), see n 9 above, 569.
[154] FSMA 2000 s 90A.
[155] FSMA 2000 s 91(1B).
[156] Gullifer and Payne (2020), see n 9 above, 613. Formerly, the UK framework was largely reshaped by EU laws, such as EC Directive 89/592/EEC of 13 November 1989 coordinating regulations on insider dealing (repealed by Directive 2003/6/EC of the European Parliament and of the Council of 28 January 2003 on insider dealing and market manipulation (market abuse)), and more recently the Market Abuse Regulation (Regulation (EU) No 596/2014). Following Brexit, the EU Regulation will continue to be relevant in the UK. See Market Abuse (Amendment) (EU Exit) Regulations 2019 (SI 310/2019). Traditionally, insider dealing had been dealt with by a predominantly company law model, as opposed to thinking in terms of market and securities law.
[157] CA 1980 ss 68–73; Part V of the Criminal Justice Act 1993; Market abuse was formerly covered by s 118 of the FSMA 2000.

treat both forms of market misconduct, namely insider dealing and market manipulation, under one umbrella called 'market abuse'. Despite the disparities between the US and EU framework, it is said that the UK still shares two notable features with the US system.[158] First, the fiduciary rationale remains central to penalising insider trading, namely that a defendant's culpability will be significantly increased where he had abused his position of trust. Second, sophisticated insider trading would warrant higher culpability. Meanwhile, criminal liability for market manipulation is stipulated by the Financial Services Act 2012.[159] There are three types of market manipulation, namely (1) misleading statements and dishonest concealment to induce someone to enter into or refrain from some investment related activity; (2) misleading impressions; and (3) misleading statements in relation to benchmarks. A person guilty of market abuse (insider trading and/or market manipulation) can face up to seven years' imprisonment and/or a fine. However, as observed by Gullifer and Payne, the criminal offences of market abuse have proved very difficult to enforce.[160] Therefore, administrative sanctions by the FCA have been a more meaningful form of public enforcement.[161] It is worth highlighting that there is currently no mechanism for private enforcement of market abuse in the UK.[162] As regards short selling, it had not been regulated until 2008 when the financial crisis happened.[163]

The FCA is the regulator of the stock market, replacing the former single regulator, the Financial Services Authority, for both the banking sector and the stock market before the financial crisis. It has been observed that during the Financial Services Authority's era the regulator was not as 'zealous' as its US counterpart, the SEC.[164] Similarly, private enforcement action has been described as 'negligible'.[165]

3.5. Protection in Switzerland

The Swiss stock market traces its origins to exchanges in Geneva (1850), Zurich (1873), and Basel (1876).[166] The SIX[167] Swiss Exchange is the main exchange of

[158] R Cheung, 'Insider Trading Sentencing: An Anglo-American Comparison' [2014] *Journal of Business Law* 566, 582. The US was the first major country to enact an insider trading law and to place restrictions on insider trading, in 1934, with France being the second country to do so, in 1967, before numerous other countries followed suit in 1980s–1990s. In the US, insider trading is largely regulated by the Securities Exchange Act of 1934. However, some commentators argue that SEC Rule 10b-5, implementing section 10(b) of the 1934 Act, does not expressly prohibit insider trading.

[159] Financial Services Act ss 89–91; originally covered by s 397 FSMA 2000.

[160] Gullifer and Payne (2020), see n 9 above, 624.

[161] MAR, arts 14–15.

[162] Gullifer and Payne (2020), see n 9 above, 640.

[163] The current regulation is in the form of the Short Selling Regulation. This is the UK version of the EU Short Selling Regulation (Regulation (EU) No 236/2012) as incorporated into UK law by the European Union (Withdrawal) Act 2018.

[164] Jackson and Roe (2009), see n 130 above.

[165] Gullifer and Payne (2020), see n 9 above, 536.

[166] Credit Suisse, 'Switzerland: A Financial Market History' (2017), available at: www.credit-suisse.com/about-us/en/reports-research/studies-publications.html (accessed on 1 February 2023).

[167] SIX is the acronym for 'Swiss Infrastructure and Exchange'.

the country. Despite the country's global reputation in finance (especially in relation to private banking and wealth management), its stock exchange is not really very large in size (compared with the three countries above). Currently, there are around 250 listed companies, with a total market capitalisation of USD 1.8 trillion, meaning that it is the fourth largest in Europe behind Euronext, the London Stock Exchange and Deutsche Börse.[168]

Up until 1995, there had been no specialist securities law in the country.[169] In 1995, the Stock Exchange and Securities Trading Act was introduced. In 2018, the Financial Services Act (FinSA) (then supplemented by the Financial Services Ordinance) was also introduced. However, in essence many aspects of the substantive regulation are still left to the Swiss Federal Code of Obligations (*Obligationenrech*) (SFCO), which for a long period of time has contained provisions normally seen in corporate law and securities law. Under the Financial Services Act, an issuer who makes a public offer of securities or who seeks the admission of securities to trading on a stock exchange must publish a prospectus.[170] The Act prescribes some essential information requirements for the prospectus.[171] But the more detailed requirements are left to the Financial Services Ordinance (FinSO).[172] Civil liability for misrepresentation is attributed in the Act.[173] Furthermore, public enforcement is enabled by the Act and those convicted can be liable for a fine of up to CHF 500,000.[174]

As regards the ongoing disclosure obligations for listed companies, under the SFCO, it is the duty of both the company and its managing directors to prepare an annual report.[175] Some basic requirements of the report are also stipulated in the law.[176] For example, the report must be clear and understandable, complete, reliable, prudent, etc. There are also some more prescriptive requirements.[177] All these are also supported by rules issued by the stock exchange such as the 'Directive on Financial Reporting', as well as the 'Directive on Ad hoc Publicity'. For example, the latter seeks to ensure that issuers provide the public with true, clear and complete information on significant events and price-sensitive changes arising in the course of their business activities. Financial reporting fraud can be punishable under the Swiss Criminal Code.[178] Furthermore, administrative sanctions can be imposed by the stock exchange.[179]

[168] As of the end of 2022, data from Statista.

[169] C Meier-Schatz and K Larsen, 'Swiss Securities Regulation and Capital Market Law: A Comprehensive Overview' (1990) 18 *Denver Journal International Law and Policy* 417.

[170] FinSA, art 35.

[171] ibid, art 40.

[172] Art 50 of the FinSO; also its Annexes 1–5.

[173] FinSA, art 69.

[174] ibid, art 90.

[175] SFCO, arts 810 and 957.

[176] ibid, art 958c.

[177] For example, see arts 959, 959a and 959b of SFCO for the content requirements for certain key financial statements.

[178] Art 146 of Swiss Criminal Code.

[179] Title V of the SIX Swiss Listing Rules. Penalties such as warning, reprimand, fine (up to CHF 10 million), and suspension can be imposed on both the issuers/listed companies, and the responsible individuals.

Meanwhile, market misconduct is regulated by the Financial Market Infrastructure Act (FinMIA). The law prohibits any person from exploiting information that they know or should know is insider information by trading securities, from disclosing such information to others, and from exploiting such information in giving investment advice.[180] Other than insider trading, market manipulation is also prohibited.[181] The law prohibits any person from publicly disseminating information and from carrying out transactions or purchase or sale orders that he or she knows or should know give false or misleading signals regarding the supply, demand or price of securities. Both insider trading and market manipulation can lead to criminal liability.[182] The penalty will be a prison term of up to five years or a fine. Burkhardt and colleagues believe that, unlike the UK, there may be scope for private enforcement against the wrongdoers under Swiss law.[183] As regards short selling, according to the SIX Swiss Exchange, 'there [were] no provisions to regulate short selling in terms of laws or stock exchange regulations' in the country as at 2013.[184] This is still the case today.

As said above, private enforcement is possible especially in relation to misrepresentation in a prospectus. However, as observed by Burkhardt and colleagues, securities litigation is rare in Switzerland. Therefore, deterrence of market misconduct is chiefly in the form of public enforcement.[185] The regulator, the Swiss Financial Market Supervisory Authority was established in 2007. In the published statistics by the regulator, in the period of 2014–21, there were an average of 100 investigations on insider trading and around 20 investigations of market manipulation per year.[186]

3.6. Concluding Remarks

There are two main roles of securities regulation: to ensure that investors can receive timely, adequate and accurate information to make an informed investment decision, as well as to protect them from unfair market behaviour. It can be said that all four jurisdictions examined have appropriate legal measures in place to achieve these two regulatory objectives. In the case of China, the Chinese Securities Law, together with other relevant Administrative Measures, manage to spell out the prospectus requirements, as well as other ongoing disclosure obligations of the

[180] Art 142 of FinMIA.
[181] Art 143 of FinMIA.
[182] Arts 154–155 of FinMIA.
[183] M Burkhardt et al, 'The Securities Litigation Review: Switzerland' (22 May 2022), available at: thelawreviews.co.uk/title/the-securities-litigation-review/switzerland (accessed on 1 February 2023). The legal basis will be a tort claim under art 41(1) of SFCO.
[184] SIX Swiss Exchange, 'Regulation of Short Selling as Part of Self-regulation' (10 October 2013), available at: www.six-group.com/dam/download/media/press-releases/2013/1010-e-Short-Selling.pdf (accessed on 1 February 2023).
[185] Burkhardt et al (2022), see n 182 above.
[186] Data from the Swiss Financial Market Supervisory Authority.

issuers. In Hong Kong, the Securities and Futures Ordinance are supplemented by the Companies (Winding Up and Miscellaneous Provisions) Ordinance as well as the Hong Kong Listing Rules. In the UK, there are specialist Prospectus Rules and Disclosure Guidance and Transparency Rules. In Switzerland, their recent Financial Services Act, together with the Financial Services Ordinance are the main source of regulation in this regard. There are also exchange-issued Directives on ongoing and ad hoc disclosures. In all four jurisdictions, there will be liability, mostly administrative and civil, for misrepresentation in initial and ongoing disclosures.

Furthermore, in all four jurisdictions, there are rules curbing problematic market behaviours, most notably insider trading and market manipulation. These financial market crimes can lead to criminal liability. There are competent public regulators to police the markets. Other than public enforcement, private enforcement can also be a way to deter wrongdoing. This is perhaps one aspect which can separate the four jurisdictions. In Hong Kong, the UK and Switzerland, there has been a general disinclination for securities-related litigation. In contrast, this is one area that has been vibrant in China. There has been a more notable number of securities-related litigations. Securities class action has recently been enabled in the country, demonstrating the country's trend to follow the line of the US, which has the reputation of being litigious.

In the context of this book, it is safe to suggest that there is no notable gap between the securities regulation of the four countries, and thereby leading to a shortfall of investor protection when compared between acquiring local securities, and foreign securities via Stock Connect. Of course, this conclusion comes with the caveat that this chapter, owing to the constraints of length, may not be able to discuss every single aspect of securities regulation, but only manage to select some 'headline' measures for comparison.

4

Regulating Connect Issuers

The previous chapter examined the state of investor protection under securities law in the four jurisdictions (China, Hong Kong, the UK and Switzerland; all involved in the Stock Connect schemes). This chapter, which is parallel to the previous one, will turn our attention to corporate law and listing rules. As explained before, despite the 'home market rules' principle under Stock Connect, there is still a notable degree of overlap between the securities law of the home and host countries, especially when depository receipts are used (as in the case of China–London/Switzerland Connect). This is seemingly more a case of co-regulation than 'home market rules'. Similarly, this overlap exists for the listing rules. Nevertheless, for the applicability of corporate law, as well as in the case of China–Hong Kong Connect where direct trading is possible, the basic principle of 'home market rules' should prevail. In this chapter, just like the previous one, I will examine the role of corporate law and listing rules in regulating the issuers/listed companies in the four jurisdictions. In the next section, I will first explain the objectives of corporate regulation in this specific regard and set out the framework of analysis in the subsequent four sections (each for one jurisdiction). The final section will conclude by reconciling how the potential difference(s) in the four jurisdictions may affect the perceived level of corporate governance and investor protection for Stock Connect participants.

4.1. Significance and Strategies of Regulation of Issuers under Corporate Law and Listing Rules

Company law generally does not function alone but together with other bodies of law, notably securities law as well as listing rules, to form a regulatory package to protect investors.[1] Company law performs two principal functions.[2] First, it establishes the structure of the corporate form, normally with standardised housekeeping rules, so as to allow users to save on transaction costs.[3] Second, it seeks to coordinate the interests of different constituencies within and outside of

[1] R Kraakman et al, *Anatomy of Corporate Law* (Oxford, OUP, 2017) 15–17.
[2] ibid, 29.
[3] For this, see the seminal work of R Coase, 'The Nature of the Firm' (1937) 4 *Economica* 386.

a company. Regarding the latter, economists refer to the concern as the agency problem. An agency relationship was defined by Jensen and Meckling as:[4] 'A contract under which one or more persons – the principals(s) – engage another person – the agent – to perform some service on their behalf which involves delegating some decision-making authority to the agent.' In a company context, the principal will be the shareholders, and the agent will be the company management. As long as both parties to the relationship are utility maximisers there is good reason to believe that the agent (company management) will not always act in the best interests of the principal (shareholders). This was viewed as a problem as early as 1776 by Adam Smith in his *Wealth of Nations*:[5]

> [The directors], however, being the managers rather of other people's money than of their own, it cannot well be expected, that they should watch over it with the same anxious vigilance with which the partners in a private copartnery frequently watch over their own.

As opposed to a classic agency problem as defined by Jensen and Meckling and Adam Smith, Kraakman and colleagues believe that there are also two other dimensions to the organisational problems.[6] One is a majority–minority conflict, under which the law should ensure that the minority shareholders' interests are not expropriated by the majority shareholders. Another is an insider–outsider conflict, under which, the interests of wider stakeholders, such as creditors, employees, consumers, and even the general public, in society should not be adversely affected by corporate activities.

The practical importance of getting investor protection laws right perhaps comes from the belief that we want to encourage investment. The correlations between law and financial development are at the core of law and finance studies.[7] La Porta and colleagues have examined legal rules covering the protection of corporate shareholders and creditors, the origin of these rules and the quality of their enforcement in 49 countries.[8] They have alleged that the legal environment, including both legal rules and their enforcement, matters for the size and extent of a country's capital market. This is because a good legal environment protects the potential financiers against expropriation by entrepreneurs. Investors are willing

[4] M Jensen and W Meckling, 'Theory of the Firm: Managerial Behaviour, Agency Costs and Ownership Structure' (1976) 3 *Journal of Financial Economics* 305, 308.

[5] As quoted in the work of Jensen and Meckling. ibid, 305.

[6] Kraakman et al (2017), see n 1 above, 29–30.

[7] M Siems, 'Legal Origins: Reconciling Law & Finance and Comparative Law' (2007) 52 *McGill Law Journal* 55, 57.

[8] See R La Porta et al, 'Legal Determinants of External Finance' (1997) 52 *Journal of Finance* 1131 and a series of related papers evolving from it. Their findings, though widely cited, are highly controversial. See for example, D Berkowitz et al, 'Economic Development, Legality and the Transplant Effect' (2003) 47 *European Economic Review* 165 and J Armour et al, 'Shareholder Protection and Stock Market Development: An Empirical Test of the Legal Origins Hypothesis' (2009) 6 *Journal of Empirical Legal Studies* 343.

to surrender funds in exchange for securities and therefore expand the scope of capital markets. The advantage of good regulation is also confirmed by the bonding hypothesis, proposed by Coffee and Stulz.[9] According to their theory, instead of going for a lower-cost and less demanding option, companies tend to choose an internationally renowned market, generally with higher entry and ongoing requirements. They comply voluntarily with a high level of disclosure and corporate governance standards. In this way, a company may potentially benefit from an increase in its share price and the ability to raise capital at a lower cost.

The importance of legal institutions in fostering a good business environment was underlined by the World Bank's 'Doing Business' project.[10] This project provided objective measures of business regulations and their enforcement across 190 economies and selected cities at the subnational and regional level. The first 'Doing Business' report, published in 2003, covered five indicator sets and 133 economies. The most recent report in 2020 covered 10 indicator sets and 190 economies,[11] amongst which, the 'protecting minority investors' indicator is perhaps the most relevant in the context of this chapter. The indicator measured the extent of protection from conflicts of interest and of shareholders' rights in corporate governance.[12] The higher the index score, the better the protection of investors' interests. The maximum score is 100. OECD high-income countries on average got a score of 68.2 in 2020. The four countries/jurisdictions (China, Hong Kong, the UK and Switzerland) that we are going to look at in this chapter had scores of 72, 84, 84 and 50 respectively. Switzerland thus did notably less well in the index.

However, this does not necessarily indicate a grave concern about the legal institutions in Switzerland. If one looks at another dataset, there can be a different conclusion. At least in the case of China, it was viewed very positively by Armour and colleagues (for the Cambridge Centre for Business Research); they discovered that a significant upward movement in the level of shareholder protection was made by China between 1995 and 2005.[13] In this period China experienced

[9] See for example J Coffee, 'Racing Towards the Top?: The Impact of Cross-Listings and Stock Market Competition on International Corporate Governance' (2002) 102 *Columbia Law Review* 1757 and R Stulz, 'Globalization, Corporate Finance, and the Cost of Capital' (1999) 12 *Journal of Applied Corporate Finance* 8.

[10] World Bank, 'Doing Business 2020' (2021), available at: www.doingbusiness.org (accessed on 1 February 2023).

[11] The project was closed down in 2021, owing to a scandal over data irregularity. It was believed that some countries (allegedly China, Saudi Arabia, the United Arab Emirates, and Azerbaijan) had tried to influence the World Bank so as to improve their rankings (and thereby international image). See a statement from the World Bank. World Bank, 'Statement on Release of Investigation into Data Irregularities in Doing Business 2018 and 2020' (16 September 2021), available at: www.worldbank.org/en/news/statement/2021/09/16/statement-on-release-of-investigation-into-data-irregularities-in-doing-business-2018-and-2020 (accessed 1 February 2023).

[12] Important parameters include the extent of disclosure, director liability, shareholder rights and available legal actions, etc.

[13] Armour et al (2009), see n 8 above.

a jump in its shareholder protection score from 5 to 6.5. According to this index (scored from 0 to 10), although the UK and the US were the top performers in 2005 (with scores of slightly more than 7), China was more protective of shareholders' interests than some developed countries such as Germany (6.25) and Switzerland (5.25). This dataset has since been updated to 2013.[14] It has been suggested that between 1990 and 2013 China experienced the 'biggest increase in shareholder protection' amongst the 30 countries studied.[15] China (7.85), Russia and France were the top performers in shareholder protection in 2013, performing even better than the UK (7.4) and the US (7.25).[16] Switzerland had a score of 5.5 and Hong Kong was not a jurisdiction studied.

To trace the root of the difference in China's performance between the two indices, Huang and Yeung examine the methodology of the indices.[17] The apparent divergence of what the two indices suggest can perhaps be explained by their differences in the choice of variables. Armour and colleagues' study concerned shareholder protection in listed companies only.[18] A typical regulatory system of the capital market entails three tiers of regulation.[19] Company law represents the bottom tier of regulation as it applies to all companies, both public and private companies. Securities law represents the second tier of regulation, in that it is only relevant to companies which issue securities to the public. Listing rules represent the top tier of regulation and are relevant only to a relatively small group of companies whose securities are admitted to public listing. So, there is a need to consider all these three tiers of regulation for a listed company. By contrast, the 'Doing Business' project overall, launched in 2002, has the aim of looking at 'domestic small and medium-sized companies and measures the regulations applying to them through their life cycle'.[20] Yet, the basic assumption in compiling the 'protecting minority investors' indicator is that the rules and regulations applicable to 'a publicly traded corporation listed on the economy's most important stock exchange' are taken into account.[21] For example, when they looked at New Zealand, a wide array of rules and regulations were taken into account, such as 'the Companies Act, Financial Reporting Act, Securities Market Act, Exchange

[14] This is available via M Siems, 'CBR Extended Shareholder Protection Index', 2nd edn (January 2016), available at: www.repository.cam.ac.uk/bitstream/handle/1810/256566/cbr-spi-30-countries-codebook-and-methodology.pdf?sequence=9&isAllowed=y (accessed 1 February 2023).

[15] D Katelouzou and M Siems, 'Disappearing Paradigms in Shareholder Protection: Leximetric Evidence for 30 Countries, 1990–2013' (2015) 15 *Journal of Corporate Law Studies* 127, 133.

[16] ibid, 134.

[17] F Huang and H Yeung, 'Shareholder Protection in China from a Numerical Comparative Law Perspective' (2019) 7(1) *Chinese Journal of Comparative Law* 124.

[18] Siems (2016), see n 14 above, 3.

[19] I MacNeil and A Lau, 'International Corporate Regulation: Listing Rules and Overseas Companies' (2001) 50 *International and Comparative Law Quarterly* 787.

[20] World Bank, 'Doing Business: About Us', available at archive.doingbusiness.org/en/about-us (accessed 1 February 2023).

[21] World Bank, 'Protecting Minority Investors Methodology', available at archive.doingbusiness.org/en/methodology (accessed 1 February 2023).

Listing Rules, Evidence Act, Limitation Act, Judicature Act, High Court Rules and Rules of Professional Conduct for Barristers and Solicitors'. By contrast, in this regard, the scope of Armour and colleagues' study was somewhat different, when the major point of reference was the company law and 'in some cases' securities law, as well as various codes, listing rules and case law.[22]

It can be seen that in the regulation of listed companies, a whole package of rules and regulations and their enforcement can be relevant. The role of securities regulation has been examined in the previous chapter. In this chapter, the focus will be more on company law and listing rules. In general, jurisdictions regulate publicly held companies in recognition of the vulnerability of public investors. The two major principles are: (1) to ensure that the prices of publicly traded securities are reasonably well-informed and (2) to ensure that public shareholders are protected by effective corporate governance arrangements once they become shareholders.[23] Accordingly, three legal strategies are employed to protect the interests of investors.

The entry strategy includes mandatory disclosure for new issues of shares and continuing disclosure requirements for listed companies.[24] An offer for the sale or subscription of shares is made via a prospectus, which is a document providing potential investors with the information they need to decide whether or not to invest. Similarly, ongoing disclosure is essential to other legal strategies used to protect shareholders. For example, the disclosure of self-dealing transactions between the company and its directors, coupled with the requirement to obtain the shareholders' approval of these transactions, can be critical to controlling the opportunistic behaviour of managers. The importance of disclosure has been discussed extensively in the previous chapter. Second, the rules and standards strategy, which is the focus of this chapter, concerns the acceptable characteristics and behaviour of listed companies.[25] There can be different ways to implement this rules and standards strategy. One example is the admission criteria prescribed by the stock exchanges via their listing rules; also, the fiduciary duties of directors, normally prescribed by company law, and the possibility of enforcing these duties via shareholder litigation is another important example of the rules and standards strategy. Finally, the trusteeship strategy involves the empowerment of a disinterested third party to screen companies that wish to enter the stock market.[26] Stock exchanges, for instance, through their listing review process, can be regarded as the guardians of quality. The strategies are usually employed in conjunction with each other. As mentioned, stock exchanges will review listing applications in accordance with certain recognisable standards stated in the listing rules. Similarly, to

[22] Armour et al (2009), see n 8 above.
[23] Kraakman et al (2017), see n 1 above, 243–45.
[24] ibid, 245–52.
[25] ibid.
[26] ibid.

ensure the reliability of corporate disclosures, what constitutes a misrepresentation must be clearly specified, and offenders must be held responsible either by public regulators (via public enforcement) and/or by the victim investors (via private enforcement) through the use of standards backed by liability. This has been covered by the previous chapter.

Therefore, the focus of this chapter will be on implementation of the rules and standards strategy via the company law and listing rules in the four chosen jurisdictions (namely China, Hong Kong, the UK and Switzerland).

4.2. Regulating China-Based Issuers

In virtually all countries, it is certain that any listing applications will be screened by the competent authorities. Screening criteria are based on objective and observable standards. These can include, but are not limited to, an incorporation requirement, a profit, capitalisation or revenue test and a minimum public float. Other ongoing requirements will also be expected. A basic requirement for listing is that an issuer must be duly incorporated or otherwise validly established according to the relevant laws of its place of incorporation (the country of domicile). This directly affects what jurisdiction will govern the affairs of the company from its formation to dissolution. The first step a company has to take in a listing is to set itself up as a 'public company'.

In China, there is a distinction between limited liability companies and joint stock companies. For the former, there can only be up to 50 shareholders.[27] Therefore, a listed company can only be a joint stock company. In theory, the laws in China do not expressly prohibit foreign companies from issuing and listing shares in China. In practice, however, except via Stock Connect, there is not a single listed foreign company in China at the moment, whether via IPO or a secondary listing. Furthermore, the basic commercial rationale for raising capital requires investors to be sufficiently interested in the company. The first thing for any company and for the stock exchange to consider is whether the company is qualified for listing. This will ensure the ex-ante quality of publicly traded securities (for ex-post quality, appropriate standards for listed companies come into play). An issuer must have been continuously operating for more than three years since it was established unless otherwise approved by the State Council.[28] However, as for other quantitative requirements, the capital, profit and revenue requirements are: (1) RMB 30 million capital immediately prior to the IPO; (2) positive net profit in each year and over RMB 30 million in aggregate in the company's three-year track

[27] Art 24 of Chinese Company Law 2018.

[28] *Administrative Measures for the Initial Public Offering and Listing of Stocks*, art 9 www.asianlii.org/cn/legis/cen/laws/amftipoalos704/.

record; and (3) over RMB 300 million revenue in aggregate in the company's three-year track record, respectively.[29]

In addition, the company should have good standing and operation compliance. As for the former, the ownership of shares and key assets in the company must be clean and clear in the sense that there have not been any major disputes over them.[30] As for the latter, the company must not have committed any material violations of laws.[31] A particular concern of the China Securities Regulatory Commission (CSRC) is that the issuer must be independent from its controlling shareholders or de facto controlling parties. For instance, the management and organisational structure of the issuer must be independent.[32]

In line with its socialist market economy, the state used to maintain a tight control over the financial markets in China. This seriously restricted access to capital for many companies. In the early days of the Chinese stock market, the CSRC imposed a quota on the maximum number of shares that could be issued each year. Its intention was to curb the potentially excessive investment demand in a premature market, where market participants had not developed an understanding of the market rules and their rights and obligations.[33] Provincial governments and industry supervising bodies were assigned quotas and they would recommend companies for listing within them.[34] The CSRC would then provide the final approval on public offerings. However, this quota system was replaced by another system in December 2003 when the *Interim Regulations on the Public Offering Review Committee of the CSRC* came into effect.[35] As discussed in the previous chapter, a more liberal registration-based system for issuers is now enabled by the Securities Law 2019.[36] In the previous approval-based IPO system, companies had to go through a strict vetting process by the CSRC. Under

[29] ibid, art 33. But these requirements mainly apply for the main boards of the exchange. For junior boards in the exchanges, such as the Sci-Tech Innovation Board, ChiNext, and the newly established stock exchange, there can be lower requirements. For example, there will be no profitability requirement as long as the issuers can meet other requirements.

[30] ibid, arts 10 and 13.

[31] According to art 11 of the *Administrative Measures*, the production and business operation of an issuer must comply with the relevant provisions of the laws, administrative regulations and its articles of association, and shall be coherent with the state's industrial policy. Furthermore, in relation to financial reporting, the Securities Law also states that the financial accounting documents of the issuer in the past three years must not contain any fraudulent entries.

[32] *Administrative Measures for the Initial Public Offering and Listing of Stocks*, arts 16 and 18. The issuer's senior management personnel shall not receive salaries from the issuer's controlling person or the affiliates controlled by such a controlling person. The functions of business operation and management of the issuer shall not mix up with its controlling shareholder, de facto controller or the affiliates.

[33] CSRC, *China Capital Markets Development Report* (Beijing, China Financial Publishing, 2008) 165–66.

[34] The total issue ceiling was based on the demand generated from China's economic development and the actual situation of the capital markets, and then was further allocated according to the nature of each province, industry sector and demand.

[35] The Review Committee consists of 25 members, 5 from the CSRC, and 20 external who mostly are senior partners from accounting or law firms.

[36] The Chinese Securities Law 2019, art 9.

the new system, the stock exchanges will be responsible for vetting IPOs with a focus on information disclosure, while the CSRC will only make sure listings are in line with national industrial policy. In general, various changes to both the Securities Law and the Company Law represent the Chinese state's commitment to a more market-based approach.[37]

After being admitted, there are various ongoing requirements; one notable example will be corporate governance. In China, regulatory requirements regarding corporate governance are reflected in the *Code of Corporate Governance for Listed Companies*, first issued in January 2002, which was developed in accordance with the OECD Principles of Corporate Governance. The principal difference between the Chinese framework and that of the likes of Hong Kong and the UK is that a 'comply or explain' principle has not been adopted.[38] A listed company is required to take the contents specified in the Code into account when formulating or revising its articles of association and detailed management rules.[39] The Code is the objective standard of measurement for the CSRC and the stock exchanges to judge whether a listed company has a favourable governance structure. It outlines the fundamental principles of the standards of conduct that should be followed by the management and requires listed companies to protect the interests of minority shareholders.

Directors' duties are another key area of ongoing corporate regulation. In general, the fiduciary duties of directors can be divided into two parts: a duty of loyalty and a duty of care. The duty of loyalty generally refers to the requirement to act bona fide for the benefit of the company; to exercise directors' powers for their proper purpose; and not to allow any conflict between their duties as directors and their personal interests. A similar concept of good faith can be found in the early Company Law, but not a duty of care. Directors of domestic companies were required to faithfully perform their duties, maintain the interests of their company and not take advantage of their positions to seek personal gain.[40] They were prohibited to engage personally or assist others in the business operation of a competing company, which might damage the interests of the company they were serving.[41] By contrast, the early Company Law had not provided for a duty of care, but it was then added to the Company Law 2005. As a result, the law now

[37] J Liu, *Modern Corporation Law* [*Xiandai Gongsi Fa*] (Beijing, Law Press China, 2015), 64–67. On the company law side, representative changes include the lowering of the minimum capital requirement by the Company Law 2013; and the relaxation of the requirements of share buyback by the Chinese Company Law 2018.

[38] 'Comply or explain' means that the adoption of the codes is voluntary but the company should explain in their annual reports why they have not adopted the codes. The principle is designed to encourage companies to develop governance processes and practices that are the most suitable for their particular circumstances and to report them in a meaningful way. See n 69 below.

[39] The Preamble of the Chinese Corporate Governance Code.

[40] Company Law 1993, art 59.

[41] ibid, art 61.

expressly commits directors, supervisors and senior officers of Chinese companies to upholding both 'duties of loyalty and care' to their companies.[42]

Whilst directors' duties are commonly seen in different jurisdiction, shareholders' duties are relatively rare. In the context of China, where a concentrated ownership pattern is predominant, the mitigation of majority–minority conflicts is perhaps more prevalent than principal–agent conflicts. Corporatisation (sometimes known as securitisation) refers to the legal and financial restructuring of SOEs through their conversion into joint stock companies. The corporatisation campaign in China was a two-step process. It first restructured SOEs into shareholding companies to be listed on a stock exchange. This caused many socio-economic and legal debates in China because such reform might change the nature of socialist public ownership. These debates involved a wide range of issues, from the fundamental principles of socialism and the efficiency of alternative economic and business forms to shareholders' rights.[43] Corporatisation was adopted, in which SOEs were converted to joint stock companies, featuring both state and non-state ownership. The goal was to improve managerial incentives by instilling in shareholders incentives and conferring on them the ability to monitor the managers. As Clarke has rightly pointed out, these diagnoses and the implementation of corporatisation as a solution are flawed.[44] The chief purpose of corporatisation is to promote higher efficiency through better management. The goal of the state owner in the new system is assumed to be profits, according to the traditional shareholder's value maximisation norm. In practice, a large number of corporatised SOEs remain dominated by a single state shareholder that exercises its control either through formal channels, such as shareholder voting, or through traditional channels, such as the appointment of key personnel.[45] It is simply too difficult for the state as the majority shareholder to effectively exercise its monitoring role.

Accordingly, one of the most important changes to the Company Law was to curb the abuse of controlling shareholders' powers in conflict with the interests of the company. The law now renders them liable to pay compensation for any loss the company suffers as a result of taking advantage of their positions.[46] It has been suggested that the intention of the regulatory authorities was to stall opportunistic affiliated transactions by imposing severe civil compensation liability on the parties to the transactions.[47] One view about imposing a duty on shareholders is that the law has effectively introduced an unfair prejudice claim or an 'oppression'

[42] Company Law 2018, art 147.

[43] J Chen, 'Securitisation of State-owned Enterprises and the Ownership Controversy in the PRC' (1993) 15 *Sydney Law Review* 59, 60.

[44] D Clarke, 'Corporate Governance in China: An Overview' (2003) 14 *China Economic Review* 494, 497–500.

[45] ibid, 499.

[46] Company Law 2005, arts 20–21. The line defining 'controlling shareholders' is drawn in the following way: they must hold half or more of the company's shares or the equivalent voting powers.

[47] J Fu and J Yuan, *PRC Company and Securities Laws: A Practical Guide* (Singapore, CCH, 2006) 48.

remedy – which is present in the UK and Hong Kong – into China.[48] The typical remedy resulting from this minority shareholder action is normally a buyout order. Indeed, an exit right is already present in the company law. In a few special cases, shareholders can request that the company buy back their shareholdings at a reasonable price.[49] Yet, this might not be a useful protection mechanism for shareholders given that there is no definition of what 'a reasonable price' really means and because shareholders need to file a petition to a people's court to enforce their exit rights. In a listed company, shareholders might avoid the hassles and be better off selling their shares on the open market.

Private enforcement mechanisms such as shareholder lawsuits serve the dual purpose of deterring potential wrongdoers and compensating injured investors. In the past, the right of shareholder action was very weak in China. Under the early Company Law, where shareholders were conferred certain rights those rights were provided mainly without any mention of civil remedies. Accordingly, a change was made to the Company Law 2005, via the introduction of a derivative-like action. For the first time, the concept of derivative action was introduced in the new Company Law to strengthen the protection of minority shareholders. Since the company is an independent legal entity, individual shareholders have not been able to bring actions against company directors under previous laws. However, Article 151 of the current Company Law gives rise to certain shareholders' rights to bring a derivative lawsuit.[50] Shareholders can sue, on behalf of the company, the directors, senior officers or supervisors who have violated any laws or administrative regulations or the company's articles of association, in the performance of their official duties, causing losses to the company. This is a derivative action-like mechanism because the right to sue still vests in the company rather than its shareholders. Accordingly, the compensation recovered belongs to the company instead of individual shareholders. Yet, it is unclear as to why the shareholders may need to rely on a derivative action, because unlike the rule in *Foss v Harbottle* under English law, the Company Law actually provides the basis for shareholders to initiate a direct action against directors and senior management personnel of the company.[51] Hence, it seems unnecessary for disgruntled shareholders to go down the derivative action route. Also, unlike the UK position, there is a shareholding

[48] C Hawes, 'The Chinese "Oppression" Remedy: Creative Interpretations of Company Law by Chinese Courts' (2015) 63 *American Journal of Comparative Law* 559.

[49] Company Law 2018, art 74. The circumstances include: (1) where the company resolves not to distribute profits to its shareholders for five consecutive years despite the company being profitable for those five years; (2) a merger or split of the company or transfer of the major assets of the company, or (3) renewal of the company's operation term after its expiration or events triggering dissolution.

[50] Under art 151, a shareholder or a group of shareholders holding one per cent or more of shares in the company for 180 consecutive days may submit a request in writing to the board of directors or board of supervisors to file a lawsuit with a people's court. The law further provides that if the request is refused or the circumstances are urgent, the shareholders shall have the right to file a lawsuit directly in their own name to protect the interests of the company.

[51] Art 152 of Company Law 2018.

threshold to meet.[52] Only shareholders holding one per cent or more of the total shares of the company for 180 consecutive days or more can invoke the action. The Chinese derivative action has been empirically appraised by Huang.[53] There has been notable number of cases following its introduction.

4.3. Regulating Hong Kong-Based Issuers

In Hong Kong, an issuer incorporated locally must not be a private company.[54] Companies that are incorporated overseas can list on the Hong Kong Exchanges and Clearing Limited (HKEX), but they are subject to the provisions of Part XII of the Companies (Winding Up and Miscellaneous Provisions) Ordinance and Listing Rule 19 (or 19A for Chinese companies; 19B for Depository Receipts; 19C for Secondary Listing). In any case, an issuer must satisfy the requirements of Chapter 8 of the Listing Rules. The HKEX will consider the suitability of the company and its business for listing. The company will need to satisfy one of three quantitative tests: the profit test, the market capitalisation test or the revenue test.[55] Broadly speaking, this means that the company must have an adequate trading record of not less than three financial years. Also, there should be a sufficient amount of profit attributable to shareholders in the most recent years. Regarding 'market capitalisation',[56] the company should have a market value of at least HKD 2 billion at the time of listing. Furthermore, it must have a turnover of at least HKD 500 million for the most recently audited financial year.[57] Lower admission requirements are in place for the Growth Enterprise Market (GEM). However, the market capitalisation of the GEM is almost negligible compared to the Main Board. Owing to its insignificance and for simplicity, the discussion of it will be skipped here.

There will be a due diligence process undertaken by underwriters to establish the completeness and accuracy of the information contained in the prospectus. Practice Note 21 of the HKEX sets out the steps a sponsor must undertake to fulfil its responsibilities. Authorisation must then be sought from the Securities and Futures Commission (SFC) of Hong Kong by providing a copy of the prospectus,

[52] Contrast this with s 260 of the UK's Companies Act 2006.

[53] H Huang, 'Shareholder Derivative Litigation in China: Empirical Findings and Comparative Analysis' (2012) 27 *Banking and Finance Law Review* 619.

[54] Hong Kong Listing Rules (HKLR) 8.03. Under CO (Cap 622) s 11, a private company is required to restrict the right of its shareholders to transfer their shares and limit the number of its members to 50. Any invitation to the public to subscribe for any shares or debentures of the company is prohibited. On the other hand, the transfer and holding of shares in public companies are not restricted.

[55] HKLR 8.05(1)–8.05(3). The HKEX may accept a shorter trading record when it is satisfied that the listing of the company is desirable in the interests of the company and investors.

[56] The total equity value of the company, namely the current market price per share multiplied by the total number of outstanding shares.

[57] HKLR 8.05(2)(e).

signed by the directors and with certain specified endorsements thereon. If this is approved, the SFC will transfer the case to the HKEX. Otherwise, the SFC is empowered to require further information from the company making the filing and raise an objection to the listing.[58] Grounds for objection can be, for instance, that the prospectus does not provide sufficiently detailed information on the company and its affairs for an investor to make an informed decision, or that the application is false or misleading as to a material fact or by omission of a material fact.[59] The reason can also be as general as that the SFC considers it 'not in the public interest' for the securities to be listed. The HKEX will also play an active role in raising questions about the contents of the prospectus. This demonstrates how the entry strategy can be employed in conjunction with the trusteeship strategy.

Although now Hong Kong-based investors can acquire Chinese shares via Stock Connect, previously they could do the same by purchasing shares from those dual listed Chinese companies. In relation to overseas issuers the general principle is that the HKEX must be satisfied that the overseas issuer is incorporated or otherwise established in a jurisdiction where the standards of shareholder protection are at least equivalent to those provided in Hong Kong.[60] Various rules should in principle apply to all issuers regardless of their country of incorporation unless otherwise stated. The company laws of Bermuda, the Cook Islands, the Cayman Islands and China were pre-vetted by the HKEX and special provisions were made for those jurisdictions, as seen in Appendix 13 of the Listing Rules. Issuers are required to make certain changes to their company constitutive documents in order to comply with Appendix 13. Also, financial statements must have been audited to a standard comparable to that required in Hong Kong.[61] The standard can be one specified by the Hong Kong Institute of Certified Public Accountants or by the International Auditing and Assurance Standards Board of the International Federation of Accountants. Furthermore, overseas issuers are required to include a summary of the provisions of their constitutive documents and the relevant regulatory provisions of the jurisdiction in which they are incorporated.[62] One notable feature of the Hong Kong regime is perhaps the inclusion of a specific chapter of listing rules for Chinese issuers, that is, Chapter 19A. Some specific provisions applying to Chinese issuers (via overseas listing, not Stock Connect) may provide additional shareholder protection; meanwhile some may represent a compromise.[63]

[58] Securities and Futures (Stock Market Listing) Rules 'SMLR' (Cap 571V) rule 6. Under SMLR rule 6(4), the HKEX is prohibited from listing any company to which the SFC has lodged an objection.

[59] SMLR rule 3(c).

[60] HKLR 19.05.

[61] HKLR 19.12.

[62] HKLR 19.10(2).

[63] For a summary, see F Huang and H Yeung, 'Regulatory Co-operation between Securities Commissions: A Reflection from Hong Kong' (2013) 1 *Chinese Journal of Comparative Law* 112, 132.

In addition to surveillance and monitoring by the stock exchanges, listed companies are required to follow a number of corporate governance requirements. The corporate governance framework in Hong Kong is derived primarily from four sources: (1) common law and equity;[64] (2) statutory legislation;[65] (3) constitutional documents of the company; and (4) soft laws.[66] These four categories are not entirely independent. For example, statutory requirements in many aspects bear a strong relationship to the directors' fiduciary duties and their common law duty of care, skills and diligence. Similarly, the Listing Rules are not legally binding, but require statutory backing by the virtue of the SMLR.[67] Although the CO and the company's constitutional documents provide the basic skeletal structure of a company (for example, the requirement that a public company has at least two directors), the Listing Rules have been the major part of a wider programme for improving the standards of corporate governance in Hong Kong. The most significant development was the adoption of the Code on Corporate Governance into the Listing Rules in January 2005.[68] The Code was essentially based on the UK's Combined Code of Corporate Governance at that time and its 'comply or explain' principle.[69]

In general, the substantive legal framework in Hong Kong to protect investors and promote market efficiency is roughly similar to that of the UK because of the influence from the English model during the colonial era before 1997. For example, both common law (including equity) and statute impose on company directors certain duties to the company. Directors owe fiduciary duties to the company, which are based upon showing the utmost good faith.[70] They should not put themselves in a position where their personal interest conflicts with those of the company.[71] Following the codification of director duties by the Companies Act 2006 in the UK, Hong Kong similarly put the director duties (partly) on a statutory footing in its current Companies Ordinance (CO) which came into operation on 3 March 2014. One change is the codification of the duty of care, skill and diligence.[72] In a similar way to its UK counterpart, a dual subjective-objective test is employed.[73] However, other fiduciary duties, including acting in good faith

[64] This, for example, is concerned with the fiduciary duties of directors.

[65] This includes the Companies Ordinance (CO) and the Securities and Futures Ordinance (SFO).

[66] This includes the Listing Rules and the Takeover Code.

[67] Rule 3(a) of the SMLR provides that a company applying for listing on the HKEX is required to comply with the rules and requirements of the HKEX.

[68] HKLR Appendices 14 and 23.

[69] A company must report on whether it has complied with the provisions in the Code and explain deviations from those provisions. For greater regulatory effects, some requirements are especially incorporated into the Listing Rules. For instance, a director is expected to have good character, experience and integrity and must be able to demonstrate a standard of competence commensurate with his position. See HKLR Appendix 14 Part 1.

[70] See for example, *Re Smith & Fawcett Ltd* [1942] Ch 304 (CA).

[71] See for example, *Aberdeen Railway Co v Blaikie Bros* (1854) 1 Macq 461 (HL).

[72] CO (Cap 622) s 465.

[73] Hong Kong Institute of Chartered Secretaries, 'Company Law Guidance Note' (November 2017), available at: www.hkcgi.org.hk/media/publication/attachment/PUBLICATION_A_2406_HKICS_Company_Law_Guidance_Note%20(Eng).pdf.pdf (accessed 1 February 2023).

in the interests of the company, exercising powers for their proper purpose, and avoiding conflict of duty and interest, remain in common law.[74]

Shareholders in Hong Kong have various ways to bring an action in the event of company maladministration, and this legal framework has a substantial resemblance to the UK model. For example, similar to the statutory protection of minority shareholders in England, any member of a company can apply to the court for an order under the Companies Ordinance on the grounds that the affairs of the company are being or have been conducted in a manner unfairly prejudicial to the interests of the members.[75] Of course, this might not be useful in a public company where shareholders can choose to sell their shares via the market. Under the CO, they can also take advantage of statutory derivative actions.[76] Even earlier than the UK did, Hong Kong placed derivative actions on a statutory footing in 2004 with a view to strengthening the position of minority shareholders.[77] As an exception to the rule in *Foss v Harbottle*,[78] a shareholder can bring legal proceedings on behalf of the company against any director in respect of misfeasance committed against the company. Furthermore, under the Securities and Futures Ordinance (SFO), shareholders have a right of action in civil proceedings for their pecuniary loss as a result of another person's contravention of market misconduct provisions.[79]

Nonetheless, in practice, these proceedings have rarely been seen. In his investigation of minority shareholder protection in Hong Kong, Lawton identified over 200 relevant shareholder actions between 1980 and 1995,[80] among which most of the cases were actions for just and equitable winding up under section 177(1)(f) of the former Companies Ordinance, which is essentially an equivalent of section 122(1)(g) of the Insolvency Act 1986 in the UK. There were a considerable number of unfair prejudice petitions under section 168A of the former Companies Ordinance in this period, but the number of derivative actions was negligible.[81] This shows that most cases were largely related to small and private companies and, therefore, should have little impact on the securities market. Nevertheless, it is incorrect to state that the law has never been enforced.

[74] ibid.

[75] CO (Cap 622) Part 14. See also the Company Act 2006 (CA 2006) of the UK s 994 (formerly CA 1985 s 459).

[76] CO (Cap 622) Part 14.

[77] It was added to the ordinance by the Companies (Amendment) Ordinance 2004 (Ordinance No 30 of 2004).

[78] *Foss v Harbottle* (1843) 2 Hare 461.

[79] SFO (Cap 571) s 281. It appears that there is no equivalent in the UK.

[80] P Lawton, 'Modeling the Chinese Family Firm and Minority Shareholder Protection: The Hong Kong Experience 1980–1995' (2007) 49 *Managerial Law* 249. This was one of the first studies to investigate the legal experience of minority shareholder protection in Hong Kong by examining the petitions and writs actually filed. A total of 275 cases were identified between the years 1980 and 1995 inclusive, by drawing upon material from a questionnaire sent to law firms and other relevant professions.

[81] See ibid. The numbers of Companies Ordinance (Cap 32) s 177 actions, s 168A actions and a mixture of both were 135, 24 and 116 respectively. There were only a very small number of cases pleaded as exceptions to *Foss v Harbottle* and these were excluded from the analysis.

For example, a case in Hong Kong, *Waddington Limited v Chan Chun Hoo Thomas*, contributed to the development of the concept of multiple derivative actions.[82] A more recent empirical examination of the statutory derivative action in Hong Kong reveals that there has been a rise in shareholder action.[83] In general, Tyler and Ho attributed the lack of cases representing minority shareholder action in Hong Kong to the Chinese disinclination for litigation and the family structure of Hong Kong companies.[84]

The predominance of family businesses in Hong Kong may have an implication for corporate governance. The rise of dispersed ownership, which has resulted from strong shareholder protection or other functional substitutes, is arguably associated with the development of stock markets.[85] Most Anglo-American corporations have a separation of management and ownership, which facilitates the growth of domestic stock markets. Despite the perception that Hong Kong is an international business centre heavily influenced by the Anglo-American model, most listed companies in Hong Kong have been controlled by families.[86] According to the International Finance Corporation, a family business is defined as 'a company where the voting majority is in the hands of the controlling family, including the founder(s) who intend to pass the business on to their descendants.'[87] Running a company in a family business form has its strengths and weaknesses.[88] In relation to strengths, the family, as the business owners, normally shows the highest dedication in seeing its business grow, prosper and get passed on to the next generations. Many family members identify with the company and usually work harder and reinvest part of their profits into the business to allow it to grow in the long term. Furthermore, accumulation of knowledge, experience and skills within families through generations is normally seen as a priority. Also, because

[82] *Waddington Ltd v Chan Chun Hoo Thomas and others* [2008] (FACV 15/2007). See also S Goo, 'Multiple Derivative Action and Common Law Derivative Action Revisited: A Tale of Two Jurisdictions' (2010) 10 *Journal of Corporate Law Studies* 255.

[83] F Mezzanotte, 'The Unconvincing Rise of the Statutory Derivative Action in Hong Kong: Evidence from its 10 Years of Enforcement' (2017) 17 *Journal of Corporate Law Studies* 469. For example, there were 54 cases in the period of 2005 to 2014, compared to just 29 in the previous decade.

[84] E Tyler and J Ho, *HKLRD Review Series 2004: Company Law* (Hong Kong, Sweet and Maxwell, 2004) 32.

[85] For a discussion on the interaction of these three spheres: law, ownership and market, see for example, J Coffee, 'The Rise of Dispersed Ownership The Roles of Law and the State in the Separation of Ownership and Control' (2001) 111 *Yale Law Journal* 1; B Cheffins, 'Does Law Matter?: The Separation of Ownership and Control in the United Kingdom' (2001) 30 *Journal of Legal Studies* 459; and M Roe, 'Legal Origins, Politics and Modern Stock Markets' (2006) 120 *Harvard Law Review* 460.

[86] Z Chen at el, 'Ownership Concentration, Firm Performance and Dividend Policy in Hong Kong' (2005) 13 *Pacific-Basin Finance Journal* 431; R La Porta et al, 'Corporate Ownership around the World' (1999) 64 *Journal of Finance* 471; S Claessens et al, 'The Separation of Ownership and Control in East Asian Corporations' (2000) 58 *Journal of Financial Economics* 81.

[87] International Finance Corporation, 'IFC Family Business Governance Handbook' (2011), available at: www.ifc.org/wps/wcm/connect/topics_ext_content/ifc_external_corporate_site/ifc+cg/resources/guidelines_reviews+and+case+studies/ifc+family+business+governance+handbook (accessed 1 February 2023).

[88] ibid, 12–14.

family businesses have their name and reputation associated with their output, they strive to increase the quality of their products or services and to maintain a good customer relationship. On the other hand, family businesses are usually complex in terms of governance and, more problematically, there is not a set of clearly articulated business practices and procedures. There are inherent conflicts between the controlling and minority shareholders of companies.[89] On the face of it, the predominance of family ownership and control of companies in Hong Kong is incompatible with its rise as an international finance centre if one believes in the nexus between shareholder protection and market growth. However, as observed by Farrar, Hong Kong represents a unique success story built on the twin foundations of Anglo-American law and finance and successful Chinese family business.[90]

4.4. Regulating London-Based Issuers

To gain a listing in the UK, companies have the choice of four routes to market: a Premium (formerly Primary) Listing, a Standard (formerly Secondary) Listing, an admission via the High Growth Segment, as well as an Alternative Investment Market (AIM) listing. Focus will be on the first two in this section. Prior to October 2009 when the Financial Conduct Authority (FCA) introduced new rules, only companies incorporated outside the UK were eligible for a standard listing. Now, standard listings are open to all companies regardless of country of domicile. However, in the case of a foreign issuer issuing depository receipts, they can go for a standard listing only, unless the issuer belongs to a specific type of company called a 'Sovereign Controlled Commercial Company'.[91]

Issuers with a premium listing are required to meet the UK's super-equivalent rules which are higher than the EU minimum requirements. In contrast, standard listings are required to comply only with the EU minimum requirements. According to the bonding hypothesis, the advantage of the former may come from a lower cost of capital through greater transparency and through building investor confidence.[92] Meanwhile, the latter may be attractive owing to lower compliance costs. For all issuers, they need to have a minimum market capitalisation of GBP 30 million; for premium listing, there is also a requirement to demonstrate a revenue-earning track record.[93]

[89] P Lawton, 'Berle and Means, Corporate Governance and the Chinese Family Firm' (1996) 6 *Australian Journal of Corporate Law* 348; and S Ho et al, *The Hong Kong Financial System* (Hong Kong, OUP, 2004) 383–88.

[90] J Farrar, 'Developing Corporate Governance in Greater China' (2002) 25 *UNSW Law Journal* 462, 464.

[91] UK Listing Rules (UKLR) 18 and 21. A Sovereign Controlled Commercial Company is 'an issuer in which a State exercises or controls 30 percent or more of the votes able to be cast on all or substantially all matters at general meetings of that company'.

[92] Coffee (2002), see n 9 above; Stulz (1999), see n 9 above.

[93] UKLR 2.2.7R and UKLR 6.3.1R.

In relation to the initial disclosure obligations, a standard listing will be the same as a premium listing in the sense that both will need to comply with Listing Rule 3. A number of documents, notably including a prospectus or listing particulars that have been approved by the FCA, must be submitted.[94] The Prospectus Rules will provide further guidance on the general contents and format of a prospectus. But for other listing requirements, both types of listings are governed by different listing rules, Listing Rule 6 for premium listings and Listing Rule 14 for standard listings. UKLR 6.1.3R(1)(a) stipulates that a new issuer under a premium listing must have published or filed historical financial information that covers at least three years. In contrast, the audited historical financial information for a standard listing should cover three years or such shorter period as the issuer has been in operation (depending on the applicable UKLR Annexes). Another notable difference between the two will be that an issuer applying for a premium listing must appoint a sponsor or have its guidance obtained. According to UKLR 8.3.1R, the role of a sponsor is two-fold: first, it provides assurance to the FCA that the responsibilities of the issuers have been met; second, it guides the issuer in understanding and meeting its responsibilities under the listing rules and other applicable listing requirements. In sharp contrast, a sponsor is not needed in a standard listing.

In relation to ongoing requirements, both premium and standard listings will be required to publish annual and semi-annual reports pursuant to the Disclosure Guidance and Transparency Rules.[95] Meanwhile, there are notable differences. First, in the case of a listed company incorporated in the UK, a company must include in its annual report a statement as to whether the listed company has complied with all relevant provisions set out in the UK Corporate Governance Code; in the case of any non-compliance, an explanation is needed why it is the case.[96] Second, ad hoc disclosures will be required in the case of significant transactions and related party transactions for 'premium' issuers only.[97] Third, with a premium listing, a disapplication of pre-emption rights is possible if it is authorised by the consent of shareholders representing a supermajority.[98] For the standard listing, none of these requirements are applicable.

Comparing the current Companies Act 2006 and its predecessor Companies Act 1985, one major change is the codification of a list of seven director duties in the UK.[99] In the view of Davies and colleagues, the codification exercise is more than 'simply a restatement of the common law'.[100] One example will be an attempt

[94] UKLR 3.3.2R.

[95] UKLR 9.2.5G. The UK's Disclosure Guidance and Transparency Rules are available on the FCA website at: www.handbook.fca.org.uk/handbook/DTR/.

[96] UKLR 9.8.6R(6).

[97] UKLR 10.2.1G; UKLR 11.1.7R and UKLR 10.4.1R.

[98] UKLR 9.3.12R(4).

[99] CA 2006 ss 171–177.

[100] P Davies et al, *Gower Principles of Modern Company Law* (London, Sweet & Maxwell, 2021) 248.

to clarify the standard of care expected of directors.[101] Historically, the common law was based upon a very low standard of care under a subjective test.[102] As discussed above in section 4.3. about Hong Kong, where a similar change was introduced, it is now a dual subjective-objective test. The central idea of this dual subjective-objective test is to use an objective test to stipulate the minimum acceptable standard, which can then be increased using a subjective test. Another new change brought about by the Companies Act 2006 is perhaps the introduction of an enlightened shareholder value approach into company law.[103] Under this enlightened shareholder value approach, a director has the duty to promote the success of the company, and in doing so, s/he needs to have regard to the interests of a spectrum of stakeholders, notably employees, suppliers, customers, the community and the environment. Although this sounds brilliant on paper, the approach has been quite heavily criticised by scholars for being vague and unenforceable.[104]

There is civil liability for a breach of any director duties.[105] Under the rule in *Foss v Harbottle*,[106] the company is the competent party to proceed against the wrongdoing director(s). However, it is also possible for the shareholders to take action. There are three types of legal action they can take, namely a derivation action,[107] an unfair prejudice claim,[108] and a just and equitable winding up petition.[109] A legal innovation brought about by the Companies Act 2006 is the introduction of a statutory derivative action. The cause of action in respect of a statutory derivative action can be quite broad, covering 'an actual or proposed act or omission involving negligence, default, breach of duty or breach of trust by a director of the company'.[110] The law now sets out some clearer procedural rules governing the management of proceedings.[111] However, as observed by Keay, there are indeed very few proceedings in the UK, and shareholders are more keen to bring an unfair prejudice claim.[112] One obvious reason will be that a derivative action, because of its nature (that the litigating shareholder is doing so on behalf of the company), can only lead to group relief. There is a 'free rider' problem. The litigating shareholder(s) will incur all the efforts and costs, but the gain will be split among all affected parties. In contrast, an unfair prejudice claim will lead to

[101] CA 2006 s 174.
[102] *Re City Equitable Fire Insurance* [1925] Ch 407 (CA).
[103] CA 2006 s 172.
[104] See eg V Harper Ho, '"Enlightened Shareholder Value": Corporate Governance Beyond the Shareholder-Stakeholder Divide' (2010) 36 *Journal of Corporation Law* 59; A Keay, *The Enlightened Shareholder Value Principle and Corporate Governance* (Abingdon, Routledge, 2014).
[105] CA 2006 s 178.
[106] *Foss v Harbottle* (1843) 2 Hare 461.
[107] CA 2006 s 260.
[108] CA 2006 s 994.
[109] Insolvency Act 1986 s 122(1)(g).
[110] CA 2006 s 260.
[111] CA 2006 ss 260–264, accompanied by the relevant Civil Procedure Rules.
[112] A Keay, 'Assessing and Rethinking the Statutory Scheme for Derivative Actions under the Companies Act 2006' (2016) 16 *Journal of Corporate Law Studies* 39.

personal relief, mostly in the form of a buyout order/an exit right.[113] Meanwhile, the use of an unfair prejudice claim can be limited in a listed company situation, as an exit right is readily available via the open market. Also, even in a private company situation, an exit right can be available outside of the court.[114] In the most radical situation, a disgruntled shareholder can also petition to wind a company up.[115] However, it is normally regarded as a 'last resort'.[116]

On the other hand, as opposed to reliance on hard laws, it is believed that the UK corporate governance landscape goes down an alternative avenue. First, the UK is a pioneer in using a non-binding corporate governance code.[117] Second, the UK regime entrusts the institutional shareholders with the guardianship of corporate governance.[118] According to government statistics, the proportion of UK shares held by UK-resident individuals fell to 12 per cent in 2020.[119] Instead, the majority of shares are held by different financial institutions, both foreign and local. The UK Stewardship Code, again a soft law, requires asset owners and asset managers to exercise different stewardship functions, including engaging with issuers and holding them to account on material issues, as well as actively exercising rights and responsibilities.

4.5. Regulating Switzerland-Based Issuers

According to SIX Swiss Exchange's listing rules, the rules seek to provide 'free and equal access' to different issuers, and at the same time to protect investors by ensuring 'transparency' and 'issuer quality'.[120] The Regulatory Board of the exchange will decide on the admission of securities to trading.[121] There are eight regulatory standards under the listing rules for different types of companies and equity securities.[122] Some of these standards were very recently introduced.[123] For example, in December 2021, SIX launched a new trading segment for small and medium enterprises, SPARKS. For this new segment, there are different listing requirements. Likewise, a special set of standards was introduced in the same year

[113] CA 2006 s 996.

[114] A Pavlovich, '"Reasonable Offers" as a Defence to Unfair Prejudice Petitions: *Prescott* v *Potamianos*' (2020) 83 *Modern Law Review* 443.

[115] Insolvency Act 1986 s 122(1)(g).

[116] Davies et al (2021), see n 100 above, 561.

[117] See the ground-breaking Cadbury Report in 1992, for example.

[118] Kraakman et al (2017), see n 1 above, 73.

[119] Data from the Office for National Statistics, UK.

[120] SIX Swiss Listing Rules (SSLR), art 1.

[121] Financial Market Infrastructure Act, art 35; SSLR art 3.

[122] SSLR, art 3. For example, there are special standards for investment and real estate companies respectively.

[123] T Härtsch and D Dedeyan, 'The Initial Public Offerings Law Review: Switzerland' (6 September 2022), available at: thelawreviews.co.uk/title/the-initial-public-offerings-law-review/switzerland (accessed 1 February 2023).

for special purpose acquisition companies. Most importantly, in the context of this book, there is also a special set of standards for depository receipts for the Stock Connect scheme with China.

For all issuers, the listing rules require that they comply with the national law to which the issuer is subject.[124] Furthermore, the issuer must have existed at least three years prior to the listing.[125] Also, the issuer's reported equity capital must be at least CHF 25 million on its first day of trading.[126]

On the other hand, as mentioned above, there are special standards for different types of companies and equity securities. For example, in relation to investment companies, the three years of operation history requirement is actually waived.[127] Similarly, for SPARKS, the requirement is shortened to two years, as opposed to three. Also, for SPARKS companies, there should be a market capitalisation of less than CHF 500 million upon listing, and a minimum equity capital of CHF 12 million on their first day of trading.[128] For the issuers of depository receipts, there are even more modifications to the usual listing rules. Firstly, there are requirements regarding the depository.[129] It must be a bank, governed by the Swiss Banking Act, or a securities firm, governed by the Financial Institutions Act, or their overseas equivalents. Second, the listing rules seek to clarify the nature of depository receipts, that the

> underlying shares [are] held by the depository on a fiduciary basis on behalf of the investors' by the depository, and 'the depository [in this arrangement] will exercise all property and membership rights attached to the underlying shares in the interests of those investors.[130]

Furthermore, the issuer is required to declare in both the prospectus and the annual report that it adheres to the corporate governance standards of its home market, as opposed to the Swiss 'Directive on Information relating to Corporate Governance'.[131]

As discussed towards the beginning of this chapter, Switzerland did not perform very well in the investor protection indices. It is crucial to see why it is the case, using the analytical framework for other three jurisdictions in the previous sections. The first focus will be the directors' duties. On the face of it, the Swiss Federal Code of Obligations (SFCO) provides a list of eight duties regarding the operation and formalities of the company.[132] The two limbs of fiduciary duty, namely the duties of care and loyalty, are jointly covered by Article 717.

[124] SSLR, art 10.
[125] ibid, art 11.
[126] ibid, art 15.
[127] ibid, art 66.
[128] ibid, arts 89b and 89d.
[129] ibid, art 92.
[130] ibid, art 93.
[131] ibid, art 101.
[132] SFCO, art 716a.

There is also a specific article addressing conflicts of interest.[133] In Switzerland, the main remedy available to shareholders is the ability to file claims against the corporation's directors and officers.[134] The law provides that the members of the board of directors and all persons engaged in the business management or liquidation of the company are liable both to the company and to the individual shareholders and creditors for any losses or damage arising from any intentional or negligent breach of their duties. As a result, there can be a personal legal action, or a derivative-like action. Nonetheless, generally, shareholder litigation has not taken off in Switzerland. A Swiss law firm attributes this to two main reasons.[135] Firstly, the standards of proof for a claim are generally high and the burden of proof is on the plaintiff. Secondly, the costs associated with civil proceedings are high and entail additional litigation risks for the plaintiff, as it will not only bear its own costs but will also have to compensate the defendant for its costs in case of loss of the legal proceedings.

To dig further regarding the quality of shareholder protection in Switzerland, it will be useful to refer back to the index prepared by the Cambridge Centre for Business Research.[136] For a breakdown of scores for the three jurisdictions (excluding Hong Kong which was not studied in their project) in the Index, see Table 4.1.

Table 4.1 Cambridge Centre for Business Research's Extended Shareholder Protection Index 2013 for Selected Countries

Variable*	**1**	**2**	**3**	**4**	**5**	**6**	**7**	**8**	**9**	**10**	**TotalScore**
China	1	0.75	0.5	1	0.6	0.5	0.75	1	1	0.75	7.85
UK	0.75	0.5	0.5	0	1	0.9	0.75	1	1	1	7.4
Switzerland	0	0.25	0.5	0.25	0.5	0.5	1	1	0.5	1	5.5

**Note*: Variables 1 to 10 are: 1) Powers of the general meeting for de facto changes; 2) Agenda-setting power; 3) Anticipation of shareholder decision facilitated; 4) Prohibition of multiple voting rights (super voting rights); 5) Independent board members; 6) Feasibility of director's dismissal; 7) Private enforcement of directors' duties (derivative suit); 8) Shareholder action against resolutions of the general meeting; 9) Mandatory bid; and 10) Disclosure of major share ownership.

Source: Cambridge Centre for Business Research.

From Table 4.1 it can be seen that Switzerland has done notably less well overall than China and the UK considering the aggregate score. In particular, that country was not doing well in the first six variables. Variable 1, for example, is about

[133] ibid, art 717a.

[134] ibid, art 754.

[135] Walder Wyss, 'Shareholders' Rights & Shareholder Activism' (2019), available at: www.walderwyss.com/user_assets/publications/019_SWITZERLAND-LP.pdf (accessed 1 February 2023).

[136] Siems (2016), see n 14 above.

the shareholder approval of large asset sales.[137] Under the Chinese Company Law, if the amount of the major assets purchased or sold or the amount of security provided by a listed company within one year exceeds 30 per cent of the total assets of the company, a resolution must be passed by the general meeting and adopted by two-thirds or more of the voting rights held by the shareholders present at the meeting.[138] By contrast, in the UK, ad hoc disclosures and approval will be required in the case of significant transactions for 'premium' issuers only.[139] A transaction is classified by assessing its size relative to that of the listed company proposing to make it.[140] In Switzerland, in light of the Directive on Ad hoc Publicity, a substantial asset sale will likely be determined to be potentially price-sensitive and therefore require disclosure. But there is no mention of approval in either the Swiss Code of Obligations or the listing rules. Conversely, Switzerland was doing better than China and the UK in relation to Variable 7, which is about private enforcement of directors' duties through a derivative claim. By scoring a perfect score of 1 in that variable, it shows that there should be almost no restrictions in Switzerland in relation to bringing a derivative claim.[141] Indeed, modernising the corporate law regime has certainly been underway in Switzerland, as exemplified by the country's recent Corporate Law Reform entering into force on 1 January 2023.[142]

4.6. Concluding Remarks

Just like the previous chapter, this chapter was unable to identify any notable regulatory gap between the four jurisdictions which could lead to a shortfall in investor protection when an investor chooses to acquire foreign securities via Stock Connect. Admittedly, Switzerland is somewhat a concern in comparison with other countries, as confirmed by some indices. However, at the same time, Switzerland has been radically overhauling its corporate and financial law regime in recent years, as exemplified by its new Financial Services Act, as well as a very recent Corporate Law Reform.

Of course, different jurisdictions may have different measures in place. As opposed to a list of seven statutory director duties in the UK, China and

[137] If the sale of more than 50 per cent of the company's assets requires approval of the general meeting, a score 1 is assigned; if the sale of more than 80 per cent of the assets requires approval, 0.5 is given; otherwise, 0 is given. If no clearly predominant opinion exists, an intermediary score is possible.

[138] Chinese Company Law 2005, art 122; Company Law 2013, art 121.

[139] UKLR 10.5.1R.

[140] UKLR 10.2.1G.

[141] Meanwhile, Siems and colleagues believe there are restrictions in the UK and China in this regards. For example, in relation to procedural restrictions (ss 260–264 CA 2006) and shareholding threshold (art 151 of Chinese Company Law).

[142] For a quick summary of key changes, refer to PwC, 'Swiss Corporate Law Reform: The Changes in a Nutshell (2021), available at: www.pwc.ch/en/publications/2021/ch-Swiss_Corporate_Law_Reform.pdf (accessed 1 February 2023).

Switzerland just have a single provision providing for the duties of care and loyalty. Hong Kong has only codified a duty of care, but a duty of loyalty is largely left to the common law. Furthermore, the UK and Hong Kong have three types of shareholder action in place, when Switzerland only has one. In relation to the Corporate Governance Code, the UK, Hong Kong and Switzerland all adopt a 'comply or explain' approach, while in China compliance is mandatory. Yet all these differences may not readily and automatically suggest that one place is better than the other.

If one believes in functionalism in comparative law, it is possible to have different approaches to dealing with the same problem.[143] Also, amidst an increasingly competitive global market for issuers, different countries are under pressure to make sure that their regimes can keep up with their competitors and demands from a modern commercial world.[144] This can mean updating their black letter rules, as well as making investments in their regulators. As the four countries all have a sizeable market, it should be no major surprise that in the two parallel chapters (Chapter three in relation to securities law and this one in relation to corporate law and listing rules) a comparable level of investor protection between the countries is seen, which is indeed the central requirement of different Stock Connect framework rules and documents.[145]

[143] K Zweigert, 'Methodological Problems in Comparative Law' (1972) 7 *Israel Law Review* 465.

[144] See Coffee (2002), n 9 above; H Hansmann and R Kraakman, 'The End of History for Corporate Law' (2001) 89 *Georgetown Law Journal* 439; M Siems, *Convergence in Shareholder Law* (Cambridge, CUP, 2007).

[145] For example, see the 'Administrative Measures for the Issuance and Trading of Depository Receipts (Trial)'.

5

Regulatory Cooperation and Enforcement

In the previous two chapters, we discussed the regulations governing cross-border investors and corporate issuers. In this chapter, we will first review the literature on the significance of regulatory cooperation. We will then examine the regulatory infrastructure in the four participant markets through Stock Connect. The focus of this chapter will be on the regulatory cooperation and enforcement between China and other regulators, such as Hong Kong, the UK, and Switzerland, under Stock Connect.

5.1. Significance and Strategies of Regulatory Cooperation

In today's global securities markets, financial activities often cross national borders. Securities regulators are responsible for supervising markets, trading, products, and market participants, which can extend beyond their borders. However, securities regulation is not global, and as Tafara and Peterson asserted, '[b]orders that have blurred for most market participants are proving as sharp as ever where market regulation is concerned'.[1]

The financial crisis of September 2008 highlighted the paramount importance for regulators to work together in overseeing the activities of globally active market participants, to identify and assess risks, and to develop a coordinated response to mitigate those risks.[2]

In contrast to purely domestic investigations, regulators in cross-border settings are often constrained by information shortfalls, jurisdictional complexities and legal limitations.[3] As suggested by Goodhart and Lastra, the boundary between regulators and jurisdictions, which is rooted in the limitations imposed

[1] E Tafara and R Peterson, 'A Blueprint for Cross-Border Access to US Investors: A New International Framework' (2007) 48 *Harvard International Law Journal* 31, 32.

[2] JG Hill, 'Regulatory Cooperation in Securities Market Regulation: Perspectives from Australia' (2020) 17(1) *European Company and Financial Law Review* 11.

[3] R Silvers, 'Cross-Border Cooperation Between Securities Regulators' (2020) 69 *Journal of Accounting and Economics* 1, 2.

by the principle of national sovereignty and territoriality, remains an obstacle to effective regulatory cooperation.[4] As a result, cross-border enforcement requires cooperation between regulators operating in different and seemingly incompatible legal systems, and differs from enforcement within a single territory.

According to a report by the International Organisation of Securities Commissions (IOSCO) of 2019, lack of international standards, or differences in the way jurisdictions implement such standards, can lead to regulatory-driven market fragmentation.[5] Regulators are hesitant to engage in broader cooperative supervision arrangements owing to their concern that by doing so they would be relinquishing their oversight responsibilities to another regulator.[6]

In the absence of any likelihood of the creation of a formal supranational regulator in the near future, regulators may enter into bilateral or multilateral memoranda of understanding (MoU) or other agreements which are built on mutual trust, assistance and reciprocity.[7] Bilateral agreements are generally underpinned by an MoU, which provides the framework for extensive continuing supervisory and enforcement cooperation between the relevant securities regulators. An MoU has been described in this context as 'an understanding among two or more states under which each recognises the adequacy of the other's regulation or supervision of an activity or institution as a substitute for its own'.[8] An MoU is also a simpler and cheaper technique for facilitating cross-border market access than complex multilateral agreements, which depend on powerful and expensive, supranational institutions.[9] However, these MoUs are expressed to be an 'understanding', in the sense that the parties do not intend to create legally binding obligations or supersede domestic laws.[10]

Many of these memoranda are influenced by the standard form created in May 2002 and earlier forms prepared by IOSCO. Established in 2002, the Multilateral Memorandum of Understanding Concerning Consultation and Cooperation and the Exchange of Information (MMoU) sets an international benchmark for cross-border cooperation. As of September 2022, there were

[4] C Goodhart and R Lastra, 'Border Problems' (2010) 13 *Journal of International Economic Law* 705, 714.

[5] IOSCO, 'Market Fragmentation & Cross-border Regulation' (June 2019), 8, available at: www.iosco.org/library/pubdocs/pdf/IOSCOPD629.pdf (accessed on 20 March 2022). The definition of market fragmentation adopted by IOSCO is the same as that used by the Financial Stability Board (FSB), namely 'global markets that break into segments, either geographically or by type of products or participants'.

[6] IOSCO, 'Principles Regarding Cross-Border Supervisory Cooperation: Final Report' (2010), p 15, available at: www.iosco.org/library/pubdocs/pdf/IOSCOPD322.pdf (accessed on 3 April 2022).

[7] PH Verdier, 'Mutual Recognition in International Finance' (2011) *Harvard International Law Journal* 52, 57.

[8] ibid, 64.

[9] C de Meijer and M Saaf, 'Mutual Recognition and the Transatlantic Dialogue: The Concept and its Progress' (2010) 3 *Journal of Securities Law, Regulation and Compliance* 124, 128.

[10] F Huang and H Yeung, 'Regulatory Cooperation between Securities Commission: A Reflection from Hong Kong' (2013) 1(1) *Chinese Journal of Comparative* Law 112, 115.

currently 129 full signatories to the MMoU, including China, Hong Kong, the UK and Switzerland.[11]

The MMoU addresses the scope, confidentiality and use of information shared between signatory regulators. The scope of assistance for signatories is set out under paragraph 7 of the MMoU. The assistance available includes: (i) providing records that identify the beneficial owner and controller of an account; (ii) providing information identifying persons who beneficially own or control companies; (iii) taking or compelling a person's statement or, where permissible, testimony under oath, regarding potential offences; and so on. Information sharing is currently an important aspect of regulatory cooperation. Signatories can execute their responsibilities under the memoranda within their legal framework.

While the MMoU is a conduit designed for regulators to increase information flows and enforcement capabilities, many scholars are sceptical of its effectiveness.[12] Similarly to the MoU, the MMoU is not a treaty but rather a cooperative arrangement structured as a statement of intent. As such, the MMoU is neither ratified by national legislatures nor approved by executive branches; any disputes that arise from it cannot be arbitrated by courts.

In addition to bilateral and multilateral agreements, regulators also develop a wide range of informal and formal tools for coordinating securities investigations, such as ad hoc cooperation, supervisory 'colleges' and regulatory networks.[13] Ad hoc cooperation can take the form of either bilateral or multilateral information sharing. The advantage of ad hoc cooperation is that it allows regulators the flexibility of addressing emerging supervisory issues in real time without the delay necessary to negotiate a more formal arrangement. On the other hand, the creation of a college of supervisors will likely entail deciding on a set number of issues that may not otherwise be present when regulators conclude a purely bilateral cooperative arrangement. The advantage of supervisory colleges is that they provide a framework for ongoing dialogue among multiple financial authorities that have direct regulatory oversight of an institution with a view to obtaining a complete risk analysis of the company.[14] A network of regulators goes even further by having more formalised agreements for coordinating the oversight of specific entities. One example would be the joint oversight of common regulated entities.

[11] China, Hong Kong, the UK and Switzerland joined the MMoU in 2007, 2003, 2003 and 2010 respectively. A list of full signatories is available on IOSCO's website at: www.iosco.org/about/?subSection=mmou&subSection1=signatories (accessed on 5 October 2022).

[12] For example, D Zaring, 'International institutional Performance in Crisis' (2010) 10(2) *Chicago Journal of International Law* 475 and E Cadmus, 'Revisiting the SEC's Memoranda of Understanding: A Fresh Look' (2011) 36(6) *Fordham International Law Journal* 1800.

[13] IOSCO (2010), see n 6 above, 31.

[14] ibid, 36.

In the context of Stock Connect, all four jurisdictions (China, Hong Kong, the UK and Switzerland) are signatories to IOSCO's MMoU, which provides a basic framework for information exchange and enforcement cooperation between them. In addition, numerous bilateral agreements have been signed between China and the other three jurisdictions as discussed in sections 5.3 and 5.4 below.

5.2. Regulatory Infrastructure in China, Hong Kong, the UK and Switzerland

Supervisory models in most countries broadly fall into three categories (sectoral, integrated or partially integrated) while the US has its own special characteristics.[15] The sectoral model consists of three separate authorities that supervise three different financial sectors: banking, insurance and securities. In the integrated model, a single agency is responsible for all oversight functions in all three sectors, whilst partially integrated models include 'Twin Peaks' and 'Two Agency' group responsibilities according to supervisory objectives or sectors.

For example, the UK was claimed to be the first major financial centre to establish a single regulator – the Financial Services Authority (FSA) – vested with the authority to regulate almost every aspect of its financial services sector, which was created by the Financial Services and Markets Act (FSMA) 2000.[16] It was argued that a single regulator responsible for all financial services activity would better reflect the composition of financial markets themselves.[17] However, in the wake of the global financial crisis of 2008, the monolithic regulator was subject to a range of excoriating criticisms for its 'inherent weaknesses and contradictions'.[18] As a result, the UK abolished the FSA and adopted a 'Twin Peaks' model (partially integrated) by splitting its functions into two new agencies in April 2013: the Financial Conduct Authority (FCA) and the Prudential Regulation Authority (PRA).

In contrast to the UK's regulatory reform, Switzerland opted to remain an integrated system by creating a single regulator, the Financial Markets Supervisory Authority (FINMA), in January 2009, shortly after the 2008 global financial crisis. The constitutional basis for FINMA's supervisory activities is provided by Article 98 of the Federal Constitution. The federal Financial Market Supervision

[15] D Calvo et al, 'Financial Supervisory Architecture: What has Changed after the Crisis?' (April 2018) Financial Stability Institute Insights on Policy Implementation No 8, pp 1 and 7, available at: www.bis.org/fsi/publ/insights8.pdf (accessed on 20 June 2022).

[16] H McVea, 'The Impact of the Global Financial Crisis upon the UK's Regulatory Architecture' in R Goddard and D Cash (eds), *Regulation and the Global Financial Crisis: Impact, Regulatory Responses, and Beyond* (Abingdon, Routledge, 2021), 45.

[17] E Ferran, 'Examining the UK Experience in Adopting the Single Financial Regulator Model' (2003) 28 *Brooklyn Journal of International Law* 257, 277–82.

[18] HM Treasury, 'A New Approach to Financial Regulation: Judgement, Focus and Stability' (July 2010), para 1.5, available at: assets.publishing.service.gov.uk/government/uploads/system/uploads/attachment_data/file/81389/consult_financial_regulation_condoc.pdf (accessed on 30 May 2022).

Act 2009 mandates FINMA to supervise banks, insurance companies, stock exchanges, securities dealers, and other financial intermediaries in Switzerland on behalf of the state.

In contrast to the integrated and partially integrated models, both China and Hong Kong employ the sectoral model, with three separate authorities for three different financial sectors (more on this later in this section). Typically, each authority has a prudential role (namely, ensuring the financial safety and stability of institutions) and a 'conduct of business' role (compliance with regulatory requirements) in the sector they supervise. This model is present in almost half of the jurisdictions and is the one most frequently applied in all regions of the world except Europe.[19]

In the US, however, supervisory functions are typically assigned to several agencies at the federal or State level. The Dodd-Frank Act of 2010 provides the basis for the creation of the inter-agency Financial Stability Oversight Council and the Consumer Financial Protection Bureau, both of which have a nationwide responsibility. The Securities and Exchange Commission (SEC) and the Commodity Futures Trading Commission (CFTC) are the primary regulators of financial markets in the US.

The US embraces a multi-enforcer approach, whereby securities regulation is jointly enforced by government agencies, self-regulatory organisations, and by private litigation.[20] While the SEC is empowered to pursue civil enforcement actions, all criminal actions under the federal securities laws are prosecuted by the Department of Justice. Self-regulatory organisations such as the Financial Industry Regulatory Authority and the securities exchanges can fine, suspend or bar their members from participating in certain aspects of the securities industry. Private litigants can sometimes rely on State and federal statutes to seek monetary damages and occasionally injunctive relief.

The multi-enforcer approach minimises the risk of under-enforcement and selective enforcement, but it is also criticised for over-enforcement.[21] It is defined as one that assigns a broad range of powers to market participants while maintaining strong oversight of market activities within a robust enforcement tradition.[22]

[19] Calvo et al (2018), see n 15, 7–8.

[20] WM Xu and GD Xu, 'Understanding Public Enforcement of Securities Law in China: An Empirical Analysis of the Enforcement Actions of the CSRC and its Regional Offices Against Informational Misconduct' (2020) 61 *International Review of Law and Economics* 1, 1.

[21] J Coffee, 'Law and the Market: the Impact of Enforcement' (2007) 156(2) *University of Pennsylvania Law Review* 229, and A Rose, 'Reforming Securities Litigation Reform: Restructuring the Relationship between Public and Private Enforcement of Rule 10B-5' (2008) 108(6) *Columbia Law Review* 1301.

[22] For example, see E Jackson and M Roe, 'Public and Private Enforcement of Securities Law: Resource-based Evidence' (2009) 93(2) *Journal of Financial Economics* 207, 214–15; J Armour et al, 'Private Enforcement of Corporate Law: An Empirical Comparison of the UK and the US' (2009) 6(4) *Journal of Empirical Legal Studies* 687, 718–20; and K Cearns and E Ferran, 'Non-enforcement-led Public Oversight of Financial and Corporate Governance Disclosures and of Auditors' (2008) 8(2) *Journal of Corporate Studies* 191.

This approach stands in sharp contrast to the UK's 'light touch' approach, which emphasises self-regulation to a greater extent.[23]

5.2.1. China's Regulatory Framework

The current financial regulatory structure in China has the defining feature of being sector-based. As the central bank, the People's Bank of China (PBOC) assumes responsibility for monetary policy and the stability of the financial system generally. The China Banking and Insurance Regulatory Commission (CBIRC) and the China Securities Regulatory Commission (CSRC) are the authorities responsible for regulating the banking and insurance sectors and the securities sector respectively.

China's public agencies that are responsible for enforcing securities law mainly include the CSRC and its regional offices, and the three stock exchanges. In accordance with the Securities Law,[24] and as duly authorised by the State Council, the CSRC oversees China's nationwide centralised securities supervisory system. It should be noted that the coverage of the Securities Law, and therefore the authority of the CSRC is broad, including the regulation of shares, corporate bonds, treasury bonds, securities investment funds, and derivative products such as futures contracts, options and warrants.[25] Thus, in terms of its regulatory remit, the CSRC is roughly equivalent to a combination of the SEC and the CFTC in the US. However, the CSRC's regulatory territory is narrower than that of its Australian counterpart, the Australian Securities and Investments Commission, which acts as both securities regulator and corporate regulator in Australia.[26]

The CSRC, a ministerial-level public institution directly under the State Council, performs a unified regulatory function. Empowered by the Securities Law,[27] the CSRC is responsible for formulating securities rules and regulations, and investigating major market misconduct or violations as well as issuing administrative and non-administrative sanctions.[28] To exercise its responsibilities, the CSRC has a number of important, semi-legislative investigative and adjudicatory powers. First, the CSRC is the primary regulatory agency responsible for

[23] C Xi and XM Pan, 'Public Enforcement of Securities Laws: A Case of Convergence?' in Y Zhao and M NG (eds), *Chinese Legal Reform and the Global Legal Order: Adoption and Adaptation* (Cambridge, Cambridge University Press, 2017), 91.

[24] The Chinese Securities Law was promulgated on 29 December 1998 and came into effect on 1 July 1999, amended in 2004, 2005, 2013, 2014 and 2019.

[25] ibid, art 2.

[26] RH Huang, 'Financial regulatory structure in China: Challenges and transitioning to Twin Peaks' in A Godwin and A Schmulow (eds), *The Cambridge Handbook of Twin Peaks Financial Regulation* (Cambridge, Cambridge University Press, 2021).

[27] Chinese Securities Law 2019, art 178.

[28] For more functions of CSRC, see the overview of the CSRC, available at <http://www.csrc.gov.cn/csrc_en/c102023/common_zcnr.shtml?channelid=e9958c689bef4d468d81dc93c8d3479f> (accessed on 10 April 2022).

overseeing the securities and futures markets in China. As a rule-making agency, the CSRC formulates regulations, rules, and guidelines that govern the conduct of market participants, including issuers, intermediaries, and investors. These rules cover a wide range of activities, from registration requirements for market participants to disclosure obligations for issuers.

Second, in addition to its rule-making function, the CSRC also has enforcement powers and conducts investigations into suspected violations of securities laws and regulations. The CSRC promulgated 'Implementation Measures for Case Investigation' on 11 March 2008 to prescribe the procedures for investigation, hearing, filing and enforcement. Pursuant to the Implementation Measures, the CSRC's Enforcement Bureau was assigned to supervise case investigation and enforcement, and to coordinate the handling of nationwide cases. To strengthen its control over listed companies' governance, the CSRC has the power

- to undertake an on-the-spot inspection of listed companies by means of photocopying documents and materials, search of property, interviewing and interrogating company officers;[29]
- to examine the capital account, security account or bank account of any relevant party concerned in or any entity or individual relating to a case under investigation;[30]
- to freeze or seal up relevant assets and/or evidence that is in jeopardy of dissipation, waste, or improper removal, with the approval of the responsible officer of the CSRC;[31] and
- to restrict the securities transactions of the parties concerned in a case under investigation when investigating any major securities irregularity such as manipulation of the securities market or insider trading, with the approval of the responsible officer of the CSRC.[32]

Third, the CSRC could decide to impose administrative sanctions and penalties on regulated entities and individuals. More specifically, the CSRC can, by way of an 'administrative sanction' (*xingzheng chufa*), impose monetary penalties (ie fines), order the disgorgement of ill-gotten profits, or issue administrative orders to cease or correct misconduct.[33] Moreover, the CSRC can issue a banning order (*shichang jinru*), to ban an individual from undertaking any securities practice or holding the post of director, supervisor or senior manager of a listed company within a prescribed term or for life.[34] Finally, if the case is serious enough to warrant criminal sanction, the CSRC will refer the case to the procuratorate to bring criminal charges.

[29] CSRC, 'Measures for the Spot Inspection of Listed Companies' issued on 13 April 2010, art 2.

[30] CSRC, 'Measures for the Implementation of Freezing and Sealing-Up' issued on 30 December 2005, and revised twice on 23 May 2011 and 20 March 2020, art 2.

[31] ibid, art 3.

[32] ibid, art 18.

[33] Chinese Securities Law 2019, Chapter 13.

[34] Chinese Securities Law 2019, art 221.

The CSRC is headquartered in Beijing with 38 regional offices in provinces and autonomous regions. The regional offices are the regional frontline supervisors who report directly to the CSRC's headquarters. In 2011, the CSRC launched a pilot project granting three regional offices in Shanghai, Guangdong and Shenzhen the authority to issue administrative sanctions against minor infractions. In October 2013, all regional offices were granted such authority.[35] There is a division of power between the CSRC and its regional offices. The CSRC is responsible for significant cases of national prominence (regardless of where the company is registered). Regional offices are mainly responsible for regulating the listed companies that are incorporated in their jurisdictions. More specifically, their duties include day-to-day supervision, prevention and handling of market risks, investigation and sanctioning of illegal activities, and investor protection and education.[36]

To restore trust in the capital market, the CSRC issued 'Interim Measures for the Supervision and Administration of Credibility of Securities and Futures Markets' in 2012 for the building of a nationally uniform securities and futures market credibility file database, the purpose of which is to curb dishonest activities such as fraud, insider dealing and market manipulation.[37] The public can access records of administrative sanctions and market-entry bans imposed on market participants via the credibility file database. All market participants including legal and financial practitioners, listed companies and their managers and major shareholders, fund companies and their managers, and financial intermediaries, are recorded in these credibility files. In addition, the CSRC and the Supreme People's Court (SPC) exchange information on dishonest individuals who are subject to enforcement actions by any courts in China. The credibility database provides confidence to investors and enhances the enforcement strategy in securities markets.[38]

However, the CSRC has been traditionally labelled as a 'toothless tiger' owing to its ineffectiveness in identifying and prosecuting frauds, its limited resources, its lack of independence from the state and its susceptibility to political

[35] Before 2011, the regional offices only were allowed to issue non-administrative sanctions. See F Huang and JH Liu, 'Enforcement Strategies in the Chinese Capital Market' in R Goddard and D Cash (eds), *Regulation and the Global Financial Crisis: Impact, Regulatory Responses, and Beyond* (Abingdon, Routledge, 2021), 176.

[36] The Provisions on the Regulatory Responsibilities of Regional Offices of the CSRC 2015, art 5.

[37] CSRC, 'Interim Measures for the Supervision and Administration of Credibility of Securities and Futures Markets' which were issued on 25 July 2012 and then replaced by the 'Measures for the Supervision and Administration of Credibility of Securities and Futures Markets' enacted on 2 November 2017, effective as of 1 July 2018 and revised 20 March 2020. The full text in Chinese is available at: www.csrc.gov.cn/csrc/c100203/c1003160/1003160/files/P020180518337990785734.pdf (accessed on 10 April 2022).

[38] JH Liu, 'Qianghua Ziben Shichang Chengxin Jianshe de Ruogan Sikao' (Some Thoughts on Enhancing Credibility in the Capital Market) (2012) 2 *Securities Law Review* 649.

pressures.[39] This can be attributed to several flaws in China's securities regulatory framework.

First, despite the fact that the CSRS is the national securities regulator, it is also a government agency operating under the Chinese Communist Party's direction. According to its annual report 2020, the CSRC is committed to implementing the Party's instructions on the capital markets and maintaining alignment with the central Party leadership.[40] In this sense, the CSRC may be susceptible to political influence, local protectionism and other forms of corruption.[41] The Chinese government is often reluctant to impose heavy administrative penalties on offenders for fear of negatively impacting the company's performance, and criminal prosecution is only invoked in particularly serious circumstances.[42] The CSRC referred more than 60 people to the judicial system for securities crime in the period of 2003–2007.[43] Only around 10 of them were prosecuted and the average sentence was six months to one year imprisonment.

Second, the CSRS and its regional offices face resource restrictions. In 2020, the annual budget of the CSRC and its regional offices was appropriately USD 220.3 million and the total number of staff was 3278.[44] 2,511 (77 per cent) employees worked at regional offices, which implies that most of the enforcement work is undertaken by regional offices. The CSRC also established an inspection division in 2007 that is responsible for major cases, but is staff number is around 300. In contrast, the SEC's annual budget was around USD 2.6 billion and its total staff was 4,411 in the fiscal year 2020.[45] The absolute level of the CSRC's budget was only around 8.5 per cent of the SEC's, whereas the absolute number of the CSRC's staff was close to that of the SEC in 2020. The reason for the co-existence of a small budget and a relatively large staff base is probably the lower average salary paid to staff members in China.[46]

Third, the monetary penalties are limited. The statutory fine imposed on listed companies for misrepresentation ranges from RMB 300,000–600,000

[39] See eg D Anderson, 'Taking Stock in China: Company Disclosure and Information in China's Stock Markets' (2000) 88 *Georgetown Law Journal* 1919; and GM Chen et al, 'Is China's Securities Regulatory Agency a Toothless Tiger? Evidence from Enforcement Actions' (2005) 24 *Journal of Accounting and Public Policy* 451.

[40] CSRC, 'Annual Report 2020', 17, available at: www.csrc.gov.cn/csrc_en/c102063/c1606114/content.shtml (28 February 2022).

[41] C Anderson and B Guo, 'Corporate Governance under the New Company Law (Part 2): Shareholder Lawsuits and Enforcement', *China Law & Practice* (May 2006).

[42] F Huang, 'Modernising the Chinese Capital Market: Old Problems and New Legal Responses' (2010) 21(1) *International Company and Commercial Law Review* 26, 34.

[43] ibid, 33.

[44] In 2020, the CSRC's financial budget was RMB 14.028 billion (approximately USD 0.22 billion), available at: www.csrc.gov.cn/csrc/c105887/c1047948/content.shtml (accessed on 10 April 2022). And the human resources of CSRC are on 'CSRC Annual Report 2020', 13, available at: www.csrc.gov.cn/csrc_en/c102063/c1606114/content.shtml (accessed on 10 April 2022).

[45] SEC, 'Agency Financial Report: Fiscal Year 2020', 7 and 34, available at: www.sec.gov/files/sec-2020-agency-financial-report_1.pdf (accessed on 10 April 2022).

[46] Xu and Xu (2020), see n 20 above, 3.

(USD 46,340–92,681), and the fine imposed on individuals for the same charge ranges from 30,000–300,000 RMB (USD 4,634–9,268).[47] Although the total amount of monetary sanctions imposed by the CSRC appears to have rapidly increased recently, reaching RMB 7.48 billion in 2017 with an annual growth rate of 75 per cent compared to 2016, the number of cases only increases by seven per cent.[48] This rapid growth in monetary penalties is mainly caused by certain high-profile cases of insider trading and malpractice in securities transactions.

In the view of Huang and Liu, at first glance China's public enforcement output (ie the number of enforcement actions and the amount of fines and disgorgement), was far below than that of the US.[49] In 2013, the CSRC took 100 enforcement actions (15 per cent of the US number) and imposed USD 102 million in financial penalties (three per cent of the US total).[50] But the ratio has dramatically increased in recent years, for instance, 87 per cent of the US in enforcement actions and 18 per cent of the US in financial penalties in 2021.[51] Taking into account the fact that the US's market capitalisation was more than five times larger than that of China at the end of 2021, China's enforcement record may not be as weak as it seems.[52] Moreover, considering that the CSRC's regulatory budget was far below than that of the SEC (roughly 8.5 per cent) mentioned above, the CSRC's enforcement intensity seems to be justifiable given the limited resources to which it has access.[53]

The CSRC is moving towards using administrative measures and sanctions in a more vigorous way, including through the imposition of larger monetary penalties and bans on the full range of market participants. In 2011 the CSRC investigated 209 cases, disqualified 11 market participants, and issued 57 administrative

[47] Chinese Securities Law 2019, art 193.

[48] The CSRC's Annual Report 2017, 45, available at: www.csrc.gov.cn/csrc_en/c102063/c1372575/content.shtml (accessed on 20 April 2022).

[49] Huang and Liu (2021), see n 35 above, 178.

[50] ibid.

[51] The CSRC investigated 609 cases and obtained RMB 4.553 billion in financial penalties. See CSRC, 'Zhongguo Zhengjianhui 2021 Fazhi Zhengfu Jianshe Qingkuang' ('CSRC's Construction of a Rule-of-Law Government Report 2021') (8 April 2022), available at: www.csrc.gov.cn/csrc/c100028/c2321617/content.shtml (accessed on 20 April 2022). In contrast, the SEC filed 697 total enforcement actions in the fiscal year 2021, including 434 new actions, 120 actions against issuers who neglected to in make required filings with the SEC, and 143 'follow-on' administrative proceedings. The SEC also obtained judgments and orders for nearly USD 2.4 billion in disgorgement and more than USD 1.4 billion in penalties. See SEC, 'SEC Announces Enforcement Results for FY2021', available at: www.sec.gov/news/press-release/2021-238 (accessed 20 April 2022).

[52] According to the World Federation of Exchanges, by 2021, China's stock market capitalisation was USD 9.9 trillion while that of the US was USD 53.4 trillion, available at: www.world-exchanges.org/our-work/statistics (accessed on 10 April 2022).

[53] This observation is also consistent with the studies by F Huang, 'In Defence of China's Public Enforcement in Equity Market' (2010) 21(10) *International Company and Commercial Law Review* 327; and TS Zhou, 'Is the CSRC Protecting a "Level Playing Field" in China's Capital Markets: Public Enforcement, Fragmented Authoritarianism and Corporatism' (2015) 15(2) *Journal of Corporate Law Studies* 377.

sanctions to the value of RMB 348 million.[54] But the administrative sanctions were intensified in 2021, with 609 case investigations and 371 administrative sanctions (6.5 times as many as in 2011), resulting in RMB 4.553 billion in fines and disgorgements (13.1 times as many as in 2011), and 95 market-entry bans against individuals.[55] 177 cases were prosecuted, a year-on-year increase of 53 per cent.[56] According to the International Monetary Fund (IMF)'s financial sector assessment on China, the CSRC's enforcement powers to impose appropriate sanctions continue to be enhanced.[57] The level of fines and penalties increased for both administrative sanctions and criminal offences, including in the latter case the prison terms. But criminal sanctions, in particular imprisonment, need to be used more vigorously to punish the most egregious violations and send a clear deterrent message to the market.

To supplement the regulatory activities of the CSRC, the stock exchanges are responsible for the self-disciplinary and front-line supervision of members, listed companies and their related securities trading activities.[58] According to Article 105 of the Securities Law 2019, Chinese stock exchanges adopt a membership system.[59] The general meeting of members (*huiyuan dahui*), as the highest authority of stock exchange, can formulate and revise the articles of association of the stock exchange; elect and remove member directors and supervisors; review and approve the work reports of the board of directors and the board of supervisors. But the articles of association must be submitted to the CSRC for approval after being adopted by the general meeting.[60]

The stock exchange's board of directors (*lishihui*) is the decision-making organ comprised of both member (securities companies) and non-member directors while the board of supervisors (*jianshihui*) is the supervisory body to oversee the managerial personnel and the financial status of the stock exchange. The exchange members elect member directors and the CSRC appoints non-member directors.[61] In addition, the CSRC nominates the chairman and deputy chairman who are then elected by the board. The CSRC also appoints and may dismiss the general manager and deputy general manager of a stock exchange.[62] In this sense, Chinese

[54] CSRC, 'Annual Report 2011', 30–31, available at: www.csrc.gov.cn/csrc_en/c102063/c1372581/content.shtml (accessed on 20 April 2022).

[55] CSRC (2021), see n 51 above.

[56] ibid.

[57] IMF, 'PRC: Financial Sector Assessment Program- Detailed Assessment of Observance of the IOSCO Objectives and Principles of Securities Regulation' (2017), 6–7, available at: www.imf.org/en/Publications/CR/Issues/2017/12/26/Peoples-Republic-of-China-Financial-Sector-Assessment-Program-Detailed-Assessment-of-45517 (accessed on 20 April 2022).

[58] Chinese Securities Law 2019, art 99.

[59] Article 105 of Chinese Securities Law 2019: 'The gains as accumulated by a stock exchange that adopts a membership system shall belong to its members. The rights and interests of a stock exchange shall be jointly shared by its members. No accumulated gains of a stock exchange may be distributed to any member within the holding term'. Also, 'Measures for the Administration of Stock Exchanges 2021', art 17.

[60] Measures for the Administration of Stock Exchanges 2021, art 19.

[61] ibid, art 23.

[62] ibid, art 27.

stock exchanges are not traditional 'mutual-help' organisations owned and run by members, as the CSRC maintains control of the stock exchange's board of directors and management.[63]

As self-regulatory bodies, Chinese stock exchanges have four primary regulatory tools for use in case of the violation of their listing rules: correction orders (*Zeling gaizheng*), circulated criticism (*Tongbao piping*), public criticism (*Gongkai qianze*) and punitive damages (*Chengfaxing weiyuejin*).[64] The first three tools are mainly reputational sanctions while punitive damages were newly introduced in 2018 as extra-compensatory damages to punish the defendant for his wrongful conduct. Correction orders are generally issued for only minor infractions. Circulated criticism is slightly more serious, but is still relatively minor notice to unusual company arrangements or activities. A public criticism (*gongkai qianze*) is the most serious form of reputational sanction taken by the exchanges against listed companies. The use of public criticism as a regulatory device originated in the London Stock Exchange, and was then borrowed by the Hong Kong Stock Exchange.[65] Chinese exchanges, in turn, modelled their practice on Hong Kong.

Despite the adoption of self-regulation, Chinese stock exchanges function under the mandate of the CSRC. The stock exchanges are required to report any abnormal trading to the CSRC in a timely way and to seek CSRC approval to formulate rules for listing, trading and membership.[66] Also, the CSRC approves the appointment and removal of the general manager of each stock exchange.[67] The exchanges can suspend, terminate, and resume bond and share trading, as the CSRC-established procedures allow.[68] The CSRC's role in the securities market is to ensure the functional operation of exchanges, but the tight control over the exchanges by the CSRC may limit their capacity for self-regulation and thus constrain their independent operation.[69]

However, a subsequent question arises: do the functions of the CSRC and the stock exchanges overlap since they both have the power to enforce securities regulations? Huang and Liu have summarised the interactions of enforcement between the CSRC and the stock exchanges from three perspectives.[70] First, the exchanges mainly take actions against the non-compliance with disclosure requirements by listed companies, while the CSRC deters major market misconduct such as

[63] CX Shi, 'Protecting Investors in China Through Multiple Regulatory Mechanisms and Effective Enforcement' (2007) 24(2) *Arizona Journal of International & Comparative Law* 451, 465–66.

[64] SSE, 'Rules Governing the Listing of Stocks on Shanghai Stock Exchange 2019', chapter 17.

[65] B Liebman and C Milhaupt, 'Reputational Sanctions in China's Securities Market' (2008) 108(4) *Columbia Law Review* 929, 948.

[66] China's Securities Law 2019, arts 111, 112 and 115.

[67] ibid, art 102.

[68] ibid, art 113.

[69] Huang (2010), see n 53 above, 331.

[70] Huang and Liu (2021), see n 35, 180–81.

manipulation and insider dealing. But the CSRC can appoint the exchanges to conduct investigation and evidence collection in serious cases.[71]

Second, in contrast to the CSRC's administrative and non-administrative sanctioning power, the exchanges, as self-regulatory organisations, have no power to issue administrative sanctions. But their non-administrative sanctions, such as public criticism, have brought significant reputational costs to listed companies.[72] In addition, the exchanges have authority to monitor listed companies' compliance with listing obligations and two powerful weapons, namely temporary suspension of trading and delisting, to discipline them.[73] All these enforcement actions taken by the stock exchanges can also serve as evidence of misrepresentation and consequently prompt securities civil suits.

Third, the stock exchanges can determine the violations of the parties and implement corresponding self-regulatory measures based on the administrative penalty decisions and regulatory actions which have been made by the CSRC or judicial judgment.[74] If there is any violation undiscovered by those CSRC sanctions and judicial judgment, the stock exchanges may further implement self-regulatory actions.

5.2.2. Hong Kong's Regulatory Framework

In line with the international trend, the sectoral model of Hong Kong's financial services has evolved and developed over the years. The principal regulators are the Hong Kong Monetary Authority (HKMA), the Securities and Futures Commission (SFC), the Insurance Authority (IA) and the Mandatory Provident Fund Schemes Authority (MPFA). They are responsible, respectively, for regulation of the banking, securities and futures, insurance, and retirement scheme industries.[75]

The existing regulatory framework for the securities and futures industry is a 'three-tiered structure'. Its genesis can be traced back to the recommendations of the 'Report of the Securities Review Committee (SRC)' published in 1988.[76]

[71] CSRC, 'CSRC Entrusts Shanghai and Shenzhen Stock Exchanges to Conduct Case Investigation' (issued on 22 September 2014 and effective as 9 January 2015), available at: www.gov.cn/gongbao/content/2015/content_2818466.htm (accessed on 20 April 2022).

[72] WM Xu et al, 'An Empirical Analysis of the Public Enforcement of Securities Law in China: Finding the Missing Piece to the Puzzle' (2017) 18(2) *European Business Organisation Law Review* 367, 371.

[73] China's Securities Law 2019, arts 48 and 110.

[74] SZSE, 'SZSE Self-Regulatory Measures and the Imposition of Disciplinary Action on Listed Companies 2022', art 7.

[75] For the overview of financial infrastructure in Hong Kong, see the HKSAR, 'Hong Kong: The Facts – Financial Services' (July 2020), available at: www.gov.hk/en/about/abouthk/factsheets/docs/financial_services.pdf (accessed on 28 February 2022).

[76] Following the stock market crash in October 1987, the then Hong Kong Governor appointed the SRC to review the constitution, powers, management and operation of the government offices responsible for regulating respectively the securities and futures markets. The SRC published its Report in May 1988 and recommended, among other things, the establishment of a new market regulator outside

Under this structure, the Hong Kong Special Administrative Region (HKSAR) government, the SFC and the Hong Kong Exchanges and Clearing Limited (HKEX) assume different roles in the operation of the securities market. Such structure is reflected in the Securities and Futures Commission Ordinance (SFO) (Cap 24), the Exchanges and Clearing Houses (Merger) Ordinance (Cap 555), the recently enacted and substantially recast SFO (Cap 571) and other related legislation.

The essence of this three-tiered structure is that the operation of the market should rest with a market operator (ie the HKEX) close to the market, under the watchful eyes of an independent regulator (ie the SFC) staffed with personnel equipped with the requisite expertise and market experience. The HKSAR government maintains a broad policy interest and concern in the development of Hong Kong's financial markets as part of Hong Kong's economy.

As the first tier, the HKSAR government has overall responsibility under Article 109 of the Basic Law to provide an appropriate economic and legal environment for the maintenance of Hong Kong as an international financial centre. Consistent with the spirit of the SRC report and international practices, the government does not interfere in the market place unless exceptional circumstances obtain. It performs its function by appointing the SFC and making sure that the SFC is, and is seen to be, a credible and independent regulatory body vested with the necessary power and equipped with professional expertise to discharge its duties.

The second tier is the SFC, which serves as the watchdog of market operators such as the stock exchange and market intermediaries. Established in 1989, the SFC is the statutory regulator of the securities and futures markets which derives its investigative, remedial and disciplinary powers from the SFO. The SFC has a statutory duty to supervise, monitor and regulate the exchanges and the performance of their listing-related functions and responsibilities. Section 4 of the SFO sets out the regulatory objectives of the SFC, which include maintaining the integrity of markets, investor protection, the prevention of financial crime and the reduction of systemic risk. Sections 5 and 6 detail the general functions and powers of the SFC, which include supervising, monitoring and regulating market activities. The SFC is a non-governmental statutory authority, with a board of directors appointed by the Chief Executive of HKSAR or by the Financial Secretary (FS) under delegated authority.

While regulators in both the US and Hong Kong have wide-ranging powers of investigation, Hong Kong's regulator is more likely to rely on cross-border regulatory cooperation in investigation and gathering evidence, in contrast to the extraterritorial SEC enforcement actions.[77] Also, public enforcement of securities

the civil service. See HKSAR, 'Chapter 3 The Three-Tiered Regulatory Framework for the Securities and Futures Industry', 13, available at www.info.gov.hk/info/pennystock/chapter3.pdf (accessed on 28 February 2022).

[77] WY Wan et al, 'Public and Private Enforcement of Corporate and Securities Laws: An Empirical Comparison of Hong Kong and Singapore' (2019) 20(2) *European Business Organization Law Review* 319, 327.

laws in Hong Kong is much more central than private enforcement. In spite of the availability of statutory derivative action and easier access to the statutory compensation scheme, almost all of the enforcement actions take place through public enforcement; private enforcement is rare in Hong Kong.[78]

At the third tier, and closest to the ground, the HKEX plays a self-regulatory role and performs certain public functions, such as risk management and market surveillance. The HKEX is the holding company of two exchanges, the Stock Exchange of Hong Kong Limited (SEHK) and Hong Kong Futures Exchange Limited (HKFE), and four recognised clearing houses. HKEX went public in June 2000 following the merger of the securities and derivatives markets of SEHK and HKFE.

Whilst stock exchanges were traditionally not-for-profit organisations that promoted mutual cooperation between members, a process called demutualisation has transformed many exchanges around the world.[79] Since the Stockholm Stock Exchange first demutualised in 1993, stock exchanges in the UK, US, Australia, Singapore, Japan and Hong Kong have followed suit. Demutualisation transforms a traditional not-for-profit mutual stock exchange into a profit-driven, demutualised company, with exchange members becoming shareholders in the new company.

On the one hand, demutualisation maximises shareholders' interests by improving corporate governance and accounting practices, enhancing professional managers' decision-making efficiency, and increasing innovation and competitiveness.[80] On the other hand, the introduction of demutualisation brings with it the conflict of shareholder interests and the interests of appropriate regulation.[81] The exchanges should be responsible for their shareholders, who are interested in profit, but they also play a key role in the functioning of the financial sector. For example, HKEX arguably plays a dual role of regulator and service provider, leading to an inherent conflict of interests. As a self-regulator, HKEX is responsible for ensuring an orderly and fair market in securities and futures contracts traded on or through the HKEX. It has important regulatory responsibilities, mainly in connection with the authorisation of prospectuses and listings. However, as a listed company, answerable to its shareholders, HKEX is a market-driven business, competing vigorously for opportunities in the region and around the world. As a result, HKEX may face multiple contingencies with diverging motivations, putting further pressure on it to satisfy multiple demands.

Although both China and Hong Kong adopt the same sectoral supervisory model, they show some disparities in their organisational structure.[82] The CSRC

[78] ibid, 353.

[79] J Elliott, 'Demutualisation of Securities Exchange: A Regulatory Perspective' (2002) *IMF working paper WP/02/119*, 3, available at www.imf.org/external/pubs/ft/wp/2002/wp02119.pdf (accessed on 20 April 2022). Both London Stock Exchange and Hong Kong Stock Exchange were demutualised in 2000.

[80] ibid, 13.

[81] ibid, 16–17.

[82] For the case of China, see Xi and Pan (2017), see n 23 above, 81–83; and for the case of Hong Kong, see Wan et al (2019) see n 77 above.

in China is closer to the hierarchical ideal, whereas the SFC in Hong Kong resembles the US's horizontal ideal.[83]

- First, the SFC primarily focuses on investor protection, maintaining the capital market and facilitating capital information.[84] By contrast, in addition to those related to the capital market, the CSRC pursues various other policy objectives under the guidance of the Communist Party, including industrial policies, state-owned enterprises reform, economic and social development and systemic risk management.[85]
- Second, as the officials of CSRC usually come from within the government, their appointment and removal are tightly controlled by the government. Thus, officials in a hierarchically organised regulator may be easily subject to political pressures and more likely to focus on political goals rather than legal matters.[86] By contrast, the officials in a horizontally structured regulatory authority are sometimes outsiders from the government and recruited only for particularly limited purposes. The outsiders are regarded as relatively insulated from political pressure, despite the concern about the 'revolving door' and 'rent-seeking' problems.[87]
- Third, unlike the stock exchange in Hong Kong, which operates independently from the SFC, the CSRC has de facto authority over the stock exchanges.[88] The CSRC has the power to appoint and remove major stock exchange personnel, including the general manager.[89] Chinese securities regulators such as the CSRC and its regional offices, monopolise securities law enforcement.

5.2.3. The UK's Regulatory Framework

The FSMA 2000 is the principal source of law concerning financial services regulation in the UK. The FSMA created the FSA (superseded in 2013 by the FCA

[83] JS Zeng, 'The Faces of Securities Regulation and State Authority: A Comparison between the United States and China' (2022), *Chinese University of Hong Kong Faculty of Law Research Paper No. 2022-16*, 39.

[84] SFC, 'Regulatory Objectives', available at: www.sfc.hk/en/About-the-SFC/Our-role/Regulatory-objectives (accessed on 20 June 2022).

[85] According to the CSRC's report, the CSRC will continue to follow the 'Xi Jingping Thought on Socialism with Chinese Characteristics for a New Era' to implement rules to advance economic and social reform and the opening up of capital markets. See CSRC, 'Annual Report 2020', 5, available at: www.csrc.gov.cn/csrc_en/c102063/c1606114/1606114/files/CSRC%20Annual%20Report%202020.pdf (accessed on 20 June 2022).

[86] Zeng (2022), see n 83 above, 9.

[87] E DeHaan et al, 'The Revolving Door and the SEC's Enforcement Outcomes: Initial Evidence from Civil Litigation' (2015) 60 *Journal of Accounting and Economics* 65.

[88] Liebman and Milhaupt (2008), see n 65 above, 940.

[89] China's Securities Law 2019, art 102.

and PRA) as a regulator for insurance, investment business and banking, and the Financial Ombudsman Service to resolve disputes as a cost-free alternative to the courts. The FSMA was considerably amended by the Financial Services Act 2012 and the Bank of England and Financial Services Act 2016.

Previously, financial regulation was based on a patchwork of statutes, with a range of regulatory bodies, many of which were self-regulatory, responsible for policing industry standards. The Financial Services Act 1986 (the 1986 Act) had started a process to rationalise regulation and provide a firmer foundation in legislation. The 1986 Act established the first statutory regulator for financial services – the Securities and Investments Board. The FSMA extended this process of rationalisation significantly, modernising financial regulatory arrangements which had previously been established under a number of different enactments.

The financial crisis of 2007–08 revealed serious flaws in the UK's system of regulation, particularly the incoherent allocation and co-ordination of responsibilities across the 'tripartite' institutions – Her Majesty's Treasury (HM Treasury), the Bank of England and the FSA. First, it placed responsibility for all financial regulation in the hands of a single financial regulator, the FSA, while leaving the Bank and Treasury with nominal responsibility; second, the FSA had too broad a remit and insufficient focus on identifying and tackling issues early; and third, the FSA relied too heavily on 'tick box' compliance with rules and directives at the expense of proper in-depth and strategic risk analysis, and no part of the framework had responsibility for monitoring the crucial link between firms' stability and the stability of the financial system as a whole.[90]

The post-crisis framework reforms were therefore focused primarily on institutional design and allocation of responsibilities, with the FSA abolished and replaced with the 'Twin Peaks' of the PRA and FCA.[91] There were also reforms to the Bank of England, most notably the creation of the Financial Policy Committee to take on responsibility for the stability of the financial system as a whole, known as 'macro-prudential' regulation. The FSMA was amended to provide more effective mechanisms for coordination across HM Treasury and the regulators, while the FSA was split into the two regulators:[92]

- the Prudential Regulation Authority (PRA) was established as the micro-prudential regulator of firms which manage significant balance-sheet risk as a core part of their business – banks, insurers and the larger, more complex investment firms. The PRA sets regulatory requirements through broad rule-making powers conferred by FSMA;

[90] HM Treasury (January 2010), see n 18, para 1.7.

[91] HM Treasury, 'Financial Services Future Regulatory Framework Review: Call for Evidence: Regulatory Coordination' (July 2019), 4, available at: assets.publishing.service.gov.uk/government/uploads/system/uploads/attachment_data/file/819025/Future_Regulatory_Framework_Review_Call_for_Evidence.pdf (accessed on 20 March 2022).

[92] ibid.

- the Financial Conduct Authority (FCA) was created to focus on 'conduct of business' regulation, with the mandate to promote the right outcomes for consumers and market participants, including through the promotion of competition. It is also responsible for the prudential regulation of firms not within the remit of the PRA. The FCA too sets regulatory requirements through broad rule-making powers conferred by FSMA.

Until the UK left the EU on 31 January 2020, EU law determined most of the regulation to which firms were actually subject, either through directly applicable regulation or via UK law implementing EU Directives. The European Union (Withdrawal) Act 2018 provides that such regulation will be 'onshored', that is, replicated in UK law and amended so that it is legally effective after the end of the Brexit implementation period on 31 December 2020. A consultation set out the government's proposals for adapting the UK regulatory framework for financial services to ensure that it remains fit for the future, and to reflect the country's new position outside the EU.[93]

Responses to the Future Regulatory Framework Review: Phase II Consultation published in October 2020 demonstrated that establishing a comprehensive model of regulation based on the FSMA, with the appropriate enhancements, was overwhelmingly supported by stakeholders.[94] As observed by International Monetary Fund (IMF) studies, when independent regulators make judgements on the design of regulatory standards, they are likely to deliver more predictable and stable regulatory approaches over time.[95]

The Financial Services Act 2021, which received Royal Assent on 29 April 2021, amended the UK Market Abuse Regulation in several ways, including the requirements related to keeping insider lists and regulations relating to managers' transactions. Particularly its section 31 increases the maximum sentence for criminal market abuse from seven years to 10 years.

5.2.4. Switzerland's Regulatory Framework

The principal financial regulator in Switzerland is the Financial Market Supervisory Authority (FINMA), an independent regulatory body responsible for the overall

[93] HM Treasury, 'Future Regulatory Framework Review: Proposals for Reform' (November 2021), available at: assets.publishing.service.gov.uk/government/uploads/system/uploads/attachment_data/file/1032075/FRF_Review_Consultation_2021_-_Final_.pdf (accessed on 13 April 2023).

[94] HM Treasury, 'Financial Services Future Regulatory Framework Review: Phase II Consultation' (October 2020), available at: assets.publishing.service.gov.uk/government/uploads/system/uploads/attachment_data/file/927316/141020_Final_Phase_II_Condoc_For_Publication_for_print.pdf (accessed on 20 March 2022).

[95] US Das et al, 'Financial Regulators Need Independence', (December 2002) 39(4) *IMF Finance & Development*, available at: www.elibrary.imf.org/view/journals/022/0039/004/article-A008-en.xml (accessed on 20 March 2022). And MG Guintyn and MW Taylor, 'Should Financial Sector Regulators be Independent?' (March 2004) *IMF Economic Issues* No. 32.

supervision of the securities exchanges and the Swiss financial market as a whole. When FINMA commenced its activities on 1 January 2009, the Swiss parliament granted it a greater degree of independence than its predecessor institutions. FINMA is the Swiss government body responsible for financial regulation, but is institutionally, functionally and financially independent from the central federal administration and the Federal Department of Finance, and reports directly to the Swiss parliament.[96] To ensure its institutional independence, FINMA was established as a public law institution in its own right. It is governed by a board of directors and managed by an executive board. Because FINMA is functionally independent of Switzerland's political authorities, neither the Swiss parliament nor the government can issue directives on how it carries out its regulatory duties. But it is subject to parliamentary scrutiny and must answer to the parliamentary commissions overseeing its work. FINMA is financed not by the taxpayer, but by the levies and fees it charges for its supervisory work. In addition, the institutions FINMA regulates are required to pay an annual levy to cover the costs incurred by FINMA which are not met by these fees. The levies relate to supervision and other FINMA services. FINMA's accounts are audited by the Swiss Federal Audit Office.

SIX Swiss Exchange operates the principal securities exchange in Switzerland and is currently the third largest exchange in Europe, with a free float market capitalisation of USD 1.87 trillion (as of September 2022). While FINMA oversees the overall capital market, the SIX Exchange and the other securities exchanges in Switzerland are authorised to issue and enforce their own regulations based on the principle of self-regulation. These rules must be approved by FINMA, which supervises the SIX Exchange. On the basis of the self-regulatory mandate prescribed under the Stock Exchange Act, SIX performs regulatory functions in stock market trading and the admission of securities as well as associated follow-up obligations.

The Swiss regulatory framework is particularly influenced by developments in the EU.[97] As an example, the EU harmonised its capital market regulation with the Markets in Financial Instruments Directive 2014/65/EU (MiFID II) and Markets in Financial Instruments Regulation (EU) No 600/2014 (MiFIR). Consequently, the Swiss legislator is following up and voluntarily harmonising certain aspects of Swiss legislation with similar provisions in the Financial Institutions Act (FinIA) and Financial Service Act (FinSA), with the aim of ensuring access to the European financial markets (which requires, among other things, a regulation that is equivalent to the EU regulation). The provisions of the FinIA on derivatives trading are significantly influenced by the respective provisions in the European

[96] The overview of FINMA is available at www.finma.ch/en/finma/finma-an-overview (accessed on 30 May 2022).

[97] Global Legal Insights, 'Banking Laws and Regulations 2022/Switzerland', available at: www.globallegalinsights.com/practice-areas/banking-and-finance-laws-and-regulations/switzerland (accessed on 30 May 2022).

Market Infrastructure Regulation (EU) No 648/2012 and by rules of other international regulatory bodies; for example, the FinIA implements the commitments assumed at the G20 summit in Pittsburgh in 2009, and adapts the Swiss regulation of its financial market infrastructure and derivatives trading to international requirements.

5.3. Cross-Border Enforcement between China and Hong Kong

Some scholars claim that the regulatory relationship between Hong Kong and Mainland China should be understood in the context of the 'One Country, Two Systems' formula, an arrangement that defines their political relationship.[98] Under the Hong Kong Basic Law and the Mainland's Constitution, except for foreign relations and defence matters, Hong Kong is guaranteed its independent legislature, judiciary and legal system, as well as full economic autonomy. However, the introduction of the National Security Law in Hong Kong in 2020 has put this formula in jeopardy.[99]

One of the main factors which facilitate the integration of the Hong Kong and Chinese stock markets is the mutual recognition of qualification of financial intermediaries of these two jurisdictions. This was partly achieved by the Closer Economic Partnership Arrangement (CEPA), the first free trade agreement concluded by China and Hong Kong on 29 June 2003, covering four areas, namely trade in goods, trade in services, investment, and economic and technical cooperation. A similar agreement between China and Macau was signed on 18 October 2003.

The conclusion of the CEPA marked a new era of cooperation in trade and investment and joint development between the two sides. There are various major initiatives under CEPA that have contributed to the utilisation of Hong Kong's financial expertise during the process of developing China's financial sectors.[100]

[98] For example, JY Wang, 'Regulatory Competition and Co-operation between Securities Markets in Hong Kong and Mainland China' (2009) 4 *Capital Markets Law Journal* 383, 388.

[99] Some critics claim that 'one country, two systems' is dead, since local democracy is being undermined, see *Financial Times*, 'The End of One Country, Two Systems in Hong Kong' (1 July 2020), available at: www.ft.com/content/5d3d7d2e-bba8-11ea-a05d-efc604854c3f (accessed on 25 April 2022). But in contrast, some argue that this system is still intact, as we need to look at the totality of the arrangement, not just particular aspects of it. See A Lo, 'One Country, Two Systems Healthier Than Ever' (*South China Morning Post*, 17 September 2021), available at: www.scmp.com/comment/opinion/article/3149181/one-country-two-systems-healthier-ever (accessed on 25 April 2022).

[100] Such initiatives include: allowing Hong Kong-licensed financial intermediaries to set up joint venture futures brokerage companies on the Mainland; allowing qualified Mainland securities, futures and fund management companies to set up subsidiaries in Hong Kong; and allowing Hong Kong securities companies to set up equity joint venture securities investment advisory companies on the Mainland.

These initiatives also benefit Hong Kong financial institutions wishing to enter China to explore and capture business opportunities.

Since then, China and Hong Kong have signed over 10 supplements and additional agreements to promote these goals and expand market liberalisation. In December 2008, the Beijing government set out a framework programme to establish the Pearl River Delta (PRD) as one of the world's most competitive regions by 2020.[101] Under the Framework, the central government vows to 'solidify' Hong Kong's position as a premier international centre for finance, trade, maritime commerce, logistics and high value-added services.

The increasing economic and financial integration between China and Hong Kong has given rise to closer communication and high-level engagement between the respective authorities and government agencies. This has resulted in more cooperative agreements signed between the Hong Kong and Mainland regulators setting out their cooperative frameworks, including investigatory and supervisory assistance, exchange of information, and market or product-related arrangements.

5.3.1. Pre-Stock Connect Regulatory Cooperation

Regulatory cooperation between China and Hong Kong can be traced back to 1993 when the five parties, namely the CSRC, SFC, Shanghai Stock Exchange (SSE), Shenzhen Stock Exchange (SZSE) and the SEHK, entered a Memorandum of Regulatory Cooperation (MORC) to facilitate mutual assistance and exchange of information for the enhancement of investment protection. The signatories to the MORC agreed to provide mutual assistance and exchange information in three areas: (i) to enhance investment protection and maintain market order; (ii) to ensure compliance with each party's relevant laws and rules; and (iii) to facilitate consultation and cooperation by means of regular liaison and exchange of personnel. On 30 March 2007, a supplement to the MORC was signed by the CSRC and the SFC, under which the SFC could require CSRC's assistance in investigation conducted on the Mainland.

Although the MORC mentions exchange of information and mutual assistance in law enforcement, it is more an expression of the desire to cooperate than a binding agreement.[102] Even if some of the provisions of the MORC are legally binding, enforcement would be difficult through dispute settlement. Additionally, the MORC does not have a dispute settlement mechanism, and it is unlikely to be politically viable to refer a dispute between the Chinese central government and the HKSAR to a third party.

[101] Guowuyuan Guojia Fazhan He Gaige Weiyuanhui, *Zhujiang Sanjiaozhou Diqu Gaige Fazhan Guihua Gangya 2008–2020* (National Development and Reform Commission, *Framework for Development and Reform Planning for the Pearl River Delta Region 2008–2020*).

[102] Wang (2009), see n 98 above, 390.

In addition to bilateral cooperation, a memorandum of understanding is the major mechanism between regulators as the basis of their cooperation. The most prominent multilateral agreement is the Multilateral Memorandum of Understanding Concerning Consultation and Cooperation and the Exchange of Information (MMoU) 2002, which is a regulatory instrument signed by a number of IOSCO members facilitating the sharing of information during the investigation of possible securities violations. Compared with the MORC, the MMoU is much more detailed, containing more specific procedures on requests for assistance and responses to such requests, as well as on consultation regarding mutual assistance and exchange of information, although the provisions of the MMoU 'are not intended to create legally binding obligations or supersede domestic laws'.[103]

5.3.2. Post-Stock Connect Regulatory Cooperation

The signing of the MoU is the main part of the CSRC and SFC's on-going attempts to strengthen their bilateral relationship in the cross-boundary cooperation. With the increasing connection between China and Hong Kong financial markets, it will not be a surprise to see more frequent collaboration and co-ordinated actions conducted by the two regulators.

The CSRC and the SFC agreed the principles and arrangements for cross-boundary regulatory and enforcement cooperation and signed the Memorandum of Understanding on Strengthening Regulatory and Enforcement Cooperation under Shanghai–Hong Kong Stock Connect (Enforcement MoU) on 17 October 2014.[104] This Enforcement MoU aims to strengthen the enforcement cooperation between the two parties and signifies their joint commitment to take effective action against cross-boundary illegal activities and market misconduct to maintain an orderly market and protect investors under Stock Connect.

Under the Enforcement MoU, the CSRC and SF have agreed to:

(a) provide for the sharing of information and data of risks and alerts about potential or suspected wrongdoing in either the Hong Kong or Shanghai stock markets under Shanghai Connect;
(b) establish a commitment and a process for joint investigations;
(c) ensure complementary enforcement action can be taken where there is wrongdoing in both jurisdictions; and
(d) make sure enforcement actions in both jurisdictions operate to protect the investing public of both China and Hong Kong, including actions that may be necessary to provide financial redress or compensation to affected investors.

[103] MMoU, art 6(a), available at: www.iosco.org/library/pubdocs/pdf/IOSCOPD386.pdf.
[104] The full text of the Enforcement MoU is available at: www.sfc.hk/web/files/ER/MOU/ENF_MOU_October2014.pdf (accessed on 24 February 2022).

The two regulators have also established arrangements and procedures for cross-boundary liaison and cooperation on any contingency or major event that affects Stock Connect and for referring and handling related investors' complaints. In addition, China's Investor Protection Bureau and Hong Kong's Investor Education Centre have established an arrangement to cooperate on investor education relating to Shanghai Connect and are continuing their efforts after the launch of Stock Connect.

On 22 May 2015, the SFC announced that it had signed a Memorandum of Regulatory cooperation on Mainland-Hong Kong Mutual Recognition of Funds with the CSRC, which allowed eligible Mainland China and Hong Kong funds to be distributed in each other's markets through a streamlined vetting process.

On 29 December 2017, the SFC and the CSRC entered into a Memorandum of Understanding on Supervisory and Enforcement Cooperation on Matters Concerning Futures, which facilitated regulatory and enforcement cooperation on the Mainland China and Hong Kong futures markets.

On 3 December 2018, the CSRC and the SFC entered into a Memorandum of Understanding on the Supervisory Cooperation and Exchange of Information in relation to Cross-Boundary Regulated Entities. The MoU facilitates the cooperation of two regulators in the interests of fulfilling their respective mandates, particularly in the areas of investor protection, promoting the integrity and financial prudence of cross-boundary regulated entities, fostering fairness of markets, reducing systemic risk and maintaining financial stability.

On 3 July 2019, the Ministry of Finance (MOF) of China, the CSRC and the SFC entered into a tripartite MoU concerning the obtaining of audit working papers from Mainland China arising from the audits of Hong Kong-listed Mainland companies. According to the SFC's press release,[105] the cooperation agreed under the tripartite MoU will facilitate the SFC's access to audit working papers created by Hong Kong accounting firms which are kept on the Mainland, when conducting investigations into Mainland-based Hong Kong issuers or listed companies (and their related entities or persons). The MOF and the CSRC have agreed to provide the fullest assistance in response to the SFC's requests for investigative assistance regarding the provision of such audit working papers.

Access by Hong Kong regulators to audit working papers kept on the Mainland has been a long-standing issue, as Chinese laws restrict the transfer of documents outside of the jurisdiction, including those which contain state secrets. On 26 May 2015, China's MOF published the 'Interim Provisions on Accounting Firms' Provision of Auditing Services for the Overseas Listing of Enterprises in Chinese Mainland', which came into force on 1 July 2015, to regulate accounting firms' provision of auditing services for the overseas listing of domestic China-based

[105] 'Memorandum of Understanding Concerning the Obtaining of Audit Working Papers in the Mainland Arising from the Audits of Hong Kong-listed Mainland Companies', see SFC, 'Signing of Tri-partite MoU on Audit Working Papers by Ministry of Finance, CSRC and SFC' (3 July 2019), available at: apps.sfc.hk/edistributionWeb/gateway/EN/news-and-announcements/news/doc?refNo=19PR61 (accessed on 25 April 2022).

enterprises.[106] Article 12 of the Interim Provisions requires Mainland Chinese companies and overseas accounting firms to strictly comply with the 'Regulation on Strengthening Confidentiality and Archives Administration Relating to Overseas Issuance and Listing of Securities 2009' (Circular [2009] No 29). The Interim Provisions therefore serve as a reminder of the 2009 Rules which prohibit the transfer of working papers containing state secrets outside of China unless specifically approved. At the same time, they confirm the need to deal with requests from overseas regulators in accordance with the supervision agreement that exists between the CSRC and the overseas regulator in question.

The 2019 tripartite MoU aims to combat instances of misconduct among Mainland businesses listed in Hong Kong and improve the quality of disclosures by listing applicants and listed companies. This is particularly significant because many companies listed in Hong Kong are based or have operations on the Mainland. The MoU is a further refinement of the existing cooperation arrangements for securities regulation between China and Hong Kong and is crucial in protecting investors' interests and maintaining market integrity.

In line with the principle of reciprocity and to assist one another in performing their regulatory functions under Stock Connect, an investor identification regime for Northbound trading was launched on 26 September 2018 and introduced for Southbound trading in 2022. The investor identification regime is also called the 'see-through' model, to give both regulators a direct and real-time line of sight into Stock Connect cross-market trades at the client level. The see-through model requires the identification of the customers of intermediaries, ie the end-investors, for each order and transaction.

The investor identification regime helps to strengthen regulatory cooperation in combating market misconduct through effective monitoring and surveillance. But it also has caused considerable controversies in China and Hong Kong, given their different regulatory systems. In contrast to China's direct holding system, having direct oversight of investor trading activities, Hong Kong adopts an indirect nominee system which is common in other developed markets such as the US, the EU and Australia.[107] As securities are held in the custody of brokers or custodians which are participants of HKSCC, a subsidiary of HKEX, the SFC normally obtains trading information by requiring individual brokers to identify

[106] The full text of the Interim Provisions in Chinese by the MOF is available at: www.gov.cn/gongbao/content/2015/content_2916962.htm (accessed on 25 April 2022).

[107] The UK has a mixed holding model with a standing register where investors may hold shares directly on the register either in dematerialised or materialised form or may use an intermediary to hold shares on their behalf. However, the EU and the US are preparing for the implementation of investor identification regimes as part of the European Market in Financial Instruments Directive II and the US Consolidated Audit Trail plan respectively. Australia has also introduced relevant clauses in its rules since March 2014 to require market participants to provide investor identification data for the purpose of placing buy and sell orders, trading and trade reporting. See the HKSAR Press Release, 'LCQ12: Real-time Investor Identification System for Northbound Cross-boundary Stock Trading' (29 November 2017), available at: www.info.gov.hk/gia/general/201711/29/P2017112800785.htm (accessed on 24 February 2022).

clients and trading. While the direct holding system raises concerns for the privacy of investors, the nominee system is criticised as lacking transparency on investor identification and making market supervision difficult, despite the gains in efficiency of securities transfer and cost reduction in securities safekeeping.[108]

The differences between Chinese and Hong Kong's regulatory and operational models have created challenges in cross-border market supervision for trading activities under Stock Connect. The SFC's traditional practice of obtaining client trading information from brokers has strained its internal resources, while the Chinese regulator lacks meaningful data for surveillance purposes when global investors trade Mainland securities through Stock Connect, and the Hong Kong regulator struggles to identify investors of Southbound trading.[109] Therefore, implementing an investor identification system will bring the Hong Kong regulatory framework more in line with Chinese efforts to increase transparency and improve cross-border market surveillance.

On 18 January 2019, China's Supreme People's Court and Hong Kong concluded a new 'Arrangement on Reciprocal Recognition and Enforcement of Judgments in Civil and Commercial Matters by the Courts of the Mainland and of the Hong Kong Special Administrative Region' (New Arrangement). Prior to the New Arrangement, the only mechanism for mutual recognition or enforcement of judgments between the two jurisdictions was the 2006 Arrangement, which applied only to commercial contracts between Mainland China and Hong Kong and placed several requirements on those contracts. However, the New Arrangement removes these limitations and broadens its scope to all civil and commercial matters under Chinese and Hong Kong law, including Stock Connect, unless expressly excluded. The New Arrangement seeks to establish a bilateral legal mechanism with greater clarity and certainty for recognition and enforcement of judgments in a wider range of civil and commercial matters between the two jurisdictions. Parties seeking to recover assets in Hong Kong or China based on judgments covered by the New Arrangement will not need to re-litigate their cases.

5.4. Cross-Border Enforcement between China and the UK

China and the UK have an extensive and growing economic relationship evidenced by the fact that China was the UK's largest import partner and sixth largest export

[108] For a summary on the benefits and drawbacks of the direct holding and indirect nominee systems, see HKEX, 'Securities Holding System and "See-Through" Market Supervision – International Experience' (January 2020), 4–5, available at: www.HKEX.com.hk/-/media/HKEX-Market/News/Research-Reports/HKEX-Research-Papers/2020/CCEO_SecHolding_202001_e.pdf?la=en (accessed on 24 February 2022).

[109] Keynote speech at the 8th Pan Asian Regulatory Summit by Ashley Alder, CEO of the SFC, 10 October 2017, available at: www.sfc.hk/web/EN/files/ER/PDF/Speeches/AIA20171010%20final.pdf (accessed on 24 February 2022).

partner for goods in 2021.[110] The economic relationship is mutually beneficial, which also creates opportunity for regulatory cooperation to tackle cross-border crimes and market misconduct. Since the first China–UK Economic and Financial Dialogue in 2008, there have been 10 dialogues between two nations thus far. Over the course of these 10 dialogues, the UK and China have reached valuable agreements in areas including macro-economic cooperation, trade and investment, financial sector regulation and development, RMB internationalisation, infrastructure, urbanisation and industrial strategy, energy and climate change, and science and innovation.[111] The launch of Shanghai–London Stock Connect was one of the achievements of the 10th dialogue.

5.4.1. Pre-Stock Connect Regulatory Cooperation

An MoU between the SSE and the London Stock Exchange (LSE) was signed in 1994 followed by an agreement with the CSRC in 1996 which allowed Chinese stocks to be listed in London for the first time.[112] By the end of 2004, six Chinese companies had gone public on the LSE with a market capitalisation of £6.3 billion, including Air China, listed in December 2004.[113] Air China was listed in both Hong Kong and London using a single prospectus owing to the legal and regulatory similarities between the two markets.

The LSE also opened its Asia-Pacific Office in October 2004 in Hong Kong, targeting large privatisation deals and other medium-to-large enterprises in China as well as other non-state-owned businesses. Hong Kong was chosen as the regional base because it was recognised as a centre of the international financial markets in Asia whilst at the same time providing direct access to the Chinese mainland. The unique position of Hong Kong and its legal, regulatory and historic links with the UK offer British companies a number of important advantages such as language, business culture, transparency and international outlook.

However, as of 2015, roughly 80 companies from China had joined the LSE's AIM (formerly the Alternative Investment Market) in the previous 10 years, but only about 45 remained, owing to their non-compliance with the exchange rules.[114] In the period of 2014–15 alone, 13 Chinese companies were de-listed. Chinese

[110] UK Government, 'UK Trade with China: 2021', available at: www.ons.gov.uk/economy/nationalaccounts/balanceofpayments/articles/uktradewithchina2021/2022-06-01 (accessed on 20 June 2022).

[111] UK Government, 'Factsheet: 10th UK China Economic and Financial Dialogue: 17 June 2019', available at: assets.publishing.service.gov.uk/government/uploads/system/uploads/attachment_data/file/809590/EFD_Factsheet_FINAL__003_.pdf_1.pdf (accessed on 20 June 2022).

[112] UK Parliament, 'Memorandum Submitted by the London Stock Exchange', Select Committee on Treasury Written Evidence (18 January 2005), available at: publications.parliament.uk/pa/cm200405/cmselect/cmtreasy/314/314we11.htm#n7 (accessed on 5 June 2022).

[113] ibid.

[114] K Burgess, 'London Stock Exchange Clamps Down on Aim-Quoted Chinese Companies' (*Financial Times*, 9 October 2015), available at: www.ft.com/content/0eee474a-6e8f-11e5-aca9-d87542bf8673 (accessed 20 April 2022).

de-listings have revealed some existing problems in Chinese financial systems, such as weak corporate governance, lack of effective accounting and auditing professionals, and poor information disclosure and investor protection.[115] But the primary responsibility may fall on the regulators who are still structurally incapable of enforcing the law across borders.[116]

5.4.2. Post-Stock Connect Regulatory Cooperation

Another MoU (Memorandum of Understanding concerning Supervisory and Enforcement Cooperation under Shanghai–London Stock Connect), signed on 17 October 2018 between the CSRC and the FCA, sets out a framework for cooperation between the two regulators to support Shanghai–London Stock Connect, which aims to protect investors and combat cross-border market abuse and other serious misconduct.[117] Jointly announced by the CSRC and the FCA, Shanghai–London Stock Connect is a landmark in cooperation between the two nations in the sphere of financial markets.[118] The programme will strengthen connectivity between China and the UK capital markets, and enhance the status of Shanghai and London as global financial centres.

The frameworks of the two MoUs on Stock Connect between China–Hong Kong and China–UK are similar, with a few minor differences.

- First, both MoUs aim to promote regulatory and investigatory cooperation under Stock Connect to achieve effective supervision in both jurisdictions.[119] The MoUs do not affect or change any existing agreements or practices related to enforcement cooperation between the parties. However, the China–Hong Kong MoU includes provisions for enforcement staff exchange and training between the two jurisdictions, which are not included in the China–UK MoU.
- Second, regarding investigatory and enforcement assistance, the parties to the two MoUs have agreed to provide each other with 'timely, sufficient, and effective assistance' within their respective statutory powers.[120] This assistance includes the provision of documentary evidence, witness statements,

[115] C Chen et al, 'Corporate Accounting Scandals in China' in MJ Jones (ed), *Creative Accounting, Fraud and International Accounting Scandals: Fraud and International Accounting Scandals* (Chichester, John Wiley & Sons, 2012), 180.

[116] D Cogman and G Orr, 'How They Fell: The Collapse of Chinese Cross-Border Listings' (*McKinsey & Co*, 1 December 2013), available at: www.mckinsey.com/business-functions/strategy-and-corporate-finance/our-insights/how-they-fell-the-collapse-of-chinese-cross-border-listings (accessed on 20 April 2022).

[117] The full text of the MoU is available on the FCA's website at: www.fca.org.uk/publication/mou/mou-fca-csrc.pdf (accessed on 20 June 2022).

[118] FCA, 'The Shanghai–London Stock Connect: A Joint Announcement by the China Securities Regulatory Commission and the UK Financial Conduct Authority' (17 June 2019), available at: www.fca.org.uk/publication/mou/joint-announcement-fca-csrc.pdf (accessed on 20 June 2022).

[119] China–Hong Kong MoU, art 1 and China–UK MoU, art II(1).

[120] China–Hong Kong MoU, art 6 and China–UK MoU, art V(2).

interview records of persons involved, and forensic opinions. In cases that are significant and urgent, the parties may initiate a joint investigation, taking into account factors such as the location of the misconduct, adverse consequences, investors, evidence, witnesses, suspects, assets, available sanctions and remedies, and any other relevant factors related to the suspects and the misconduct.[121]

- Third, with regard to information exchange, the China–UK MoU specifies that requests for information must follow the process outlined in paragraph 8 of IOSCO's MMoU.[122] In contrast, the China–Hong Kong MoU does not include this procedural requirement, which suggests that either the CSRC or SFC may request any information regarding suspected misconduct from the other party without using a specific written format. However, the parties are obligated to keep requests made confidential under the MoUs.[123] They should also immediately alert each other to any information regarding suspected misconduct and notify each other when they commence a cross-border investigation.[124] Additionally, the parties agree to hold regular exchanges of views on cross-boundary market surveillance and analysis, the progress of enforcement cooperation, and matters of mutual concern or common interests.
- Fourth, compared to the China–Hong Kong MoU, the MoU between China and the UK places more emphasis on investor protection. It recognises that investor protection is a key priority when taking enforcement action under Stock Connect and encourages the use of various means to disseminate educational information and investment know-how to Shanghai–London Stock Connect investors.[125] This is because mutual access to international and Chinese investors beyond Greater China (ie beyond the Mainland, Hong Kong, Macau and Taiwan) is a new development, and many investors may be unfamiliar with the rules and policies of the other market.

While the MoU has much promise, there are also inherent risks for UK authorities in working with China, and limitations on what they can do with their Chinese counterparts. Concerns are often raised about China's political and judicial system, as well as human rights protections. These concerns have been instrumental in discouraging the British government from ratifying an extradition treaty with

[121] China–Hong Kong MoU, art 6 and China–UK MoU, art V(5).

[122] Pursuant to paragraph 8 of IOSCO's MMoU, requests for assistance should be made in writing (telephone or facsimile are only acceptable in urgent circumstances), and include a description of the facts of the investigation, the assistance sought, any information that might assist the requested authority in investigation, and an indication of any special precautions needed as well as the relevant laws related to the subject-matter of the request. Available at: www.iosco.org/library/pubdocs/pdf/IOSCOPD386.pdf.

[123] China–Hong Kong MoU, art 8 and China–UK MoU, art VI(2).

[124] China–Hong Kong MoU, arts 3 and 4 and China–UK MoU, art IV (5) and (6).

[125] China–UK MoU, art VII (2) and (3).

the Chinese government.[126] The debate about whether to ratify the treaty is an instructive case study on the concerns and risks of working with China. Given the divergent jurisdictions and lack of extradition between the UK and China, cross-border enforcement remains a significant issue.

5.5. Cross-Border Enforcement between China and Switzerland

5.5.1. Pre-Stock Connect Regulatory Cooperation

Switzerland was one of the first western states to recognise Communist China in 1950. In 2007, Switzerland and China signed an MoU aimed at intensifying high-level political consultations and deepening all aspects of bilateral relations.[127] In addition to regular official contact between Beijing and Bern, projects are carried out in partnership with various Swiss cantons and communes. At the civil society level, close, regular exchanges have been established by various experts, academic institutions and artistic groups.

Since 2010, China has been Switzerland's biggest trading partner in Asia and its third-largest globally after the EU and the US.[128] A bilateral free trade agreement was signed in Beijing in 2013 and entered into force on 1 July 2014.[129] This agreement contains provisions on trade in goods and services, non-tariff barriers to trade, intellectual property protection, and sustainable trade and development.

Furthermore, the initiation of financial dialogue between Switzerland and China was agreed upon 24 May 2013, with the signing of an MoU.[130] The objective of this regular dialogue is to foster and enhance cooperation between the two countries in the area of finance. The talks touched upon greater involvement of Switzerland in the international use of the Renminbi. Topical issues such as regulation and supervision, financial service provision, and cooperation in international bodies were also addressed.

[126] *The Guardian*, 'MPs Call for Overhaul of China Policy After UK Suspends Hong Kong Extraditions' (20 July 2020), available at www.theguardian.com/world/2020/jul/20/uk-risks-chinas-wrath-by-suspending-hong-kong-extradition-treaty (accessed on 20 June 2022).

[127] 'Memorandum of Understanding on Promoting Dialogue and Cooperation 2007' is available at: www.eda.admin.ch/eda/en/fdfa/representations-and-travel-advice/china/switzerland-china.html (accessed on 1 August 2022).

[128] The Federal Department of Foreign Affairs of Switzerland (2021), 'China Strategy 2021–24', 16, available at: www.eda.admin.ch/eda/en/fdfa/fdfa/publikationen.html/content/publikationen/en/eda/schweizer-aussenpolitik/China_Strategie_2021-2024.html (accessed on 1 August 2022).

[129] The full text of free trade agreement between Switzerland and China 2013 is available at: www.fedlex.admin.ch/eli/treaty/2013/16301001/en (accessed on 1 August 2022).

[130] Switzerland's Federal Department of Finance, 'Switzerland and China Commence Financial Dialogue', available at: www.sif.admin.ch/sif/en/home/dokumentation/medienmitteilungen/medienmitteilungen.msg-id-51238.html (accessed on 1 August 2022).

On 8 June 2015, the SIX Swiss Exchange and the SSE signed an MoU to formalise the regular exchange of information, promote business relations, and strengthen regulatory standards.[131] In April 2019, SIX Swiss Exchange renewed its MoU with the SSE, intending to deepen the collaboration which was initiated in 2015.[132] The amended MoU aims to further intensify cooperation between the two financial centres, assess the feasibility of listing securities such as depository receipts on each other's markets, and allow companies listed on either exchange to tap into each other's liquidity pools. The MoU also includes the consideration of collaborating on further matters of mutual interest, such as digitalisation. Later, in October 2019, SIX Swiss Exchange signed a similar MoU with the SZSE to connect the investors' community and companies in both countries.[133] These two 2019 MoUs provide a foundation for the launch of Stock Connect between China and Switzerland by establishing capital formation possibilities. This development paves the way for greater financial cooperation between the two countries.

5.5.2. Post-Stock Connect Regulatory Cooperation

Since the signing of the 2019 MoUs, SIX Swiss Exchange has been collaborating closely with the Shanghai and Shenzhen Stock Exchanges to establish Stock Connect, which would offer market access equally to Chinese and Swiss market participants. But unfortunately, China's CSRC and the Swiss FINMA haven't signed any agreement thus far, which leaves their cooperation limited to the stock exchange level instead of higher securities authority level.

5.6. Enforcement Data and Cases

While bilateral arrangements, complementing the multilateral platform, are recognised as 'an essential tool in assisting regulators to enforce securities laws globally and locally',[134] they are faced with mounting criticism. All these memoranda constitute more an expression of a desire to cooperate than a binding agreement.[135]

[131] The 2015 MoU between SIX Swiss Exchange and Shanghai Stock Exchange is available at: www.six-group.com/dam/download/media/press-releases/2015/0806-e-mou-china.pdf (accessed on 1 August 2022).

[132] SIX Swiss Exchange, 'SIX and Shanghai Stock Exchange Sign an Updated Memorandum of Understanding' (23 April 2019), available at: www.six-group.com/en/newsroom/media-releases/2019/20190423-mou-six-sse.html (accessed on 1 August 2022).

[133] SIX Swiss Exchange, 'SIX and Shenzhen Stock Exchange Sign a Memorandum of Understanding' (10 October 2019), available at: www.six-group.com/en/newsroom/media-releases/2019/20191010-szse-six-mou.html (accessed on 1 August 2022).

[134] R Cunha, 'The IOSCO Multilateral Memorandum of Understanding MMoU: An International Benchmark for Securities Enforcement' (2010) 15 *Uniform Law Review* 677, 685.

[135] Wang (2009), see n 98 above, 390.

Hence, whether to cooperate or not is largely left to the regulators who should have an incentive to do so to preserve their reputation and credibility.[136] China has long been blamed for its reluctance to allow overseas regulators to inspect audit documents relating to Chinese companies due to national security concerns. In a media interview in 2020, Jay Clayton, chairman of the SEC, indicated that the regulator's accounting oversight arm, the Public Company Accounting Oversight Board had been unable to access audits of US-listed Chinese companies from the Chinese government for almost a decade.[137] Even in a better-established relationship between China and Hong Kong, China has consistently in the past rejected requests for information by Hong Kong regulators investigating locally-listed Chinese companies, particularly in high-profile corporate scandals such as Liu Jinbao, the former chief executive of the Bank of China (Hong Kong), Yang Bin, chairman of Euro-Asia Agricultural Holdings, an orchid grower in north-east China, and Zhou Zhengyi, chairman of Shanghai Land Holdings.[138]

Stock Connect has changed China's incentive to engage in regulatory cooperation, which is reflected by the enforcement-related requests between China and Hong Kong in the 10 years 2011–20. Prior to 2014, only a few requests were sent out by the CSRC each year, compared to being on the receiving end of numerous requests for investigatory assistance. But after the launch of Stock Connect, the requests made by the CSRC (mainly to the SFC) has jumped to dozens. By contrast, the in-and-out requests by the SFC (mainly with the CSRC) were consistently at around 100–160. Particularly in 2019, the CSRC received 224 requests for enforcement assistance and information exchange, of which 182 requests (81.2 per cent) were from Hong Kong. Meanwhile, the CSRC made 53 outbound requests in the same year, including 40 requests (75.5 per cent) to the SFC and the other 13 requests (24.5 per cent) to nine foreign securities regulators, a record high in recent years.[139]

On the other hand, the UK's FCA received around 1,000 requests from international counterparts while the requests made by the FCA itself were not published in 2018–19.[140] In Switzerland, FINMA can request information and documents from foreign financial market supervisory authorities to help with its enforcement activities. It also receives several hundred requests for assistance from

[136] J Austin, 'IOSCO's Multilateral Memorandum of Understanding Concerning Consultation, Cooperation and the Exchange of Information' (2012) 23 *Criminal Law Forum* 393, 416.

[137] K Johnson, 'US Securities Regulator Warns Investors over Chinese Company Disclosures (Reuters, 22 April 2020), available at: www.reuters.com/article/us-health-coronavirus-sec-china-idUSKCN2242A1 (accessed on 20 June 2022).

[138] D Donald, *A Financial Centre for Two Empires* (Cambridge: Cambridge University Press, 2014), 252–53.

[139] CSRC, 'Annual Report 2019', 71, available at: www.csrc.gov.cn/csrc_en/c102063/c1606308/content.shtml (accessed on 25 April 2022).

[140] FCA, 'Enforcement Annual Performance Report 2018/19' (2019), 20, available at: www.fca.org.uk/publication/corporate/annual-report-2018-19-enforcement-performance.pdf (accessed on 25 April 2022).

foreign authorities every year. FINMA received 384 incoming requests and made 34 outgoing requests annually during the period of 2016–20.[141] However, the number of requests communicated between China and the UK/Switzerland was unknown due to the shortage of data.

Table 5.1 Enforcement-Related Requests for Regulatory Cooperation in China and Hong Kong (2011–20)

	Requests	2011	2012	2013	2014	2015	2016	2017	2018	2019	2020
CSRC	Received	75	54	90	97	130	174	184	125	224	97
	Made	5	3	6	13	30	37	N/A	24	53	23
SFC	Received	104	112	103	94	92	155	136	113	103	110
	Made	104	146	113	111	160	112	104	99	95	108

Sources: Various Annual Reports of the CSRC and SFC 2011–20.

5.6.1. *Tang Hanbo v SFC* [2017] HKEC 2442 – The First Securities Violation under Stock Connect

This case is noteworthy because it is the first enforcement action under Shanghai–Hong Kong Stock Connect since its launch in October 2014. The CSRC levied one of its largest ever fines for manipulation by penalising a businessman, Tang Hanbo, and his associates. This case also signifies the joint forces to tackle cross-border market misconduct between the CSRC and the SFC.

5.6.1.1. *On the CSRC's Side*

On 10 March 2017, the CSRC published two related decisions concerning Tang Hanbo and his associates for the manipulative trading of securities. According to the decision ([2017] No 21), Tang Hanbo and Wang Tao controlled four different securities accounts (three Hong Kong accounts and one Mainland onshore account) and used such accounts to carry out manipulative trading of the shares of Zhejiang China Commodities City Group (SHA:600415), a stock company listed in Shanghai that also traded under Shanghai–Hong Kong Stock Connect.[142] The decision described the different stages of their position building, price maintenance, overweighting, and sell-off at great length, and identified their activities such as 'churning', intra-day trading, fictitious quotation, and quote revocation.

[141] FINMA, 'National and International Cooperation', available at: www.finma.ch/en/enforcement/national-and-international-cooperation/ (accessed on 25 April 2022).

[142] CSRC's Administrative Sanction Decision (*Tang Hanbo and Wang Tao*) [2017] No 21 (published by CSRC on 10 March 2017), available at: www.csrc.gov.cn/csrc/c101928/c1042724/content.shtml (accessed on 25 April 2022).

The CSRC found that Tang and Wang illegally gained about RMB 42 million and it held that both committed manipulation activities contrary to Article 77 of the Securities Law 2005, including continuous trading manipulation, wash trade manipulation, and manipulation through other methods. The use by Tang of Hong Kong accounts was allegedly intended to disguise his activity. Whereas regulators and stock exchanges on the Mainland maintain a system for identifying traders in real time, the SFC requests the identities of investors after trades have taken place.

The CSRC also found that Tang was involved in manipulating the prices of five other domestic stocks unrelated to Stock Connect from 2014 to 2015 and as a result made an illicit gain of around RMB 250 million ([2017] No 20).[143] The CSRC alleged that Tang and others artificially ramped up and maintained trading prices and volumes with a view to misleading market investors into trading in the same stock. The CSRC said these violations had severely disrupted market order and damaged the interests of other investors.

In arguing against the sanctions imposed by the CSRC's decision ([2017] No 21), Tang and Wang submitted that:

(1) the evidence of the case came from SFC, hence there was doubt as to whether such evidence, obtained by CSRC, was legal and valid;
(2) as the incident took place in Hong Kong, the CSRC would not have any jurisdiction to sanction;
(3) there was no concrete evidence to show that Tang took the leading role; and
(4) the Securities Law does not govern acts such as manipulation of opening price and intra-day trading.[144]

In rebuttal, the CSRC stated the following:

(1) As both Tang and Wang were Chinese citizens, the CSRC had jurisdiction over their unlawful activities;
(2) The evidence obtained from Tang's apartment in Hong Kong showed that Tang was responsible for making payments and that the computers used for the manipulative trading were also found in his apartment.
(3) Tang and Wang, in order to bypass regulatory oversight and to control the public market in subtle means, traded in Hong Kong as offshore traders. Hence a reduction of penalty, as requested by Wang, was not given.

The CSRC dismissed the defendants' argument that because the evidence in the case was collected by the SFC there were issues regarding the legality and validity of the evidence. The CSRC likewise dismissed their argument that since the place of the unlawful acts was Hong Kong, the CSRC did not have jurisdiction.

[143] CSRC's Administrative Sanction Decision (*Tang Habbo, Tang Yuanzi, Yuan Hailin etc five persons*) [2017] No 20 (published by CSRC on 10 March 2017), available at: www.csrc.gov.cn/csrc/c101928/c1042725/content.shtml (accessed on 25 April 2022).

[144] CSRC's Administrative Sanction Decision (*Tang Hanbo and Wang Tao*) [2017] No 21.

The CSRC went out of its way to comment on the SFC's evidence as being trustworthy, having been compiled in exercise of the latter's investigatory powers under the SFO. It also recognised the SFC's rights to conduct its own investigation into the case. It cited a number of Chinese regulations under which the CSRC may cooperate with overseas securities regulatory authorities to carry out duties regarding cross-border supervision and administration of the securities market. These included the Memorandum of Understanding on Strengthening and Expanding Cross-Boundary Regulatory and Enforcement Cooperation, issued on 26 August 2016. It also relied on the fact that both the CSRC and the SFC are members of IOSCO. The evidence provided by the SFC had strictly complied with the relevant procedural requirements concerning the handing over of evidence as well as relevant laws and regulations.

Based on the above findings and the social harm to the parties involved, the CSRC ordered the confiscation of Tang's illegal income of about RMB 42 million and further imposed a monetary fine of RMB 209 million pursuant to Article 203 of the Securities Law ([2017] No 21). This represents the 'maximum penalty' permitted under the Securities Law, being five times of the amount of the illegal gain. Wang was given a RMB 600,000 fine over the offending transaction. The discrepancy in their penalties was owing to Tang being the person who controlled the accounts and implemented the manipulation, while Wang was only a trader. Tang's high penalty also took into account the facts that Tang was a repeat offender and played a core leading role in this case.[145]

In the two cases, the total illegal income confiscated from Tang and his associates amounted to RMB 290 million and the total fine imposed was RMB 952 million. Although Tang appealed to the CSRC against the decision to impose the administrative sanction, the CSRC upheld the decision after the reconsideration.[146]

Although the CSRC sanction against Tang and Wang is the first sanction for market manipulation under Stock Connect, the offences committed and the trading activities concerned are no different from those committed by domestic market investors under the Securities Law. Prohibition of manipulative securities trading was codified in China's Securities Law, and in 2007 the CSRC issued its 'Guidance on the Determination of Securities Market Manipulative Activities (Trial)'.[147] Later in 2019, China's Supreme People's Court and the Supreme People's Procuratorate jointly issued 'Interpretation of Several Issues Concerning the Application of law in the Handling of Criminal Cases Regarding

[145] *Bloomberg*, 'China Fines Repeat Offender $170 Million for Stock Manipulation' (13 March 2017), available at: www.bloomberg.com/news/articles/2017-03-13/china-fines-trader-170-million-makes-first-stock-link-penalty (accessed on 25 April 2022).

[146] CSRC's Administrative Reconsideration Decision (*Tang Hanbo*) [2017] 99 (published by CSRC on 2 August 2017), available at: www.csrc.gov.cn/csrc/c105938/c1044079/content.shtml (accessed on 25 April 2022).

[147] The Trial Guidance was issued on 27 March 2007 and then abolished by the CSRC on 30 October 2020.

the Manipulation of Securities and Futures market', to harmonise the laws and practices on imposing punishment for securities and futures-related crimes.[148] In addition, other securities trading activities not having all the characteristics of market manipulation, and thus not punishable under the Securities Law, can nevertheless be 'abnormal trading activities' under the rules of the SSE and the SZSE. The SSE and SZSE can each take disciplinary measures against investors and suspend trading of their securities accounts. Tang and Wang were punished by CSRC for stock manipulation, and the CSRC decision also identified their activities as 'abnormal trading activities' (ie intra-day trading of the shares on 29 trading days).

5.6.1.2. On the SFC's Side

Tang's case also provides an interesting insight into the SFC's increasingly close cooperation with the CSRC and illustrates the SFC's power to share information with the CSRC and other regulators outside Hong Kong.

On 8 December 2017, the Hong Kong Court of First Instance refused a judicial review application against the SFC and a Magistrate sitting at the Eastern Magistracy. The application was made by Tang Hanbo, a PRC national resident in Hong Kong. Tang sought to quash a search warrant obtained by the SFC from the Magistrate and the SFC's decision to transmit materials seized during its search to the CSRC.

The SFC commenced an investigation against Tang and his wife in relation to suspected breaches of the Hong Kong Codes on Takeovers and Mergers and Share Buy-backs, and suspected offences under the Securities and Futures Ordinance (Cap 571) (SFO) for the trading of shares in two Hong Kong-listed companies. Meanwhile, the CSRC was investigating Tang and another person for alleged market misconduct in Mainland China in relation to the trading of shares in a Shanghai-listed company.

In June 2016, the CSRC sent a request to the SFC for investigatory assistance. Subsequent to the CSRC's request, the SFC obtained a search warrant from the Magistrate and, in execution of the search warrant, seized notebook computers, mobile phones and documents at Tang's residence. When the SFC applied for the search warrant, the Magistrate was informed that the warrant was for investigating breaches of Hong Kong laws and regulatory codes. The SFC did not disclose to the Magistrate the CSRC's investigation, nor did it mention the CSRC's interest in Tang and the materials to be seized. However, when the SFC was conducting the search, the SFC officers tried to get Tang to speak with the CSRC officers on the phone and also (through their superior in the SFC's office) kept the CSRC officers updated as to what had been seized and what appeared to be on the computers.

[148] The Interpretation was issued on 27 June 2019 and came into effect on 1 July 2019.

After the search, the CSRC sent several requests to the SFC for further assistance, and the SFC transmitted the requested materials (which included materials seized during the search) to the CSRC.

Tang filed to challenge the search warrant on the basis that it had been obtained by deliberate non-disclosure and a misleading description of the true purpose behind it, which Tang alleged was to assist the CSRC's investigation.[149] Tang also sought to challenge the SFC's decision to transmit materials to the CSRC based on the same illegality, which tainted the search warrant.

The SFC argued that there was no reason for it to have deliberately misled the Magistrate by withholding the true purpose of the search warrant when they had the right to render assistance to the CSRC. The SFC also pointed out that the transmission of information was based on the CSRC's request after the search warrant.

The Court upheld the validity of the SFC's search warrant used to assist CSRC's investigation. The judgment affirms the SFC's power to provide investigatory assistance to foreign regulators pursuant to section 186 of the SFO and the IOSCO's MMoU, and confirms that the SFC may pass on what it has gathered in its investigations to the CSRC, even if the information was collected by the SFC for its own investigations in the first place.[150]

In summary, Tang's case was the first time the Memorandum of Understanding on Strengthening and Expanding Cross-Boundary Regulatory and Enforcement Cooperation 2016 was seen in action, with the CSRC making use of the SFC investigation findings and giving credit to the SFC for its help in the investigation. Collaboration of this sort was hailed by Thomas Atkinson, the SFC's Executive Director of Enforcement, in his speech to the 7th Pan-Asian Regulatory Summit in Hong Kong on 9 November 2016. Atkinson commented on the joint investigations between the two regulators which he said 'provide excellent opportunities for officers of both organisations to build trust and establish long-term working relationships.'[151]

With the increasing volume of trading through Stock Connect, collaboration between the SFC and the CSRC will significantly increase. In a press release issued in June 2017, the CSRC disclosed that it had already commenced 365 cross-border enforcement matters as a result of the cooperation with the SFC since the beginning of the Shanghai–Hong Kong Stock Connect in November 2014.[152] Tang's case is a further testament to the close collaboration between the SFC and the CSRC in assisting each other's investigations.

[149] *Tang Hanbo v SFC* [2017] HKEC 2442.

[150] ibid.

[151] SFC, 'Speech at 7th Pan Asian Regulatory Summit' by Mr Thomas Atkinson, Executive Director, Enforcement (9 November 2016), available at: www.sfc.hk/-/media/EN/files/ER/PDF/Speeches/Atkinson_20161109.pdf (accessed on 1 June 2022).

[152] CSRC, 'Zhongguo Zhengjianhui he Xianggang Zhengjianhui Juxing Disici Liangdi Zhifahezuo Gongzuohuiyi' (CSRC and SFC's Fourth Enforcement and Cooperation Meeting) (30 June 2017), available at www.gov.cn/xinwen/2017-06/30/content_5207057.htm (accessed on 25 April 2022).

After Tang's case, the CSRC probed another market manipulation incident under Stock Connect.[153] From December 2015 to July 2016, LV Le, a private equity fund manager, and Chen Zhilong used Shanghai–Hong Kong Stock Connect accounts to manipulate three stock companies including 'Feida Environmental Science & Technology Co., Ltd (600526)' which is a Shanghai-listed company and traded under Stock Connect, making a total profit of more than RMB 15 million. On 14 November 2019 the CSRC imposed a penalty on LV and Chen for their market misconduct by confiscating the illegal gain of about RMB 15 million and further imposing a monetary fine of RMB 30 million.[154]

5.7. Concluding Remarks

Over the past several decades, securities markets and market participants have become fully globalised, with operations stretching across borders, drawing on investment capital around the world and looking for investment opportunities in many different countries. The increasing mobility of financial markets calls for greater cross-border regulatory cooperation. Without enhanced supervisory cooperation and information sharing among the world's securities authority regulators, many of the regulatory reforms may prove insufficient to the tasks for which they are being designed.[155] Among the different types of collaborative mechanisms between securities regulators, supervisory MoUs have become increasingly popular forms of cross-border regulatory cooperation.

In the context of Stock Connect, the four participant jurisdictions of China, Hong Kong, the UK and Switzerland adopt different supervisory infrastructures in the financial markets. On the one hand, the securities regulators of the UK and Switzerland exercised their powers via the integrated model for the regulation of banks, securities markets and insurance companies, but their regulatory approaches have been on increasingly divergent paths after the global financial crisis. The UK has moved towards the 'Twin Peaks' model of financial regulation so that the FSA was split into two new prudential and conduct agencies, whereas, the Swiss Confederation strengthened the single regulatory framework by creating FINMA after the financial turmoil.

On the other hand, China and Hong Kong use the sectoral supervisory model with separate authorities for different financial sectors, but they also show certain disparities. China's CSRC is regarded as a typical example of hierarchically

[153] CSRC, 'Zhengjianhui Chahuo Yiqi Liyong Hugangtong Zhanghu Kuajing Caozong Shichang Anjian' (CSRC Seizes a Case of Cross-Border Market Manipulation Using Shanghai-Hong Kong Stock Connect Accounts) (18 May 2018), available at: www.csrc.gov.cn/csrc/c100200/c1000477/content.shtml (accessed on 1 June 2022).

[154] CSRC's Administrative Sanction Decision (*L v Le and Chen Zhilong*) [2019] No 125, available at: www.csrc.gov.cn/csrc/c101928/c1042381/content.shtml (accessed on 1 June 2022).

[155] IOSCO (2010), see n 6 above, 3.

structured regulators, which tend to consider state goals as their priority and have direct authority over the stock exchanges. By contrast, Hong Kong is similar to the US's horizontal structure, mainly seeking to protect investors and facilitate capital formation.

Despite different supervisory structures, China has maintained collaborative relationships with the other three jurisdictions in the financial markets. With further development and optimisation, Stock Connect is playing an increasingly significant role in the opening-up of Chinese capital markets and regulatory collaboration. This is reflected in numerous MoUs signed between China and overseas authorities and increasing cross-border enforcement actions. The securities violation cases of *Tang* and *LV/Chen* have highlighted the enhancement of mutual understanding on both sides and the joint investigations between the regulators. They also mark the first time we have seen the MoU in action and a significant step for the CSRC, which uses international cooperation to deter cross-border securities violations.

6

Impacts and Limitations of Stock Connect on Local and Global Financial Markets

Along with the rapid development of the Chinese capital market, China has been actively implementing a series of policies to open its financial markets since 2014. Amid the ongoing risks of US–China trade and de-listing, Chinese companies have been turning to other markets to raise funds while fending off the fallout caused by China–US geopolitical tensions. Starting with the launch of Shanghai–Hong Kong Stock Connect (Shanghai Connect) in November 2014, China's programme was expanded to include three more links: the Shenzhen–Hong Kong Stock Connect (Shenzhen Connect) in December 2016, the Shanghai–London Stock Connect (London Connect) in June 2019, and the China–Switzerland Stock Connect (Switzerland Connect) in July 2022.

With the rapid expansion of Stock Connect, it also needs constant enhancements to broaden the range of investment opportunities, improve efficiency, and facilitate the two-way flow of capital between China and the world. In the nine years since the commencement of Stock Connect, there have been a series of new enhancements, including: the addition of more eligible stocks to expand investor choice; the addition of public holiday trading on Stock Connect; technological advances for trading checking and price execution, such as Master Special Segregated Accounts and Synapses; and the launch of Morgan Stanley Capital International (MSCI) China A50 Connect Futures, offering investors an effective A-share exposure risk management tool.[1]

The breakthroughs are notable in opening-up Chinese onshore markets for international investors and foreign markets for Mainland Chinese investors. Existing literature has studied the short-term effects of Stock Connect with a focus on the China–Hong Kong link.[2] Yet, few papers investigate its long-term implications for and limitations on the local and global financial markets. Therefore, this chapter will fill the gap by providing a comprehensive picture of the impacts

[1] For more developments of Stock Connect, see HKEX, 'Our Connect Story: A New Chapter Begins' (October 2022), 2–3, available at: www.hkex.com.hk/-/media/HKEX-Market/Mutual-Market/Stock-Connect/Reference-Materials/Resources/HKEX-Connect-Story.pdf (accessed on 3 January 2023).

[2] See the discussion in Section 6.1 below.

of Stock Connect on all participant markets (China, Hong Kong, the UK, and Switzerland) and its limitations.

6.1. Literature Review

The Chinese government has gradually adopted a series of policies for opening-up to the world in the context of economic globalisation and financial liberalisation. It is generally recognised that Stock Connect, as a major liberalisation initiative, provides opportunities for the Chinese stock market to strengthen its ties with international markets. This initiative has inspired a voluminous body of scholarship from different perspectives and levels of understanding on the effects on Stock Connect, in particular on market quality, A–H-share price premium and co-integration between China and other markets.

6.1.1. Market Quality

How does Stock Connect affect market quality in Chinese stock markets? Academic studies find that capital market openness has controversial effects on market quality. Brogaard and Garriott find that opening the market to more foreigners can increase competition for liquidity provision.[3] Similarly, Meng and others employ a dataset of 17,086 Chinese listed firms, covering 2009 to 2018, to demonstrate that stock market liberalisation has improved the market efficiency of the Chinese stock market.[4] In particular, stock price informational efficiency and corporate governance quality have been significantly increased after the launch of Stock Connect.

However, opening the market to more sophisticated foreign investors leads to more cross-market arbitrage activities that intensify adverse selection, thus putting upward pressure on liquidity and volatility.[5] In the context of Stock Connect, using the difference-in-difference approach, Wu and Ohk find that market quality, as reflected by the market illiquidity and market volatility measures of constituent stocks, is worse than that of non-constituent stocks after the launch of the Shanghai–Hong Kong programme in the Shanghai A-shares market.[6] However, the differences in market quality between constituent and non-constituent stocks gradually diminish over time. In contrast, no significant market quality effects have generally occurred in the Hong Kong market.

[3] J Brogaard and C Garriott, 'High-frequency Trading Competition' (2019) 54 *Journal of Financial and Quantitative Analysis* 1469.

[4] Y Meng et al, 'The Effect of Overseas Investors on Local Market Efficiency: Evidence from the Shanghai/Shenzhen-Hong Kong Stock Connect' (2023) 9 *Financial Innovation* 42.

[5] J Hasbrouck, 'High-frequency Quoting: Short-term Volatility in Bids and Offers' (2018) 53(2) *Journal of Financial and Quantitative Analysis* 613.

[6] M Wu and KY Ohk, 'Who Benefits More? Shanghai-Hong Kong Stock Connect – "Through Train"' (2023) 84 *International Review of Economics and Finance* 409.

6.1.2. Price Disparity of A–H-Shares

A prominent feature of China's financial market is the prevalence of cross-listed firms, which constitute a sizable proportion of the total market capitalisation. These firms are concurrently listed in Mainland Chinese and Hong Kong markets (as A-shares and H-shares, respectively).[7] Their widely varying price disparities have been one of the most interesting puzzles in the Chinese financial market, resulting from liquidity and a lack of market circulation on both sides.[8] Because foreign investors may trade H-shares, the shares are more liquid than A-shares. As a result, A-shares typically trade at a premium compared to H-shares of the same company. In addition, differences between local and foreign investors in required returns, relative stock supply, information asymmetry and exchange rate changes also have significant influence on the price difference between the China and Hong Kong stock markets.[9] Building on a sample of 63 listed companies from 2014 to 2017, Bai and others argue that the premiums of many shares are becoming narrower in recent years, which might pave the way to convergence after closer links between the Mainland and Hong Kong stock exchanges.[10] Likewise, Chan and Kwok used longitudinal data to investigate abnormal systematic changes in the price disparity of cross-listed stocks between Hong Kong and Shanghai markets, and found that Stock Connect had caused the price disparity to reduce by one-sixth.[11] But the empirical research is also subject to the limitations on the sample size and duration of the study as well as other factors influencing stock prices such as policy announcements and global market environment.[12]

6.1.3. Market Co-movement

Will the launch of the Stock Connect programme result in a closer correlation between stock markets in China and other participant markets? Though there is growing literature on the effects of market liberalisation policies in China, scholars have not yet reached a consensus. Most scholars argue that these market liberalisation policies have positive effects on market integration – that is, they have

[7] As discussed in Chapter 2, A-shares are generally only available for trading to mainland Chinese citizens. H-shares of Chinese companies listed on the HKEX are quoted and traded with a face value of Hong Kong dollars. H-shares are open for trading to all investors.

[8] K Chan and J Kwok, 'Market Segmentation and Share Price Premium: Evidence from Chinese Stock Markets' (205) 4(1) *Journal of Emerging Market Finance* 43.

[9] Q Su et al, 'On the Convergence of the Chinese and Hong Kong Stock Markets: A Cointegration Analysis of the A and H Shares' (2007) 17 *Applied Financial Economics* 1349.

[10] Y Bai et al, 'Analysis of Price Differences between A and H Shares' (2019) 26 *Asia-Pacific Financial Market* 529.

[11] MK Chan and S Kwok, 'Connecting the Markets? Recent Evidence on China's Capital Account Liberalisation' (2018) 70 *Economic Modelling* 417, 428.

[12] HC Huang and JH Lin, 'The Impact of Shanghai-Hong Kong Stock Connect Policy on Price Differences and Announcement Effects' (2016) 10(3) *Global Journal of Business Research* 1, 7.

increased integration between the Mainland Chinese and other stock markets. For example, Su and others suggest that the stock prices of China and Hong Kong started to co-integrate as early as the launch of the Closer Economic Partnership Agreement in 2003.[13] After the 2008 financial crisis, their relationships transformed from one-way causation into two-way causation, and the influence of Mainland stock markets on the Hong Kong market, which was little in the past, became significant.[14] In recent years, Stock Connect has considerably intensified the short-run co-movements between the markets in Shanghai, Shenzhen and Hong Kong, which was vague before. Huo and Ahmed examine the volatility spill-over effect and stock markets correlation between Shanghai and Hong Kong after the launch of Shanghai–Hong Kong Stock Connect using high frequency data.[15] They find significant spill-over effect from Shanghai to Hong Kong stock market and the effect is strengthened after the launch of the programme. Their results also show that there has been a significant long-term co-integration relationship between these two markets after the programme, but no co-integration relationship before the programme.

However, different views persist. Ma and others point out that previous studies' failure to separate the influence of financial liberalisation from that of other factors may thus overvalue the former's effect on co-movement among financial markets. One major drawback of those studies is that they are unable to distinguish financial liberalisation-induced co-movement from that induced by other factors, such as economic integration, culture, religion, and others.[16] By investigating the changes in co-movements among the Mainland Chinese, Hong Kong and US stock markets before and after launching China–Hong Kong Stock Connect, Li and Chen contend that the Connect programme does not substantively enhance the daily price co-movements among the examined markets except between the Hong Kong–US markets.[17] The Shanghai and Shenzhen stock markets react severely to the new policy, while the response of the Hong Kong market is lukewarm.[18] Stock Connect affects the participant markets differently because of their distinct characteristics such as different investor structure, entry thresholds, and regulatory requirements.

[13] Su et al (2007), see n 9 above.

[14] J Shi et al, 'An Empirical Study on the Linkage and Causality between Stock Markets of Mainland and Hong Kong before and after American Financial Crisis' (2011) 26(2) *Statistics & Information Forum* 42.

[15] R Huo and AD Ahmed, 'Return and Volatility Spillovers Effects: Evaluating the Impact of Shanghai-Hong Kong Stock Connect' (2017) 61 *Economic Modelling* 260.

[16] RF Ma et al, 'Does Shanghai-Hong Kong Stock Connect Drive Market Comovement between Shanghai and Hong Kong: A New Evidence' (2019) 50 *North American Journal of Economics and Finance* 1, 2.

[17] S Li and Q Chen, 'Do the Shanghai–Hong Kong & Shenzhen–Hong Kong Stock Connect Programs Enhance Co-movement between the Mainland Chinese, Hong Kong, and US Stock Markets?' (2021) 26(2) *International Journal of Finance & Economics* 2871.

[18] YC Wang et al, 'The Influence of Shanghai-Hong Kong Stock Connect on the Mainland China and Hong Kong Stock Markets' (2016) 10(3) *International Journal of Business and Finance Research* 1.

In summary, although numerous studies in the literature have been devoted to investigating the influences of Stock Connect, the majority of the literature has been focused on the Chinese and Hong Kong markets and little investigation pertains to other connected markets such as London and Switzerland. Given the size and dynamism of the Chinese economy as well as the expansion of Stock Connect, China's connect programme will inevitably affect the global financial system, especially other participant markets. Instead, this chapter covers *all* Stock Connect links in order to present a comprehensive picture of how this whole programme influences local and global capital markets.

6.2. China–Hong Kong Stock Connect: Towards 'One Country, One Market'

There is an objective need for Mainland China to further raise the level of opening-up in order to adapt to the new international status quo. The active implementation of opening-up in the capital market will optimise the market structure as well as improve the quality and enhance the competitiveness of the capital market. This way, the capital market can better serve the real economy. As the second largest economy in the world, China has been relatively cautious in financial openness compared with its openness in the trade sector. China's approach to its financial liberalisation in past decades has been one of gradualism and experimentation,[19] whereas, in recent years, it has accelerated its liberalisation of capital accounts and gradually relaxed the regulation to allow foreign investors to enter its stock markets.

6.2.1. Broadening Mutual Market Access

Market access has always been an important issue for international companies and investors with an interest in the Chinese domestic capital market. Most observers still consider China to be an emerging financial market despite its huge size and potential (the Shanghai Stock Exchange (SSE) was the third-largest stock exchange in the world by market capitalisation in 2022).[20] This is partly due to the fact that China's securities markets are still much more tightly regulated than those in most developed countries, and foreign participation is strictly controlled.

On the investor side, it had previously been very difficult for overseas investors to trade Chinese stocks, bonds, derivatives and other financial instruments

[19] P Harrold, 'China's Reform Experience to Date' (1992), *World Bank discussion paper, WDP 180.*

[20] Eg JN Carpenter and RF Whitelaw, 'The Development of China's Stock Market and Stakes for the Global Economy' (2017) 9 *Annual Review of Financial Economics* 233; and C Lo, *Demystifying China's Mega Trends: The Driving Forces That Will Shake Up China and the World* (Bingley, Emerald Publishing, 2017), Ch 6 'Capital Account Liberalisation Realities versus Myths'.

as China set strict criteria for foreign investors who intended to acquire financial assets in China. The main reason was that the central government was wary of the stability of currency exchange rates relating to Renminbi (RMB) and the potential control of foreign capital over some Chinese companies in key sectors.[21] On the issuer side, no foreign companies were yet allowed to be listed on China's domestic stock exchanges. The initiative of an International Board on the SSE was raised in 2009 by the Shanghai government and its exploration was supported by the central government in its 12th Five-Year Plan for National Economic and Social Development, released in 2011. However, little progress has been observed so far.[22]

In the 1980s, 1990s and early 2000s, China's annual GDP growth frequently exceeded 10 per cent, propelling China to become the second largest economy in the world. China's economic growth was also associated with its ambition to integrate with the global economy. Meanwhile, more investment channels are needed to meet international investor demand for exposure to China's onshore stock markets. But for a long time, for inbound investment, foreign institutions were only allowed to invest in Chinese stock market through the Qualified Foreign Institutional Investor scheme (QFII), established in 2002, and after December 2011, through the Renminbi Qualified Foreign Institutional Investor (RQFII) scheme, but only with government-approval for selected institutional investors. For example, QFII only allowed some licensed international institutional investors (approximately 300) to enter the Chinese capital market, with a quota of up to USD 80 billion.[23] The quotas were granted by China's State Administration of Foreign Exchange (SAFE), and could be reviewed at any time in response to the country's current economic and financial conditions. The key difference between the QFII scheme and the RQFII scheme is that QFIIs remit foreign currency, which is then converted into RMB, whereas RQFIIs use offshore RMB.

For outbound investment, prior to the launch of Stock Connect, the Qualified Domestic Institutional Investors (QDII) scheme, established in 2006, was the only official channel for Chinese institutional investors to convert RMB into foreign currencies to buy overseas securities, but it was subject to the investment quota approved by the SAFE. While Mainland qualified institutional investors could directly invest overseas after obtaining QDII licences and the authorised quota, Mainland retail investors who wanted to invest in overseas markets could do so

[21] LR Lu and NY Ye, 'Shanghai-London Stock Connect: Operating Mechanism, Opportunities, and Challenges' (2019) 34 *Journal of International Banking and Financial Law* 684, 684.

[22] HKEX, 'Primary Equity Connect – A breakthrough Opportunity for Mainland-Hong Kong Mutual Market Connectivity and RMB Internationalisation' (August 2017), Research Report, availableat: www.hkex.com.hk/-/media/HKEX-Market/News/Research-Reports/HKEx-Research-Papers/2017/CCEO_Rpt(PEC)_201708_e.pdf?la=en.

[23] The quota was increased from USD 30 billion to USD 80 billion in 2012, and topping out at USD 300 billon in 2019. But it was finally removed in 2020. See the 'Regulations on Funds of Securities and Futures Investment by Foreign Institutional Investors' (PBOC & SAFE Announcement [2020] No 2) was jointly issued by the People's Bank of China (PBOC) and the State Administration of Foreign Exchange (SAFE) on 7 May 2020, available at: www.safe.gov.cn/en/2020/0507/1677.html (accessed on 12 December 2022).

through available QDII products. Later, the RMB Qualified Domestic Institutional Investor (RQDII) programme was promulgated in 2014 to allow Chinese institutional investors to invest in overseas RMB-denominated products using their own RMB funds. But this was soon suspended unofficially in late 2015, along with several other outbound schemes amid fears of 'capital flight' and worries of rapid RMB depreciation.[24] Although RQDII investment is not subject to any quota restrictions, it did not attract much market attention or interest because traditional RMB-denominated products were relatively limited in scope and size in the international market. Both the (R)QFII and (R)QDII schemes have undergone various reforms over the years as discussed in Chapter two, in particular QFII and RQFII have been converted into a single system – the Qualified Foreign Investor (QFI).

As the Chinese economy grew, investors and companies on both sides demanded a more efficient process, less restrictive rules, more flexibility and a safe channel through which to gain exposure to each other's markets. Due to the poor performance of QFII and QDII funds, the focus of Chinese market liberalisation has moved from institutional to retail investors to further encourage the outflow of domestic capital. As a major institutional innovation of the two-way opening-up of China's capital markets, the Stock Connect programme created a new mutual market model for cross-border securities investment in 2014, linking onshore markets and international investors, and vice versa. It furnishes Mainland investors with more opportunities to invest overseas and gives international investors greater access to the Mainland China markets.

Under the mutual market model, overseas products of interest to Mainland investors could be offered to the Mainland investors and vice versa for offering Mainland products of interest to global investors. Southbound trading opens up a regularised channel for Mainland investors, both individuals and institutions, to invest in overseas assets. As the eligible instruments under Stock Connect are expandable, this will offer an increasingly diversified scope of investment tools to Mainland investors. In addition, Southbound trading is effectively investment in a foreign currency, ie the Hong Kong dollar (HKD) which is pegged to the US dollar (USD), for Mainland investors. At a time of expected depreciation of the RMB, Southbound investment could offer a possibly better protection of investment returns in terms of currency value.[25]

Global investors also have an increasing appetite for investment in Chinese stocks through Northbound trading. Their investment is not limited to large-cap blue-chips but also includes smaller-sized stocks in various industries. Shenzhen

[24] Reuters, 'Update 1- China Bank Signals Resumption of RQDII Outbound Investment Scheme' (3 May 2018), available at: www.reuters.com/article/china-investment-rqdii-idINB9N1S000Q (accessed on 12 December 2022).

[25] HKEX, 'Stock Connect – Towards A 'Mutual Market' for the Interests of Mainland and Global Investors' (November 2016), 12, available at: www.hkex.com.hk/-/media/HKEX-Market/News/Research-Reports/HKEx-Research-Papers/2016/CCEO_Rpt(StkConnect)_201611.pdf?la=en (accessed on 12 December 2022).

Connect covers more small-sized stocks to meet the needs of both Mainland and global investors. In addition to investors, international issuers will not only get the full benefits of a listing in Hong Kong, but will also gain access to an enhanced and significant regional investor base.

6.2.2. Enhancement of Investor Base and Diversification of Investment

As discussed above, either QFI or (R)QDII is only a paralleled one-way investment channel for international or Chinese institutional investors to invest. In contrast to these two schemes, Stock Connect is a two-way cross-border investment channel for both individuals and institutions without aggregate quota. Stock Connect is a closed-loop system with prudential real-time monitoring of the usage of the Daily Quota, and yet with considerable flexibility in the absence of an aggregate quota. As the Daily Quota applies on a net-buy basis and is reset every day (once it is reached during the day, only cross-border sell orders of eligible securities are accepted), there is virtually no limitation of stock turnover during the day.[26] The mutual market under Stock Connect therefore effectively extends the universe of investable assets for Mainland and international investors, which could possibly offer investment opportunities with good potential returns to them.

Since the launch of Stock Connect, the scope of underlying stocks eligible for trading under Hong Kong Connect has been constantly expanding. In recent years, with the joint efforts of relevant parties, the Hong Kong-listed companies with a dual-class structure, the biotech companies, and the corresponding H-share companies of those issuing A+H-shares on the SSE Science and Technology Innovation Board (or STAR Market), as well as the exchange-traded funds (ETFs) and foreign company stocks have been included within the scope of underlying stocks eligible for Southbound trading under Hong Kong Connect.[27]

On 27 May 2022, the China Securities Regulatory Commission (CSRC) and the Hong Kong Securities and Futures Commission (SFC) jointly announced the launch of the trading of eligible ETFs in Stock Connect commencing on 4 July 2022.[28] Since then, Chinese and Hong Kong investors have been able to

[26] HKEX, 'CES Stock Connect Hong Kong Select 100 Index-A Key Measure of Hong Kong Market Investment under Stock Connect' (November 2017), 3, Research Report, available at: www.hkex.com.hk/-/media/HKEX-Market/News/Research-Reports/HKEx-ResearchPapers/2017/CES_SCHK100(201711)_e.pdf?la=en (accessed on 12 December 2022).

[27] SZSE, 'Q&A on the Expansion of Scope of Underlying Stocks Eligible for Trading Under Chinese Mainland-Hong Kong Stock Connect Mechanisms' (21 December 2022), available at: www.szse.cn/English/about/news/szse/t20221221_597925.html (accessed on 3 January 2023).

[28] CSRC, 'Joint Announcement of the China Securities Regulatory Commission and the Hong Kong Securities and Futures Commission' (27 May 2022), available at: www.csrc.gov.cn/csrc_en/c102030/c3046291/content.shtml (accessed on 3 January 2023).

trade eligible ETFs listed on each other's exchanges through local brokers. The Hong Kong Exchanges and Clearing Limited (HKEX) has published an initial list of eligible ETFs for Northbound trading which will be updated from time to time, and has also published amendments to the Rules of the Exchange for the purpose of facilitating the inclusion of eligible ETFs listed on the SSE and the Shenzhen Stock Exchange (SZSE) as eligible securities for Northbound trading under Stock Connect. But certain regulatory requirements applicable to the trading of A-shares may not apply to the trading of ETFs. For example, disclosures of interest in shares and the short-swing profit rule applicable to A-share trading would not apply to trading in ETFs. In addition, overseas investors' indirect holdings in the A-shares constituting an ETF will not be counted towards the foreign ownership limits applicable to A-shares.[29]

The inclusion of ETFs is noteworthy because it reflects the global trend towards passive investing, and provides more investment opportunities and convenience for Chinese and global investors. 83 onshore and four Hong Kong-listed ETFs were included on the Northbound and Southbound Stock Connect, respectively, with Northbound-eligible ETFs accounting for 73 per cent of market capitalisation and 58 per cent of turnover on the Mainland China ETF market, while the Southbound eligible ETFs covered 57 per cent of aggregate assets under management ETFs listed in Hong Kong.[30]

In addition to the inclusion of ETFs, the China–Hong Kong Connect keeps broadening the scope of qualifying equities as discussed in Chapter two. On 19 December 2022, to further deepen mutual stock market access between China and Hong Kong and promote the development of both capital markets, the CSRC and the SFC reached a consensus that the stock exchanges on both sides would further expand the scope of eligible stocks under Stock Connect.[31]

Specifically, the scope of eligible stocks for Northbound trading under Stock Connect will be changed to (1) constituent stocks of the SSE A-Share Index and the SZSE Composite Index which have a market capitalisation of RMB 5 billion or above and which meet certain requirements such as liquidity criteria; and (2) SSE/SZSE-listed stocks of companies which have issued both A-shares and H-shares.

Southbound trading is expanded to include stocks of international companies that are primary-listed in Hong Kong and meet relevant criteria, while the existing scope of other underlying stocks eligible for the same will remain unchanged.

[29] With respect to the trading of A-shares (under Northbound Stock Connect and other channels such as Qualified Foreign Investor (QFI)), the shareholding of a single foreign investor in a listed company is not allowed to exceed 10% of the company's total issued shares, and the aggregate shareholdings of all foreign investors in the A-shares of a listed company is not allowed to exceed 30% of its total issued shares. A-shares constituting an ETF and held by overseas investors under ETF Connect will not be counted towards these limits.

[30] HKEX (October 2022), see n 1 above, 6.

[31] SFC, 'Joint announcement of the China Securities Regulatory Commission and the Hong Kong Securities and Futures Commission' (19 December 2022), available at: www.sfc.hk/en/News-and-announcements/Policy-statements-and-announcements/Joint-announcement-of-the-CSRC-and-SFC-Dec-2022 (accessed on 3 January 2023).

The specific criteria are that the stocks of such foreign companies are (1) constituent stocks of the Hang Seng Composite LargeCap Index or Hang Seng Composite MidCap Index, or (2) constituent stocks of the Hang Seng Composite SmallCap Index with a market capitalisation of HKD 5 billion or above. In addition, the scope of eligible stocks for Southbound trading under Shanghai–Hong Kong Stock Connect will be expanded to include constituents of the Hang Seng Composite SmallCap Index with a market capitalisation of HKD 5 billion or above, which will align with the existing scope of eligible stocks for Southbound trading under the Shenzhen–Hong Kong Stock Connect. After obtaining the consent from the CSRC and the SFC, the stock exchanges will set out the specific requirements for the inclusion of eligible stocks, adjustment mechanism etc.

The latest expansion is a game-changer for Mainland Chinese retail investors to purchase foreign equities in Hong Kong for the first time ever. It would make Hong Kong's listing platform more alluring to foreign issuers seeking to access the enormous pools of cash on the Mainland. In turn, it provides international investors access to an extra 3,000 stocks listed in Shanghai and Shenzhen through Hong Kong Connect. By the end of 2020, Mainland investors owned a total of RMB 205 trillion (USD 29.35 trillion) worth of financial assets. The volume is anticipated to increase by a compound annual growth rate (CAGR) of 10 per cent by 2025, reaching an estimated RMB 328 trillion (USD 46.96 trillion).[32] The addition of foreign firms will give investors new choices for diversification in addition to the wide variety of already available international products at HKEX, such as the MSCI futures product suite with underlying products from a broad range of Asian and emerging markets. This promotes effective risk management and the overall soundness of the local and international financial systems.

As appraised by Laura M Cha, HKEX Chairman, the new expansion is another exciting milestone for the Stock Connect programme,

> providing Mainland investors with more opportunities to invest overseas and enabling international investors to enjoy wider access to the Mainland China markets. This latest enhancement to Stock Connect will help boost the healthy development of both Mainland China and Hong Kong financial markets by bringing new connectivity, liquidity and vibrancy.[33]

6.2.3. Cross-border Investment Flow

Stock Connect has integrated Mainland China's markets more closely into the global financial system, with Hong Kong acting as the primary gateway. More than

[32] China Briefing, 'Mainland China and Hong Kong to Expand their Stock Connect Scheme' (23 December 2022), available at: www.china-briefing.com/news/mainland-china-and-hong-kong-to-expand-their-stock-connect-scheme/ (accessed on 3 January 2023).

[33] HKEX, 'HKEX Welcomes Further Expansion of Stock Connect' (19 December 2022), available at: www.hkex.com.hk/News/News-Release/2022/2212192news?sc_lang=en (accessed on 3 January 2023).

that, the innovative, pioneering Stock Connect programmes have made China accessible as an asset class, provided new diversification opportunities for the sizeable investor base in Mainland China, facilitated two-way capital flow between China and the world, and paved the way for Chinese assets to be included in key global benchmarks such as the MSCI Emerging Market Index and Bloomberg Barclays Global Bond Aggregate. FTSE Russell, for the first time in its history, included A-share stocks in its global equity benchmarks in June 2019. China A-shares now constitute approximately six per cent of the Financial Times Stock Exchange (FTSE) Emerging Index, which is tracked by around USD 140 billion in investor assets.[34]

From the Chinese central government's website, global investors have shown increasing interest in pursuing RMB-denominated assets to diversity their investment portfolios over the past few years. From 2018 to 2021, the total net increase in the holdings of Chinese domestic stocks and bonds by global investors exceeded USD 700 billion, with an annual growth rate of 34 per cent.[35] And it's a similar picture for onshore investors, who had increased their overseas investments from RMB 4.9 trillion in 2014 to an estimated RMB 22.8 trillion at the end of 2021.[36] In 2021, the cross-border RMB settlement under the capital account totalled RMB 36.61 trillion with a year-on-year increase of 29 per cent, of which receipts and payments stood at RMB 18.51 trillion and RMB 18.10 trillion respectively.[37] The direct investments, portfolio investments and cross-border financing accounted for 17.7 per cent, 76.4 per cent and 4.3 per cent of the total settlement under the capital account respectively.

The accessibility of China's equity market has greatly improved recently, as the country ramped up efforts to upgrade the Shanghai–Hong Kong and Shenzhen–Hong Kong Stock Connect schemes and promote the steady increase of A-shares' proportion in global equity indices. Looking at China–Hong Kong Stock Connect alone (Figure 6.1), total trade value (buy and sell) on the Northbound and Southbound channels has grown over the years, with Northbound total trading growing from HKD 193 billion in 2014 to HKD 24.54 trillion in 2022, and with Southbound total trading increasing from HKD 26 billion to 6.35 trillion in 2022. The total trading values of Northbound and Southbound trading have increased 127 times and 244 times during the 10-year period since the launch of Stock Connect.

[34] FTSE Russell, 'FTSE Russell Completes Landmark Inclusion of China A Shares' (22 June 2020), available at: www.ftserussell.com/press/ftse-russell-completes-landmark-inclusion-china-shares (accessed on 12 December 2022).

[35] China's State Council, 'RMB Assets Show Growing Appeal for Global Investors' (7 June 2022), available at: english.www.gov.cn/news/topnews/202206/07/content_WS629f46d8c6d02e533532bd04.html (accessed on 12 December 2022).

[36] HKEX (October 2022), see n 1 above, 5.

[37] PBOC, '2022 RMB Internationalisation Report' (26 September 2022), 3, available at: www.gov.cn/xinwen/2022-09/24/5711660/files/003e0bd04d4742a5a06869fdc37ea8c8.pdf (accessed on 3 January 2023).

Figure 6.1 Total Trade Value on China-Hong Kong Stock Connect 2014–2022

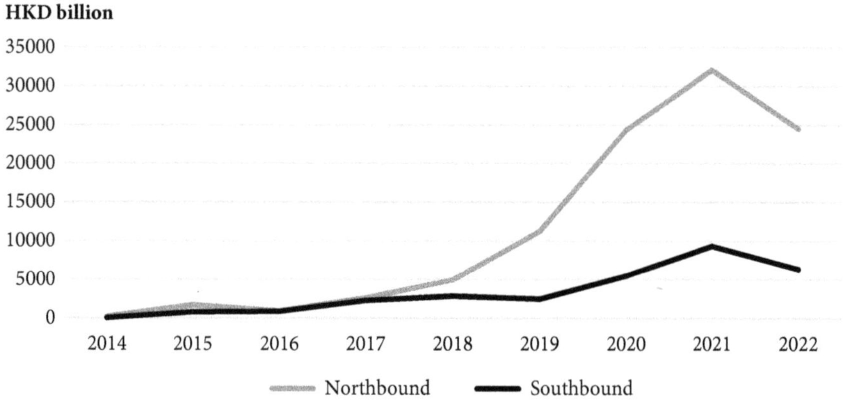

Source: HKEX, 'Annual Market Statistics' (2014–2022).

6.2.4. Institutional Reforms

As discussed in Chapter three, a fundamental principle of Stock Connect is that 'home market rules' – that is the laws and rules of the home market of the applicable securities – shall apply to investors in such securities. This principle avoids the need to significantly alter home rules and regulations, which could be a very lengthy process. For instance, with respect to purchasing Chinese Stock Connect securities, China is the home market and thus its law applies. Conversely, Chinese investors trading foreign securities via Stock Connect should refer predominantly to the destination market laws such as the laws of Hong Kong, the UK and Switzerland.[38]

In order to implement the 'home market rules', China has made efforts to incorporate Stock Connect into its legal system, for instance, the new Chinese Securities Law 2019,[39] the amended Stock Connect Rules and many initiatives in regulatory enforcement between China and other regulators.[40] Article 2 of the new Chinese Securities Law 2019 defines securities to encompass stocks, bonds, depository receipts (DRs), asset management products, investment funds and other securities of similar nature. DRs as part of Stock Connect products have been embedded into the Securities Law for the first time. The expanded coverage of the Securities Law is intended to resolve the previous inconsistency between the old Securities Law and the Stock Connect rules.

[38] F Huang, 'Stock Connect: Integration, Internationalisation and Implementation' (2021) 7 *Journal of Business Law* 558, 569–70.

[39] The first Chinese Securities Law was enacted in 1998 and then amended four times in 2005, 2013, 2014 and 2019. The New Chinese Securities Law came into force on 1 March 2020.

[40] F Huang (2021), see n 38 above, 559. Chinese regulatory cooperation and enforcement with other regulators have been examined in Chapter 5.

Another issue for investors using Stock Connect is whether investors have any proprietary rights or beneficial ownership in the shares. Under the Stock Connect trading scheme, SSE/SZSE-listed shares are held in a separate account controlled by the Hong Kong Securities Clearing Company (HKSCC) on behalf of investors. This raises concerns about the ambiguity of share ownership, since the securities are neither HKSCC's assets nor owned by the investors. In other words, foreign investors are concerned about whether they have any proprietary rights to or beneficial ownership of shares in Chinese companies under Chinese law. Under Hong Kong's law, it is well established that HKSCC holds the shares on trust for investors and investors thus would undoubtedly have beneficial ownership.[41] Such rights include, among others, the right to call shareholders' meetings, to exercise voting rights, to subscribe for allocated rights and entitlements, and to receive dividends and distributions, which are all substantive rights normally enjoyed by beneficial owners of shares. The remaining question then is whether Chinese law contains comparable provisions for such ownership. Unlike the common law system, China, with a civil law system, has traditionally not contained equitable ownership and trust concepts.[42]

The notion of 'nominee holder' was first introduced into the CSRC's 'Administrative Measures for the Securities Registration and Settlement of Securities' 2006 (Settlement Measures).[43] This provision establishes the legal basis upon which QFII/RQFII asset managers hold A-shares (as the nominee holders) for their investors (the beneficial owners). In response to the concerns arising from the market, the CSRC further released 'FAQ on Beneficial Ownership' in 2015 and 'Q&A Regarding Certain Provisions on Stock Connect between the Mainland and Hong Kong Stock Markets' in 2016 to recognise the concepts of 'nominee holder' and 'beneficial ownership' under Chinese laws.[44]

Article 18 of the Settlement Measures stipulates that 'securities shall be recorded in the accounts of the securities holders, unless laws, administrative regulations or CSRC rules prescribe that the securities shall be recorded in accounts opened in the name of nominee holders'.[45] Hence, the Settlement Measures

[41] General Rules 824 (Chapter 8) of the Hong Kong Central Clearing and Settlement System stipulates that HKSCC as the nominee holder to provide services to the relevant Chinese authority/Chinese clearing house.

[42] P Jiang, *Zhongmei Wuquanfa de Xianzhuang yu Fazhan* (*The Presence and Development of Sino-US Property Law*) (Tsinghua University Press, 2003), 20; and M Chang, 'Hugangtong Mingyi Chiyou Gupiao Falv Wenti Chutan' ('Discussion on Beneficial Ownership under Shanghai-Hong Kong Stock Connect') (2015) *Company Law Review* 109, 116.

[43] Article 18 of CSRC's Administrative Measures for the Securities Registration and Settlement (re-issued and effective as of 20 November 2009).

[44] CSRC, 'FAQ on Beneficial Ownership' (15 May 2015), available at: www.csrc.gov.cn/csrc_en/c102035/c1371508/content.shtml (accessed on 10 January 2023) and 'Q&A regarding Certain Provisions on Stock Connect between the Mainland and Hong Kong Stock Markets' (27 October 2016), available at: www.csrc.gov.cn/csrc_en/c102035/c1371506/content.shtml (accessed on 10 January 2023).

[45] The Settlement Measures was promulgated by the CSRC on 7 April 2006 and revised a few times 20 November 2009, 7 December 2017, 15 August 2018 and 20 June 2022, respectively.

expressly provide for the concept of nominee shareholding. Meanwhile, Article 13 of the 'Certain Provisions on Stock Connect between the Mainland and Hong Kong Stock Markets' 2016 (Certain Provisions) states that, among other things,

> investors are entitled to the rights and interests of the securities acquired through the Northbound Trading Links of the Stock Connect between the Mainland and Hong Kong Stock Markets. … Securities acquired through the Northbound Trading Links shall be registered in the name of HKSCC …[46]

Hence, it has been set out explicitly that in Northbound trading, overseas investors shall hold Stock Connect securities in the name of HKSCC and enjoy the proprietary interests of shareholders.

The overseas investors as beneficial owners of Connect securities could exercise their shareholder rights under the Hong Kong law. Pursuant to the Central Clearing and Settlement System (CCASS) Rules and the CCASS Operational Procedures issued by HKSCC, beneficial owners of Connect securities shall exercise their rights over Connect securities through HKSCC, which is the nominee holder, covering the right to call and participate in shareholders' meetings, the right to propose matters for voting at shareholders' meetings, the right to exercise voting rights at shareholders' meetings and the right to receive dividends and the distribution of earnings from investment, among others.

On the Hong Kong side, the launch of Stock Connect provides an important catalyst in further strengthening the importance of Hong Kong as a capital raising centre. In September 2014, Alibaba debuted its IPO on the New York Stock Exchange (NYSE), raising a total of USD 25 billion and becoming the largest initial public offering (IPO) in history, prior to Saudi Aramco's USD 29.4 billion listing in 2019. The decision to list in the US was taken because Hong Kong did not permit weighted voting right (WVR) structures and, Hong Kong having lost out on Alibaba's IPO, the issue on whether to allow companies with such structures to list on HKEX reignited. Following this, on 18 June 2014, the Financial Services Development Council (FSDC) of Hong Kong published 'Positioning Hong Kong as an International IPO Centre of Choice' and suggested that WVR should be introduced, noting that modifications and partial relaxations might be appropriate and that regulators should keep an open mind to ensure the Hong Kong market is up to date.[47] The concept of proportionality between the voting power and equity interest of shareholders, commonly known as the 'one-share, one-vote' principle, is an important aspect of investor protection. It helps align controlling shareholders'

[46] The Certain Provisions were issued by the CSRC on 30 September 2016 and came effective on the same day. A full text in Chinese is available at CSRC's website: www.csrc.gov.cn/csrc/c106256/c1654020/1654020/files/6dc3bca009924c9ba18e72b62f1869ed.pdf (accessed on 10 January 2023).

[47] FSDC, 'Positioning Hong Kong as an International IPO Centre of Choice' (June 2014), *FSDC Paper No 09*, available at: www.fsdc.org.hk/media/jg1hulyd/ipo4-2-final-17-6-2014.pdf (accessed on 10 January 2023).

interests with those of other shareholders, and makes it possible for incumbent management to be removed, if they underperform, by those with the largest equity interest in the issuer. In contrast, WVR (also called 'dual class shares') offers additional classes of shares that provide holders with greater voting rights, which has been long criticised for violating the 'one share, one vote' principle and destroying shareholder democracy. Despite the debates, WVR are likely to persist and succeed in many jurisdictions, and have been widely adopted in technology companies such as Google, Groupon, Meta Platforms (formerly Facebook), Alibaba, and Meituan.[48]

HKEX consulted the market in February 2018 on proposed amendments to its Listing Rules to expand the original listing regime to facilitate the listing of companies from emerging and innovation sectors.[49] The goal of this reform was to strategically enhance Hong Kong's position as a hub for technology and biotech firms looking to raise capital, and enable it to become a truly international IPO centre. As part of the 2018 reforms, the HKEX added three new chapters in the Main Board Listing Rules and made consequential changes to the current Rules: (a) Chapter 18A permits listings of biotech issuers that do not meet any of the Main Board financial eligibility tests; (b) Chapter 8A permits listings of companies with WVR structures; and (c) Chapter 19C establishes a new concessionary secondary listing route for Greater China[50] and international companies that wish to secondary list in Hong Kong. Since the new listing rules were introduced in 2020, 51 of the total 154 IPOs were new economy companies, raising HKD 257.4 billion, accounting for 64 per cent of IPO funds raised in the Hong Kong market, compared with 49 per cent in both 2018 and 2019.[51] On 31 March 2021, the market capitalisation of new economy companies listed on HKEX since the new listing regime took effect totalled HKD 14.45 trillion, accounting for 27 per cent of Hong Kong's total market capitalisation. HKEX also welcomed 13 'homecoming' secondary listings under Chapter 19C in the same period, raising a total of HKD 285.8 billion.[52]

China's regulators have also taken a further step towards the broadening of the Stock Connect share trading scheme with Hong Kong after Hong Kong revised its listing rules permitting WVR shares eligible through the trading link.

[48] For the debates on WVR and the worldwide application of WVR, see F Huang, 'Dual Class Shares Around the Top Global Financial Centres' [2017] *Journal of Business Law* 137.

[49] HKEX, 'Hong Kong's Listing Regime Enters New Era, Featuring Emerging and Innovative Firms' (24 April 2018), available at: www.hkex.com.hk/News/RegulatoryAnnouncements/2018/180424news?sc_lang=en (accessed on 10 January 2023).

[50] Greater China being the Chinese Mainland along with Hong Kong, Macau and Taiwan.

[51] HKEX, 'Celebrating the 3rd Anniversary of HKEX's new Listing Regime' (15 June 2021), available at: www.hkex.com.hk/News/Media-Centre/Special/HKEX-Celebrates-Third-Anniversary-of-New-Listing-Regime?sc_lang=en (accessed on 20 December 2022).

[52] ibid.

On 2 August 2019, the HKEX, the SSE and SZSE reached consensus on the criteria for Hong Kong-listed companies with WVR to be included for the first time in Southbound Trading of Stock Connect.[53] Subsequently, the SSE and SZSE revised the 'Measures of the Shanghai Stock Exchange for the Implementation of the Shanghai–Hong Kong Stock Connect' and 'Measures of the Shenzhen Stock Exchange for the Implementation of the Shenzhen–Hong Kong Stock Connect' respectively and conducted public market consultations.[54]

The relevant amendments specify that the stocks of companies listed on the HKEX with WVR structures (except for the H-shares of A+H listed companies) have to satisfy not only the existing conditions for the inclusion of their shares in the Southbound trading of Stock Connect, but also the following conditions at the time of their initial inclusion in the same:

(1) have been listed for six months and been traded on the HKEX for 20 trading days;
(2) reach the daily average market capitalisation of no less than HKD 20 billion and a total volume of transactions on the Hong Kong stock market of no less than HKD 6 billion during the 183-day period prior to the date of assessment (inclusive); and
(3) compliance conditions, ie after the stock listing, the issuer and the WVR beneficiaries must not have been publicly condemned by the HKEX, been publicly sanctioned in any other way or triggered the termination of WVR as a result of any violation of the regulations on corporate governance, information disclosure and investor protection measures.[55]

To conclude, Stock Connect is the biggest step towards integrating the stock markets of Mainland China and Hong Kong. It creates a single 'China' stock market that ranks as one of the biggest in the world measured by market capitalisation and daily trading turnover. Stock Connect has opened-up mutual market access and provided more opportunities for domestic and international investors with fewer restrictions than previous channels like QDII and QFI. Statistics show that there is a strongly growing cross-border flow and holding of RMB-denominated assets. For international investors, the continued expansion of the programme adds more than 3,000 companies to the investable universe. These moves help diversify the portfolios of Chinese investors, increase efficiencies for trading in Chinese

[53] HKEX, 'HKEX Welcomes Public Consultation by SSE and SZSE on WVR-Related Rules Changes) (2 August 2019), available at: www.hkex.com.hk/News/News-Release/2019/1908022news?sc_lang=en (accessed on 20 December 2022).

[54] The two measures are constantly revised and the most recent versions are dated 2022.

[55] Art 67 of SSE's 'Measures of the Shanghai Stock Exchange for the Implementation of the Shanghai-Hong Kong Stock Connect' of 2022 and art 66 of SZSE's 'Measures of the Shenzhen Stock Exchange for the Implementation of the Shenzhen-Hong Kong Stock Connect' of 2022.

companies, and increase the inclusion of Chinese shares in global benchmark stock indices. Apart from the integration of Chinese and Hong Kong markets, Stock Connect also promotes institutional reforms to minimise the regulatory gaps in both jurisdictions.

6.3. Hong Kong as a Superconnector between East and West

Hong Kong's traditional role has been as a trading and market entrepôt linking China and the rest of the world in the mid-nineteenth century. Since then it has taken a developmental route of its own, flourishing first as an entrepôt and a centre of commerce and finance for Chinese business, then as an industrial city, and subsequently as a regional and international financial centre.[56] Its location in the South Asian Pacific region makes it well placed as a transport and trade hub. Trade activities in Hong Kong are also supported by its no-tariff regime. Following Deng Xiaoping's historic visit to Shenzhen in 1992, Hong Kong's capital market went on to play a privotal role in Chinese overseas listings, starting in 1993, which paved the way for enormous investment in China's economy and the growth of China's own capital markets. 1 July 1997 marked the official transfer of sovereignty over Hong Kong from Britain to China, and Hong Kong became a Special Administrative Region (SAR) of China. Since then, the socio-economic integration of Hong Kong and Mainland China has been an ongoing process. In 1993 HKEX revealed its intention to become the 'Manhattan of China' by playing a bigger role in raising equity funds for China's economic development.[57] It envisioned China remaining HKEX's main source of growth.

With its image as a robust financial market, largely thanks to the institutions inherited from its colonial era, Hong Kong is able to attract a number of financial activities from China and has firmly established itself as a leading international financial centre.[58] The Hong Kong government has sought to maintain a 'big market, small government' approach, allowing businesses to thrive. The government imposes a low and straightforward tax regime, with one of the lowest tax rates in the world. Hong Kong is consistently ranked among the top five global financial centres, supported by its robust ecosystem which provides a conducive

[56] For an overview of capital market development in Hong Kong, see F Huang and H Yeung, *Chinese Companies and the Hong Kong Stock Market* (Abington, Routledge, 2014), 46.

[57] *South China Morning Post*, 'The Risk Behind Mainland Firms' (20 June 1993), available at: www.scmp.com/article/33937/risk-behind-mainland-firms (20 July 2022).

[58] H Yeung and F Huang, '"One Country, Two Systems" as Bedrock of Hong Kong's Continued Success: Fiction or Reality?' (2015) 38(2) *Boston College International & Comparative Law Review* 191.

environment for companies to do business, a sound regulatory framework, deep and diverse capital markets, strong talent bases, and accessibility to the Asia-Pacific region.[59]

In recent years, Hong Kong's role as a superconnector, an extension of its entrepôt function, has developed as China's economy and need for capital continues to grow. The pivotal role Hong Kong continues to play as an international financial centre makes it the superconnector for international businesses to access mainland China markets and opportunities. In March 2022, HKEX articulated its vision to build the 'Marketplace of the Future', underpinned by three strategic pillars: 'Connecting China and the World, Connecting Capital with Opportunities and Connecting Today with Tomorrow.'[60] These three initiatives are significant foundational pillars for Hong Kong's status of international financial centre and the city's global role as an East/West superconnector.

Although Hong Kong has one of the most active stock markets in the world, Chinese companies account for a substantial portion of the Hong Kong-listed market. As shown in Table 6.1, Hong Kong is among the world's largest stock markets in terms of IPO fundraising and market capitalisation. It has been ranked top IPO venue globally for seven of the past 14 years.[61] It also is the favoured platform of Mainland corporations raising funds and the window for international investors seeking exposure to the fast-growing Mainland markets. Even during the global pandemic in 2020, the Hong Kong IPO market achieved a historic high in terms of global funds raised of USD 51.28 trillion, ranking second globally. The number of companies listed on HKEX's Main Board has grown from 812 in 2002 to 2,257 in 2022, approximately a threefold increase.[62]

According to KPMG's 2022 report, global markets had seen a drop in IPO activities in 2022, with the number of deals and total proceeds falling by around 50 per cent and 60 per cent, respectively.[63] This has been led by declines in major stock exchanges: proceeds from IPOs in the US stock exchanges dropped by over 90 per cent. However, Mainland China and Hong Kong IPO markets performed relatively well amid a broader environment of geopolitical and economic uncertainty.

[59] Hong Kong ranked 3rd and 4th in the Global Financial Centres Index in 2021 and 2022, respectively. See Z/Yen Group, 'The Global Financial Centre Index 32' (September 2022), available at: www.longfinance.net/media/documents/GFCI_32_Report_2022.09.22_v1.0_.pdf (accessed on 15 December 2022).

[60] HKEX, 'HKEX in 2022: Year in Review' (20 December 2022), available at: www.hkex.com.hk/News/News-Release/2022/221220news?sc_lang=en (accessed on 4 January 2023).

[61] Hong Kong ranked 1st in 2009–11, 2015–16 and 2018–19. See HKEX's website, 'We are a World Leading IPO Venue', available at: www.hkex.com.hk/Join-Our-Market/IPO/Listing-with-HKEX?sc_lang=en (accessed on 3 January 2023).

[62] HKEX, 'Hong Kong and Mainland Market Highlights', available at: www.hkex.com.hk/Mutual-Market/Stock-Connect/Statistics/Hong-Kong-and-Mainland-Market-Highlights?sc_lang=en#select3=0&select2=0&select1=16 (accessed on 5 January 2023).

[63] KPMG, 'Hong Kong is Set to Regain Top-three IPO Ranking in 2022' (8 December 2022), available at: home.kpmg/cn/en/home/media/press-releases/2022/12/hong-kong-is-set-to-regain-top-three-ipo-ranking-in-2022-says-kpmg-china.html (accessed on 5 January 2023).

HKEX ranked third globally in terms of total funds raised while the top two rankings were taken by China's SSE and SZSE in 2022.[64] The A-share market was the key driver for the global IPO market in 2022, accounting for nearly half of total proceeds.

However, some observers worry that Hong Kong will be turned into a 'one-dimensional market' as the high level of reliance placed on Chinese companies may undermine the HKEX's status as an 'international' market and its long-term development.[65] In the 2000s, China-related stocks including H-share, red chip and Mainland private enterprises accounted for around 50 per cent of the market capitalisation and over 60 per cent of the equity turnover value of all Hong Kong listings (Main Board and Growth Enterprise Market combined).[66] But in the recent years from 2017 to 2022, the ratio of China-related stocks on the Hong Kong market had slightly decreased to around 30 per cent, as appears in Table 6.1. While Hong Kong continues to benefit from its position as China's gateway to the world (and the world's gateway to China), the regulators have made significant efforts to reform the listing rules as discussed above so as to diversity their client base and actively open-up to quality companies from all the world.

Table 6.1 Market Capitalisation and IPOs of Hong Kong's Equity Market (2017–22)

Year	Number of IPOs	IPO Equity Funds Raised (USD million)	Global IPO Fundraising Ranking	Market Capitalisation (USD million)	China-related Stocks (% of HK Market)	Largest Stock Exchanges in the World
2022	73	31,864	3	4,550,262	29.69 %	7
2021	98	42,297	4	5,405,968	27.06 %	5
2020	154	51,279	2	6,060,750	23.65 %	4
2019	183	40,055	1	4,867,166	31.18 %	4
2018	218	36,563	1	3,801,215	38.06 %	5
2017	174	49,346	3	4,11,890	37.03 %	7

Sources: Data from HKEX and the World Federation of Exchange.

Apart from being a connector between China and the world through capital markets, Hong Kong has also already developed itself into a leading offshore Renminbi (RMB) centre in the world. From both geographical and strategic points

[64] ibid.
[65] FSDC (June 2014), see n 47 above, 6.
[66] HKEX, 'China Dimension', available at: www.hkex.com.hk/Market-Data/Statistics/Consolidated-Reports/China-Dimension?sc_lang=en#select1=0&select2=2 (accessed on 5 January 2023).

of view, Hong Kong has maintained its competitive edge with the largest pool of liquidity from retail and wholesale RMB deposits and financial products in RMB. RMB business in Hong Kong began in 2004 after China's Central Bank, the People's Bank of China (PBOC), and the Hong Kong Monetary Authority (HKMA) signed a Memorandum of Understanding in November 2003 which allowed Hong Kong banks to conduct RMB business for individuals.[67]

The introduction of the pilot scheme for RMB cross-border trade settlement in July 2009 was a watershed as RMB business in Hong Kong moved into its second stage of development. It expanded from serving personal customers to enterprises and institutions, and transformed from just one-way repatriation of RMB cash to two-way flows of RMB, marking a crucial step forward to the internationalisation of RMB. With the deepening of the use of RMB in cross-border trade and investment activities since 2009, there have been more and more bridges linking the onshore and offshore markets, enabling RMB to be increasingly used, circulated and accumulated in overseas markets.[68] In 2012, the access to the cross-border RMB settlement of the trade in goods was extended to the whole nation.

The course of RMB to becoming an international currency is the course for it to be extensively used in global trade settlement, cross-border investment and national reserves.[69] Before the implementation of Stock Connect, Chinese government and media promoted the expected benefits, such as increasing new volumes of international investment into the SSE, increased integration of China's capital markets into the global economy, providing investors from both sides with greater access to a broader range of equities and enhancing Hong Kong's role as an offshore RMB trading hub.[70] However, there are also uncertainties including tax, legal, and operational issues that may lead some investors to delay their full participation. In order to increase the usage of RMB under the capital account by global participants and to provide greater convenience for cross-border investment and finance in RMB, China still needs a bridge to effectively connect the domestic and international markets before achieving the full convertibility of the RMB.

The Stock Connect programme between Mainland China and Hong Kong is warmly welcomed by international investors and is helpful to further develop an important platform in Hong Kong to offer RMB-denominated assets as well

[67] HKMA, 'Hong Kong as offshore Renminbi Centre-Past and Prospects' (18 February 2014), available at: www.hkma.gov.hk/eng/news-and-media/insight/2014/02/20140218/ (accessed on 3 January 2023).

[68] When the Renminbi trade settlement pilot scheme was launched in 2009, it only covered five Mainland cities (Shanghai, Guangzhou, Shenzhen, Zhuhai and Dongguan), and many operational arrangements, such as tax rebates for exporters, were not yet in place.

[69] ibid.

[70] Y Bai and D Chow, 'Shanghai-Hong Kong Stock Connect: An Analysis of Chinese Partial Stock Market Liberalisation Impact on the Local and Foreign Markets' (2017) 50 *Journal of International Financial Markets, Institutions & Money* 182, 183.

as promote the process of RMB internationalisation. It gives international investors direct access to A-shares denominated in RMB, resulting in a significant broadening of the currency's use among an investor base beyond China's borders. The scheme is designed to ensure that RMB which is used to trade SSE/SZSE shares via the programme cannot be used for other purposes: Stock Connect is sealed from the rest of China's market. When a position acquired through Stock Connect is sold, the RMB is returned to the seller in Hong Kong, thus preventing RMB acquired for Stock Connect purchases from being redeployed for other purposes in China.[71]

Currently Hong Kong offers the largest number and scope of RMB securities and derivatives products among world exchanges outside Mainland China. Offshore RMB services in Hong Kong now embrace RMB retail and corporate banking, RMB capital markets, RMB money and FX market and RMB insurance. These services are supported by the formation of a large RMB liquidity pool, and together are conducive to the development of a wide range of RMB products. In terms of financial infrastructure, the connectivity scheme is a major step taken by the Chinese government in financial liberalisation for retail investors and the broader scheme of RMB internationalisation. The Connect scheme covers equities, bonds and ETFs, along with an efficient, globally integrated financial infrastructure for cross-border RMB payment and settlement. With all these advantages, Hong Kong can better serve the needs of Chinese and global issuers and investors through further enhancements and innovations of RMB products and services.[72]

On July 2022, the PBOC and HKMA executed an agreement to upgrade the monetary swap agreement, first entered in 2009, to a long-standing swap arrangement with no need for renewal. Its size has also been expanded from RMB 500 billion / HKD 590 billion to RMB 800 billion / HKD 940 billion. On this basis, Hong Kong will further enhance the RMB Liquidity Facility, including increasing the size and streamlining the operation, to support the continued development of Hong Kong's offshore RMB market. Eddie Yue, Chief Executive of the HKMA, commented:

> Enhancing the Currency Swap Agreement with the PBOC and the HKMA's RMB Liquidity Facility will ensure the availability of ample RMB liquidity in Hong Kong as an offshore RMB market, further reinforcing Hong Kong's unique edge and leading position in developing our offshore RMB business.[73]

[71] ASIFMA, 'The Through Train: Stock Connect's Impact and Future' (December 2014), 11, available at: www.asifma.org/wp-content/uploads/2018/05/asifma-tr-stock-connect-white-paper.pdf (accessed on 1 December 2022).

[72] HKEX, 'Leveraging Hong Kong as an Offshore Renminbi Centre for Advancing Renminbi Internationalisation' (18 March 2021), 1, Research Report.

[73] HKMA, 'Enhanced Currency Swap Agreement between People's Bank of China and Hong Kong Monetary Authority' (4 July 2022), press release, available at: www.hkma.gov.hk/eng/news-and-media/press-releases/2022/07/20220704-5/ (accessed on 1 December 2022).

On 13 December 2022 HKEX introduced a new HKD–RMB Dual Counter Model in its securities market, further supporting the listing, trading and settlement of RMB counters in Hong Kong.[74] Under the proposed Model, investors will be able to interchange securities listed in both HKD and RMB counters, following enhancements to be made to existing trading and settlement arrangements. To support the liquidity of RMB counters and minimise price discrepancies between the two counters, HKEX also introduced a new Dual Counter Market Making Programme. Dual Counter Market Makers engaged to conduct market making and liquidity-providing activities may be qualified for stamp duty exemption for their eligible transactions, subject to the relevant legislative amendments being passed by Hong Kong's Legislative Council.

The inclusion of RMB trading counters under Stock Connect would make it possible for Mainland Chinese investors to trade shares of Hong Kong-listed companies in either HKD or RMB, streamlining settlement procedures and attracting more retail investors to the Southbound Stock Connect. The project can increase Hong Kong's offshore RMB market's liquidity and accelerate the long-term internationalisation of the RMB by opening new channels for two-way cross-border RMB capital circulation. The start of the RMB counter project will provide Hong Kong with a unique position in pushing RMB trade to the global market at a time when other international financial centres are vying for RMB business. As commented by Wilfred Yiu, HKEX Chief Operating Officer and Co-head of Markets, these initiatives have the potential to help further facilitate and attract dual counter listings and help develop even greater synergies with the current China-related products.[75] As a result, it will deepen liquidity in Hong Kong's offshore RMB market and drive the long-term RMB internalisation process in order to strengthen Hong Kong's role as the world's premier offshore RMB hub.

According to the PBOC's '2022 RMB Internationalisation Report', RMB overtook the Japanese yen to become the fourth global payment currency by value in December 2021, with a share up to 2.7 per cent, which then continuously climbed to a historical high point at 3.2 per cent in January 2022.[76] RMB accounted for 2.88 per cent of global foreign exchange reserves in the first quarter of 2022, up 1.8 percentage points from 2016 when it first entered the International Monetary Fund (IMF)'s Special Drawing Rights (SDR) basket in 2015, ranking fifth among

[74] HKEX, 'HKEX to Introduce HKD-RMB Dual Counter Model and Dual Counter Market Making Programme in Hong Kong Securities Market' (13 December 2022), available at: www.hkex.com.hk/News/News-Release/2022/221213news?sc_lang=en (accessed on 3 January 2023). The HKD-RMB Dual Counter Model means that the same issuer can offer the simultaneous IPO and listing of two tranches of shares in different trading currencies (i.e. RMB and HKD). Shares of both RMB tranche and the HKD tranche are of the same class. Shareholders under these two tranches are expected to be treated equally.

[75] ibid.

[76] PBOC (26 September 2022), see n 37 above, 1.

major reserve currencies along with the US dollar, the euro, the Japanese yen, and the British pound. In May 2022, IMF increased RMB's share in SDR from 10.92 to 12.28 per cent, reflecting a growing recognition worldwide of the improvement in the free use of RMB.[77] The growth in the cross-border use of the RMB was partly due to the facilitation of cross-border RMB settlement under the current account and direct investment, and progress was made in such real economy sectors as commodities trading and surrounding areas such as the Association of Southeast Asian Nations (ASEAN).

As a superconnector between Mainland China and the international market, Hong Kong has a high degree of flexibility to tackle the interactions between Mainland China and the international market during the course of the RMB's internationalisation. This unique role as the gateway between Mainland China and the rest of the world is hard to replace or replicate. With the strong support of the Chinese government's policies, Hong Kong's can improve its RMB products and services, thereby strengthening its position as a global financial centre and offshore RMB hub.

6.4. Impacts and Limitations on Other International Markets

As previously discussed in Chapter two, unlike eligible equities in ordinary stocks and ETFs under China–Hong Kong Connect, the London/Switzerland Connects use depository receipts (DRs), a type of transferable financial security which represents a claim on a bundle of a company's shares. Chinese companies would be the ones issuing Global Depository Receipts (GDRs) on the LSE and Swiss stock exchange. On the other hand, international companies would be issuing Chinese Depository Receipts (CDRs) on China's markets.

As shown in Table 6.2 below, there were 387 eligible Southbound stocks and 646 eligible Northbound stocks (for both sell and buy) under Shanghai Connect, representing around 17.1 per cent of stocks on the HKEX Main Board and 29.7 per cent of the number of A-shares listed on the SSE as of the end of 2022. The scope of eligible shares for Shenzhen Connect is extended to cover a group of shares on both the SME Board and ChiNext market of the SZSE and to include the constituents of the SmallCap Index in the HKEX. So the number of Shenzhen Connect stocks was larger than those under Shanghai Connect, increasing to 553 Southbound and 926 Northbound stocks.

In contrast to the successful growth of China–Hong Kong Connect, the London/Switzerland Connects have attracted little interest thus far. As of the end

[77] ibid.

of 2022, only eight SSE-listed companies had issued GDRs in London.[78] Huatai Securities was the first company to list under the London Connect scheme, raising USD 1.54 billion of GDRs in London on 20 June 2019.[79] This was also the first time for international investors to gain access to China A-shares on an exchange outside Greater China using an international trading and settlement mechanism. The initiative of an International Board on the SSE was raised in 2009 to attract foreign companies to raise funds on China's stock market. However, slow progress has been made so far, pending the convertibility of Chinese currency and the removal of the foreign ownership limit in firms providing securities and fund management services. After Huatai Securities' first step, seven more Chinese companies also made use of London Connect to issue GDRs (three in 2020 and four in 2022). The listings were suspended in 2021, likely owing to the China–Britain political tension over Hong Kong and the market turbulence caused by the global coronavirus pandemic, but this was denied by China.[80]

Switzerland Connect seems to have progressed better than London Connect in terms of the number of listings and the pace of growth. Whilst London is possibly still perceived as somewhat scattered due to Brexit ramifications, Chinese issuers seem currently to prefer a Swiss listing. Switzerland, being a world-leading financial centre, has held a top spot in the heart of Europe in terms of innovation, a stable political and economic environment and a predictable, market-oriented regulatory framework for decades. Four Chinese companies – namely, GEM, Gotion High-tech, Keda Industrial Group and Ningbo Shanshan – became the first to issue GDRs in Switzerland via Stock Connect, raising around USD 1.6 billion in total. The four companies operate in new energy or manufacturing industries. By the end of 2022, nine GDR listings from SSE/SZSE were recorded on the SIX Swiss Exchange only in six months after the launch of China–Switzerland Stock Connect.

However, while several Chinese companies found new opportunities to raise capital in London or Switzerland, there has been no reciprocal issuance by UK and Swiss firms in China. HSBC, along with British luxury brand Burberry, were planning to become the first CDR issuers but to no avail as yet. Although Stock Connect is designed as a two-way programme, it appears to be a one-way channel for Chinese companies to go abroad at the moment.

[78] The details of GDRs on the SSE's website, www.sse.com.cn/assortment/stock/slsc/home/ (accessed on 5 January 2023).

[79] LSE, 'Shanghai-London Stock Connect welcomes its first issuer: Huatai Securities' (17 June 2019), available at: www.lseg.com/en/media-centre/press-releases/2019/shanghai-london-stock-connect-welcomes-its-first-issuer-huatai-securities (accessed on 5 January 2023).

[80] XC Zhang and A Galbraith, 'China Regulator Denies Report of Halt to Shanghai–London Stock Connect Listings' (*Reuters*, 3 January 2020), available at: www.reuters.com/article/us-china-markets-regulator/china-regulator-denies-report-of-halt-to-shanghai-london-stock-connect-listings-idUSKBN1Z20U5 (accessed 2 January 2023); and C Cohn and O Hirt, 'China Pacific Insurance to Press on With London Listing Under Connect Scheme' (*Reuters*, 2 June 2020), available at: www.reuters.com/article/cpic-listing-london-idUSL8N2DF47Y (accessed on 2 January 2023).

Table 6.2 Securities Listings under Stock Connect in December 2022

	Shenzhen–Hong Kong Stock Connect		**Shanghai–Hong Kong Stock Connect**		**Shanghai–London Stock Connect**		**China–Switzerland Stock Connect**	
Trading Links	South-bound Hong Kong Trading Link	North-bound Shenzhen Trading Link	South-bound Hong Kong Trading Link	North-bound Shanghai Trading Link	East-bound Shanghai Business Link	West-bound London Business Link	East-bound China Business Link	West-bound Swiss business Link
Number of Securities	553	926	387	646	0	8	0	9

Sources: The websites of SSE, SZSE, HKEX, LSE and SIX Swiss Exchange.

The overall impact of the London/Switzerland Connects on partner markets has been limited, causing some to question the scheme and its viability. There are several factors that may hinder the progress of the London and Switzerland Connects.[81]

First, extra regulations applicable to foreign issuers may lead to limited participation in Stock Connect. Under the initial agreement, UK-listed companies could only issue CDRs backed by existing shares but not new shares, falling short of meeting their financing needs. This implied that they gave the Chinese market access only to shares that were already traded in London. On the other hand, Chinese firms issuing GDRs are not constrained by this requirement and can raise capital. This would inevitably be a massive disincentive for UK-listed companies who would not be able to raise fresh capital from the Chinese market due to China's attempt to curb capital outflows and prevent capital inflows of fresh equity from flooding the domestic markets.[82]

Meanwhile, not all SSE-listed companies can join this connectivity scheme due to the requirement of a minimum market capitalisation of RMB 20 billion (around USD 2.9 billion) and approval from the CSRC under London Connect. This means that only large Chinese companies (appropriately 260 companies of the 1500 SSE-listed companies) would be eligible.[83] It was natural to expect that those who would seriously consider London GDR listing would be firms with global expansion ambitions and with strong confidence in their financial credibility, corporate governance and European investor relations management capabilities.[84] However, in accordance with Chapter 2 of the modified Listing Rules of the LSE,

[81] Huang (2021), see n 38 above, 575–78.

[82] S Shen and A Galbraith, 'China Constricts Capital Outflows with Eye on Yuan Stability' (*Reuters*, 11 October 2018), available at: www.reuters.com/article/us-china-markets-soft-landing-analysis/china-constricts-capital-outflows-with-eye-on-yuan-stability-idUSKCN1ML1SW (accessed on 3 January 2023).

[83] *BBC*, 'UK to Launch Ground-Breaking China Stock Market Link' (17 June 2019), www.bbc.co.uk/news/business-48658844> (accessed on 12 December 2022).

[84] S Wei, 'What Shanghai-London Connect Means for European Investors' (ATC Initiative, 22 June 2020), available at: www.atcinitiative.org/what-shanghai-london-stock-connect-means-for-european-investors (accessed on 12 December 2022).

which requires that the expected aggregate market value of all securities – including equity shares and depository receipts – to be listed on the Main Market is at least GBP 30 million (approximately USD 38.4 million).[85] This could imply that the capital eligibility criterion for Chinese GDRs in London has been reduced to GBP 30 million (around 1.3 per cent of the previous capital requirement).

In contrast to the requirements under London Connect, the eligibility criteria for issuer capital are much lower under Switzerland Connect. SIX Swiss Exchange introduced the new GDR trading segment and amended its listing and trading rules with regard to GDRs to make GDRs more attractive, while at the same time ensuring that the interests of investors are protected. The requirements to be fulfilled by issuers of GDRs remain unchanged and are the same as for the main market segment. These requirements include: the rules on the required minimum equity capital of at least CHF 25 million (around USD 26.9 million), a company track record of three years, application of the recognised account standards, and compliance with the rules regarding auditors and audit reports (see Articles 11–15 of SIX Listing Rules). With respect to Chinese GDRs, SIX accepts the Accounting Standard of the People's Republic of China for Business Enterprises (ASBE) as an accounting standard.

The restrictions are not only on corporate issuers but also on Chinese investors. Initially qualified Chinese individual investors should hold at least RMB 3 million (USD 440,000) in their cash or securities accounts over 20 trading days before applying for a licence to trade CDRs. Data released in 2019 by the SSE showed that about 820,000 stock trading account-holders in China met the standards for CDR trading, which accounts for merely 2.1 per cent of the total.[86] Institutional investors wishing to obtain a licence to trade CDRs should submit an application to CDR cross-border conversion institutions in accordance with related rules released by the CSRC.

Recognising the narrow scope of application of Stock Connect, on 22 February 2022, the CSRC issued 'Provisions on the Supervision and Administration of Depository Receipts under the Stock Connect Scheme between Domestic and Overseas Stock Exchange' (the 2022 Provisions), No 28 [2022] of CSRC, which came into effect immediately on the day of issuance.[87] Later, the SSE and SZSE issued, respectively, the 'Notice on Issuing the Interim Measures for the Listing and Trading of Depository Receipts under the Stock Connect Scheme between Shanghai Stock Exchange and Overseas Stock Exchanges' and the 'Notice on Issuing the Interim Measures for the Listing and Trading of Depository Receipts under the Stock Connect Scheme between Shenzhen Stock Exchange and Overseas Stock Exchanges' on 25 March 2022 to revise their listing rules for DRs accordingly.

[85] LSE, 'Main Market – Key Eligibility Criteria', available at: docs.londonstockexchange.com/sites/default/files/documents/main-market-key-eligibility-criteria.pdf (accessed on 12 December 2022).

[86] XY Li, 'New Connection' (*Beijing Review*, 24 June 2019), available at: www.bjreview.com/Business/201906/t20190624_800171443.html (accessed on 25 April 2021).

[87] The Provisions is available at: www.csrc.gov.cn/csrc_en/c102030/c1885850/content.shtml (accessed on 3 January 2023).

According to CSRC's 2022 Provisions, on the domestic front, qualified companies listed on the SZSE, in addition to the SSE, are also allowed to apply for the issuance of GDRs in overseas markets, which are further expanded from the UK to include also Switzerland and Germany. On the overseas front, the Provisions permit overseas issuers to raise capital in the Chinese domestic market through CDR offerings and adopt a market-driven book-building mechanism, but these arrangements will be subject to certain requirements governing the use of proceeds complying with Chinese regulations regarding foreign capital and foreign exchange controls. By expanding and optimising the Stock Connect scheme between domestic and overseas capital markets, the Provisions broaden channels for two-way cross-border financing and advance opening-up of the Chinese market. However, the Provisions only relax the restrictions on CDR issuers raising new capital and do not touch on other entry requirements for Chinese companies and investors.

Regarding the investor suitability, the entry requirements for Chinese individual investors participating in CDRs have been relaxed by the 2022 Notices of the SSE and SZSE: the required daily average value of assets in an investor's securities account and funds account over the 20 trading days before applying for trading CDRs is at least RMB 500,000 (previously RMB 3 million) excluding the funds and securities acquired from margin trading and short-selling transactions.[88]

Second, London/Switzerland Connects have minimal impact on local markets due to more appealing channels that already exist. As discussed above, before November 2014, the only way to invest in China's stock market was through buying equities of Chinese overseas listings and the QFII scheme, which enables foreign institutional investors to gain access to trade A-shares in China. The launch of China–Hong Kong Stock Connect allows international investors to directly buy and trade A-shares from companies based in Shanghai or Shenzhen which are listed on the HKEX, whilst also giving Chinese investors access to Hong Kong stocks. Whereas London/Switzerland Connects would only allow investors to access DRs, the already existing link with between China and Hong Kong lets investors trade shares through local brokerages and offers a much wider menu of stock selection. London Connect is probably considered 'more incremental than revolutionary' because international investors have already had access to Chinese shares through the existing avenues such as China–Hong Kong Stock Connect and Chinese overseas listings.[89] These stocks give investors the chance to invest

[88] Art 48 of SSE's 'Notice on Issuing the Interim Measures for the Listing and Trading of Depository Receipts under the Stock Connect Scheme between Shanghai Stock Exchange and Overseas Stock Exchanges' of March 2022, available on SSE's website: english.sse.com.cn/start/sserules/icbb/slsc/c/5700286.pdf; and art 48 of SZSE's 'Notice on Issuing the Interim Measures for the Listing and Trading of Depository Receipts under the Stock Connect Scheme between Shenzhen Stock Exchange and Overseas Stock Exchanges' of March 2022, available at: www.szse.cn/lawrules/rule/inno/t20220325_592080.html (accessed on 3 January 2023).

[89] J Fioretti, 'Launch of Shanghai-London Stock Link Stalled amid Doubts on Demand' (*Reuters*, 20 December 2018), available at: uk.reuters.com/article/uk-china-listings-analysis/launch-of-shanghai-london-stock-link-stalled-amid-doubts-on-demand-idUKKCN1OJ00B (accessed on 3 January 2023).

in all Chinese prominent economic sectors like the industrial, financial and utilities sectors. It is in doubt whether international investors will choose to access A-shares through London Connect or Switzerland Connect, which has been criticised for being 'just a watered-down version of Hong Kong's programme', when they can already access them easily through Hong Kong, a free market open to traders worldwide.[90]

Third, the complex process of fungibility of DRs may also dampen the interests of overseas investors. A DR is a certificate issued by a depository bank, representing underlying shares in a foreign company and traded on a local stock exchange. The term fungibility means the interchangeability of any securities of a class. The DRs under Stock Connect include a two-direction business: CDRs, referring to the qualifying companies listed on overseas stock exchanges listing CDRs in China; and GDRs, referring to the A-share companies in China listing GDRs on overseas stock exchanges. The DRs and the shares are fungible, and realise the interconnection between the two markets. The issuance and listing of DRs under Stock Connect are subject to local regulatory requirements, and issuers must fulfil information disclosure obligations. Unlike the China–Hong Kong Stock Connect, under which investors in China and Hong Kong may trade shares directly on each other's markets, the DRs under Stock Connect have to be converted into the shares of each other's markets so as to enable investors to trade locally.

However, this is where it gets a bit complicated because in order to do this, investors need to use a designated broker who is licensed to trade in both markets and convert GDRs and A-shares or CDRs and overseas shares. In practice, the UK and Switzerland have few restrictions over the selection of depository institutions and custodian institutions. However, China has introduced strict criteria in this area and allows few institutions to act as depository institutions of CDR issuers and custodian institutions of GDR issuers. For example, the depository banks for CDR issuers and custodian institutions for A-share issuers must be served by China Clear, with issuers' subsidiaries, commercial banks, and securities companies approved by the CSRC.[91]

Also, the ability of CDRs to be interchangeable with the stocks of London-listed or Switzerland-listed companies is still under question, because of China's capital controls that prevent RMB-denominated assets from being converted into overseas currency. Some have speculated that the chance for free conversion of CDRs is almost zero, and renamed CDRs as 'depositories with Chinese characteristics', because the interchangeability would break China's capital control. The inability

[90] N Gopalan, 'London's Shanghai Dream is a Bridge to Nowhere' (*Bloomberg*, 13 April 2018), available at: www.bloomberg.com/opinion/articles/2018-04-13/london-s-shanghai-stock-connect-dream-is-a-bridge-to-nowhere (accessed on 3 January 2023).

[91] Arts 24 and 25 of the 2022 Provisions on the Supervision and Administration of Depository Receipts under the Stock Connect Scheme between Domestic and Overseas Stock Exchange by the CSRC.

to convert the CDRs would make the receipts 'pointless', making them more like a secondary listing, said Ba Shusong, Chief China Economist of the HKEX.[92]

Fourth, another compelling argument has been made by those who claim that this programme is unlikely to be as successful as it could be because of divergence in information disclosure and investor protection in both sides.[93] Under the initial Shanghai–London Stock Connect programme, CDR issuers had an obligation to release all information required by the SSE. This could make CDR issuers overburdened with various information disclosure obligations, which may impact on the enthusiasm of potential CDR issuers and jeopardise the competitiveness of the Chinese stock market.[94] Also, China has long been blamed for its reluctance to allow overseas regulators to inspect audit documents relating to Chinese companies due to national security concerns. In a media interview, Jay Clayton, Chairman of the US Securities and Exchange Commission (SEC), indicated that the regulator's accounting oversight arm, the Public Company Accounting Oversight Board (PCAOB) has been unable to access audits of US-listed Chinese companies from the Chinese government for almost a decade.[95] The SEC has even warned of the risks of Chinese listings, because the SEC and other authorities often have substantial difficulties in bringing and enforcing actions against such Chinese companies for false disclosure around the nature and quality of financial information, including financial reporting and audits.[96]

The disclosure problem also casts doubt on whether current regulations can offer good protection for investors who trade cross-border DRs. The regulatory loophole in cross-border securities transactions and the classic problem of information asymmetry due to the different corporate cultures and legal systems as well as geographical locations, also makes it more difficult for investors to acquire the information they need to make informed investment decisions. Considering the long and complex transactional chain relating to DRs, the bankruptcy of any parties in the chain such as overseas-listed companies, custodian institutions, or depository institutions will result in financial loss to investors, who have limited remedies.[97]

Taking into account the differences in the regulatory rules and practices of listed companies between domestic and overseas markets, the CSRC has adjusted

[92] X Yu, 'Questions Remain as Countdown Begins on Depositary Receipts with Chinese Characteristics' (*South China Morning Post*, 19 June 2018), available at: www.scmp.com/business/companies/article/2151293/questions-remain-countdown-begins-depositary-receipts-chinese (accessed on 12 December 2022).

[93] Huang (2021), see n 38 above.

[94] Lu and Ye (2019), see n 21 above, 687.

[95] K Johnson, 'US Securities Regulator Warns Investors over Chinese Company Disclosures' (*Reuters*, 22 April 2020), available at: www.reuters.com/article/us-health-coronavirus-sec-china-idUSKCN2242A1 (accessed on 12 December 2022).

[96] SEC, 'Emerging Market Investments Entail Significant Disclosure, Financial Reporting and Other Risks, Remedies are Limited' (21 April 2020), available at: www.sec.gov/news/public-statement/emerging-market-investments-disclosure-reporting (accessed on 12 December 2022).

[97] Lu and Ye (2019), see n 21 above.

the ongoing supervision requirements such as those on information disclosure, in CSRC's 2022 Provisions. It clarifies that an overseas issuer that adopts equivalent accounting standards does not need to make additional disclosure of the differences between the accounting standards it adopts and the Chinese ASBE; nor does it need to disclose the difference adjustment information according to the Chinese accounting standards.[98] Also, on 26 August 2022, the CSRC and the SEC signed a historic agreement on audit oversight cooperation to allow the PCAOB to inspect and investigate audit firms based in China and Hong Kong whose clients trade on American exchanges.[99] This agreement marks the first time the CSRC has made such detailed and specific commitments to allow an overseas regulator to inspect and investigate Chinese firms. But unfortunately no such agreement has been signed between China and the UK/Switzerland.

6.5. Concluding Remarks

Stock Connect is a major channel for foreign investors to participate in China's capital markets, and it will continue to expand and open-up in the coming years. This could involve expanding the number of stock exchanges participating or relaxing rules to facilitate stock listings on different exchanges. In the short and medium term, Stock Connect is a simple and straightforward way for international investors to trade in a number of Chinese equities without having to apply for individual licences and quotas, and for domestic Chinese investors to invest in overseas markets. In the long term, it represents further integration of the Chinese market into the global economy. Through China–Hong Kong Stock Connect, China is creating a single 'one country, one market' by bridging the divisions in their markets and institutions between two economies. This is done with a view to widening mutual market access, diversifying investor bases and investment opportunities, and growing trans-border capital flow, as well as harmonising their listing regulations and Stock Connect rules.

Hong Kong plays a remarkable role in China's financial liberalisation. Over the past decades, Hong Kong has served as a superconnector between the East and West, enabling global capital to gain access to China's dynamic economic growth while also allowing Chinese capital to invest in international markets. Hong Kong's unique combination of a common law legal system, listing requirements, a large talent pool, and proximity with China facilitate investment flows between Hong Kong and Mainland China. To reinforce its attractiveness to the international

[98] CSRC, 'Revision Notes on the Provisions on the Supervision and Administration of Depository Receipts under the Stock Connect between Domestic and Overseas Stock Exchanges' (11 February 2022), available at: www.csrc.gov.cn/csrc_en/c102034/c1885832/content.shtml (accessed on 12 December 2022).

[99] SEC, 'Statement on Agreement Governing Inspections and Investigations of Audit Firms Based in China and Hong Kong' (26 August 2022), available at: www.sec.gov/news/statement/gensler-audit-firms-china-hong-kong-20220826 (accessed on 12 December 2022).

business and financial community, Hong Kong has adopted a series of business-friendly market initiatives, such as the reform of listing rules to broaden and deepen its 'superconnector' role.

However, opening-up will take time. While China–Hong Kong Stock Connect shows its importance to the international market, London and Switzerland Connects have not progressed very well. None of the British and Swiss issuers have used Stock Connect to issue CDRs in China yet, and these links seem to be a one-way passage for Chinese companies to go abroad rather than the other way around.

The limited participation in London/Switzerland Connects is caused by higher restrictions, more appealing existing investment channels, the complex process of fungibility of DRs, and regulatory differences in investor protection and information disclosure. The Chinese government is wary of the impact that fast and uncontrolled opening will have on the economy and wants foreign capital to help serve its economic goals. Foreign capital should help develop the sectors of the economy deemed the most important and should be kept away from 'sensitive' industries linked to national security.[100] But as the Connect scheme matures and evolves to embrace additional exchanges and asset classes and relax the restrictions on both sides of the border, its impact and significance will spread.

[100] *China Briefing*, 'China Stock Connect: Expanding the Shanghai-London Programme to Germany and Switzerland' (5 January 2022), available at: www.china-briefing.com/news/china-stock-connect-expanding-shanghai-london-program-to-germany-switzerland/ (accessed on 4 January 2023).

7

Capital Market Connectivity Across the World

In Chapter six we assessed the profound impacts of Stock Connect on the local and global capital markets. Stock Connect not only creates a single 'China' stock market that ranks as one of the biggest capital markets in the world by market capitalisation and daily trading turnover, but also enhances mutual market connectivity between Chinese and global markets. In addition to Stock Connect, there is an increasing tendency to create new global and regional integration schemes. The European Union (EU) is one of the most prominent examples. Integration could also be achieved by different means, such as cross-listing (ie a company lists on a foreign exchange), multinational funds (ie a pension or mutual fund is located in one jurisdiction but invests in another jurisdiction), or direct market connectivity, such as the US and EU integration projects.[1] This chapter discusses the different stages and the various mechanisms of capital market integration in areas of the world such as the US, EU, Asia, Africa and the Middle East. It also provides a comparative analysis of these market connectivity mechanisms.

7.1. The US Regulation National Market System (Reg NMS)

Before the creation of a national market system in 1975, no consolidated data feeds existed to ensure uniform stock price quotations across all trading exchanges in the US. The same stock was sometimes traded at different prices at different trading venues. It presented a major problem in equity trading, as some traders would receive more favourable pricing than other traders. In 1975, Congress passed the Securities Acts Amendments by inserting section 11A into the text of the Securities Exchange Act of 1934. Section 11A contained an explicit statutory commitment to the establishment of a 'national market system' and clarified and strengthened the Securities and Exchange Commission (SEC)'s authority to implement such a system. The 1975 Amendments vested substantial discretion in the SEC to implement Congress's vision of what a national market system ought to be.

[1] DC Donald, 'Bridging Finance Without Fragmentation: A Comparative Look at Market Connectivity in the US, Europe and Asia' (2015) 16 *European Business Organization Law Review* 173.

Congress directed the SEC: first, to encourage better communication among the various markets; and second, to eliminate inappropriate burdens on competition among securities trading market centres.[2]

Werner observed that neither the SEC nor Congress ever defined what it meant by the term 'national market system' (NMS).[3] But Congress set forth the goals of establishing a national market system as follows:

(1) The economically efficient execution of transactions;
(2) Fair competition among broker-dealers, among exchanges, and between exchanges and other markets;
(3) The ready availability of quotation and transaction information to broker-dealers and investors;
(4) The ability of broker-dealers to execute orders in the best market; and
(5) The opportunity, consistent with the other goals, for investors to execute orders without the participation of a dealer.[4]

However, the definition has been long debated since the introduction of the concept of NMS. Advocates of the NMS believed that through the establishment of a communication system linking all national exchanges, there would be a consolidation of order flows and sufficient competition amongst brokers, dealers, and securities markets.[5] The anticipated result of this system would be a reduction in trading and execution costs for local market participants, an increase in market depth and liquidity, and an increase in the overall efficiency of the securities markets and investor confidence.[6] Moreover, it is expected that general investor confidence could also be improved as a result of this system.

While proponents of the NMS foresaw a consolidation of the national securities markets as fundamentally beneficial to investors, others believed the system would lead to the opposite of the intended effects. Regulatory mechanisms designed to link trading venues stifle competition and innovation by requiring that all markets conform to the linkage mechanism. Formal linkages also are likely to fail in the long run because no individual market has an incentive to improve or maintain the mechanism.[7] Opponents of the NMS also expressed a concern that the consolidation of order flows might lead to a reduction in the volumes on specific exchanges and, as a result, the liquidity in certain securities.[8] The net

[2] Section 11A(a)(2) of the Securities Exchange Act of 1934, 15 U.S.C. 78K-1.

[3] W Werner, 'The SEC as Market Regulator' (1984) 70(4) *Virginia Law Review* 775, 776.

[4] The Securities and Exchange Act of 1934, s 11A(a)(1)(C), 15 U.S.C. 78k-1(a)(1)(C).

[5] KJ Cohen and RM Conroy, 'An Empirical Study of the Effect of Rule 19c-3' (1990) 33(1) *Journal of Law and Economics* 277.

[6] P Atkins, 'Speech by SEC Commissioner: Enhancement and Modernisation of the National Market System', April 2005, available at: www.sec.gov/news/speech/spch040605psa.htm (accessed 20 August 2021).

[7] Stoll notes that the Intermarket Trading System, which provides for order routing between venues trading equity securities, 'is a good example of linking that has not kept pace with technology.' See H Stoll, 'Market Fragmentation' (2001) 56 *Financial Analysts Journal* 16, 16.

[8] NS Poser, 'Restructuring the Stock Markets: A Critical Look at the SEC's National Market System' (1981) 56 *New York University Law Review* 883, 905–6.

result would be a stifling of innovation in securities as a result of the dominance of certain exchanges for various securities. The potential failure of NMS is owing to the motivation of the SEC, not driven a concern for the 'public interest', but rather by the varying power dynamics of special interest groups.[9] But these arguments have been refuted by assertions that there would remain sufficient competition amongst markets in securities and the unintended effects of lower order flows among markets would be minimal.[10]

At the heart of the debate regarding the implementation of an NMS within the US is a wider discussion of the choice between fragmentation and consolidation of a securities market. To some, an NMS represents an embracing of the consolidation viewpoint over that of fragmentation. Taking this into account, the SEC aimed to achieve a compromise system that sufficiently consolidates order flows while maintaining the benefits of competition.

The promulgation of Regulation National Market System (Reg NMS) provides an opportunity to gauge the extent to which the goals of the SEC have been met. As the offspring to the 1975 Amendments, the SEC ultimately adopted Reg NMS, a set of rules that instigated major changes in the structure of US equity markets in 2005. Reg NMS covers all entities and facilities such as stock exchanges, trade clearing houses, and market price quotation providers, both public and private, that are involved in the buying and selling of stocks. Its regulations govern how stock market prices are quoted and how stock trades are executed.

In addition to re-designating the national market system rules previously adopted under section 11A of the 1934 Securities Exchange Act, Reg NMS includes new substantive rules that are designed to modernise and strengthen the regulatory structure of the US equity markets, including the following four key provisions:[11]

- First, the 'Order Protection Rule' aims to ensure that investors receive the best price when their order is executed by removing the ability to have orders 'traded through'. This rule requires trading centres to establish, maintain, and enforce written policies and procedures in place to prevent trade-throughs for NMS stock, which occur when trades are executed without regard for immediately available and better-priced quotations in other trading centres.[12] To be protected, a quotation must be immediately and automatically accessible. Reg NMS also created the National Best Bid and Offer (NBBO) requirement that requires brokers to route their orders to the venues offering the best-displayed price. But there are many exceptions to the rule, for example, for inter-market sweep orders (block transactions), 'flickering quotes' and benchmark trades, which may raise questions about enforcement.

[9] JR Macey and DD Haddock, 'Shirking at the SEC: The Failure of The National Market System' (1985) *University of Illinois Law Review* 315, 316.

[10] R Battalio et al, 'Toward a National Market System for US Exchange-Listed Equity Options' (2004) 2 *Journal of Finance* 933, 959–61.

[11] SEC, 'Reg NMS', available at: www.sec.gov/rules/final/34-51808.pdf (accessed on 20 August 2022).

[12] For more on this rule see text to nn 18–19 below.

- Second, the 'Access Rule' seeks to improve access to quotations from trading centres in the NMS by requiring greater linking and lower access fees. This rule includes a mandate that each national securities exchange and national securities association adopts, maintains, and enforces written rules prohibiting their members from displaying cross-automated quotations or quotations that lock.
- Third, the 'Sub-Penny Rule' sets the minimum quotation increment of all stocks over USD 1.00 per share to at least USD 0.01. It prohibits market participants from accepting, ranking, or displaying orders, quotations, or indications of interest in a pricing increment smaller than a penny (one cent).
- Finally, the 'Market Data Rules' update the requirements for consolidating, distributing and displaying market information, as well as amending the joint industry plans for disseminating market information to modify the formulas for allocating plan revenues and broaden participation in plan governance.

Combined, these four rules made up Reg NMS, which the SEC hoped would create a true national market system in which key rules could be applied uniformly across market centres and ultimately protect the rights of individual investors. As explained by William Donaldson, former Chairman of the SEC,

> the Commission is acting pursuant to the mandate Congress gave us in 1975 to use our rulemaking authority to further the goals of the national market system – among them to enhance competition among markets and to enhance opportunities for the interaction of investor orders.[13]

Likewise, in adopting the rule, the Commission celebrated what its 30-year old mandate had accomplished and would achieve in the future:

> The Commission believes that the NMS approach adopted by Congress is a primary reason that the U.S. equity markets are widely recognized as being the fairest, most efficient, and most competitive in the world. The rules that the Commission is now adopting represent an important and needed step forward in its continuing implementation of Congress's objectives for the NMS.[14]

The primary focus of Reg NMS is on ensuring transparency and full disclosure in relation to equity price quotations and trade execution. The objectives of NMS that are spelled out in the statute are essentially fivefold:[15]

(1) Fair market competition – to ensure fair competition among all stock trading exchanges and markets, including over-the-counter trading;

[13] W Donaldson, former Chairman of SEC, 'Speech by SEC Chairman: Opening Statement at Commission Opening Meeting) (21 April 2004), available at: www.sec.gov/news/speech/spch042104whd.htm (accessed on 25 November 2022).

[14] Reg NMS, 70 Fed. Reg. at 37, 497.

[15] 15 U.S.C. § 78k-1(a)(1)(C) (2012) and also see a summary from Corporate Finance Institute, 'National Market System (NMS)' (23 October 2022), available at: corporatefinanceinstitute.com/resources/wealth-management/national-market-system-nms/ (accessed on 23 November 2022).

(2) Efficient order execution – to ensure that all equity trading orders are executed in a timely and efficient manner;
(3) Transparency in price quotations – to ensure that all price quotations of securities and buy and sell equity transactions are freely and equally available to all market participants;
(4) Best price execution – to ensure that all stock trading orders are executed at the best possible price for both buyers and sellers;
(5) Direct matching of buy and sell orders – to ensure that buy and sell orders for stocks are executed, whenever possible in keeping with the other four goals of the National Market System, without using a dealer (which usually increases transaction costs for investors). Since the advent of electronic trading, nearly all stock trading transactions are executed by direct matching of buyers and sellers.

While Reg NMS has been largely successful in accomplishing its objective of reducing stated transaction costs for investors,[16] it also shares much of the blame for being 'excessively protectionist, prescriptive and anti-competitive'.[17] For example, Rule 611 of Reg NMS includes what is known as the 'Order Protection Rule' or the 'Trade-through Rule'. The rule basically states that an order entered on one trading exchange, such as the New York Stock Exchange (NYSE), must be executed on a different exchange, such as the NASDAQ, if doing so offers a better price. Such rule is blamed as being both redundant to best execution and an 'overly-proscriptive' requirement for marketplace connectivity that is no longer needed in today's environment.[18] It has made markets more fragile and less resilient by requiring all markets to interconnect on rigid terms, increasing the risk of market disruption. And by declaring price the most important component of execution – as opposed to liquidity or anonymity or other considerations deemed valuable by competitive forces – it has reduced the incentive for exchanges to innovate. Likewise, SEC Commissioners Glassman and Atkins criticise Rule 611 for imposing government-controlled competition, increasing barriers to competition and representing a misguided attempt to micro-manage the markets.[19] They even argue that narrowing down best execution to the price criterion reduces competition to the detriment of other factors of execution, and to the detriment of the market structure and innovation.

[16] JJ Angel et al, 'Equity Trading in the 21st Century' (2015) 1(1) *Quarterly Journal of Finance* 1, 1.

[17] JP Casey and K Lannoo, *The MiFID Revolution* (New York, Cambridge University Press, 2009), ch 11 'MiFID and Reg NMS: A Test-case for 'Substituted Compliance'?', 207.

[18] FIA Principal Traders Group, 'Reg NMS: A Retrospective Review & Practical Reforms for Improvement' (17 September 2018), 4, available at: www.fia.org/sites/default/files/2020-02/FIA-PTG-Reg-NMS-A-Retrospective-Review-Practical-Reforms-for-Improvement.pdf (accessed on 25 November 2022).

[19] CA Glassman and PS Atkins (SEC Commissioners), 'Dissent to the Adoption of Regulation NMS' (9 June 2005), available at: www.sec.gov/rules/final/34-51808-dissent.pdf (accessed on 25 November 2022).

Critics of Reg NMS have also pointed out that transparency rules requiring that all bids and offers for a stock be publicly available have led to the creation of 'dark pools', which are private trading exchanges that enable large institutional investors to hide their trades until after the trades have been executed.[20] In short, the rules intended to create greater trading transparency have, in fact, created less transparency. An increasing amount of trading occurs off-exchange in dark pools and other 'non-lit' venues, and hidden costs proliferate. Most importantly, the rising share of data revenue generated by the exchanges functions as a sort of tax on traders, and by extension investors, who are forced to pay for enhanced data feeds if they are to remain competitive and meet their duty of best execution.

In a speech at the Economic Club of New York dated 12 July 2017, Jay Clayton, SEC Chairman, set forth eight principles to guide the work of the SEC and emphasised the need for retroactive review of Reg NMS.[21] From the perspective of equity market structure, notable among these eight principles were the fourth – 'regulatory actions drive change, and change can have lasting effects' – and the sixth – 'effective rulemaking does not end with rule adoption'. Reg NMS has been a central feature of the equity trading landscape for over a decade and is a prime candidate for the retroactive review of past policy-making efforts encouraged by Chairman Clayton's sixth principle.

Several initiatives have been undertaken to reform market data and equity market overhaul. Pursuant to section 11A of the 1975 amendment to the Securities Exchange Act of 1934, market data is made widely available to investors through the NMS. This system features a centralised consolidation model in which the self-regulatory organisations such as national stock exchanges and the Financial Industry Regulatory Authority act jointly under the Equity Data Plans to provide specified NMS market data for each NMS stock to exclusive securities information processors (SIPs). The exclusive SIPs then consolidate that information and disseminate a national best bid and national best offer and last sale information. However, technologies, as well as business and trading practices, have changed dramatically since their initial implementation in the late 1970s. In particular, the combination of technological advances and order routing and trading strategies has greatly increased the speed and automation of markets, making trading more market-data-dependent, in terms of content, access and processing speed. In response, the SEC adopted new rules intended to modernise the infrastructure for the collection, consolidation and dissemination of market data for exchange-listed national market system stocks (NMS market data) on 9 December 2020.[22] The adopted rules update and significantly expand the content of NMS market

[20] S McNamara, 'The Stock Exchange as Multi-sided Platform and the Future of the National Market System' (2018) 5 *Brigham Young University Law Review* 969, 972.

[21] J Clayton, SEC Chairman, 'Remarks to the Economic Club of New York' (9 September 2019), available at www.sec.gov/news/speech/speech-clayton-2019-09-09 (accessed on 25 August 2022).

[22] SEC, 'SEC Adopts Rules to Modernise Key Market Infrastructure Responsible for Collecting, Consolidating, and Disseminating Equity Market Data', Press Release 9 December 2020, available at: www.sec.gov/news/press-release/2020-311 (accessed on 25 August 2022).

data to better meet the diverse needs of investors in today's equity markets. The rules also update the method by which NMS market data is consolidated and disseminated, by fostering a competitive environment and providing for a new decentralised model that promises reduced latency and other new efficiencies.

Moreover, on 14 December 2022, the SEC proposed new rules and rule amendments relating to five aspects of the US equity market structure: (i) new 'Regulation Best Execution' (new Reg NMS Rules 1100, 1101, and 1102 establishing a best execution standard and requiring robust policies and procedures for firms engaging in certain conflicted transactions with retail customers); (ii) new Reg NMS Rule 615 'Order Competition Rule' (including requiring certain retail equity orders to be exposed in auctions before being internalised); (iii) amendments to Rule 610 and 612 (including tick size, access fees, odd lots and round lots); (iv) amendments to Rule 605 (enhancing broker disclosure of order execution information); (v) amendments to Rule 10b5-1 of Reg NMS (adopting insider trading arrangements and related disclosures).[23]

Comments on the proposals can be made to the SEC until at least 31 March 2023. The proposals are widely welcome as evidenced by commentaries that the reforms represent a constructive and positive effort to improve transparency and fairness while increasing competition for investors' stock orders.[24]

7.2. The EU Markets in Financial Instruments Directive (MiFID)

A wealth of regulatory changes, combined with the swiftly changing operational environment, has created an increasingly complex compliance landscape in the EU. For instance, MiFID is the term referring to the Markets in Financial Instruments Directive (2004/39/EC) that requires investment firms and banks operating across the EU's financial markets to provide investment services transparently, to facilitate fair competition. The original directive (MiFID I) was introduced in the EU on 1 November 2007, replacing the 1993 Investment Service Directive that was not particularly effective. As its updated response to the 2008 financial crisis, Directive (2014/65/EU) (MiFID II) was introduced to accommodate additional investment regulations, which was supplemented by the Markets in Financial Instruments Regulation (MiFIR, Regulation EU No 600/2014). Both MiFID II and MiFIR were published in the Official Journal of the European Union

[23] C Crenshaw, SEC Commissioner, 'Statement on Proposals related to Equity Market Structure' (14 December 2022), available at: www.sec.gov/news/statement/crenshaw-insider-trading-20221214-0 (accessed on 20 December 2022).

[24] Eg J Mccrank, 'US SEC Votes to Advance Stock Market Overhaul Proposals' (*Reuters*, 14 December 2022), available at: www.reuters.com/markets/us/us-sec-vote-proposal-overhaul-stock-market-rules-2022-12-14/ (accessed on 20 December 2022).

on 12 June 2014 and entered into force on 3 January 2018. To avoid misunderstandings, we consistently refer to either MiFID II/MiFIR, or MiFID I where the old directive is concerned.

MiFID I was claimed to be a cornerstone of the EU's regulation of financial markets.[25] It included an updated and expanded passport system so as to create a level playing-field and eliminate remaining barriers to the provision of cross-border financial services.[26] It sought to improve the competitiveness of EU financial markets by creating a single market for investment services and activities, and ensuring a high degree of harmonised protection for investors in financial instruments. Several main areas were covered in MiFID I:

(1) Conduct of business requirements for firms, for example, their obligation towards each category of client as defined ('eligible counterparties' 'professional' and 'retail'), their obligation to assess whether the products and services which they provide are 'suitable' or 'appropriate' for their client, and their obligation to secure 'best execution' for their client;
(2) Organisational requirements for firms and markets, for example, compliance, risk management and internal audit functions that operate independently, identification and management of conflicts of interest, and limitations on out-sourcing, especially to third countries;
(3) Transaction reporting to relevant competent authorities of buying and selling transactions in all financial instruments;
(4) Transparency requirements for the trading of shares.[27]

MiFID I was adopted a year before the US mortgage market meltdown in 2008. It was then realised that the directive could not provide adequate regulations in the investment field, which saw MiFID II come into effect as the new arrangement, taking into account the lessons learned during the crisis. MiFID I focused primarily on stocks, which was seen as a limitation, because it did not include the vast amount of financial products available in the market, such as over-the-counter (OTC) derivatives products.[28] The 2008 global financial crisis revealed the destabilising effects of OTC derivative products. OTC transactions leave counterparties with direct credit exposure to each other, since there is no exchange market between the users to oversee transactions. Previously, there was less regulatory oversight concerning the reporting of derivatives transactions to increase transparency between engaging parties. Closing such a gap is necessary to bolster

[25] EC, 'Markets in Financial Instruments Directive (MiFID II): Frequently Asked Questions' (15 April 2014), available at: ec.europa.eu/commission/presscorner/detail/en/MEMO_14_305 (accessed on 20 November 2022).

[26] F Haas (2007), 'The Markets in Financial Instruments Directive: Banking on Market and Supervisory Efficiency', *IMF Working Paper WP/07/250*, October, 2–25.

[27] Casey and Lannoo (2009), see n 17 above, ch 2 'Origins and Structure of MiFID', 34.

[28] EC, 'Review of the Markets in Financial Instruments Directive (MiFID): Frequently Asked Questions', EC MEMO/11/716, 20 October 2011, available at: ec.europa.eu/commission/presscorner/detail/en/MEMO_11_716 (accessed on 20 November 2022).

investor confidence and ensure a more robust framework of regulation to address the more complex market reality we are now faced with. Therefore, MiFID II introduces more financial products, thereby expanding the original MiFID scope to monitor counterparties' total financial exposure.

Another issue in MiFID I was that the regulatory approach in dealing with countries outside of the EU was left up to each Member State. This meant that some firms outside of the EU could have a competitive advantage over firms inside the Union because of their lighter regulatory oversight. This issue was addressed through MiFID II, which was implemented in January 2018 and harmonised the rules for all firms with EU clients.

Despite claims of benefiting from more competition, wider investor choice, lower transaction costs, and deeper integration, the European Commission (EC) in 2011 highlighted that the benefits of competition were not flowing efficiently to all market participants and were not always passed on to end users.[29] Market fragmentation had further rendered the trading environment more complex and opaque, while MiFID I's classification of trading avenues had been outpaced by innovations. These circumstances led to EC's proposal for a fresh directive (MiFID II) to address these flaws and deficiencies comprehensively.[30]

Compared to MiFID I, MiFID II/MiFIR are much wider-ranging pieces of legislation. They represent the biggest overhaul of the European financial markets in a decade, impacting global client trading in European venues, in European financial instruments and with European investment firms.[31] The main objectives of MiFID II/MiFIR include the pursuit of harmonised regulation across EU financial markets, increased competition between EU financial markets, ensuring appropriate levels of investor protection, and strengthening of supervisory powers.

7.2.1. Market Infrastructure

MiFID II/MiFIR make a range of significant changes in relation to market infrastructure. In order to make EU financial markets more transparent and efficient and to level the playing-field for the various venues offering multilateral trading services, a new execution venue called an organised trading facility (OTF) was created.[32] The rules around regulated markets (RMs) and multilateral trade

[29] ibid.

[30] EC, 'Proposal for a Directive of the European Parliament and of the Council on Markets in Financial Instruments Repealing Directive 2004/39/EC of the European Parliament and of the Council', COM(2011) 656 final, 2011/0298 (COD), 20 October 2011, available at: eur-lex.europa.eu/legal-content/EN/TXT/?uri=CELEX:52012AP0406 (accessed on 20 November 2022).

[31] ESMA, 'MiFID II', available at: www.esma.europa.eu/policy-rules/mifid-ii-and-mifir (accessed on 20 November 2022).

[32] Recital 8 MiFIR and art 4(1)(23) MiFID II contain the definition of an OTC: a multilateral system which is not a regulated market or an MTF and in which multiple third-party buying and selling

facilities (MTFs) have been aligned, and a range of organisational requirements previously applying to RMs and MTFs have been extended to the newly introduced OTFs. Pursuant to Recital 8 MiFIR, the term 'OTF' has been internationally broadly defined so that now and in the future it should be able to capture all types of organised execution and arranging of trading that have not so far been subject to requirements applied to RMs and MTFs. For this reason an OTF is often perceived as a catch-all category of trading venue, ensuring that any system trading in financial instruments is properly regulated.[33] The trading of standardised OTC contracts is intended to come within the scope of OTFs. This fulfils the G20 obligation to move trading in standardised OTC derivative contracts to exchanges or electronic trading platforms.[34]

Requirements are imposed on operators of OTFs and transactions concluded on an OTF have to be submitted to pre- and post-trade transparency provisions similar to RMs and MTFs, creating a level playing-field. An investment firm or market operator operating an OTF should be able to exercise discretion at two different levels: (a) when deciding to place an order on the OTF or to retract it again; and (b) when deciding not to match a specific order with the orders available in the system at a given point in time, provided that that complies with specific instructions received from clients and with best execution obligations.[35] In the view of Busch, the OTF is a hybrid concept: operating an OTF is an investment activity, but matching client orders with each other through an OTF constitutes an investment service, which the 'conduct of business' rules should also apply to.[36]

However, it is noted that Recital 8 of MiFIR clarifies that an OTF should not include facilities where there is no genuine interaction of trading interest, such as bulletin boards used for advertising buying and selling interests, other entities aggregating or pooling potential buying or selling interests, electronic post-trade confirmation services, or portfolio compression. Any system that only receives, pools, aggregates and broadcasts indications of interest, bids and offers or prices shall not be considered a multilateral system for the purpose of MiFID II. This is because there is no reaction of one trading interest to another within these systems – they do not 'act reciprocally'.[37]

MiFID II also harmonised the regime for third-country firms. When serving retail clients or professional clients on request in the EU, third-country firms

interests in bonds, structured finance products, emission allowances or derivatives are able to interact in the system in a way that results in a contract in accordance with Title II of MiFID II (Authorisation and operating conditions for investment firms).

[33] Recital 6 MiFIR.

[34] Recital 25 MiFIR.

[35] Art 20(6) in conjunction with Art 27 MiFID II; Recital 9, first paragraph, MiFIR.

[36] D Busch, 'MiFID II and MiFIR: Stricter Rules for the EU Financial Markets' (2017) 11 *Law and Financial Markets Review* 126, 128.

[37] Financial Conduct Authority, 'Markets in Financial Instruments Directive II Implementation – Consultation Paper I', December 2015, CP15/43, 49, available at: www.fca.org.uk/publication/consultation/cp15-43.pdf (accessed on 22 November 2022).

have to establish a branch in each EU country where they operate. Branches will be subject to authorisation and supervision in the Member States. In turn, when serving eligible counterparties or per se professional clients in the EU, investment firms will directly register with the European Securities and Markets Authority (ESMA).[38] This registration will be first subject to the third country receiving a positive equivalence assessment from the EC. No EU branch is required and the EU passport still applies.

7.2.2. Stricter Governance Requirements and Enhanced Investor Protection

Under the MiFID I framework, investment firms are required to take 'reasonable steps' to obtain the best possible results for their clients in Article 21. Under Article 27 of MiFID II, the term 'reasonable steps' has been replaced with 'all sufficient steps', thus raising the bar for compliance. ESMA requires firms to ensure that the intended outcomes can be successfully achieved on an on-going basis when designing their execution policies and establishing their execution arrangements.[39] This is likely to involve the strengthening of front-office accountability and systems and controls, according to which firms will ensure that their detection capabilities are able to identify any potential deficiencies.

Article 27 MiFID II also requires firms to monitor not only the execution quality obtained but also the quality and appropriateness of their execution arrangements and policies on an ex-ante and ex-post basis to identify circumstances under which changes may be appropriate. An example of ex-ante monitoring would be to ensure that the policy design and review process is appropriate and takes into account new services or products offered by the firms. Accordingly, an ex-post monitoring may be to check whether the firm has correctly applied its execution policy and if client instructions and preferences are effectively passed along the entire execution chain when using smart orders routers or any other means of execution.[40]

MiFID II also introduces the differentiation between 'independent' and 'non-independent' investment advice. Advice from investment firms must meet two criteria in order to be 'independent': (i) they must assess a sufficient range of financial instruments (ie not limited to in-house products) and (ii) they must refrain from accepting or retaining inducements from third parties.[41] MiFID II

[38] Art 3(1) MiFID II.

[39] ESMA, 'Questions and Answers on MiFID II and MiFIR Investor Protection and Intermediaries Topics', Q 1, available at: www.esma.europa.eu/sites/default/files/library/esma35-43-349_mifid_ii_qas_on_investor_protection_topics.pdf> (accessed on 22 November 2022).

[40] ibid.

[41] Art 24(7) MiFID II.

ensures that clients receive better information about the cost of financial services. Investment firms have to inform clients about the total costs of investing and its impact on the yield, broken down into product costs and service costs.

A new concept of 'management body' has been introduced: the governing body of an investment firm or a data services provider, including the supervisory and the managerial functions (ie all persons who effectively direct the business).[42] Also, MiFID II imposed strengthened criteria for qualified senior management, the role of directors and supervisors, who must commit sufficient time to perform their function and take into account diversity in their composition.[43]

7.2.3. Extended Market Transparency and Transaction Reporting

MiFID I already imposed pre-trade and post-trade transparency requirements for trading on regulated markets and MTFs and for trading that takes place through internalisation or systematic internalisation. However, the transparency obligations are greatly expanded and harmonised in MiFID II. Key system changes are required to capture additional reporting requirements on new instruments such as bonds and derivatives, and additional information (65 fields, versus 23 previously) including identification of individuals, or computer algorithms where relevant, responsible for the investment decision.

Transaction reporting now also becomes the responsibility of the counterparty who initiates the transaction – typically buy-side firms, as under the new regime all investment firms have responsibility for ensuring that transaction information is accurate. Title IV of MiFIR (transaction reporting) sets out the obligation of investment firms and trading venues to keep data relating to transactions in financial instruments and then to report these details to the competent authorities. The reporting obligations are much wider than under MiFID I and therefore cover a wider range of execution venues and more types of financial instruments.[44] Transaction reports also need to be published through approved publication arrangement firms, which are subject to authorisation and certain organisational requirements.[45] This aim is to enable the competent authorities, in coordination with ESMA, to use these data to monitor the activities of investment firms to ensure that they act honestly, fairly and professionally and in a manner which promotes the integrity of the market.[46]

[42] Art 4(36) MiFID II.
[43] Art 4(37) MiFID II.
[44] Art 25 MiFID II and Arts 9–16 Commission Regulation (EC) No 1287/2006 of 10 August 2006 implementing Directive 2004/39/EC (MiFID Implementing Regulation).
[45] Art 20(1) MiFIR (equity) and Art 21(1) MiFIR (non-equity).
[46] Art 24 MiFIR.

7.2.4. Strengthened Prudential Surveillance

MiFID II/MiFIR empower national competent authorities (NCAs) throughout Europe to prohibit or restrict the marketing, distribution and sale of financial instruments.[47] In coordination with ESMA, NCAs have powers to permanently ban financial products, activities or practices, and limit the ability of any person to enter into commodity derivatives.[48] Administrative sanctions, fines and penalties will be made public, and be sufficiently high to offset any benefit and to be dissuasive also for larger institutions.

Market regulators also could use formal position management powers to deal with position limits for commodity derivatives. NCAs set position limits for each type of derivative traded on trading venues and for economically equivalent OTC contracts, on the basis of a method of calculation determined by ESMA.[49] The aims of imposing position limits are (a) to prevent market abuse, and (b) to support orderly pricing and settlement conditions, including preventing market distorting positions, and ensuring, in particular, convergence between the prices of derivatives in the delivery month and spot prices for the underlying commodity, without prejudice to price discovery on the market for the underlying commodity.[50] The investment firm or market operator operating the trading venue must inform the NCAs of the details of position management controls.[51] The NCAs communicate the same information, as well as the details of the position limits it has established, to ESMA, which then publishes and maintains on its website a database with summaries of the position limits and position management controls.[52]

7.3. ASEAN Trading Link

In the wake of the Asian financial crisis of 1997, the Association of Southeast Asian Nations (ASEAN) set up the ASEAN Capital Markets Forum (ACMF) in 2004, comprising securities regulators of all ASEAN states. The ACMF has introduced an Implementation Plan (2009–15) and Action Plans (2016–20 and 2021–25) to provide a clear roadmap for an integrated regional capital market.[53] Capital market integration was seen as vital to reduce vulnerabilities to external shocks

[47] Recital 125 MiFID II.

[48] Art 52 MiFID II.

[49] ESMA has developed regulatory technical standards to determine whether an OTC contract is economically equivalent to an OTC contract traded on a trading venue. See Art 57(12)(c) MiFID II and the Commission Delegated Regulation (EU) 2017/591, [2016] OJ L 87/479–91, Art 6.

[50] Art 57(1)(a) and (b) MiFID II; Recital 127 MiFID II.

[51] Art 57(10), first paragraph, MiFID II.

[52] Art 57(10), second paragraph, MiFID II.

[53] ACMF, 'About ACMF', available at: www.theacmf.org/about/about-acmf (accessed on 9 November 2022).

and market volatility following financial crises and to provide issuers with 'liquidity, scale and capacity to compete globally'.[54] The cooperation could result in the region having a greater voice in respect of global initiatives relating to financial stability and development. Financial integration in ASEAN accelerated with the establishment of the ASEAN Trading Link in 2012 and the ASEAN Economic Community (AEC) in 2015 to build ASEAN as a single market and production base, in which securities market integration was one of the key goals.[55]

The ASEAN Trading Link was a stock trading link established among the stock exchanges of Malaysia, Singapore and Thailand, launched in September 2012. This initiative was one of the measures driven by the ASEAN Exchanges, a collaboration of six stock exchanges within ASEAN.[56] The ASEAN Trading Link was initially created to mirror MiFID in Europe to break the barriers to cross-border trade and offer a single entry-point to three of Southeast Asia's biggest stock markets, with thousands of listed companies. Stockbrokers and international investors were allowed to connect directly to the three bourses through one sole broker in any of the three countries. Before the foundation of the trade link, the investor's broker had to establish a relationship with an additional vendor in the country they wished to invest in. With an additional broker involved, the client would have to pay more in brokerage fees. It was initially anticipated that the ASEAN Trading Link would connect all six equities markets of the ASEAN Exchanges by 2015.

However, the ASEAN Trading Link suffered from several drawbacks.[57] First, trading volume via the ASEAN Trading Link had not been particularly strong, given low regional investor interest and because brokers in each of Malaysia, Singapore and Thailand were, in any case, able to transact on other ASEAN exchanges before the establishment of the ASEAN Trading Link. Second, it lacked a centralised clearing and settlement system, which made it not fully operational as an end-to-end platform and undesirable for day-trading investors. Third, the lack of harmonisation in market regulation was also an issue. Different capital controls and exchange jurisdictions for each market deterred international investors.

Indeed, there were already measures emerging to solve these issues. For example, in 2014, the ASEAN Exchanges appointed Deutsche Bank to provide

[54] ACMF, 'Implementation Plan to Promote the Development of an Integrated Capital Market to Achieve the Objectives of the AEC Blueprint', 3, available at: www.theacmf.org/images/downloads/pdf/ACMF%20Implementation%20Plan%202009–2015.pdf (accessed on 9 November 2022).

[55] G Almekinders et al, 'ASEAN Financial Integration' (2015) International Monetary Fund (IMF) *Working Paper WP/15/34*, available at: www.imf.org/external/pubs/ft/wp/2015/wp1534.pdf (accessed on 9 November 2022).

[56] ASEAN Exchanges is a collaboration of the six exchanges from Indonesia, Malaysia, the Philippines, Singapore, Thailand and Vietnam. The collaboration aims to promote the growth of the ASEAN capital market by bringing more ASEAN investment opportunities to more people. See ASEAN Exchange's website: www.aseanexchanges.org/#/AboutUs (accessed on 9 November 2022).

[57] O Ward, 'The Missed Opportunity of the ASEAN Trade Link' (*ASEAN Today*, 21 October 2017), available at: www.aseantoday.com/2017/10/the-missed-opportunity-of-the-asean-trade-link/ (accessed on 9 November 2022).

clearing services. The better standardisation of clearing services was a step closer to launching an ASEAN clearing house in the future. Also, in 2015, Singapore, Malaysia and Thailand launched the Collective Investment Scheme (CIS) Framework to increase harmonisation and streamline the cross-border movement of funds.[58]

Despite the signs of progress, Singapore Exchange announced in a consultation paper that the ASEAN Trading Link was no longer in operation, with effect from 6 October 2017, and consequently Chapter 10A of the securities trading rules relating to the ASEAN Trading Link was also deleted.[59] With the termination of the ASEAN Trading Link, the integration of ASEAN's capital markets will have to start from scratch again and seek an alternative to closer integration and market standardisation.

Later, a plan to restore the trading link between Singapore and Malaysia was announced on 6 February 2018.[60] Learning from the failure of the ASEAN Trading Link and the successful experience of China–Hong Kong Stock Connect, the bilateral link not only covered trading, but also included post-trade arrangements such as the clearing and settlement of the stocks traded. The two regulators also planned to set up cross-border supervisory and enforcement arrangements, and formulate listing, trading and clearing rules for such link. But sadly, the bilateral trading link was called off following a regime change in Malaysia. The link is no longer 'a major priority' in its existing form for Malaysia's new government, according to the CEO of Bursa Malaysia, interviewed in 2022.[61] The more immediate task for Malaysia's government is boosting trading volumes and retaining customers by improving its service and attracting more initial public offerings in the technology and healthcare sectors. Instead, one notion being discussed by regional bourses is an 'ASEAN Connect' providing brokers and investors with one-stop access to the Indonesia, Thailand, Malaysia and Singapore stock markets, although this is an idea 'still a little ahead of its time'.[62]

[58] The ASEAN CIS Framework is one of the initiatives undertaken by the ASEAN Capital Markets Forum (ACMF). The Memorandum of Understanding on the ASEAN CIS Framework was first signed by the signatories in October 2013, and implemented in August 2014. More details at the ACMF, 'Framework for Cross-Border offering of ASEAN Collective Investment Schemes', available at: www.theacmf.org/initiatives/collective-investment-schemes/framework-for-cross-border-offering-of-asean-collective-investment-schemes (accessed on 6 November 2022).

[59] Singapore Exchange, 'Consultation Paper: Proposed Changes to the SGX-ST Rules and Other Rulebooks' 10 October 2017, paragraph 15.4, available at: api2.sgx.com/sites/default/files/public-consultations/migration/ST%2BRules%2BReview%2BPC.pdf (accessed on 9 November 2022).

[60] Monetary Authority of Singapore, 'Malaysia and Singapore to Set Up Stock Market Trading Link' (2 February 2018), available at: www.mas.gov.sg/news/media-releases/2018/malaysia-and-singapore-to-set-up-stock-market-trading-link (accessed on 6 November 2022).

[61] *The Star*, 'Trading Link with SGX Not Priority Now, Says Bursa CEO' (4 February 2022), available at: www.thestar.com.my/business/business-news/2022/02/04/trading-link-with-sgx-not-priority-now-says-bursa-ceo (accessed on 6 November 2022).

[62] ibid.

7.4. Intra-African Trade and Investment

African stock exchanges have undergone tremendous development in the past several decades. Many developments have been witnessed, such as the introduction of automated trades, demutualisation of several African exchanges, introduction of derivative products in several countries, and the introduction of exchange-traded funds and launch of US-dollar denominated trades, among others.[63] The past few years have also seen some newly created exchanges and an increase in cross-listings within Africa. From only eight stock exchanges in 1989, the number of African stock exchanges has grown to 25, representing 37 nations' capital markets with over 1100 listed companies.[64]

Despite African stock markets becoming comparatively deeper and more sophisticated, African capital markets remain underdeveloped. Excluding South Africa (235 per cent of GDP), the highest stock market capitalisation in Africa was in Mauritius (69 per cent of GDP) in 2018, which was below the average market capitalisation in the East Asia and Pacific region (83 per cent of GDP) and in high income countries (119 per cent of GDP).[65] Many factors could be contributing to the underdevelopment of capital markets in Africa, including the small size of the domestic economies, macroeconomic and business environment, quality of institutions, financial infrastructure, the shortage of talent and the lack of transparency in some marketplaces.[66]

A growing body of literature has evaluated the integration of African stock markets with emerging and global markets, given that most of these markets were recently established and are generally small. While some studies take a bilateral approach to determine the extent of integration between two exchanges, others use a continent-wide approach including the countries with the major African exchanges.[67] Some studies show a linkage between Africa and the global markets. For example, Alagidede examined four countries (South Africa, Egypt, Nigeria and Kenya) with some of the largest equity markets in Africa, and observed that these markets were working towards a pan-African stock exchange through the African Stock Exchanges Association (ASEA) and integration with the world economy.[68] The four countries have common colonial experience and common investment

[63] A Kunle and P Omoruyi, 'Empirics of Demutualization of African Stock Exchanges: Lesson from Nigeria' (2014) 3(2) *Journal of Finance and Investment Analysis* 14.

[64] The data is from the website of the African Securities Exchanges Association, available at: african-exchanges.org (accessed on 10 November 2022).

[65] I Soumaré et al, 'Capital Market Development in Sub-Saharan Africa: Progress, Challenges and Innovations' (May 2021) *Working Paper 2*, The ODI Research Series for Financial Development in Africa, 7.

[66] I Soumaré, 'Innovations in Equity and Stock Market Financing' (2020) Background Paper for Economic Report on Africa 2020, UNECA.

[67] K Nyakurukwa and Y Seetharam, 'Stock Market Integration in Africa: Further Evidence from an Information-Theoretic Framework' (2023) 26(1) *International Finance* 2, 3.

[68] P Alagidede, 'African Stock Market Integration: Implications for Portfolio Diversification and international Risk Sharing', *Proceedings of the African Economic Conference 2008*, 25–54.

policies, such as harmonising trading practices, encouraging cross-border listing of shares, developing computerised trading systems and promoting greater inter and intra-regional trade.

But most research supports a general perception that most of the African stock markets are isolated from the world market and weakly integrated within the continent.[69] Wang and others examined integration between five major African stock markets (South Africa, Egypt, Morocco, Nigeria and Zimbabwe) and the US market (used as a proxy for the rest of the world) during the financial crisis 1997–98.[70] They found that the US was significantly affected only by the South African market but not by other African markets. Hence, the degree of global integration of African stock markets was very limited, with the exception of South Africa. Similarly, Atenya used a dataset of stock index prices to examine the flow of information between the South African and East African Exchanges between 2008 and 2017. The study found that African exchanges were not influenced by each other despite increased efforts from various economic reforms and financial liberalisation.[71] This may be the outcome of political instability and investment barriers that have existed in many African countries, weak accounting and disclosure standards, differences in social and cultural practices, and information asymmetries.[72]

Regionalisation could be a route to deepening African capital markets, given that most local markets in Africa are very small in size, as suggested by Soumaré.[73] Regionalisation or regional financial integration can be defined as a market- or institutionally-driven process of broadening and deepening the financial interrelationships within a region. Integrated capital markets, if managed properly, will allow savings to be pooled across the region; cost and information sharing among members; diversification of risks; enhanced competition and innovation across financial institutions; wider choices of financial products provided to regional and foreign investors; and more integration into the global economy, facilitated by increased attractiveness of markets.[74]

Indeed, there are several initiatives to create regional stock exchanges in Africa. One of the most accomplished is the establishment of the West African Capital Markets Integration Council (WACMIC) on 18 January 2013 as the governing body for the integration of capital markets in the Economic Community of West African States (ECOWAS). The over-arching objective of the Council is to establish

[69] O Kodongo and K Ojah, 'Foreign Exchange Risk Pricing and Equity Market Segmentation in Africa' (2011) 35 *Journal of Banking & Finance* 2295.

[70] Z Wang et al, 'Financial Crisis and African Stock Market Integration' (2003) 10 *Applied Economics Letters* 527.

[71] MK Atenya, 'The Status Quo of East African Stock Markets: Integration and Volatility' (2019) 13(5) *African Journal of Business Management* 176.

[72] NA Boamah et al, 'Investigating Temporal Variation in the Global and Regional Integration of African Stock Markets' (2016) 36 *Journal of Multinational Financial Management* 103, 103.

[73] Soumaré et al (2021), see n 65 above, 26.

[74] J Irving, 'Regional Integration of Stock Exchanges in Eastern and Southern Africa: Progress and Prospects' (2005) *IMF Working Paper 05/122*.

a harmonised regulatory environment for the issuance and trading of financial securities across the region, as well as to develop a common platform for cross-border listing and trading of such securities in the sub-regions. It will deepen the West African capital markets, enabling them achieve scale to attract institutional and retail investors, and broaden the range of capital market instruments, corporate and sovereign issuances available for mobilisation of funding into private and public enterprises.

The WACMIC seeks to implement the integration of financial markets in three phases.[75] Phase 1 facilitates Sponsored Access trading between ECOWAS Member States' bourses, where a home country stockbroker can act as a sponsor of a foreign broker in transactions in the home country. Based on recognised agreements, the ECOWAS Member State brokers can trade and settle securities in markets other than their own jurisdiction through local brokers in those markets. The first step is seen as important because it requires a level of agreement and coordination not before seen in the regional capital markets. Sponsored Access trading began on 1 April 2015 and the first transactions were executed on 15 July 2015, which means that Phase 1 is already being implemented.

Phase 2 is scheduled to establish a common passport system to harmonise and validate regulations for trading and settlement of securities in West African capital markets as well as implement other related activities. The qualified brokers who receive a common passport will be mutually recognised by stock exchanges, regulators and depositories. These Qualified West African Brokers (QWAB) will then be able to deal directly in the securities markets across the other ECOWAS Member States without having to conclude a partnership with a local broker. This is a major step in the full dematerialisation of securities in the region, which will allow for the easier settling of shares cross-border and ultimately the unification of markets.

Phase 3 aims to fully integrate West African Capital markets. At this stage, all WACMIC member exchanges will be linked in a virtual West African Single Market (WASM), and QWABs will have access to listed securities and related market information to enable them to execute transactions in the region. The settlement banks will be able also to raise capital across the region. Currently, WACMIC is still in Phase 2 where the West Africa Securities Regulators Association has approved the documents and rules for the common passport and it is likely moving to Phase 3, the implementation stage.[76] But much is quite technical at this point, although the technicalities are very important if the markets are to work together. For example, trading hours have been harmonised (9am to 3pm), and a standard settlement

[75] *Bourse Régionale des Valeurs Mobilières* (Regional Stock Exchange) – the regional stock market for all the eight Member States in the West African Economic and Monetary Union, 'UEMOA', available at: www.brvm.org/en/wacmic (accessed on 25 November 2022).

[76] Ghanaian German Economic Association, 'West Africa Stock exchanges integration implementation likely this year – GSE MD' (14 February 2020), available at: ggea.net/news/west-africa-stock-exchanges-integration-implementation-likely-this-year-gse-md/ (accessed on 10 November 2020).

cycle has been agreed upon: T+3 (trade date plus three days) for equities and T+2 for bonds.

Another similar initiative to integrate capital markets is the launch of the East African Community (EAC), an intergovernmental organisation composed of seven countries in the Great Lakes region of East Africa. The broad goal of the EAC is to enhance cooperation in all areas for the mutual benefit of the Partner States. In the Treaty for the Establishment of the East African Community,[77] the Partner States committed to establishing a common market with free movement of capital. Specifically, the treaty calls for (i) removal of controls on capital transactions among the member countries (Article 86); and (ii) harmonisation of capital market infrastructure including regulations, taxation, accounting, trading systems, and cross-listings of securities (Article 85). The common market was officially launched in June 2010 as the second regional integration milestone of the EAC. To accelerate economic growth and development, the EAC Partner States maintain a liberal stance towards the four freedoms of movement (goods, persons/labour, services and capital) for all the factors of production and two rights (rights of establishment and residence) between themselves. The Common Market Protocol requires legislation by each member to fully implement the common market by 2015 and provides timetables of actions to be undertaken by each state, including capital account liberalisation.

Since the launch of the common market in EAC, concrete progress has been made, for example in a common procedure for cross-border listings, while further progress in wide areas including taxes, financial reporting, trading systems, and financial education is expected, despite the lack of a common currency.[78] Three of the markets (Uganda Securities Exchange, Dar es Salaam Stock Exchange, Rwanda Stock Exchange) have connected their trading systems and linked with the EAC Capital Markets Infrastructure platform.[79] But the requirements for full liberalisation still have been hampered by tariff and non-tariff barriers, red tape and non-compliance by the Partner States.[80] As the integration is partly politically driven, successful implementation of the Common Market Protocol largely depends on political goodwill among the EAC regional governments.[81] A degree of mistrust has resulted in delays in implementing the Common Market Protocol.

[77] The Treaty Establishing the East African Community was signed on 30 November 1999 and entered into force on 7 July 2000 following its ratification by the original three Partner States – Kenya, Uganda and Tanzania. The EAC was formally launched on 15 January 2001. The full text of the Treaty is available at: investmentpolicy.unctad.org/international-investment-agreements/treaty-files/2487/download (accessed on 10 November 2020).

[78] M Yabara, 'Capital Market Integration: Progress Ahead of the East African Community Monetary Union' (2012) *IMF Working Paper, WP/12/18.*

[79] EAC, 'Capital Markets infrastructure Adding Value to East Africans', available at: www.eac.int/financial/capital-markets-infrastructure (accessed on 10 November 2022).

[80] EAC, 'EAC Reviews Common Market Protocol Ahead of DRC Entry' (20 March 2022), available at: www.theeastafrican.co.ke/tea/news/east-africa/eac-reviews-common-market-protocol-ahead-of-drc-entry-3753502 (accessed on 10 November 2022).

[81] EAC, 'Report for an On-spot Assessment on the Challenges of Implementation of the Common Market Protocol along the Northern and Central Corridors by the Committee on Regional Affairs

Moreover, another attempt to deepen African capital markets is represented by the African Continental Free Trade Area (AfCFTA) agreement signed by 44 African Heads of State to establish a single continental market for goods and services on 21 March 2018. The AfCFTA is one of the flagship projects of the African Union's Agenda 2063, a blueprint toward transforming the continent to compete globally and deliver inclusive and sustainable development for African Union members. Since the inception of Africa's first continent-wide grouping, the Organisation of African Unity, in 1963, various initiatives have been explored toward ensuring the creation of a fully-fledged economic integration framework on the continent. These initiatives (for example, the 1979 Monrovia Summit, the 1980 Lagos Plan of Action and the 1991 Abuja Treaty) have largely failed to produce economic integration.[82]

The AfCFTA agreement entered into force on 30 May 2019, after 24 Member States deposited their instruments of ratification following a series of continuous continental engagements dating back to 2012. It has brought renewed hope for a continent-wide economic integration framework. The Member States commit to remove tariffs on 90 per cent of goods, progressively liberalise trade in services, and address a host of other non-tariff barriers.[83] If successfully implemented, the agreement will create a single African market of over a billion consumers with a total GDP of over USD 3 trillion. This will make Africa the largest free trade area in the world. The scope of AfCFTA exceeds that of a traditional free trade area – which generally focuses on trade in goods – to include trade in services, investment, intellectual property rights and competition policy, and possibly e-commerce.

The AfCFTA is regarded as a stepping-stone toward achieving the African Union Agenda 2063 and the establishment of a pan-African exchange. In line with the AfCFTA agreement, the interconnection of stock exchanges forms part of Africa's major economic and financial integration projects. As part of the AfCFTA negotiations, African countries are currently negotiating services-related commitments in five priority sectors: business services (including areas such as accounting, legal, and ICT-related services, among others), financial services, communication, transportation, and tourism. As of January 2022, 46 countries had submitted services offers. The parties are still working to try to finalise these negotiations. Nevertheless, some concerns about AfCFTA have been raised, including low intra-African trade and infrastructure too weak to support seamless economic integration.[84] An initiative toward regional integration based on the establishment

and Conflict Resolution' (November 2012), 8, available at www.eala.org/documents/view/report-on-common-market-protocol-implementation-challenges-along-the-northe (accessed on 10 November 2022).

[82] M Hailu, 'Regional Economic Integration in Africa: Challenges and Prospects' (2015) 8(2) *Mizan Law Review* 299.

[83] AfCFTA, 'About the AfCFTA', available at: au-afcfta.org/about/ (accessed on 12 November 2022).

[84] ET Aniche, 'African Continental Free Trade area and African Union Agenda 2063: The Roads to Addis Ababa and Kigali' (2020) *Journal of Contemporary African Studies* (online) 1.

of a pan-African stock exchange would be capable of driving transnational mergers, but the successful establishment of a pan-African stock exchange requires increased integration among existing African stock exchanges.[85]

7.5. Gulf Cooperation Council (GCC)

The Cooperation Council for the Arab States of the Gulf, commonly known as the GCC was founded on 25 May 1981, consisting of six members: Bahrain, Kuwait, Oman, Qatar, Saudi Arabia and the United Arab Emirates (UAE). The GCC countries form an oil-based region with the largest proven oil reserves in the world, 34 per cent of the world's total crude oil reserves in 2022. The GCC Charter states that the basic objectives are:

(i) to effect coordination, integration and inter-connection between Member States in all fields in order to achieve unity between them;
(ii) to deepen and strengthen relations, links and areas of cooperation now prevailing between their peoples in various fields;
(iii) to formulate similar regulations in various fields;
(iv) to stimulate scientific and technological progress in the fields of industry, mining, agriculture, water and animal resources; to establish scientific research; to establish joint ventures and encourage cooperation by the private sector for the good of their peoples.[86]

Economic integration is considered to be the cornerstone of the GCC. The first effort towards economic integration in the GCC countries was through the 1981 Unified Economic Agreement.[87] The Agreement draws the plan for the joint economic action and the phases of the economic integration and cooperation among the GCC states. Even though the Agreement was the GCC's major success on the economic side, most of its clauses have not been implemented. For instance, restrictions on capital and labour still existed in most Member States. Moreover, this Agreement was in place for 20 years without change or update in spite of dramatic change in economic conditions for Member States and the world economy in those two decades. Thus, an updated Economic Agreement was adopted in 2001, which has shifted the joint action approach from the stage of coordination to the stage of integration according to specific mechanisms and schemes.[88] According to the 2001 Economic Agreement, the Gulf Customs Union was created

[85] ibid.

[86] Article 4 of the GCC Charter. The Charter was signed on 25 May 1981.

[87] The Unified Economic Agreement 1981 was adopted by the GCC Supreme Council at its 2nd session in November 1981.

[88] GCC, 'Joint Action Process – the Economic Agreement 2001', available at: www.gcc-sg.org/en-us/CooperationAndAchievements/Achievements/EconomicCooperation/JointActionProcess/Pages/TheEconomicAgreement2001.aspx (accessed on 22 November 2022).

in January 2003, moving Member States to a single customs area in which trade barriers, taxes and related procedures are eliminated among them. This represents an important step in the process of economic integration, following the launch of a common market in 2008 and proposals for single currency by 2010.

At the same time, GCC countries accumulated large amounts of oil income during the 1980s and 1990s, giving impetus to the development of financial markets in these countries. The years of the setting up of the individual GCC stock markets differ, but the early 1990s marked the real beginning of these markets. In the 1990s most GCC countries attempted to diversity their economy and enhance financial infrastructure by privatising public sectors, utilising sophisticated technology in stock trading and modernising legal systems.[89] As Middle East economies work to diversify away from oil and gas, the capital markets become more and more important to fund this diversification. However, it is worth highlighting that the region is cash-rich and that the major companies are government owned, so the main function of the equity market is to privatise state assets/shares with citizens, rather than to raise funds to finance business.[90]

Most of the GCC stock markets were relatively small and virtually closed to foreign investors, a situation that blocked foreign portfolio investment inflows, even though the GCC Supreme Council in 1988 called for free participation in the GCC stock markets among Member States. The Supreme Council's resolution (9th session, December 1988) allowed GCC nationals to own shares in stock-companies and transfer ownership.[91] But those rules were amended by the Supreme Council's resolution (15th session, December 1994) to exclude some corporations such as insurance companies and banks. The amendment also allows for imposing other restrictions on the stock ownership and formation of corporations. At the same time, GCC countries adopted policies that led to greater openness of the respective capital markets to foreign investors and institutions. There is no doubt that the GCC countries are joining the global trend in trying to remove capital flow restrictions and to allow greater mobility than ever before. But variation in governmental policies applying to trading on these exchanges has led to different degrees of openness in these markets.

Bahrain, an Arabic island state in the Persian Gulf, has always been an important financial and banking centre, both in the Gulf region and internationally. The Bahrain Bourse (BHB, previously called the Bahrain Stock Exchange before

[89] M Fernandez and NM Sahawneh, 'GCC Stock Markets: A Comparative Analysis' (2010) 6(1) *Skyline Business Journal* 17, 17.

[90] CFA Institute Research Foundation, 'Middle East Capital Markets: Challenges and Opportunities' (2022), xiii, available at: www.cfainstitute.org/-/media/documents/article/rf-brief/rfbr-middle-east-capital-markets.pdf (accessed on 22 November 2022).

[91] GCC, 'Steps Have Been Taken to Achieve Economic Citizenship', IX Stock Ownership and Formation of Corporations, available at: www.gcc-sg.org/en-us/CooperationAndAchievements/Achievements/EconomicCooperation/TheGCCCommonMarketandEconomicnationality/Stepshavebeentakentoachieveeconomiccitizenship/Pages/IXStockOwnershipandFormationof.asp (accessed on 20 November 2022).

January 2011) was established in 1987 and officially commenced operations on 17 June 1989 with 29 listed companies. The BHB is the most liberalised market in this region. In 1999, the government lifted the restrictions on foreign ownership by issuing Amiri Decree No 10/1999, allowing GCC nationals to own up to 100 per cent (increased from 49 per cent) of the shares of listed Bahraini companies, and raising the permitted non-GCC investment from 24 per cent to 49 per cent with the exception of two state-owned companies (Bahrain Flour Mills and Delmon Poultry Company).[92]

Kuwait is the second largest country among the GCC states after Saudi Arabia. The Kuwait Stock Exchange (KSE), which was inaugurated in 1977, is the oldest exchange in the Gulf region, but was not fully liberalised until 2013. Non-GCC investors were previously forbidden to trade on the KSE, except through mutual funds. In 2013, the Kuwaiti authorities issued the Direct Investment Promotion Law (Decree Law No 116 for 2013) to allow foreign investors to own up to 100 per cent equity in a Kuwaiti company (previously restricted to 49 per cent).[93] Kuwait now follows the 'Negative List' approach, by which investments in sectors outside the Negative List are eligible for 100 per cent foreign ownership. Article 1 of Ministerial Resolution No 75 of 2015 sets out the Negative List that includes 10 different sectors in which investments by foreign entities are not permitted.

Oman is a middle-income economy with notable oil and gas resources and substantial trade and budget surpluses. Its Muscat Securities Market (MSM), established in 1988 and reorganised as an automated trading and settlement system in 1989, has the lowest capitalisation of the six GCC stock markets. Subject to certain exceptions, the Foreign Capital Investment Law (FCIL) No 102/1994 capped foreign ownership at 49 per cent of an Omani company's share capital. This threshold was increased to 70 per cent upon Oman's accession to the World Trade Organization. By repealing the old FCIL, the 2019 FICL No 50/2019 removes these restrictions on foreign ownership. As a result, a foreign investor now can generally own 100 per cent of an Omani company's share capital. But certain business activities remain closed to foreign investment in the 'Negative List'.

Qatar is one the smallest Gulf countries in terms of population and geographical area, but has the second largest gas reserves in the world, representing more than five per cent of the world total. The GDP per capita income in Qatar (USD 93,508) ranked fourth in the world in 2022.[94] Trading on the Doha Securities Market (DSM) in Qatar started manually in 1997, with electronic central clearing

[92] WTO, 'Trade Policy Reviews – Bahrain: October 2000' (13 October 2000), available at: www.wto.org/english/tratop_e/tpr_e/tp139_e.htm (accessed on 20 November 2022).

[93] Article 12 of Kuwait Direct Investment Promotion Law 2013, the full text of law is available at: e.kdipa.gov.kw/main/law1162013.pdf (accessed on 25 November 2022).

[94] IMF, 'GDP per Capita', available at: www.imf.org/external/datamapper/NGDPDPC@WEO/OEMDC/ADVEC/WEOWORLD (accessed on 25 November 2022).

and settlement, and became fully automated in 2002. The market started operations with 17 companies. At the beginning of its operation, DSM allowed only Qatari citizens to trade the stocks. However, on 7 January 2019, Foreign Capital Investment Law No 1 of 2019, regulating the investment of non-Qatari capital in economic activity, became effective, repealing Law No 13 of 2000. The new law permits foreign ownership of up to 100 per cent in all economic sectors, but certain activities remain excluded, namely banking and insurance, unless exempted by a Council of Ministers' decision.[95]

Saudi Arabia is an oil-based economy with the largest proven oil reserves in the world, representing 54.5 per cent of the GCC countries' reserves, 28.4 per cent of those of OPEC, and 20 per cent of the world's total reserves. By far the largest stock market is Saudi Arabia, with a market capitalisation of USD 2.7 trillion at the end of 2022.[96] The Saudi Arabia Investment Fund, which was launched by the Saudi American Bank in 1997, is traded on the London Stock Exchange, allowing foreign investors to trade indirectly in Saudi shares. On 26 June 2019, the 'Instructions for Foreign Strategic Investors' Ownership in Listed Companies', issued by the Capital Market Authority, became effective.[97] The Instructions removed the existing limit (49 per cent) on foreign ownership of a Saudi-listed company for foreign strategic investors. Under the new regulations, foreign ownership of stocks will no longer be limited to qualified foreign investors (ie financial firms with at least USD 500 million in assets under management). Also, the previous minimum or maximum ownership limits for strategic investors have been abolished.

The UAE is located in the middle of the Persian Gulf. The Dubai Financial Market was founded in March 2000, and the combined market capitalisation of Dubai and Abu Dhabi plus NASDAQ Dubai that was founded on 26 September in 2005, have already elevated the UAE stock market to the second largest stock market in the GCC region. With Dubai becoming the financial and economic hub of the Gulf region, most investors in UAE securities focus on the Dubai Financial Market, which already accounts for about three-quarters of the country's total trading volume. In the view of Yeung and Huang, common law financial centres including Dubai, Abu Dhabi and Doha arise in Islamic countries owing to their

[95] UNCTAD, 'Investment Policy Hub – Qatar: New Law Regulating Foreign Investment Allows Up to 100 Percent Foreign Ownership' (7 January 2019), available at: investmentpolicy.unctad.org/investment-policy-monitor/measures/3360/new-law-regulating-foreign-investment-allows-up-to-100-percent-foreign-ownership (accessed on 25 November 2022).

[96] The data from Saudi Exchange, 'Market Summary', available at: www.saudiexchange.sa/wps/portal/tadawul/home/!ut/p/z1/04_Sj9CPykssy0xPLMnMz0vMAfIjo8zijYycLQwtTQx83D39zA0cAx09wtzCQowNDEz1w_Wj9KPwKTGBKjDAARwN9IMTi_QLsrPTHB0VFQEBEmvK/dz/d5/L0lHSkovd0RNQUZrQUVnQSEhLzROVkUvZW4!/ (accessed on 25 November 2022).

[97] Capital Market Aauthority, 'Instructions for Foreign Strategic Investors' Ownership in Listed Companies' (June 2019), available at: cma.org.sa/en/RulesRegulations/Regulations/Documents/Instructions-FSI-Ownership-Listed-Companies-en.pdf. UNCTAD, 'Investment Policy Hub – Saudi Arabia: Relaxes Ownership Limits for Foreign Investors' (26 June 2019), available at: investmentpolicy.unctad.org/investment-policy-monitor/measures/3415/saudi-arabia-relaxes-ownership-limits-for-foreign-investors (accessed on 25 November 2022).

transplantation and operation of laws based on the English common law, independent of their national legal systems (civil law systems influenced by Islamic tradition).[98]

Historically, UAE law provided that foreign investors could only own up to 49 per cent of a UAE mainland company, subject to limited exceptions. At least 51 per cent of the shares in a UAE mainland company had to be owned by one or more UAE nationals, or by a company which was itself wholly owned by one or more UAE nationals. In 2017, the UEA implemented a legislative change to the Commercial Companies Law No 2 of 2015, permitting 100 per cent foreign ownership of certain onshore companies. In September 2018, the Federal Decree Law No 19 of 2018 regarding foreign direct investment was issued, which provided a Negative List for sectors in which an application for foreign direct investment may not be made. Also, in March 2020, the UAE Cabinet issued a 'Positive List of Economic Sectors and Activities in which Foreign Direct Investment is Permitted' to provide the much-awaited list of business activities that would allow 100 per cent ownership in companies by foreign investors (subject to the satisfaction of certain criteria).[99]

In the last decade, stock markets in the Middle East were largely ignored by international investors due to restrictions imposed on foreign stock ownership and the lack of common accounting standards and corporate transparency, or dismissed simply on the basis of economic and political uncertainty.[100] But with the continued economic reform and further liberalisation of financial markets, this region has become one of the world's fastest growing markets in the banking and capital market sector. Various studies have been conducted on stock market integration in the Middle East and North Africa (MENA) region and the GCC countries. For example, some scholars analysed MENA market subsets but could not find any significant cross-linkages despite market proximity.[101] Others have tried to determine the market dynamics and contemporaneous interactions of the GCC stock markets and concluded that GCC market integration is increasing.[102] But Qatar and the UAE are more financially integrated, while there is evidence of

[98] H Yeung and F Huang, 'The Rise of Distinct Common Law Commercial Zones in Islamic Countries' (December 2019) Law and Development Conference, Dubai, UAE, available at: www.lawanddevelopment.net/img/2019papers/yeung.pdf (accessed on 25 November 2022).

[99] UAE Government Portal, 'Federal Law on Commercial Companies', available at: u.ae/en/information-and-services/business/full-foreign-ownership-of-commercial-companies (accessed on 22 November 2022).

[100] J Bley and KH Chen, 'Gulf Cooperation Council (GCC) Stock Markets: The dawn of a New Era' (2006) 17 *Global Finance Journal* 75, 77.

[101] Eg T Lagoarde-Segot and BM Lucey, 'Capital Market Integration in the Middle East and North Africa' (2007) 43(3) *Emerging Markets Finance and Trade* 34; JS Yu and MK Hassan, 'Global and Regional Integration of the Middle East and North African (MENA) Stock Markets' (2008) 48(3) *Quarterly Review of Economics and Finance* 482.

[102] Eg Bley and Chen (2006), see n 100 above; and T Alshammari, 'Integration of the GCC Stock Markets' (2020) 11(5) *Research in World Economy* 24.

relatively weak financial linkages for all the other cases. Despite the great progress made in the field of economic cooperation and integration between the GCC economies, the capital market integration process still faces some challenges, as evidenced by the relative weakness of stock market integration between these countries.[103]

7.6. Comparison of Different Market Connectivity Mechanisms

7.6.1. Reg NMS vs. MiFID

Reg NMS and MiFID represent major changes in the structure of the markets for equities trading in the US and EU respectively. At their cores, the goals of the SEC and the European Commission are the same: to create a more efficient, transparent and fair market for investors. But Reg NMS is more targeted, while MiFID takes on a broader range of issues. MiFID, in part, attempts to create a more unified European equities market with greater convergence in terms of business practice, market structure and regulation in Member States. Reg NMS seeks to address specific shortcomings in the existing structure of the US equities markets.

Although MiFID and Reg NMS share the common objectives of enhancing competition in securities markets, a closer look reveals very substantial differences in many ways, such as best execution, the consolidation of market data and the disclosure of trades execution information.

First, a major difference lies in the best execution standards. In defining best execution, MiFID takes a series of criteria and characteristics into account, thus allowing best execution requirements to be tailored to each investor's profile, whereas Reg NMS emphasises strict price priority.[104] In other words, Reg NMS covers a number of factors, with price being typically the most important, while price is just one factor among others in assessing whether the client has obtained the best possible result for the execution of its trade under MiFID.

MiFID I introduced in its Article 21 the obligation to execute orders on terms most favourable to the client and to take all reasonable steps to obtain the best possible result for clients when executing orders. MiFID II reinforces the best execution criteria in Article 27 that 'price, costs, speed, likelihood of execution and settlement, size, nature or any other consideration relevant to the execution of the order' must be evaluated against the background of the client and the circumstances of an order. When an order comes from a retail client, the investment firm is obliged to take into account total consideration, representing the price of a

[103] J Jouini, 'Does Economic Cooperation Lead to Great Stock Market Integration in the GCC Region?' (March 2020), *Arab Monetary Fund Research Paper No 3/2020*.

[104] Casey and Lannoo (2009), see n 17 above, 207.

financial instrument and transaction costs. The EU acknowledges best execution as the multiple dimensions of market quality and also implies that heterogeneity in traders' needs is protected under MiFID, unless there are other reasons to think otherwise. Also, the term 'reasonable steps' in MiFID I was replaced with 'sufficient steps' in MiFID II to set a higher bar for firms' compliance in ensuring the best possible result for their clients when executing orders.

Moreover, in accordance with Article 64 of the MiFID II Delegated Regulation, investment firms need to take into account the following when they determine the relative importance of the factors from Article 27 of MiFID II:

(1) the characteristics of the client including the categorisation of the client as retail or professional;
(2) the characteristics of the client order, including where the order involves a securities financing transaction;
(3) the characteristics of financial instruments that are the subject of that order; and
(4) the characteristics of the execution venues to which that order can be directed.

In contrast, price alone matters under Reg NMS, provided that the quote is automated and immediately executable. Quotes from a non-automated market like NYSE specialists and floor brokers could be traded-through. Obviously, this rule creates a huge competitive gap between fast markets and slow, whose quotations can be traded through markets, and also generates opportunities for new trading venues to compete on the basis of price only, rather than relationships or other factors.[105]

Besides, Reg NMS Rule 602b obliges trading centres to execute each order at the best available price and if they cannot fill an order at the best price they are expected to route it to a competing trading venue displaying better quotes. Therefore, it is the responsibility of the trading venue to pass on the orders it cannot fill at the best price. This provision implies that market centres in the US need to link and route orders to each other. Under MiFID II, by contrast, investment firms only are responsible for the best execution of their clients' orders and, consequently, markets do not need to be interconnected and route orders to each other.

Second, the SEC and the EU have taken different approaches to the consolidation of market data. Reg NMS institutes a single data consolidator with a complex method for allocating fees, whereas MiFID just opens market data to competition.[106] Prior to MiFID I, equity quotes and trade data were concentrated in just one exchange. Following MiFID I, quotes and trade information had been split between multiple trading venues and reporting platforms. MiFID I only required trading venues to make public price, volume and time of trades as close to

[105] G Petrella, 'MiFID, Reg NMS and Competition Across Trading Venues in Europe and the USA' (2010) 18(3) *Journal of Financial Regulation and Compliance* 257, 262.
[106] Casey and Lannoo (2009), see n 17 above, 206.

real time as possible on a reasonable commercial basis. This approach liberalised the market for security data and allowed businesses to offer services aggregating data from different trading venues. However, in order to improve access to market data and increase market liquidity, MiFID II proposed the creation of a consolidated tape (CT) which would act as a single price-comparison tool consolidating data across the EU, assisting market participants in analysing market liquidity and increasing investors' capacity to evaluate the quality of execution of their orders.[107]

The third difference lies in the disclosure of execution information. Reg NMS requires both markets and intermediaries to regularly publish statistics on execution quality, whereas European trading venues face no comparable requirement under MiFID I. Reg NMS gives more freedom to trading venues to disseminate their trade reports independently, but still requires them to communicate best prices to the data consolidator. To facilitate the comparison of execution costs across markets, Reg NMS Rule 605 requires market centres (such as exchanges, electronic communication networks and dealers) to publish, on a monthly basis, statistics on several dimensions of execution quality (probability of orders' execution, speed of execution, execution costs, price improvement) and Reg NMS Rule 606 requires intermediaries too to make public, on a quarterly basis, the market centres to which they route the orders received from customers. The consolidation of best quotes and trades benefits investors, since it enables them to assess the quality of execution prices and evaluate the best execution of their orders by obtaining data from a single source that is reliable and comprehensive.[108]

MiFID II also introduced the obligation for firms and execution venues to produce a number of periodic reports to demonstrate the quality of executions and compliance with its best execution obligations. In accordance with the obligations set out in the Commission Delegated Regulation (EU) 2017/5754 (RTS 27), execution venues are required to produce quarterly reports with regard to the quality of their execution including the publication of data on price, costs and likelihood of execution.[109] In turn, investment firms are also required to publish an assessment of execution quality obtained in relation to all execution venues used by the firm.

7.6.2. Stock Connect vs. Other Market Connectivity Mechanisms

China has three national government-owned securities exchanges in Shanghai, Shenzhen and Beijing, plus the exchange of Hong Kong Special Administrative

[107] ESMA, 'Final Guidelines on the MiFID II/MiFIR Obligations on Market Data' (18 August 2021), ESMA70-156-4263.

[108] Petrella (2010), see n 105 above, 263.

[109] The European Commission is empowered to adopt a delegated Regulation to specify the content, the format and the periodicity of data on the quality of execution, to be published by execution venues under Art 27(10) (a) of MiFID II.

Region. As the world's second largest economy, China needs to open-up its onshore market to offshore funds, while enhancing its exchanges' international reputation. Stock Connect is a mutual market access service to link Chinese stock exchanges to foreign exchanges, but it does not lead to a common market between them, which is the major distinction to separate Stock Connect from other market connectivity. This can be traced back to their roots in divergent purposes and visions.

Most economic and political unions such as the EU, ASEAN, the African regional unions and GCC have multiple and profound purposes of removing trade barriers and establishing a single market with free flow of goods, services, investments, capital and labour. Following the successful example of the EU, many unions have made major steps towards economic unity. While free trade is still the main focus of these unions, they also recognise the proven tangible economic benefits associated with a significant degree of financial integration. Capital market integration is the highest form of their economic integration, which demands agreement on adjustment, or even harmonisation, of national policies. Thus, deeper integration necessarily implies surrendering some national autonomy.[110] In contrast, Stock Connect is purely a cross-boundary investment channel that connects Chinese and non-Chinese bourses, which requires regulatory cooperation on both sides but does not reduce national autonomy in states' investment and capital market policies.

Also, unlike the US and EU models which create 'destabilising levels of complexity' through multilateral competition, Stock Connect does not advocate competition among trade-matching platforms.[111] Both Reg NMS and MiFID use legally imposed competition for order flows among trading venues, which will drive down trading costs while providing large broker-dealers with new business opportunities. Competition among trading centres may, however, lead to a fragmented marketplace and this may arguably damage market quality.[112] In contrast, Stock Connect uses the same systems of transparency, oversight and price discovery that are developed in traditional exchanges, with the addition of a further concentrated pool of partner exchanges. It allows broker-dealers from each participant exchange to place orders on the other participant exchange, stimulating competition among brokers rather than among exchanges. The direct connection between exchanges through Stock Connect allows even small brokers to execute trades on distant markets without the kind of proprietary connection usually exercised only by large competitors. China's model preserves network externalities while giving a larger portion of the national economy access to each of the exchanges within the national territory. This approach of granting reciprocal access to existing exchanges' matching systems retains the monopoly position of

[110] U Koester, 'Market Integration: How it Works' in A Burrell and A Oskam (eds), *Agricultural Policy and Enlargement of the European Union* (Wageningen, Wageningen Pers, 2000).
[111] Donald (2015), see n 1 above, 176.
[112] Petrella (2010), see n 105 above, 257.

traditional exchanges, allowing them to escape the competitive pressure stimulated by the US and EU models.

The ASEAN Trading Link was the predecessor of Stock Connect, allowing licensed brokers to execute orders on all participant stock exchanges, thus multiplying network externalities. Such link advances further financial integration through common trading rules and platforms so as to avoid the pitfalls of market fragmentation and 'regulatory hollowing' while consolidating a large regional market.[113] But the failure of the ASEAN Trading Link was attributed to the lack of centralised clearing and settlement and the divergence of market regulations. Instead, Stock Connect well makes up for those shortcomings of the ASEAN Trading Link by establishing centralised clearing links whereby the parties will undertake to each other to perform their settlement obligations. Also, China's market regulators stay committed to enhancing regulatory cooperation with other securities authorities by signing many Memoranda of Understanding to set up common legal frameworks and cross-border enforcement commitments for Stock Connect as addressed in Chapter five.

7.7. Concluding Remarks

Connectivity among securities exchanges has progressed, along with advances in technology and economic integration. Among different market connectivity mechanisms, the US's Reg NMS and the EU's MiFID are the most directly comparable since they share similar objectives aiming to maintain fair and orderly markets, protect investors, and provide price transparency. Although both markets have become more integrated – the US within its national territory and the EU within its treaty area – there are many differences in securities rules and approaches on both sides of the Atlantic. The unprecedented scope of harmonisation of securities markets legislation and the resulting open architecture ushered in by Reg NMS and MiFID, especially in trade execution and reporting, have caused a profound upheaval within existing market structures.

Seen from the EU perspective, Reg NMS is more protective of US exchanges and execution venues providing automated execution, applies a narrow definition of best execution and maintains a monopolistic data consolidator. MiFID, on the other hand, is more orientated towards market opening, but it may lead to a higher degree of order fragmentation, and hence reduce liquidity, if connectivity is not assured.[114] It has a broad and flexible definition of best execution, but this may cause the enforceability issue for national authorities. However, the disparities between the two securities regulatory regimes appear to have become smaller with the implementation of MiFID II/MiFIR.

[113] Donald (2015), see n 1 above, 195.
[114] Casey and Lannoo (2009), see n 17 above, 213.

Other regions follow in the EU's steps to develop a common market to promote economic and financial integration, along with significant divergence of developmental stages across the regions. The common constraint in African and Middle Eastern capital markets is that their markets are generally underdeveloped with relatively small-sized and illiquid markets as well as insufficient market infrastructure. The GCC countries and African unions such as ECOWAS and EAC have been actively pursuing regional integration of domestic capital markets by removing capital restrictions and harmonising market infrastructure. These efforts achieved some outputs such as a common procedure for cross-border listings and harmonising some technical standards as well as relaxing restrictions for foreign investors. Despite the authorities' efforts, capital market integration in these regions is still limited, with some countries showing signs of increasing divergence. In Asia, as part of capital market integration, the ASEAN Trading Link was initially established to mirror MiFID in Europe to become a single entry point for the ASEAN exchanges. Nevertheless, the ASEAN Trading Link was terminated in 2017 due to the low liquidity, the absence of a centralised clearing system and the lack of harmonisation in market regulation.

Improved from the ASEAN Trading Link, China's Stock Connect preserves concentrated trading and clearing settlement while multiplying network externalities. As a form of quasi-public infrastructure, Stock Connect is also diametrically opposed to the US and EU arrangements of multiplying private platforms, and this is extremely important both for the economics of trading and for the structure of regulation. While the US and EU integration programmes seek to place exchanges under competitive pressure, they in fact offer large broker-dealers the new business opportunity of opening trading facilities. Stock Connect, on the other hand, protects exchanges but places larger broker-dealers under competition by removing the advantages they have gained through building proprietary connections to other markets. China's model that multiplies network externalities while retaining transparency offers an alternative for regulators in all regions to consider.

8

Conclusion

8.1. Summary of the Findings

This book offers a comprehensive and comparative analysis of Stock Connect, discussing its legal and implementation challenges, and examining the impacts it has had on both local and global financial markets. Established initially in 2014 as a link between the Shanghai and Hong Kong stock exchanges, Stock Connect has expanded to include four links and five stock exchanges, namely Shanghai–Hong Kong Stock Connect (Shanghai Connect), Shenzhen–Hong Kong Stock Connect (Shenzhen Connect), Shanghai–London Stock Connect (London Connect) and China–Switzerland Stock Connect (Switzerland Connect).

8.1.1. Uniqueness of Stock Connect

The four existing Stock Connect links are different from each other, and also distinct from other Chinese liberalisation schemes. To consolidate the different links, in 2022 China expanded the investment scopes of both Shanghai and Shenzhen Connects, bringing them in line with each other in terms of investment opportunities and business models as well as clearing and settlement.[1] Additionally, China has unified the depository receipt rules for London and Switzerland Connects. The China Securities Regulatory Commission (CSRC) has set out guidelines in its 'Provisions on the Supervision and Administration of Depository Receipts under the Stock Connect Scheme between Domestic and Overseas Stock Exchanges 2022' that require international issuers to meet the same liquidity and compliance criteria for offering and trading Chinese depository receipts (CDRs) in the Chinese domestic markets under London and Switzerland Connects.[2] However, the listing and trading requirements for London/Switzerland Connects are still higher than those of Shanghai/Shenzhen Connects in terms of financial criteria for issuers and investor suitability, as well as the regulatory approval.

Compared to other Chinese financial liberalisation schemes such as Qualified Foreign Investor (QFI, a collective regime that includes Qualified Foreign Institutional

[1] HKEX, 'HKEX Welcomes Further Expansion of Stock Connect' (19 December 2022), available at: www.hkex.com.hk/News/News-Release/2022/2212192news?sc_lang=en (accessed on 20 February 2023).

[2] Issued by the CSRC on 11 February 2022 (CSRC Announcement [2022] No 28).

Investor and RMB Qualified Foreign Institutional Investor schemes)) and Qualified Domestic Institutional Investors (QDII), Stock Connect is generally considered to be more liberalised in capital markets and more accessible to international investors.

While all financial liberalisation schemes in China aim to facilitate investment flows between China and overseas financial markets, the most significant differences between Stock Connect and others lie in market access, investor suitability, types of investment, and regulatory restrictions. Stock Connect allows a wider range of participants, including both institutional and individual investors, to invest in the Chinese stock market. This is in contrast to the QFI/QDII schemes, which are primarily designed for institutional investors. Also, compared to the QFI/QDII schemes, which require investors to obtain quotas from the government and face restrictions on the types of investments they can make, Stock Connect offers investors a more open and streamlined access to the Chinese stock market. Under Stock Connect, investors can trade eligible securities directly on the counterpart stock exchange without the need to obtain a quota from the Chinese government, and without facing the same investment restrictions as under the other schemes, despite the limited selection of investable securities to which Stock Connect applies.

8.1.2. Home Market Rules or Co-regulation?

In addition to the unique features of Stock Connect, this book has thoroughly examined the three-tier regulatory regimes (investors, issuers, and regulators) in the four participant markets. The fundamental principle of Stock Connect, known as 'home market rules', on the face of it, requires investors in securities to comply with the laws and regulations of the market where those securities originate. The home market rule ensures that investors follow the regulations in each market and protects the integrity and stability of the markets involved in Stock Connect. However, in the case of Stock Connect, it is more likely that co-regulation is in fact in place rather than purely relying on home market rules.

For instance, when international investors purchase Chinese securities through Stock Connect, Chinese securities law and listing rules should prevail because China is considered the home market. However, host market laws and regulations may also apply concurrently because trading and clearing participants in Hong Kong are still in principle subject to the Securities and Futures Ordinance (SFO) of Hong Kong, and the issuance of global depository receipts (GDRs) is subject to the securities law and listing rules in the UK and Switzerland.[3] Conversely, Chinese investors who trade securities through the Hong Kong or London/Switzerland links must comply with the laws and regulations of those markets while still being subject to Chinese law.

[3] F Huang, 'Stock Connect: Integration, Internationalisation and Implementation' (2021) 7 *Journal of Business Law* 558, 569.

Under London/Switzerland Connect, companies listed on the London and SIX Swiss exchanges are primarily regulated by their respective home market rules including company law, securities law and listing rules. However, they are also subject to the CSRC and exchange rules when issuing CDRs. Similarly, Chinese GDR issuers must adhere to the regulations of the two Connect markets. In contrast, under Shanghai/Shenzhen Connect, companies in Mainland China and Hong Kong are only governed by their respective home market rules. This is because investors on both sides can directly purchase and sell stocks in the other market, with the products remaining local under Shanghai/Shenzhen Connect. On the other hand, under London/Switzerland Connect, depository receipts that are converted from stocks in the counterpart market are listed and traded in the local market, with the products crossing borders while investors remain local.

Co-regulation is even more apparent in regulatory enforcement, where Stock Connect has brought significant changes to the incentives of the CSRC from being a passive recipient of enforcement requests to actively collaborating with overseas regulators. Despite different supervisory structures in the Connect markets, China has maintained collaborative relationships with the other three jurisdictions in the financial markets. As Stock Connect continues to develop and improve, it is increasingly important in opening-up Chinese capital markets and promoting regulatory collaboration. This is evidenced by numerous memorandums of understanding (MoUs) signed between China and overseas authorities, as well as the growing number of cross-border enforcement actions. These enforcement actions also represent a significant milestone for the CSRC, as it employs international cooperation to prevent cross-border securities violations.

It is also observed that all four jurisdictions reviewed in this context have appropriate legal frameworks to protect investors and regulate corporate issuers. Each jurisdiction has its own regulatory measures, with some variations in the codification of director duties, shareholder actions, information disclosure and the prohibition of market misconduct. But there is no significant regulatory disparity between them. The level of investor protection for domestic securities is not significantly different from that for foreign securities acquired through Stock Connect. Switzerland might have raised some concerns in comparison to other countries, but it has undertaken a significant transformation of its corporate and financial legal framework in recent years. Therefore, it can be concluded that these variations do not necessarily point to any substantial discrepancies in investor protection and corporate governance standards that warrant concern.

8.1.3. 'One Country, One Market' but Limited Impacts on Global Markets

Stock Connect has had a significant impact on local and global financial markets. In the short and medium term, it has improved liquidity by providing access to a larger pool of investors and facilitated greater investment flows between Mainland China and Hong Kong. This has led to increased capital flows and greater financial integration between the two regions. Over the long term, Stock Connect has played a crucial role in promoting legal and institutional reforms in Mainland China and Hong Kong, with the ultimate goal of creating a unified market in the region. Moreover, it has enhanced market connectivity between China and the rest of the world by enabling investors to trade Chinese stocks through local brokers. This has resulted in the integration of China into the global financial system and promoted trade and investment between China and other countries. Additionally, Stock Connect has allowed for increased participation of international investors in China's currency, the Renminbi (RMB), contributing to the internationalisation of the RMB and further integrating China into the global financial system.

Out of the four links, two are connected with Hong Kong, while the other two are connected with overseas exchanges. The links with Hong Kong seem to be more successful in terms of trading volume and the number of issuers. Stock Connect has created a single 'China' stock market that ranks among the world's largest, measured by market capitalisation and daily trading turnover. Hong Kong has traditionally been a significant financial hub in the Asia-Pacific region, and its status as a Special Administrative Region of China, along with its historical links to the British Empire, has allowed it to establish close relationships with both regions, making it a natural 'superconnector' between them.[4] Its strategic location, well-developed financial infrastructure, and regulatory framework make it an attractive destination for investors from both regions.

The impact of Stock Connect on the global financial markets has been positive but also limited thus far, with the potential to drive greater market integration and promote economic growth. However, none of the British or Swiss issuers have utilised Stock Connect to list on Chinese stock exchanges. Limited participation in London/Switzerland Connects is due to greater listing and regulatory restrictions, more appealing existing investment channels, the complex process of fungibility of DRs, and regulatory differences in investor protection and information disclosure. Therefore, Stock Connect appears to have more strategic significance than practical use concerning the global financial markets. With the expansion of the Connect scheme to embrace additional exchanges and asset classes and the relaxation of restrictions on both sides of the border, its impact and significance will continue to spread.

8.1.4. Better Options for Market Connectivity in the World

In recent years, global capital market connectivity has been steadily increasing due to advancements in technology, regulatory reforms, and the growing demand for

[4] HKEX, 'Our Connect Story: A New Chapter Begins' (October 2022), available at: www.hkex.com.hk/-/media/HKEX-Market/Mutual-Market/Stock-Connect/Reference-Materials/Resources/HKEX-Connect-Story.pdf (accessed on 20 February 2023).

cross-border investment opportunities.[5] However, this connectivity is not evenly distributed across the world, as certain regions and countries face significant barriers to entry and limited access to international capital markets. Political instability, weak regulatory frameworks, and insufficient infrastructure are some factors that can hinder the growth of capital market connectivity in these areas.[6]

The US's Regulation National Market System (Reg NMS) and the EU's Markets in Financial Instruments Directive (MiFID) are the most comparable market connectivity mechanisms owing to the similar objectives of maintaining fair and orderly markets, protecting investors, and providing price transparency. Despite differences in their securities rules and approaches, the disparities have become smaller with the implementation of MiFID II and the Markets in Financial Instruments Regulation (MiFIR). Other regions, such as Africa and the Middle East, are following the EU's lead in developing a common market to promote economic and financial integration, but they generally have underdeveloped, illiquid markets with insufficient infrastructure. In Asia, the Association of Southeast Asian Nations (ASEAN) Trading Link was terminated due to low liquidity and lack of harmonisation in market regulation.

By contrast, as a system improving on the ASEAN Trading Link, China's Stock Connect maintains concentrated trading and clearing settlement, while also increasing network externalities. Unlike the US and EU models, which rely on private platforms, Stock Connect is a quasi-public infrastructure that regulators may consider an alternative. The US and EU systems have yet to restore adequate transparency, oversight, and price discovery, but China's model increases liquidity by multiplying network externalities while preserving transparency.[7] Stock Connect exemplifies how a link between securities markets can bridge capital markets without fragmentation, which may offer a superior option for securities regulators in the rest of the world. For example, Taiwan has considered using the Stock Connect model to link Singapore, Japan and London.[8]

8.2. The Future of Stock Connect

The future of Stock Connect looks promising, as it has already gained significant traction since its launch. The link has seen increasing trading volumes and

[5] P Gomber et al, 'Competition between Equity Markets: A Review of the Consolidation versus Fragmentation Debate' (2016) 31(3) *Journal of Economic Surveys* 792, 792–93.

[6] C Guervo et al, 'Strengthening Capital Markets Regulation-National Progress and Gaps' (June 2022), *IMF Monetary and Capital Market Department Paper DP/2022/012*, 1–5.

[7] D Donald, 'Bridging Finance Without Fragmentation: A Comparative Look at Market Connectivity in the US, Europe and Asia' (2015) *European Business Organisation Law Review* 173, 200.

[8] R Tung, 'Taiwan Stock Connect Link with Singapore May be Ready Near Year End' (*Reuters*, 19 March 2015), available at: www.reuters.com/article/taiwan-markets-singpaore-idUSL3N0WL1JS20150319 (accessed 20 February 2023).

growing interest from global investors, which suggests that it is likely to continue to expand in the years ahead.

One of the key factors driving the future growth of Stock Connect is the continued liberalisation of the Chinese financial markets. Chinese regulators have been taking steps to open up the markets to foreign investors, including relaxing restrictions on foreign ownership of domestic companies and increasing access to financial services.[9] This trend is expected to continue, which will make it easier for international investors to access the Chinese markets through Stock Connect.

Another factor that will drive the future growth of Stock Connect is the increasing demand for exposure to the Chinese markets. The Chinese economy has been growing rapidly over the past few decades, and its stock markets are now some of the largest in the world. As the Chinese economy continues to grow, more investors will be looking for opportunities to invest in Chinese companies and gain exposure to this growth.

There are some potential trends that could shape the future of Stock Connect such as the inclusion of more asset classes, the continued expansion to more exchanges, potential for increased regulatory cooperation.

- First, since the start of Stock Connect nine years ago, there have been several expansions to make it more accessible to global investors. These include abolishing the aggregate quotas in 2016 and increasing the daily trading quota in 2018; adding Exchange Traded Funds (ETFs) listed in Hong Kong, Shanghai, and Shenzhen in 2022, making it easier for investors to diversify their portfolios and gain exposure to a broader range of assets; and expanding the scope of eligible stocks under Shanghai/Shenzhen Connect in response to the high demand for access to the Chinese stock markets in 2022.

  The Stock Connect model is also replicated in other areas such as bonds and commodities. Bond Connect, established in 2017, allows investors from Mainland China and overseas to trade in each other's bond markets through a market infrastructure linkage in Hong Kong. The Hong Kong Exchanges and Clearing Limited (HKEX) has also successfully launched futures contracts on gold, precious metals, base metal, and ferrous metals. It aims to establish a direct Commodities Connect scheme with Mainland China to accelerate the internationalisation of China's commodities market.[10] These expansions and developments have contributed to the growth of cross-border investment

[9] CSRC, 'Q&A on Further Opening Up the Capital Market' (17 June 2019), available at: www.csrc.gov.cn/csrc_en/c102035/c1371505/content.shtml (accessed on 20 February 2023); and S Shen and R Woo, 'China to Push on with Opening Capital Markets to Foreign Investors' (*Reuters*, 6 September 2021), available at www.reuters.com/world/china/china-will-improve-opening-up-capital-market-securities-regulator-2021-09-06/ (accessed on 20 February 2023).

[10] HKEX, 'The Connectivity Platform Offered by the HKEX Commodities Market for the Mainland and the World' (March 2020), research paper, 10, available at: www.hkex.com.hk/-/media/HKEX-Market/News/Research-Reports/HKEx-Research-Papers/2020/CMD_HK_CommConnect_e_202003.pdf (accessed on 21 February 2023).

flows and have made it easier for international investors to access the Chinese markets.

- Second, the expansion of Stock Connect has enabled it to cover multiple international stock exchanges at a rapid pace. It all started with the Shanghai–Hong Kong Stock Connect and has spread to four links bridging five different exchanges. Furthermore, a new China–Germany Stock Connect may pave the way for Chinese companies to tap European markets for fundraising. There have also been speculations that Stock Connect may expand to include other markets like Singapore and Japan, thereby giving investors more options to diversify their portfolios and access a broader range of Asian markets.[11]
- Third, given the cross-border nature of Stock Connect, it is important for regulators in different jurisdictions to cooperate effectively. By standardising regulations and procedures, investors can be assured of consistent and predictable rules governing their investments, reducing compliance costs and increasing transparency. Many MoUs have been signed between China and overseas regulators, which has resulted in an increasing number of cross-border enforcement actions. As a result, the CSRC's attitude has shifted from being a passive enforcement receiver to an active enforcement requester. However, achieving effective regulatory cooperation can be challenging due to differences in regulatory frameworks and legal systems, the lack of international standards and harmonisation, and market conditions across different jurisdictions.[12] Regulators must navigate these differences while ensuring that their regulatory objectives are met, which can require considerable coordination and collaboration. As such, there is a need for continued efforts to promote regulatory cooperation and standardisation in order to facilitate cross-border investment and support the continued growth of Stock Connect.

In conclusion, the launch of Stock Connect has played a crucial role in boosting investor confidence in China's financial markets, as it has signalled the country's commitment to liberalising its financial sector and opening-up to foreign investment. Stock Connect has also facilitated greater market integration between China's domestic capital markets and global markets, reducing market fragmentation and promoting greater cross-border trade. The future of Stock Connect looks bright, as it continues to play a crucial role in opening-up the Chinese markets to international investors. With the continued liberalisation of the Chinese financial markets, increasing demand for exposure to the Chinese markets, and the potential for further expansions of the scheme, Stock Connect is likely to continue to

[11] E Yiu, 'Singapore to establish ETF link with Shenzhen, joining Hong Kong, London in tie-ups with Chinese exchanges' (*South China Morning Post*, 29 December 2021), available at: www.scmp.com/business/banking-finance/article/3161389/singapore-establish-etf-link-shenzhen-joining-hong-kong (accessed on 21 February 2023).

[12] IOSCO, 'Market Fragmentation & Cross-border Regulation' (June 2019), 8, available at: www.iosco.org/library/pubdocs/pdf/IOSCOPD629.pdf (accessed on 20 February 2023).

grow and evolve in the coming years and become an increasingly vital part of the global investment landscape.

While Stock Connect offers many benefits, it also poses risks and challenges, including regulatory complexity, trading limitations, market volatility, information asymmetry, and political and economic risks.[13] Stock Connect involves multiple regulators across different jurisdictions, which can create challenges for investors and issuers who must navigate a complex regulatory environment. Cross-border investments can be more volatile than domestic investments due to differences in market conditions and regulatory environments. Trading limitations, such as daily quotas and participant eligibility, can impact liquidity and trading volumes. Access to timely and accurate information about companies listed on Stock Connect exchanges can be challenging, which may impact investors' decisions. Additionally, investors must also consider political and economic risks, such as changes in government policies, geopolitical tensions, and currency fluctuations, which could impact the performance of their investments. The biggest challenge for the future of Stock Connect is geopolitical tensions between China and other countries. The ongoing trade tensions between China and the US, for example, could have an impact on the demand for access to the Chinese markets. However, given the significant growth potential of the Chinese economy, it is likely that investors will continue to look for ways to gain exposure to the Chinese markets through Stock Connect.

[13] CSRC, 'Capital Markets Connectivity: Opportunities and Challenges' (August 2019), available at: www.carecprogram.org/uploads/Capital-Markets-Connectivity-Opportunities-and-Challenges-Developments-in-China.pdf (accessed on 20 February 2023).

BIBLIOGRAPHY

Books

Armour, J et al, *Principles of Financial Regulation* (Oxford, OUP, 2016).
Casey, JP and Lannoo, K, *The MiFID Revolution* (New York, Cambridge University Press, 2009).
Chen, CH and Shih, HT, *The Evolution of The Stock Market in China's Transnational Economy* (Cheltenham, Edward Elgar, 2002).
Davies, P et al, *Gower Principles of Modern Company Law* (London, Sweet & Maxwell, 2021).
Donald, D, *A Financial Centre for Two Empires* (Cambridge, Cambridge University Press, 2014).
Deng, XP, *Selected Words by Deng Xiaping* (Beijing, People's Publishing House, 1993).
Fu, J and Yuan, J, *PRC Company & Security Laws: A Practical Guide* (Singapore, CCH Asia, 2006).
Green, S, *China's Stockmarket: A Guide to its Progress, Players and Prospects* (London, Profile Books, 2003).
Gu, M, *Understanding Chinese Company Law* (Hong Kong, Hong Kong University Press, 2006).
Gullifer, L and Payne, J, *Corporate Finance Law* (Oxford, Hart Publishing, 2020).
Ho, S et al, *The Hong Kong Financial System* (Hong Kong, OUP, 2004).
Huang, F and Yeung, H, *Chinese Companies and the Hong Kong Stock Market* (Abingdon, Routledge, 2014).
Jiang, P, *Zhongmei Wuquanfa de Xianzhuang yu Fazhan* (*The Presence and Development of Sino-US Property Law*) (Beijing, Tsinghua University Press, 2003)
Keay, A. *The Enlightened Shareholder Value Principle and Corporate Governance* (Abingdon, Routledge, 2014).
Kraakman, R et al, *Anatomy of Corporate Law* (Oxford, OUP, 2017).
Law, J and Martin, E, *A Dictionary of Law* (Oxford, OUP, 2014).
Li, D, *Zhengquan Jianguan Falun (Securities Regulation Law Theory)* (Beijing, Peking University Press, 2019).
Liu, J, *Xiandai Gongsi Fa (Modern Corporation Law)* (Beijing, Law Press China, 2015)
Lo, C, *Demystifying China's Mega Trends: The Driving Forces That Will Shake Up China and the World* (Bingley, Emerald Publishing, 2017).
Lu, L, *Private Lending in China: Practice, Law and Regulation of Shadow Banking and Alternative Finance* (Abingdon, Routledge, 2019).
Manne, H, *Insider Trading and the Stock Market* (New York, The Free Press, 1966).
Michie, R, *The London Stock Exchange: A History* (Oxford, OUP, 2001).
Robson, P, *The Economics of International Integration* (London, Allen and Unwin, 1980).
Siems, M, *Convergence in Shareholder Law* (Cambridge, CUP, 2007).
SFC, *Securities Regulation in Hong Kong* (Hong Kong, Securities and Futures Commission, 2002).
Tyler, E and Ho, J, *HKLRD Review Series 2004: Company Law* (Hong Kong, Sweet and Maxwell, 2004).
Zhen, Y, *China's Capital Markets* (Oxford, Chandos Publishing, 2013).
Zhou, Y, *Zhengjuanfa Xinlun* (*New Study on Securities Law*) (Beijing, Law Press China, 2020).

Chapters in books

Chen, C et al, 'Corporate Accounting Scandals in China' in MJ Jones (ed), *Creative Accounting, Fraud and International Accounting Scandals: Fraud and International Accounting Scandals* (Chichester, John Wiley & Sons, 2012).

Donald, DC, 'Networked Securities Markets: From Cross-listing to Direct Connection' in DW Warner et al (eds), *Research Handbook on Asian Financial Law* (Cheltenham, Edward Elgar, 2020).
Hasenstab, M, 'Financial System Reform and Implications' in R Garnart and LG Song (eds), *China: Twenty Years of Economic Reform* (Canberra, Australian National University E Press, 2012).
Huang, RH, 'Financial regulatory structure in China: Challenges and transitioning to Twin Peaks' in A Godwin and A Schmulow (eds), *The Cambridge Handbook of Twin Peaks Financial Regulation* (Cambridge, Cambridge University Press, 2021).
Huang, H, 'The Regulation of Insider Trading in China: Law and Enforcement' in S Bainbridge (ed), *Research Handbook on Insider Trading* (Cheltenham, Edward Elgar, 2013).
Koester, U, 'Market Integration: How it Works' in A Burrell and A Oskam (eds), *Agricultural Policy and Enlargement of the European Union* (Wageningen, Wageningen Pers, 2000).
McVea, H, 'The Impact of the Global Financial Crisis upon the UK's Regulatory Architecture' in R Goddard and D Cash (eds), *Regulation and the Global Financial Crisis: Impact, Regulatory Responses, and Beyond* (Abingdon, Routledge, 2021).
Stoll, H, 'Market Microstructure', in G Constantinides et al (eds), *Handbook of the Economics of Finance*, Vol 1A, (Amsterdam, Elsevier, 2003).
Tang, X, 'Protecting Minority Shareholders in China: A Task for Both Legislation and Enforcement' in H Kanda et al (eds), *Transforming Corporate Governance in East Asia* (London, Taylor & Francis, 2008).
Xi, C, 'CSRC Enforcement of Securities Laws: Preliminary Empirical Findings' in S Griffith et al (eds) *Research Handbook on Representative Shareholder Litigation* (Cheltenham, Edward Elgar, 2018).
Xi, C and Pan, XM, 'Public Enforcement of Securities Laws: A Case of Convergence?' in Y Zhao and M NG (eds), *Chinese Legal Reform and the Global Legal Order: Adoption and Adaptation* (Cambridge, Cambridge University Press, 2017).

Journal Articles

Aitken, M et al, 'The Impact of Fragmentation, Exchange Fees and Liquidity Provision on Market Quality' (2017) 41 *Journal of Empirical Finance* 140.
Alagidede, P, 'African Stock Market Integration: Implications for Portfolio Diversification and international Risk Sharing', *Proceedings of the African Economic Conference 2008.*
Alshammari, T, 'Integration of the GCC Stock Markets' (2020) 11(5) *Research in World Economy* 24.
Almekinders, G et al, 'ASEAN Financial Integration' (2015) *IMF Working Paper WP/15/34.*
Anderson, D, 'Taking Stock in China: Company Disclosure and Information in China's Stock Markets' (2000) 88 *Georgetown Law Journal* 1919.
Anderson, C and Guo, B, 'Corporate Governance under the New Company Law (Part 2): Shareholder Lawsuits and Enforcement', *China Law & Practice* (May 2006).
Aniche, ET, 'African Continental Free Trade area and African Union Agenda 2063: The Roads to Addis Ababa and Kigali' (2020) *Journal of Contemporary African Studies* online) 1.
Angel, JJ et al, 'Equity Trading in the 21st Century' (2015) 1(1) *Quarterly Journal of Finance* 1.
Armour, J et al, 'Private Enforcement of Corporate Law: An Empirical Comparison of the UK and the US' (2009) 6(4) *Journal of Empirical Legal Studies* 687.
——, 'Shareholder Protection and Stock Market Development: An Empirical Test of the Legal Origins Hypothesis' (2009) 6 *Journal of Empirical Legal Studies* 343.
Art, R and Gu, MK, 'China Incorporated: The First Corporation Law of the People's Republic of China' (1995) 20 *Yale Journal of International Law* 273.
Atenya, MK, 'The Status Quo of East African Stock Markets: Integration and Volatility' (2019) 13(5) *African Journal of Business Management* 176.
Austin, J, 'IOSCO's Multilateral Memorandum of Understanding Concerning Consultation, Cooperation and the Exchange of Information' (2012) 23 *Criminal Law Forum* 393.

Bai, Y and Chow, D, 'Shanghai-Hong Kong Stock Connect: An Analysis of Chinese Partial Stock Market Liberalisation Impact on the Local and Foreign Markets' (2017) 50 *Journal of International Financial Markets, Institutions & Money* 182.

Bai, Y et al, 'Shanghai-Hong Kong Stock Connect: An Analysis of Chinese Partial Stock Market Liberalisation Impact on the Local and Foreign markets' (2017) 50 *Journal of International Financial Markets, Institutions & Money* 182.

—— 'Analysis of Price Differences between A and H Shares' (2019) 26 *Asia-pacific Financial Market* 529.

Battalio, R et al, 'Toward a National Market System for US Exchange-Listed Equity Options' (2004) 2 *Journal of Finance* 933.

Bekaert, G and Harvey, CR, 'Emerging Equity Market Volatility' (1997) 43(1) *Journal of Financial Economics* 29.

Beltratti, A et al, 'the Stock Market Reaction to the 2005 Non-Tradable Share Reform in China' (2011) *European Central Bank Working Paper Series No 1339.*

Bennett, P and Wei, L, 'Market Structure, Fragmentation, and Market Quality' (2006) 9(1) *Journal of Financial Markets* 49.

Berkowitz, D et al, 'Economic Development, Legality and the Transplant Effect' (2003) 47 *European Economic Review* 165.

Bhattacharya, U and Daouk, H, 'The World Price of Insider Trading' (2022) 57 *Journal of Finance* 75.

Biais, B and Foucault, T, 'HFT and Market Quality' (2014) 128 *Bankers, Markets & Investors* 5.

Bley, J and Chen, KH, 'Gulf Cooperation Council (GCC) Stock Markets: The dawn of a New Era' (2006) 17 *Global Finance Journal* 75.

Boamah, NA et al, 'Investigating Temporal Variation in the Global and Regional Integration of African Stock Markets' (2016) 36 *Journal of Multinational Financial Management* 103

Boskovia, T, Cerruti, C and Noel, M, 'Comparing European and US Securities Regulations: MiFID versus Corresponding US Regulations' (2009), *World Bank Working Paper No 184.*

Brogaard, J and Garriott, C, 'High-frequency Trading Competition' (2019) 54 Journal of Financial and Quantitative Analysis 1469.

Burkhardt, M et al, 'The Securities Litigation Review: Switzerland' (22 May 2022), available at: thelawreviews.co.uk/title/the-securities-litigation-review/switzerland (accessed on 1 February 2023).

Busch, D, 'MiFID II and MiFIR: Stricter Rules for the EU Financial Markets' (2017) 11 *Law and Financial Markets Review* 126.

Cadmus, E, 'Revisiting the SEC's Memoranda of Understanding: A Fresh Look' (2011) 36(6) *Fordham International Law Journal* 1800.

Calvo, D et al, 'Financial Supervisory Architecture: What has Changed after the Crisis?' (April 2018) Financial Stability Institute Insights on Policy Implementation No 8, available at: www.bis.org/fsi/publ/insights8.pdf (accessed on 20 June 2022).

Carpenter, JN and Whitelaw, RF, 'The Development of China's Stock Market and Stakes for the Global Economy' (2017) 9 *Annual Review of Financial Economics* 233.

Carlton, D and Fischel, D, 'The Regulation of Insider Trading' (1983) 35 *Stanford Law Review* 857.

Cearns, K and Ferran, E, 'Non-enforcement-led Public Oversight of Financial and Corporate Governance Disclosures and of Auditors' (2008) 8(2) *Journal of Corporate Studies* 191.

Chan, K and Kwok, J, 'Market Segmentation and Share Price Premium: Evidence from Chinese Stock Markets' (2005) 4(1) *Journal of Emerging Market Finance* 43.

Chan, MK and Kwok, S, 'Connecting the Markets? Recent Evidence on China's Capital Account Liberalisation' (2018) 70 *Economic Modelling* 417.

Chang, M, 'Hugangtong Mingyi Chiyou Gupiao Falv Wenti Chutan' ('Discussion on Beneficial Ownership under Shanghai-Hong Kong Stock Connect') (2015) *Company Law Review* 109.

Chari, A and Henry, PB, 'Risk Sharing and Asset Prices: Evidence from a Natural Experiment' (2002) 59 *Journal of Finance* 1295.

Cheffins, B, 'Does Law Matter?: The Separation of Ownership and Control in the United Kingdom' (2001) 30 *Journal of Legal Studies* 459.

Chen, F, 'Special Representative Litigation System; The Chinese-style Securities Class Action Mechanism for Investor Protection: Context, Content, Comparison and Consequence' (2022) 30 *Asia Pacific Law Review* 287.

Chen, GM et al, 'Is China's Securities Regulatory Agency a Toothless Tiger? Evidence from Enforcement Actions' (2005) 24 *Journal of Accounting and Public Policy* 451.

Chen, J, 'Securitization of State-owned Enterprises and the Ownership Controversy in the PRC' (1993) 15 *Sydney Law Review* 59.

Chen, Z at el, 'Ownership Concentration, Firm Performance and Dividend Policy in Hong Kong' (2005) 13 *Pacific-Basin Finance Journal* 431.

Cheung, R, 'Insider Trading Sentencing: An Anglo-American Comparison' [2014] *Journal of Business Law* 566.

Claessens, S et al, 'The Separation of Ownership and Control in East Asian Corporation' (2000) 58 *Journal of Financial* Economics 81.

Clarke, D, 'Corporate Governance in China: An Overview' (2003) 14 *China Economic Review* 494.

Click, RW and Plummer, MG, 'Stock Market Integration in ASEAN After the Asian Financial Crisis' (2005) 16(1) *Journal of Asian Economics* 5.

Coase, R, 'The Nature of the Firm' (1937) 4 *Economica* 386.

Coffee, J, 'The Rise of Dispersed Ownership The Roles of Law and the State in the Separation of Ownership and Control' (2001) 111 *Yale Law Journal* 1.

—— 'Racing Towards the Top? The Impact of Cross-Listing and Stock Market Competition on International Corporate Governance' (2002) 102 *Columbia Law Review* 1757.

—— 'Law and the Market: the Impact of Enforcement' (2007) 156(2) *University of Pennsylvania Law Review* 229.

Cogman, D and Orr, G, 'How They Fell: The Collapse of Chinese Cross-Border Listings' (*McKinsey & Co*, 1 December 2013), available at: www.mckinsey.com/business-functions/strategy-and-corporate-finance/our-insights/how-they-fell-the-collapse-of-chinese-cross-border-listings (accessed on 20 April 2022).

Cohen, KJ and Conroy, RM, 'An Empirical Study of the Effect of Rule 19c-3' (1990) 33(1) *Journal of Law and Economics* 277.

Cunha, R, 'The IOSCO Multilateral Memorandum of Understanding MMoU: An International Benchmark for Securities Enforcement' (2010) 15 *Uniform Law Review* 677

Das et al, US, 'Financial Regulators Need Independence', (December 2002) 39(4) *IMF Finance & Development*, available at: www.elibrary.imf.org/view/journals/022/0039/004/article-A008-en.xml (accessed on 20 March 2022).

DeHaan, E et al, 'The Revolving Door and the SEC's Enforcement Outcomes: Initial Evidence from Civil Litigation' (2015) 60 *Journal of Accounting and Economics* 65.

Donald, DC, 'Bridging Finance Without Fragmentation: A Comparative Look at Market Connectivity in the US, Europe and Asia' (2015) 16 *European Business Organisation Law Review* 173.

Donald, D and Cheuk, P, 'Hong Kong's Public Enforcement Model of Investor Protection' (2017) 4 *Asian Journal of Law and Society* 349.

Easterbrook, F and Fischel, D, 'Mandatory Disclosure and the Protection of Investors' (1984) 70 *Virginia Law Review* 669.

Elliott, J, 'Demutualisation of Securities Exchange: A Regulatory Perspective' (2002) IMF working paper WP/02/119, available at: www.imf.org/external/pubs/ft/wp/2002/wp02119.pdf (accessed on 20 April 2022).

Fama, E, 'Efficient Capital Markets: A Review of Theory and Empirical Work' (1970) 25(2) *Journal of Finance* 383.

Fernandez, M and Sahawneh, NM, 'GCC Stock Markets: A Comparative Analysis' (2010) 6(1) *Skyline Business Journal* 17.

Ferran, E, 'Examining the UK Experience in Adopting the Single Financial Regulator Model' (2003) 28 *Brooklyn Journal of International Law* 257.

Ferrell, A, 'The Case for Mandatory Disclosure in Securities Regulation around the World' (2007) 2 *Brooklyn Journal of Corporate, Financial & Commercial Law* 81.

Foerster, SR and Karolyi, GA, 'The Effects of Market Segmentation and Investor Recognition on Asset Prices: Evidence from Foreign Stocks Listing in the United States' (1999) 54 (3) *Journal of Finance* 981.

Foucault, T and Menkveld, AJ, 'Competition for order flow and smart order routing systems' (2008) 63(1) *Journal of Finance* 119.

Furman, J et al, 'Economic Crises: Evidence and Insights from East Asia' (1998) 29(2) *Brookings Papers on Economic Activity* 1.

Gajewski, JF and Gresse, C, 'Centralised Order Books versus Hybrid Order Books: A Paired Comparison of Trading Costs on NSC (Euronext Paris) and SETS (London Stock Exchange)' (2007) 31(9) *Journal of Banking & Finance* 2906.

Gilson, R, 'The Mechanisms of Market Efficiency' (1984) 70 *Virginia Law Review* 549.

Gilson, RJ and Gordon, JN, 'Controlling Controlling Shareholders' (2003) 152(2) *University of Pennsylvania Law Review* 785.

Gleeson, S and Bloomenthal, H, 'The Public Offer of Securities in the United Kingdom' (1999) 27 *Denver Journal International Law and Policy* 359.

Gomber, P et al, 'Competition between Equity Markets: A Review of the Consolidation versus Fragmentation Debate' (2016) 31(3) *Journal of Economic Surveys* 792.

Goo, S, 'Multiple Derivative Action and Common Law Derivative Action Revisited: A Tale of Two Jurisdictions' (2010) 10 *Journal of Corporate Law Studies* 255

Goodhart C and Lastra, R, 'Border Problems' (2010) 13 *Journal of International Economic Law* 705.

Gu, MK and Art, R, 'Securitisation of State Ownership: Chinese Securities Law' (1996) 18 *Michigan Journal of International Law* 115.

Guervo, C et al, 'Strengthening Capital Markets Regulation-National Progress and Gaps' (June 2022), *IMF Monetary and Capital Market Department Paper DP/2022/012.*

Guintyn, MG and Taylor, MW, 'Should Financial Sector Regulators be Independent?' (March 2004) *IMF Economic Issues No 32.*

Gunningham, N, 'Moving the Goalposts: Financial Market Regulation in Hong Kong and the Crash of October 1987' (1990) 15 *Law and Social Inquiry* 1.

Haas, F 'The Markets in Financial Instruments Directive: Banking on Market and Supervisory Efficiency', *IMF Working Paper WP/07/250* (2007).

Hailu, M, 'Regional Economic Integration in Africa: Challenges and Prospects' (2015) 8(2) *Mizan Law Review* 299.

Hansmann, H and Kraakman, R, 'The End of History for Corporate Law' (2001) 89 *Georgetown Law Journal* 439.

Harper Ho, V, '"Enlightened Shareholder Value": Corporate Governance Beyond the Shareholder-Stakeholder Divide' (2010) 36 *Journal of Corporation Law* 59.

Härtsch, T and Dedeyan, D, 'The Initial Public Offerings Law Review: Switzerland' (6 September 2022), available at: thelawreviews.co.uk/title/the-initial-public-offerings-law-review/switzerland (accessed 1 February 2023).

Hasbrouck, J, 'High-frequency Quoting: Short-term Volatility in Bids and Offers' (2018) 53(2) *Journal of Financial and Quantitative Analysis* 613.

Harrold, P, 'China's Reform Experience to Date' (1992), *World Bank discussion paper, WDP 180.*

Harris, LE, 'Consolidation, Fragmentation, Segmentation, and Regulation' (1993) 48(3) *Journal of Finance* 1092.

Hawes, C, 'The Chinese "Oppression" Remedy: Creative Interpretations of Company Law by Chinese Courts' (2015) 63 *American Journal of Comparative Law* 559.

Hill, JG, 'Regulatory Cooperation in Securities Market Regulation: Perspectives from Australia' (2020) 17(1) *European Company and Financial Law Review* 11.

Howson, N, 'Enforcement without Foundation? – Insider Trading and China's Administrative Law Crisis' (2012) 60(4) *American Journal of Comparative Law* 955.

Hu, GX et al, 'Chinese Capital Market: An Empirical Overview' (2018) *NBER Working Papers 24346.*

Huang, F, 'Modernising the Chinese Capital Market: Old Problems and New Legal Responses' (2010) 21(1) *International Company and Commercial Law Review* 26.

—— 'In Defence of China's Public Enforcement in Equity Market' (2010) 21(10) *International Company and Commercial Law Review* 327.

—— 'Dual Class Shares around the Top Financial Centres' [2017] *Journal of Business Law* 137.

—— 'Stock Connect: Integration, Internationalisation and Implementation' [2021] *Journal of Business Law* 558.

Huang, F and Yeung, H, 'Regulatory Cooperation between Securities Commission: A Reflection from Hong Kong' (2013) 1(1) *Chinese Journal of Comparative Law* 112.

—— 'Shareholder Protection in China from a Numerical Comparative Law Perspective' (2019) 7(1) *Chinese Journal of Comparative Law* 124.

Huang, H, 'Insider Trading and the Regulation on China's Securities Market: Where are We Now and Where do We Go from Here?' (2012) 5 *Journal of Business Law* 379.

—— 'Private Enforcement of Securities Law in China: A Ten-Year Retrospective and Empirical Assessment' (2013) 61 *American Journal of Comparative Law* 757.

—— 'Enforcement of Chinese Insider Trading Law: An Empirical and Comparative Perspective' (2020) 68(3) *American Journal of Comparative Law* 517.

—— 'Rethinking the Relationship between Public Regulation and Private Litigation: Evidence from Securities Class Action in China' (2018) 19 *Theoretical Inquiries in Law* 333.

—— 'Shareholder Derivative Litigation in China: Empirical Findings and Comparative Analysis' (2012) 27 *Banking and Finance Law Review* 619

Huang, HC and Lin, JH, 'The Impact of Shanghai-Hong Kong Stock Connect Policy on Price Differences and Announcement Effects' (2016) 10(3) *Global Journal of Business Research* 1.

Huo, S, 'The Company Law of the People's Republic of China' (1995) 13 *Pacific Basin Law Journal* 373.

Huo, R and Ahmed, AD, 'Return and Volatility Spillovers Effects: Evaluating the Impact of Shanghai-Hong Kong Stock Connect' (2017) 61 *Economic Modelling* 260.

Hutchens, W, 'Private Securities Litigation in China: Material Disclosure about China's Legal System' (2003) 24 *University of Pennsylvania Journal of International Economic* Law 599.

Irving, J, 'Regional Integration of Stock Exchanges in Eastern and Southern Africa: Progress and Prospects' (2005) *IMF Working Paper 05/122.*

Jackson, E and Roe, M, 'Public and Private Enforcement of Securities Law: Resource-based Evidence' (2009) 93(2) *Journal of Financial Economics* 207.

Jappelli, T and Pagano, M, 'Financial market Integration under EMU' (March 2008) *European Commission Economic Papers 312.*

Jensen, M and Meckling, W, 'Theory of the Firm: Managerial Behaviour, Agency Costs and Ownership Structure' (1976) 3 *Journal of Financial Economics* 305.

Johnson, S et al, 'Tunnelling' (2000) 90 (2) *American Economy Review* 22.

Jouini, J, 'Does Economic Cooperation Lead to Great Stock Market Integration in the GCC Region?' (March 2020) *Arab Monetary Fund Research Paper, No 3/2020.*

Katelouzous, D and M Siems, M, 'Disappearing Paradigms in Shareholder Protection: Leximetric Evidence for 30 Countries, 1990–2013' (2015) 15 *Journal of Corporate Law Studies* 127.

Ke, B and Zhang, X, 'Does Public Enforcement Work in Weak Investor Protection Countries? Evidence from China' (2021) 38 *Contemporary Accounting Research* 1231.

Keay, A, 'Assessing and Rethinking the Statutory Scheme for Derivative Actions under the Companies Act 2006' (2016) 16 *Journal of Corporate Law Studies* 39.

King, MR and Segal, D, 'The Long-Term Effects of Cross-Listing, Investor Recognition, and Ownership Structure on Valuation' (2009) 22(6) *Review of Financial Studies* 2393.

King, M and Roell, A, 'Insider Trading' (1988) 6 *Economic Policy* 165.

Knauss, R, 'Securities Regulation in the United Kingdom: A Comparison with United States Practice' (1974) 5 *Vanderbilt Law Review* 47.

Kodongo, O and Ojah, K, 'Foreign Exchange Risk Pricing and Equity Market Segmentation in Africa' (2011) 35 *Journal of Banking & Finance* 2295.

Kunle, A and Omoruyi, P, 'Empirics of Demutualization of African Stock Exchanges: Lesson from Nigeria' (2014) 3(2) *Journal of Finance and Investment Analysis* 14.

Lagoarde-Segot, T and Lucey, BM, 'Capital Market Integration in the Middle East and North Africa' (2007) 43(3) *Emerging Markets Finance and Trade* 34.
La Porta, R et al, 'Legal Determinants of External Finance' (1997) 52 *Journal of Finance* 1131.
—— 'Law and Finance' (1998) 106(6) *Journal of Political Economy* 1113.
—— 'Corporate Ownership around the World' (1999) 64 *Journal of Finance* 471.
—— 'The New Comparative Economics' (2003) 31 *Journal of Comparative Economics* 595.
—— 'What Works in Securities Laws?' (2006) 61 *Journal of Finance* 1.
—— 'The Economic Consequences of Legal Origins' (2008) 46 *Journal of Economic Literature* 285.
Lane, PR et al, 'International Financial Integration in the Aftermath of the Global Financial Crisis' (2017), *IMF Working Paper WP/17/115*.
Lawton, P, 'Berle and Means, Corporate Governance and the Chinese Family Firm' (1996) 6 *Australian Journal of Corporate Law* 348.
—— 'Modeling the Chinese Family Firm and Minority Shareholder Protection: The Hong Kong Experience 1980–1995' (2007) 49 *Managerial Law* 249.
Li, S and Chen, Q, 'Do the Shanghai–Hong Kong & Shenzhen–Hong Kong Stock Connect programs enhance co-movement between the Mainland Chinese, Hong Kong, and U.S. stock markets?' (2020) 26 *International Journal of Financial & Economics* 2871.
—— 'Do the Shanghai–Hong Kong & Shenzhen–Hong Kong Stock Connect Programmes Enhance Comovement between the Mainland Chinese, Hong Kong, and US Stock Markets?' (2021) 26 *International Journal of Finance & Economics* 2871.
Licht, AN, 'Cross-Listing and Corporate Governance: Bonding or Avoiding?' (2003) 4(1) *Chicago Journal of International Law* 141.
Liebman, B and Milhaupt, C, 'Reputational Sanctions in China's Securities Market' (2008) 108(4) *Columbia Law Review* 929
Liu, JH, 'Qianghua Ziben Shichang Chengxin Jianshe de Ruogan Sikao' ('Some Thoughts on Enhancing Credibility in the Capital Market') (2012) 2 *Securities Law Review* 649.
Lu, L, 'PRC Securities Law 2020: Promoting More Efficient and Transparent Capital Markets in China' (2021) 36 *Journal of International Banking and Financial Law* 237.
Lu, LR and Ye, NY, 'Shanghai-London Stock Connect: Operating Mechanism, Opportunities, and Challenges' (2019) 34 *Journal of International Banking and Financial Law* 684
Ma, RF et al, 'Does Shanghai-Hong Kong Stock Connect Drive Market Comovement between Shanghai and Hong Kong: A New Evidence' (2019) 50 *North American Journal of Economics and Finance* 1.
Macey, JR and Haddock, DD, 'Shirking at the SEC: The Failure of The National Market System' (1985) *University of Illinois Law Review* 315.
MacNeil, I and Lau, A, 'International Corporate Regulation: Listing Rules and Overseas Companies' (2001) 50 *International and Comparative Law Quarterly* 787.
Madhavan, A, 'Consolidation, Fragmentation, and the Disclosure of Trading Information' (1995) 8(3) *Review of Financial Studies* 579.
Mahoney, P, 'Mandatory Disclosure as a Solution to Agency Problems' (1995) 62 *The University of Chicago Law Review* 1047.
McNamara, S, 'The Stock Exchange as Multi-sided Platform and the Future of the National Market System' (2018) 5 *Brigham Young University Law Review* 969.
McVea, H, 'What's Wrong with Insider Dealing' (1995) 15 *Legal Studies* 390.
Meier-Schatz, C and Larsen, K, 'Swiss Securities Regulation and Capital Market Law: A Comprehensive Overview' (1990) 18 *Denver Journal International Law and Policy* 417.
de Meijer, C and Saaf, M, 'Mutual Recognition and the Transatlantic Dialogue: The Concept and its Progress' (2010) 3 *Journal of Securities Law, Regulation and Compliance* 124.
Meng, Y et al, 'The Effect of Overseas Investors on Local Market Efficiency: Evidence from the Shanghai/Shenzhen-Hong Kong Stock Connect' (2023) 9 *Financial Innovation* 42.
Mezzanotte, F, 'The Unconvincing Rise of the Statutory Derivative Action in Hong Kong: Evidence from its 10 Years of Enforcement' (2017) 17 *Journal of Corporate Law Studies* 469.

Nyakurukwa, K and Seetharam, Y, 'Stock Market Integration in Africa: Further Evidence from an Information-Theoretic Framework' (2023) 26(1) *International Finance* 2.

O'Hara, M and Ye, M, 'Is Market Fragmentation Harming Market Quality?' (2011) 100 *Journal of Financial Economics* 459.

Pavlovich, A, '"Reasonable Offers" as a Defence to Unfair Prejudice Petitions: Prescott v Potamianos' (2020) 83 *Modern Law Review* 443.

Petrella, G, 'MiFID, Reg NMS and Competition across Trading Venues in Europe and the USA' (2010) 18(3) *Journal of Financial Regulation and Compliance* 257.

Pistor, K, 'Rethinking the 'Law and Finance' Paradigm' (2009) *BYU Law Review* 1647.

Poser, NS, 'Restructuring the Stock Markets: A Critical Look at the SEC's National Market System' (1981) 56 *New York University Law Review* 883.

Raju, GA and Pavto, VS, 'Stock Market Integration: A Review of Literature from a Global Perspective' (2019) 25 (3) *Journal of Applied Finance* 66.

Roe, M, 'Legal Origins, Politics and Modern Stock Markets' (2006) 120 *Harvard Law Review* 460.

Rose, A, 'Reforming Securities Litigation Reform: Restructuring the Relationship between Public and Private Enforcement of Rule 10B-5' (2008) 108(6) *Columbia Law Review* 1301.

Rose, AD and Spiegel, MM, 'A Gravity Model of Sovereign Lending: Trade, Default, and Credit' (2004) *IMF Staff Papers, special issue vol 51.*

Schenk, C, 'Banks and the Emergence of Hong Kong as an International Financial Centre' (2002) *Journal of International Financial Markets, Institutions and Money* 321.

Sharma, A and Seth, N, 'Literature Review of Stock Market Integration: A Global Perspective' (2012) 4(1) *Qualitative Research in Financial Markets* 84.

Shi, CX, 'Protection Investors in China Through Multiple Regulatory Mechanisms and Effective Enforcement' (2007) 24(2) *Arizona Journal of International & Comparative* Law 451.

Shi, J et al, 'An Empirical Study on the Linkage and Causality between Stock Markets of Mainland and Hong Kong before and after American Financial Crisis' (2011) 26(2) *Statistics & Information Forum* 42.

Siems, M, 'Legal Origins: Reconciling Law & Finance and Comparative Law' (2007) 52 *McGill Law Journal* 55.

—— 'CBR Extended Shareholder Protection Index', 2nd edn (January 2016), available at: www.repository.cam.ac.uk/bitstream/handle/1810/256566/cbr-spi-30-countries-codebook-and-methodology.pdf?sequence=9&isAllowed=y (accessed 1 February 2023).

Silvers, R, 'Cross-Border Cooperation Between Securities Regulators' (2020) 69 *Journal of Accounting and Economics* 1.

Smith, C, 'The Early History of the London Stock Exchange' (1929) 19 *American Economic Review* 206.

Soumaré, I, 'Innovations in Equity and Stock Market Financing' (2020) Background Paper for Economic Report on Africa 2020, UNECA.

Soumaré, I et al, 'Capital Market Development in Sub-Saharan Africa: Progress, Challenges and Innovations' (May 2021) *Working Paper 2*, The ODI Research Series for Financial Development in Africa, 7.

Stiglitz, JE, 'Capital Market Liberalization, Economic Growth, and Instability' (2000) 28 *World Development* 1075.

Stoll, HR, 'Market fragmentation' (2001) 56 *Financial Analysts Journal* 16.

—— 'Future of Securities Markets: Consolidation or Competition?' (2008) 64(6) *Financial Analysts Journal* 15.

Strudler, A and Orts, E, 'Moral Principle in the Law of Insider Trading' (1999–2000) 78 *Texas Law Review* 375.

Stulz, R, 'Globalization, Corporate Finance, and the Cost of Capital' (1999) 12 *Journal of Applied Corporate Finance* 8

Su, Q et al, 'On the Convergence of the Chinese and Hong Kong Stock Markets: A Conintegration Analysis of the A and H Shares' (2007) 17 *Applied Financial Economics* 1349.

Tafara, E and Peterson, R, 'A Blueprint for Cross-Border Access to US Investors: A New International Framework' (2007) 48 *Harvard International Law Journal* 31.

Tam, OK, 'Capital Market Development in China' (1991) 19(5) *World Development* 511.
Torbert, P, 'Broadening the Scope of Investment' (1994) 21 *China Business Review* 48.
Ventoruzzo, M, 'Comparing Insider Trading in the United States and in the European Union: History and Recent Developments' (2014) 11 *European Company and Financial Law Review* 554.
Verdier, PH, 'Mutual Recognition in International Finance' (2011) 52(1) *Harvard International Law Journal* 52.
Wan, WY et al, 'Public and Private Enforcement of Corporate and Securities Laws: An Empirical Comparison of Hong Kong and Singapore' (2019) 20(2) *European Business Organisation Law Review* 319.
Wang, JY, 'Regulatory Competition and Co-operation between Securities Markets in Hong Kong and Mainland China' (2009) 4 *Capital Markets Law Journal* 383.
Wang, L, 'Who Moves East Asian Stock Markets? The Role of the 2007-2009 Global Financial Crisis' (2014) 28 *International Financial Markets, Institutions and Money* 182.
Wang, YC et al, 'The Influence of Shanghai-Hong Kong Stock Connect on the Mainland China and Hong Kong Stock Markets' (2016) 10(3) *International Journal of Business and Finance Research* 1.
Wang, Z et al, 'Financial Crisis and African Stock Market Integration' (2003) 10 *Applied Economics Letters* 527.
Weng, C, 'Who is an Insider? A Case Study on Chinese Insider Trading Enforcement Principles' (2014) 22 *Asia Pacific Law Review* 85.
Werner, W, 'The SEC as Market Regulator' (1984) 70 (4) *Virginia Law Review* 775.
Wurgler, J, 'Financial Markets and the Allocation of Capital' (2000) 58 *Journal of Financial Economics* 187.
Wu, M and Ohk, KY, 'Who Benefits More? Shanghai-Hong Kong Stock Connect – "Through Train"' (2023) 84 *International Review of Economics and Finance* 409.
Xu, WM, et al, 'An Empirical Analysis of the Public Enforcement of Securities Law in China: Finding the Missing Piece to the Puzzle' (2017) 18(2) *European Business Organisation Law Review* 367.
Xu, WM and Xu, GD, 'Understanding Public Enforcement of Securities Law in China: An Empirical Analysis of the Enforcement Actions of the CSRC and its Regional Offices Against Informational Misconduct' (2020) 61 *International Review of Law and Economics* 1.
Yabara, M, 'Capital Market Integration: Progress Ahead of the East African Community Monetary Union' (2012) *IMF Working Paper, WP/12/18.*
Yang, S and Shi, Q, 'Eyi Zuokong de Shengcheng Luoji Falu Guizhi (The Logic and Regulation of "Malicious Short Selling)' [2017] *Jingji Fa Yanjiu* (*Studies on Economic Law*) 68.
Yeung, H and Huang, F, '"One Country, Two Systems" as Bedrock of Hong Kong's Continued Success: Fiction or Reality?' (2015) 38(2) *Boston College International & Comparative Law Review* 191.
—— 'The Rise of Distinct Common Law Commercial Zones in Islamic Countries' (December 2019) Law and Development Conference, Dubai, UAE.
Yu, JS and Hassan, MK, 'Global and Regional Integration of the Middle East and North African (MENA) Stock Markets' (2008) 48(3) *Quarterly Review of Economics and Finance* 482.
Zaring, D, 'International institutional Performance in Crisis' (2010) 10(2) *Chicago Journal of International Law* 475.
Zeng, JS, 'The Faces of Securities Regulation and State Authority: A Comparison between the United States and China' (2022), *Chinese University of Hong Kong Faculty of Law Research Paper No 2022-16.*
Zhang, XC, 'The Old Problems, The New Law, and the Developing market – A Preliminary Examination of the First Securities Law of the People's Republic of China' (1999) 33(4) *The International Lawyer* 983.
Zhou, TS, 'Is the CSRC Protecting a "Level Playing Field" in China's Capital Markets: Public Enforcement, Fragmented Authoritarianism and Corporatism' (2015) 15(2) *Journal of Corporate Law Studies* 377.
Zhu, S, 'Civil Litigation Arising from False Statements on China's Securities Market' (2005) 31 *North Carolina Journal of International Law and Commercial Regulation* 377.
Zweigert, K, 'Methodological Problems in Comparative Law' (1972) 7 *Israel Law Review* 465.

Reports

ACMF, 'Implementation Plan to Promote the Development of an Integrated Capital Market to Achieve the Objectives of the AEC Blueprint', available at: www.theacmf.org/images/downloads/pdf/ACMF%20Implementation%20Plan%202009-2015.pdf (accessed on 9 November 2022).

ASIFMA, 'The Through Train: Stock Connect's Impact and Future' (December 2014), available at: www.asifma.org/wp-content/uploads/2018/05/asifma-tr-stock-connect-white-paper.pdf (accessed on 1 December 2022).

Capital Market Aauthority, 'Instructions for Foreign Strategic Investors' Ownership in Listed Companies' (June 2019), available at: cma.org.sa/en/RulesRegulations/Regulations/Documents/Instructions-FSI-Ownership-Listed-Companies-en.pdf.

China Securities Regulatory Commission, *China Capital Markets Development Report* (Beijing, China Financial Publishing, 2008).

CSRC, 'Annual Report 2011', available at: www.csrc.gov.cn/csrc_en/c102063/c1372581/content.shtml (accessed on 20 April 2022).

—— 'CSRC Annual Report 2012', available at: www.csrc.gov.cn/csrc_en/c102063/c1372580/1372580/files/P020130716403852654782.pdf> (accessed on 4 June 2022).

—— 'Annual Report 2019', available at: www.csrc.gov.cn/csrc_en/c102063/c1606308/content.shtml (accessed on 25 April 2022).

—— 'Annual Report 2020', available at: www.csrc.gov.cn/csrc_en/c102063/c1606114/content.shtml (28 February 2022).

—— 'Zhongguo Zhengjianhui 2021 Fazhi Zhengfu Jianshe Qingkuang' CSRC's Construction of a Rule-of-Law Government Report 2021' (8 April 2022), available at: www.csrc.gov.cn/csrc/c100028/c2321617/content.shtml (accessed on 20 April 2022).

EAC, 'Report for an On-spot Assessment on the Challenges of Implementation of the Common Market Protocol along the Northern and Central Corridors by the Committee on Regional Affairs and Conflict Resolution' (November 2012), 8, available at: www.eala.org/documents/view/report-on-common-market-protocol-implementation-challenges-along-the-northe (accessed on 10 November 2022).

EC, 'Review of the Markets in Financial Instruments Directive (MiFID): Frequently Asked Questions', EC MEMO/11/716, 20 October 2011, available at: ec.europa.eu/commission/presscorner/detail/en/MEMO_11_716 (accessed on 20 November 2022).

—— 'Proposal for a Directive of the European Parliament and of the Council on Markets in Financial Instruments, Repealing Directive 2004/39/EC of the European Parliament and of the Council', COM(2011) 656 final, 2011/0298 (COD), 20/10/11, available at: eur-lex.europa.eu/legal-content/EN/TXT/?uri=CELEX:52012AP0406 (accessed on 20 November 2022).

FIA Principal Traders Group, 'Reg NMS: A Retrospective Review & Practical Reforms for Improvement' (17 September 2018), 4, available at: www.fia.org/sites/default/files/2020-02/FIA-PTG-Reg-NMS-A-Retrospective-Review-Practical-Reforms-for-Improvement.pdf (accessed on 25 November 2022).

Freshfields Bruckhaus Deringer, 'Enforcement Trends – 2021 Year in Review and Looking Ahead' (4 March 2022), available at: www.freshfields.com/en-gb/our-thinking/knowledge/briefing/2022/03/hong-kong-regulatory-enforcement-trends/ (accessed on 1 February 2023).

ESMA, 'MiFID II', available at: www.esma.europa.eu/policy-rules/mifid-ii-and-mifir (accessed on 20 November 2022).

—— 'Questions and Answers on MiFID II and MiFIR Investor Protection and Intermediaries Topics', Q1, available at: www.esma.europa.eu/sites/default/files/library/esma35-43-349_mifid_ii_qas_on_investor_protection_topics.pdf (accessed on 22 November 2022).

FCA, 'Enforcement Annual Performance Report 2018/19' (2019), 20, available at: www.fca.org.uk/publication/corporate/annual-report-2018-19-enforcement-performance.pdf (accessed on 25 April 2022).

FSDC, 'Positioning Hong Kong as an International IPO Centre of Choice' (June 2014), *FSDC Paper No 09*, available at: www.fsdc.org.hk/media/jg1hulyd/ipo4-2-final-17-6-2014.pdf (accessed on 10 January 2023).

GCC, 'Steps Have Been Taken to Achieve Economic Citizenship', IX Stock Ownership and Formation of Corporations, available at: www.gcc-sg.org/en-us/CooperationAndAchievements/Achievements/EconomicCooperation/TheGCCCommonMarketandEconomicnationality/Stepshavebeentakentoachieveeconomiccitizenship/Pages/IXStockOwnershipandFormationof.asp (accessed on 20 November 2022).

HKEX, 'Primary Equity Connect-A breakthrough Opportunity for Mainland-Hong Kong Mutual Market Connectivity and RMB Internationalisation' (August 2017), Research paper.

—— 'CES Stock Connect Hong Kong Select 100 Index-A Key Measure of Hong Kong Market Investment under Stock Connect' (November 2017), Research Report, available at: www.hkex.com.hk/-/media/HKEX-Market/News/Research-Reports/HKEx-Research Papers/2017/CES_SCHK100(201711)_e.pdf?la=en (accessed on 12 December 2022).

—— 'Securities Holding System and "See-Through" Market Supervision – International Experience' (January 2020), available at: www.HKEX.com.hk/-/media/HKEX-Market/News/Research-Reports/HKEX-Research-Papers/2020/CCEO_SecHolding_202001_e.pdf?la=en (accessed on 24 February 2022).

—— 'The Connectivity Platform Offered by the HKEX Commodities Market for the Mainland and the World' (March 2020), Research Report, available at: www.hkex.com.hk/-/media/HKEX-Market/News/Research-Reports/HKEx-Research-Papers/2020/CMD_HK_CommConnect_e_202003.pdf (accessed on 21 February 2023).

—— 'Leveraging Hong Kong as an Offshore Renminbi Centre for Advancing Renminbi Internationalisation' (18 March 2021), 1, Research Report.

—— 'HKEX in 2022: Year in Review' (20 December 2022), available at: www.hkex.com.hk/News/News-Release/2022/221220news?sc_lang=en (accessed on 4 January 2023).

—— 'Our Connect Story: A New Chapter Begins' (October 2022), 2–3, available at: www.hkex.com.hk/-/media/HKEX-Market/Mutual-Market/Stock-Connect/Reference-Materials/Resources/HKEX-Connect-Story.pdf (accessed on 3 January 2023).

HM Treasury, 'A New Approach to Financial Regulation: Judgement, Focus and Stability' (July 2010), available at: assets.publishing.service.gov.uk/government/uploads/system/uploads/attachment_data/file/81389/consult_financial_regulation_condoc.pdf (accessed on 30 May 2022).

—— 'Financial Services Future Regulatory Framework Review: Call for Evidence: Regulatory Coordination' (July 2019), available at: assets.publishing.service.gov.uk/government/uploads/system/uploads/attachment_data/file/819025/Future_Regulatory_Framework_Review_Call_for_Evidence.pdf (accessed on 20 March 2022).

—— 'Financial Services Future Regulatory Framework Review: Phase II Consultation' (October 2020), available at: assets.publishing.service.gov.uk/government/uploads/system/uploads/attachment_data/file/927316/141020_Final_Phase_II_Condoc_For_Publication_for_print.pdf (accessed on 20 March 2022).

—— 'Future Regulatory Framework Review: Proposals for Reform' (November 2021), available at: www.gov.uk/government/consultations/future-regulatory-framework-frf-review-proposals-for-reform (accessed on 20 March 2022).

International Finance Corporation, 'IFC Family Business Governance Handbook' (2011), available at: www.ifc.org/wps/wcm/connect/topics_ext_content/ifc_external_corporate_site/ifc+cg/resources/guidelines_reviews+and+case+studies/ifc+family+business+governance+handbook (accessed on 1 February 2023)

IMF, 'PRC: Financial Sector Assessment Program- Detailed Assessment of Observance of the IOSCO Objectives and Principles of Securities Regulation' (2017), available at: www.imf.org/en/Publications/CR/Issues/2017/12/26/Peoples-Republic-of-China-Financial-Sector-Assessment-Program-Detailed-Assessment-of-45517 (accessed on 20 April 2022).

IOSCO, 'Objectives and Principles of Securities Regulation' (May 2017), available at: www.iosco.org/library/pubdocs/pdf/IOSCOPD561.pdf.

—— 'Principles Regarding Cross-Border Supervisory Cooperation: Final Report' (2010), available at www.iosco.org/library/pubdocs/pdf/IOSCOPD322.pdf (accessed on 3 April 2022).

—— 'Market Fragmentation & Cross-border Regulation' (June 2019), available at: www.iosco.org/library/pubdocs/pdf/IOSCOPD629.pdf (accessed on 20 March 2022).

PBOC, '2022 RMB Internationalisation Report' (26 September 2022), available at: www.gov.cn/xinwen/2022-09/24/5711660/files/003e0bd04d4742a5a06869fdc37ea8c8.pdf (accessed on 3 January 2023).

PwC, 'Swiss Corporate Law Reform: The Changes in a Nutshell (2021), available at: www.pwc.ch/en/publications/2021/ch-Swiss_Corporate_Law_Reform.pdf (accessed on 1 February 2023).

SAFE, 'Abolish Restrictions on the Investment Quota of Qualified Foreign Investors (QFII/ RQFII) and Further Expand the Opening up of Financial Markets', 10 September 2019, available at: www.safe.gov.cn/en/2019/0910/1552.html (accessed on 3 August 2021).

SEC, 'Agency Financial Report: Fiscal Year 2020', available at: www.sec.gov/files/sec-2020-agency-financial-report_1.pdf (accessed on 10 April 2022).

—— 'SEC Announces Enforcement Results for FY2021', available at: www.sec.gov/news/press-release/2021-238 (accessed 20 April 2022).

—— 'Emerging Market Investments Entail Significant Disclosure, Financial Reporting and Other Risks, Remedies are Limited' (21 April 2020), available at: www.sec.gov/news/public-statement/emerging-market-investments-disclosure-reporting (accessed on 12 December 2022).

—— 'Statement on Agreement Governing Inspections and Investigations of Audit Firms Based in China and Hong Kong' (26 August 2022), available at: www.sec.gov/news/statement/gensler-audit-firms-china-hong-kong-20220826 (accessed on 12 December 2022).

Singapore Exchange, 'Consultation Paper: Proposed Changes to the SGX-ST Rules and Other Rulebooks' 10 October 2017, paragraph 15.4, available at: api2.sgx.com/sites/default/files/public-consultations/migration/ST%2BRules%2BReview%2BPC.pdf (accessed on 9 November 2022).

Trade and Industry Department of Hong Kong, 'Mainland and Hong Kong Closer Economic Partnership Arrangement', available at: www.tid.gov.hk/english/cepa/cepa_overview.html (accessed on 3 December 2022).

UK government, 'Competition and Innovation in Digital Markets' (2021), BEIS Research Paper Number: 2021/040, 12, available at: assets.publishing.service.gov.uk/government/uploads/system/uploads/attachment_data/file/1003985/uae-ccp-report__1_.pdf (accessed on 20 November 2022).

UNCTAD, 'Investment Policy Hub- Saudi Arabia: Relaxes Ownership Limits for Foreign Investors' (26 June 2019), available at: investmentpolicy.unctad.org/investment-policy-monitor/measures/3415/saudi-arabia-relaxes-ownership-limits-for-foreign-investors (accessed on 25 November 2022).

—— 'Investment Policy Hub- Qatar: New Law Regulating Foreign Investment Allows Up to 100 Percent Foreign Ownership' (7 January 2019), available at: investmentpolicy.unctad.org/investment-policy-monitor/measures/3360/new-law-regulating-foreign-investment-allows-up-to-100-percent-foreign-ownership (accessed on 25 November 2022).

WTO, 'Trade Policy Reviews- Bahrain: October 2000' (13 October 2000), available at: www.wto.org/english/tratop_e/tpr_e/tp139_e.htm (accessed on 20 November 2022).

Z/Yen, 'The Global Financial Centre Index 32' (September 2022), available at: www.longfinance.net/media/documents/GFCI_32_Report_2022.09.22_v1.0_.pdf (accessed on 15 December 2022).

News

Atkins, P, 'Speech by SEC Commissioner: Enhancement and Modernisation of the National Market System', April 2005, available at: www.sec.gov/news/speech/spch040605psa.htm (accessed on 20 August 2021).

BBC, 'UK–China Stocks Link Plan Unveiled' (22 September 2015), available at: www.bbc.co.uk/news/business-34322446 (accessed on 11 April 2023).

—— 'UK to Launch Ground-Breaking China Stock Market Link' (17 June 2019), www.bbc.co.uk/news/business-48658844 (accessed on 12 December 2022).

Bloomberg, 'China Fines Repeat Offender $170 Million for Stock Manipulation' (13 March 2017), available at: www.bloomberg.com/news/articles/2017-03-13/china-fines-trader-170-million-makes-first-stock-link-penalty (accessed on 25 April 2022).

Burgess, K, 'London Stock Exchange Clamps Down on Aim-Quoted Chinese Companies' (*Financial Times*, 9 October 2015), available at: www.ft.com/content/0eee474a-6e8f-11e5-aca9-d87542bf8673 (accessed 20 April 2022).

CFA Institute Research Foundation, 'Middle East Capital Markets: Challenges and Opportunities' (2022), xiii, available at: www.cfainstitute.org/-/media/documents/article/rf-brief/rfbr-middle-east-capital-markets.pdf (accessed on 22 November 2022).

China Briefing, 'China Stock Connect: Expanding the Shanghai-London Programme to Germany and Switzerland' (5 January 2022), available at: www.china-briefing.com/news/china-stock-connect-expanding-shanghai-london-program-to-germany-switzerland/ (accessed on 4 January 2023).

—— 'Mainland China and Hong Kong to Expand their Stock Connect Scheme' (23 December 2022), available at: www.china-briefing.com/news/mainland-china-and-hong-kong-to-expand-their-stock-connect-scheme/ (accessed on 3 January 2023).

China's Government, 'Decision of the Central Committee of the Communist Party of China on Some Major Issues Concerning Comprehensively Deepening the Reform' is available at: www.china.org.cn/china/third_plenary_session/2014-01/16/content_31212602.htm (accessed on 6 August 2021).

—— 'We Will Give Policy Support to Small and Medium-sized Enterprises' (1 April 2021), available at: www.gov.cn/zhengce/2020-04/01/content_5497938.htm (accessed on 6 January 2022).

China's State Council, 'RMB Assets Show Growing Appeal for Global Investors' (7 June 2022), available at: english.www.gov.cn/news/topnews/202206/07/content_WS629f46d8c6d02e533532bd04.html (accessed on 12 December 2022).

Clayton, J, SEC Chairman, 'Remarks to the Economic Club of New York' (9 September 2019), available at: www.sec.gov/news/speech/speech-clayton-2019-09-09 (accessed on 25 August 2022).

Cohn, C and Hirt, O, 'China Pacific Insurance to Press on With London Listing Under Connect Scheme' (*Reuters*, 2 June 2020), available at: www.reuters.com/article/cpic-listing-london-idUSL8N2DF47Y (accessed on 2 January 2023).

Crenshaw, C, SEC Commissioner, 'Statement on Proposals related to Equity Market Structure' (14 December 2022), available at: www.sec.gov/news/statement/crenshaw-insider-trading-20221214-0 (accessed on 20 December 2022).

CSRC, 'FAQ on Beneficial Ownership' (15 May 2015), available at: www.csrc.gov.cn/csrc_en/c102035/c1371508/content.shtml (accessed on 10 January 2023).

—— 'Q&A regarding Certain Provisions on Stock Connect between the Mainland and Hong Kong Stock Markets' (27 October 2016), available at: www.csrc.gov.cn/csrc_en/c102035/c1371506/content.shtml (accessed on 10 January 2023).

—— 'Revision Notes on the Provisions on the Supervision and Administration of Depository Receipts under the Stock Connect between Domestic and Overseas Stock Exchanges' (11 February 2022), available at www.csrc.gov.cn/csrc_en/c102034/c1885832/content.shtml (accessed on 12 December 2022).

—— 'Joint Announcement of the China Securities Regulatory Commission and the Hong Kong Securities and Futures Commission' (27 May 2022), available at: www.csrc.gov.cn/csrc_en/c102030/c3046291/content.shtml (accessed on 3 January 2023).

—— 'China-Switzerland Stock Connect Officially Launched' (28 July 2022), available at: www.csrc.gov.cn/csrc_en/c102030/c4885446/content.shtml (accessed on 12 December 2022).

—— 'CSRC Entrusts Shanghai and Shenzhen Stock Exchanges to Conduct Case Investigation' (9 January 2015), available at: www.gov.cn/gongbao/content/2015/content_2818466.htm (accessed on 20 April 2022).

—— 'Zhongguo Zhengjianhui he Xianggang Zhengjianhui Juxing Disici Liangdi Zhifahezuo Gongzuohuiyi' (CSRC and SFC's Fourth Enforcement and Cooperation Meeting) (30 June 2017), available at: www.gov.cn/xinwen/2017-06/30/content_5207057.htm (accessed on 25 April 2022).

—— 'Zhengjianhui Chahuo Yiqi Liyong Hugangtong Zhanghu Kuajing Caozong Shichang Anjian' (CSRC Seizes a Case of Cross-Border Market Manipulation Using Shanghai-Hong Kong Stock Connect Accounts) (18 May 2018), available at: www.csrc.gov.cn/csrc/c100200/c1000477/content.shtml (accessed on 1 June 2022).

—— 'Q&A on Further Opening Up the Capital Market' (17 June 2019), available at: www.csrc.gov.cn/csrc_en/c102035/c1371505/content.shtml (accessed on 20 February 2023).

—— 'Capital Markets Connectivity: Opportunities and Challenges' (August 2019), available at: www.carecprogram.org/uploads/Capital-Markets-Connectivity-Opportunities-and-Challenges-Developments-in-China.pdf (accessed on 20 February 2023).

CSRC and SFC, 'Joint Announcement of the China Securities Regulatory Commission and the Securities and Futures Commission' (16 August 2016), available at: apps.sfc.hk/edistributionWeb/gateway/EN/news-and-announcements/news/doc?refNo=16PR80 (accessed on 2 December 2020).

Donaldson, W, former Chairman of SEC, 'Speech by SEC Chairman: Opening Statement at Commission Opening Meeting) (21 April 2004), available at: www.sec.gov/news/speech/spch042104whd.htm (accessed on 25 November 2022).

EAC, 'EAC Reviews Common Market Protocol Ahead of DRC Entry' (20 March 2022), available at: www.theeastafrican.co.ke/tea/news/east-africa/eac-reviews-common-market-protocol-ahead-of-drc-entry-3753502 (accessed on 10 November 2022).

EC, 'Markets in Financial Instruments Directive (MiFID II): Frequently Asked Questions' (15 April 2014), available at: ec.europa.eu/commission/presscorner/detail/en/MEMO_14_305 (accessed on 20 November 2022).

FCA, 'The Shanghai-London Stock Connect: A Joint Announcement by the China Securities Regulatory Commission and the UK Financial Conduct Authority' (17 June 2019), available at: www.fca.org.uk/publication/mou/joint-announcement-fca-csrc.pdf (accessed on 20 June 2022).

Financial Times, 'The End of One Country, Two Systems in Hong Kong' (1 July 2020), available at: www.ft.com/content/5d3d7d2e-bba8-11ea-a05d-efc604854c3f (accessed on 25 April 2022).

Fioretti, J, 'Launch of Shanghai-London Stock Link Stalled amid Doubts on Demand' (*Reuters*, 20 December 2018), available at: uk.reuters.com/article/uk-china-listings-analysis/launch-of-shanghai-london-stock-link-stalled-amid-doubts-on-demand-idUKKCN1OJ00B (accessed on 3 January 2023).

FTSE Russell, 'FTSE Russell Completes Landmark Inclusion of China A Shares' (22 June 2020), available at: www.ftserussell.com/press/ftse-russell-completes-landmark-inclusion-china-shares (accessed on 12 December 2022).

GCC, 'Joint Action Process- the Economic Agreement 2001', available at: www.gcc-sg.org/en-us/CooperationAndAchievements/Achievements/EconomicCooperation/JointActionProcess/Pages/TheEconomicAgreement2001.aspx (accessed on 22 November 2022).

Ghanaian German Economic Association, 'West Africa Stock Exchanges Integration Implementation Likely This Year – GSE MD' (14 February 2020), available at: ggea.net/news/west-africa-stock-exchanges-integration-implementation-likely-this-year-gse-md/ (accessed on 10 November 2020).

Glassman, CA and Atkins, PS (SEC Commissioners), 'Dissent to the Adoption of Regulation NMS' (9 June 2005), available at: www.sec.gov/rules/final/34-51808-dissent.pdf (accessed on 25 November 2022).

Gopalan, N, 'London's Shanghai Dream is a Bridge to Nowhere' (*Bloomberg*, 13 April 2018), available at: www.bloomberg.com/opinion/articles/2018-04-13/london-s-shanghai-stock-connect-dream-is-a-bridge-to-nowhere (accessed on 3 January 2023).

HKEX, 'HKEX to Introduce HKD-RMB Dual Counter Model and Dual Counter Market Making Programme in Hong Kong Securities Market' (13 December 2022), available at: www.hkex.com.hk/News/News-Release/2022/221213news?sc_lang=en (accessed on 3 January 2023).

HKMA, 'Enhanced Currency Swap Agreement between People's Bank of China and Hong Kong Monetary Authority' (4 July 2022), press release, available at: www.hkma.gov.hk/eng/news-and-media/press-releases/2022/07/20220704-5/ (accessed on 1 December 2022).

Guardian, 'MPs Call for Overhaul of China Policy After UK Suspends Hong Kong Extraditions' (20 July 2020), available at: www.theguardian.com/world/2020/jul/20/uk-risks-chinas-wrath-by-suspending-hong-kong-extradition-treaty (accessed on 20 June 2022).

Global Legal Insights, 'Banking Laws and Regulations 2022/Switzerland', available at: www.globallegalinsights.com/practice-areas/banking-and-finance-laws-and-regulations/switzerland (accessed on 30 May 2022).

HKEX, 'Four-Party Agreement for Shanghai-Hong Kong Stock Connect Signed' is available at: www.HKEX.com.hk/News/News-Release/2014/1409042news?sc_lang=en (accessed on 22 November 2020).

—— 'HKEX Comments on Stock Connect Daily Quota Expansion' (11 April 2018), available at: www.HKEX.com.hk/News/News-Release/2018/180411news?sc_lang=en (accessed on 2 December 2020).

—— 'Hong Kong's Listing Regime Enters New Era, Featuring Emerging and Innovative Firms' (24 April 2018), available at: www.hkex.com.hk/News/RegulatoryAnnouncements/2018/180424news?sc_lang=en (accessed on 10 January 2023).

—— 'Celebrating the 3rd Anniversary of HKEX's new Listing Regime' (15 June 2021), available at: www.hkex.com.hk/News/Media-Centre/Special/HKEX-Celebrates-Third-Anniversary-of-New-Listing-Regime?sc_lang=en (accessed on 20 December 2022).

—— 'HKEX Welcomes Public Consultation by SSE and SZSE on WVR-Related Rules Changes) (2 August 2019), available at: www.hkex.com.hk/News/News-Release/2019/1908022news?sc_lang=en (accessed on 20 December 2022).

—— 'HKEX to Include ETFs in Stock Connect on 4 July' (28 June 2022), available at: www.hkex.com.hk/News/News-Release/2022/220628news?sc_lang=en (28 December 2022).

—— 'HKEX Welcomes Further Expansion of Stock Connect' (19 December 2022), available at: www.hkex.com.hk/News/News-Release/2022/2212192news?sc_lang=en (accessed on 2 January 2023).

—— 'Stock Connect – Towards A 'Mutual Market' for the Interests of Mainland and Global Investors' (November 2016), 12, available at: www.hkex.com.hk/-/media/HKEX-Market/News/Research-Reports/HKEx-Research-Papers/2016/CCEO_Rpt(StkConnect)_201611.pdf?la=en (accessed on 12 December 2022).

—— 'We are a World Leading IPO Venue', available at: www.hkex.com.hk/Join-Our-Market/IPO/Listing-with-HKEX?sc_lang=en (accessed on 3 January 2023).

HKMA, 'Hong Kong as offshore Renminbi Centre-Past and Prospects' (18 February 2014), available at: www.hkma.gov.hk/eng/news-and-media/insight/2014/02/20140218/ (accessed on 3 January 2023).

HKSAR Press Release, 'LCQ12: Real-time Investor Identification System for Northbound Cross-boundary Stock Trading' (29 November 2017), available at: www.info.gov.hk/gia/general/201711/29/P2017112800785.htm (accessed on 24 February 2022).

—— 'Chapter 3 The Three-Tiered Regulatory Framework for the Securities and Futures Industry', available at: www.info.gov.hk/info/pennystock/chapter3.pdf (accessed on 28 February 2022).

Johnson, K, 'US Securities Regulator Warns Investors over Chinese Company Disclosures (*Reuters*, 22 April 2020), available at: www.reuters.com/article/us-health-coronavirus-sec-china-idUSKCN2242A1 (accessed on 20 June 2022).

KPMG, 'Hong Kong is Set to Regain Top-three IPO Ranking in 2022' (8 December 2022), available at: home.kpmg/cn/en/home/media/press-releases/2022/12/hong-kong-is-set-to-regain-top-three-ipo-ranking-in-2022-says-kpmg-china.html (accessed on 5 January 2023).

Leng, C, 'Hong Kong and Mainland China to Expand Stock Connect Scheme' (*Financial Times*, 20 December 2022), available at: www.ft.com/content/8983e7fe-3e88-4fc1-9e13-46add87ff9c2 (accessed on 2 January 2023).

Li, XY, 'New Connection' (*Beijing Review*, 24 June 2019), available at: www.bjreview.com/Business/201906/t20190624_800171443.html (accessed on 25 April 2021).

LSE, 'Shanghai-London Stock Connect welcomes its first issuer: Huatai Securities' (17 June 2019), available at: www.lseg.com/en/media-centre/press-releases/2019/shanghai-london-stock-connect-welcomes-its-first-issuer-huatai-securities (accessed on 5 January 2023).

Lo, A, 'One Country, Two Systems Healthier Than Ever' (*South China Morning Post*, 17 September 2021), available at: www.scmp.com/comment/opinion/article/3149181/one-country-two-systems-healthier-ever (accessed on 25 April 2022).

Monetary Authority of Singapore, 'Malaysia and Singapore to Set Up Stock Market Trading Link' (2 February 2018), available at: www.mas.gov.sg/news/media-releases/2018/malaysia-and-singapore-to-set-up-stock-market-trading-link (accessed on 6 November 2022).

Mccrank, J, 'US SEC Votes to Advance Stock Market Overhaul Proposals' (*Reuters*, 14 December 2022), available at: www.reuters.com/markets/us/us-sec-vote-proposal-overhaul-stock-market-rules-2022-12-14/ (accessed on 20 December 2022).

McMorrow, R et al, 'China's Didi to delist from New York and switch to Hong Kong', (*Financial Times*, 3 December 2021), available at: www.ft.com/content/c30cf911-51da-4b40-a969-161351de6f04 (accessed on 5 January 2022).

Ping, CK and Osipovich, A, 'NYSE to Delist Chinese Telecom Carriers After Rejecting Appeals' (Wall Street Journal, 7 May 2021), available at: www.wsj.com/articles/nyse-to-delist-chinese-telecoms-carriers-afterrejecting-appeals-11620394719 (accessed on 5 January 2022).

Reuters, 'Update 1- China Bank Signals Resumption of RQDII Outbound Investment Scheme' (3 May 2018), available at: www.reuters.com/article/china-investment-rqdii-idINB9N1S000Q (accessed on 12 December 2022).

SEC, 'Reg NMS', available at: www.sec.gov/rules/final/34-51808.pdf (accessed on 20 August 2022).

—— 'SEC Adopts Rules to Modernise Key Market Infrastructure Responsible for Collecting, Consolidating, and Disseminating Equity Market Data', Press Release on 9 December 2020, available at: www.sec.gov/news/press-release/2020-311 (accessed 25 August 2022).

SFC, 'Speech at 7th Pan Asian Regulatory Summit" by Mr Thomas Atkinson, Executive Director, Enforcement (9 November 2016), available at: www.sfc.hk/-/media/EN/files/ER/PDF/Speeches/Atkinson_20161109.pdf (accessed on 1 June 2022).

—— 'Signing of Tri-partite MoU on Audit Working Papers by Ministry of Finance, CSRC and SFC' (3 July 2019), available at: apps.sfc.hk/edistributionWeb/gateway/EN/news-and-announcements/news/doc?refNo=19PR61 (accessed on 25 April 2022).

—— 'Joint announcement of the China Securities Regulatory Commission and the Hong Kong Securities and Futures Commission' (19 December 2022), available at: www.sfc.hk/en/News-and-announcements/Policy-statements-and-announcements/Joint-announcement-of-the-CSRC-and-SFC-Dec-2022> (accessed on 3 January 2023).

Shen, S and Galbraith, A, 'China Constricts Capital Outflows with Eye on Yuan Stability' (*Reuters*, 11 October 2018), available at: www.reuters.com/article/us-china-markets-soft-landing-analysis/china-constricts-capital-outflows-with-eye-on-yuan-stability-idUSKCN1ML1SW (accessed on 3 January 2023).

Shen, S and Woo, R, 'China to Push on with Opening Capital Markets to Foreign Investors' (*Reuters*, 6 September 2021), available at: www.reuters.com/world/china/china-will-improve-opening-up-capital-market-securities-regulator-2021-09-06/ (accessed on 20 February 2023).

SIX Swiss Exchange, 'SIX and Shenzhen Stock Exchange Sign a Memorandum of Understanding' (10 October 2019), available at: www.six-group.com/en/newsroom/media-releases/2019/20191010-szse-six-mou.html (accessed on 1 August 2022).

South China Morning Post, 'Britain and China Promise to Speed Up Work on London-Shanghai Stock Connect' (16 December 2017), available at: www.scmp.com/news/china/diplomacy/article/2124601/britain-and-china-promise-speed-work-london-shanghai-stock (accessed on 21 June 2021).

SZSE, 'SZSE Releases Rules on Shenzhen-Hong Kong Stock Connect Programme' (12 October 2016), available at: www.szse.cn/enSzhk/introduction/news/t20161013_558113.html (accessed on 30 November 2020).

—— 'Q&A on the Expansion of Scope of Underlying Stocks Eligible for Trading Under Chinese Mainland-Hong Kong Stock Connect Mechanisms' (21 December 2022), available at: www.szse.cn/English/about/news/szse/t20221221_597925.html (accessed on 3 January 2023).

Sun, SW, 'Securities Law Giving overwhelming Approval' (*China Daily*, 30 December 1998).

The Star, 'Trading Link with SGX Not Priority Now, Says Bursa CEO' (4 February 2022), available at: www.thestar.com.my/business/business-news/2022/02/04/trading-link-with-sgx-not-priority-now-says-bursa-ceo (accessed on 6 November 2022).

Tung, R, 'Taiwan Stock Connect Link with Singapore May be Ready Near Year End' (*Reuters*, 19 March 2015), available at: www.reuters.com/article/taiwan-markets-singpaore-idUSL3N0WL1JS20150319 (accessed 20 February 2023).

Walder Wyss, 'Shareholders' Rights & Shareholder Activism' (2019), available at: www.walderwyss.com/user_assets/publications/019_SWITZERLAND-LP.pdf (accessed 1 February 2023).

Ward, O, 'The Missed Opportunity of the ASEAN Trade Link' (*ASEAN Today*, 21 October 2017), available at: www.aseantoday.com/2017/10/the-missed-opportunity-of-the-asean-trade-link/ (accessed on 9 November 2022).

Wei, S, 'What Shanghai-London Connect Means for European Investors' (ATC Initiative, 22 June 2020), available at: www.atcinitiative.org/what-shanghai-london-stock-connect-means-for-european-investors (accessed on 12 December 2022).

Xinhua News Agency, 'Full text of Chinese President Xi Jinping's remarks at Global Trade in Services Summit of 2021 China International Fair for Trade in Services' (*China Daily*, 2 September 2021), available at: www.chinadaily.com.cn/a/202109/02/WS6130dc6ea310efa1bd66cfc1.html (accessed on 31 December 2021).

Yiu, E, 'Singapore to establish ETF link with Shenzhen, joining Hong Kong, London in tie-ups with Chinese exchanges' (South China Morning Post, 29 December 2021), available at: www.scmp.com/business/banking-finance/article/3161389/singapore-establish-etf-link-shenzhen-joining-hong-kong (accessed on 21 February 2023).

Yu, X, 'China Resumes Outbound Investment Scheme but With Tighter Controls' (*South China Morning Post*, 3 May 2018), available at: www.scmp.com/business/global-economy/article/2144575/china-resumes-outbound-investment-scheme-tighter-controls (accessed on 4 August 2021).

—— 'Questions Remain as Countdown Begins on Depositary Receipts with Chinese Characteristics' (*South China Morning Post*, 19 June 2018), available at: www.scmp.com/business/companies/article/2151293/questions-remain-countdown-begins-depositary-receipts-chinese (accessed on 12 December 2022).

Zhang, XC and Galbraith, A, 'China Regulator Denies Report of Halt to Shanghai-London Stock Connect Listings' (*Reuters*, 3 January 2020), available at: www.reuters.com/article/us-china-markets-regulator/china-regulator-denies-report-of-halt-to-shanghai-london-stock-connect-listings-idUSKBN1Z20U5 (accessed 2 January 2023

Zhen, W, 'Emerging Markets Since China a Shares' Inclusion' (5 December 2019), available on the MSCI's website: www.msci.com/www/blog-posts/emerging-markets-since-china-a/01662775315 (accessed on 2 December 2020).

The Websites of International Organisations and Governments

ACMF, 'About ACMF', available at: www.theacmf.org/about/about-acmf (accessed on 9 November 2022).

—— 'Framework for Cross-Border offering of ASEAN Collective Investment Schemes', available at: www.theacmf.org/initiatives/collective-investment-schemes/framework-for-cross-border-offering-of-asean-collective-investment-schemes (accessed on 6 November 2022).

AfCFTA, 'About the AfCFTA', available at: au-afcfta.org/about/ (accessed on 12 November 2022).

ASEAN Exchange's website, www.aseanexchanges.org/#/AboutUs (accessed on 9 November 2022).

Bourse Régionale des Valeurs Mobilières (Regional Stock Exchange), 'WACMIC', available at: www.brvm.org/en/wacmic (accessed on 25 November 2022).

Credit Suisse, 'Switzerland: A Financial Market History' (2017), available at: www.credit-suisse.com/about-us/en/reports-research/studies-publications.html (accessed 1 February 2023).

CSRC, 'The overview of the CSRC', available at: www.csrc.gov.cn/csrc_en/c102023/common_zcnr.shtml?channelid=e9958c689bef4d468d81dc93c8d3479f (accessed on 10 April 2022).

EAC, 'Capital Markets infrastructure Adding Value to East Africans', available at: www.eac.int/financial/capital-markets-infrastructure (accessed on 10 November 2022).

FINMA, 'National and International Cooperation', available at: www.finma.ch/en/enforcement/national-and-international-cooperation/ (accessed on 25 April 2022).

—— 'Overview', available at: www.finma.ch/en/finma/finma-an-overview (accessed on 30 May 2022).

HKEX, 'Information Book for Investors' (4 July 2022), Section 2 'Investor and participant Eligibility', available at: www.hkex.com.hk/-/media/HKEX-Market/Mutual-Market/Stock-Connect/Getting-Started/Information-Booklet-and-FAQ/Information-Book-for-Investors/Investor_Book_En.pdf (accessed on 2 January 2023).

—— 'Hong Kong and Mainland Market Highlights', available at: www.hkex.com.hk/Mutual-Market/Stock-Connect/Statistics/Hong-Kong-and-Mainland-Market-Highlights?sc_lang=en#select3=0&select2=0&select1=16 (accessed on 5 January 2023).

—— 'China Dimension', available at: www.hkex.com.hk/Market-Data/Statistics/Consolidated-Reports/China-Dimension?sc_lang=en#select1=0&select2=2 (accessed on 5 January 2023).

Hong Kong Institute of Chartered Secretaries, 'Company Law Guidance Note' (November 2017), available at: www.hkcgi.org.hk/media/publication/attachment/PUBLICATION_A_2406_HKICS_Company_Law_Guidance_Note%20(Eng).pdf.pdf (accessed on 1 February 2023)

HKSAR, 'Hong Kong: The Facts-Financial Services' (July 2020), available at: www.gov.hk/en/about/abouthk/factsheets/docs/financial_services.pdf (accessed on 28 February 2022).

IMF, 'GDP per Capita', available at: www.imf.org/external/datamapper/NGDPDPC@WEO/OEMDC/ADVEC/WEOWORLD (accessed on 25 November 2022).

Investor and Financial Education Council of Hong Kong, 'Understand Stock Connect', available at: www.ifec.org.hk/web/en/investment/investment-products/stock/stockconnect/understand-stock-connect.page (accessed on 1 February 2023).

LSE, 'Trading through Shanghai-London Stock Connect' available at: www.lseg.com/markets-products-and-services/our-markets/shanghai-london-stock-connect/trading-through-shanghai-london-stock-connect (accessed on 21 June 2022).

—— 'Main Market – Key Eligibility Criteria', available at: docs.londonstockexchange.com/sites/default/files/documents/main-market-key-eligibility-criteria.pdf (accessed on 12 December 2022).

Saudi Exchange, 'Market Summary', available at: www.saudiexchange.sa/wps/portal/tadawul/home/!ut/p/z1/04_Sj9CPykssy0xPLMnMz0vMAfIjo8zijYycLQwtTQx83D39zA0cAx09wtzCQowNDEz1w_Wj9KPwKTGBKjDAARwN9IMTi_QLsrPTHB0VFQEBEmvK/dz/d5/L0lHSkovd0RNQUZrQUVnQSEhLzROVkUvZW4!/ (accessed on 25 November 2022).

SFC, 'Regulatory Objectives', available at: www.sfc.hk/en/About-the-SFC/Our-role/Regulatory-objectives (accessed on 20 June 2022).

SIX Swiss Exchange, 'Regulation of Short Selling as Part of Self-regulation' (10 October 2013), available at: www.six-group.com/dam/download/media/press-releases/2013/1010-e-Short-Selling.pdf (accessed 1 February 2023)

SSE, 'STAR Market', available at: english.sse.com.cn/aboutsse/overview/ (accessed on 7 February 2023).

Switzerland's Federal Department of Finance, 'Switzerland and China Commence Financial Dialogue', available at: www.sif.admin.ch/sif/en/home/dokumentation/medienmitteilungen/medienmitteilungen.msg-id-51238.html (accessed on 1 August 2022).

SZSE, 'Market Overview', available at: www.szse.cn/market/overview/index.html (accessed on 7 February 2023).

The Federal Department of Foreign Affairs of Switzerland (2021), 'China Strategy 2021–24', available at: www.eda.admin.ch/eda/en/fdfa/fdfa/publikationen.html/content/publikationen/en/eda/schweizer-aussenpolitik/China_Strategie_2021-2024.html (accessed on 1 August 2022).

UAE Government Portal, 'Federal Law on Commercial Companies', available at: u.ae/en/information-and-services/business/full-foreign-ownership-of-commercial-companies (accessed on 22 November 2022).

UK Government, 'Chancellor: 'Let's Create a Golden Decade for the UK-China Relationship' (22 September 2015), available at: www.gov.uk/government/speeches/chancellor-lets-create-a-golden-decade-for-the-uk-china-relationship (accessed on 21 June 2021).

—— 'UK Trade with China: 2021', available at: www.ons.gov.uk/economy/nationalaccounts/balanceofpayments/articles/uktradewithchina2021/2022-06-01 (accessed on 20 June 2022).
—— 'Factsheet: 10th UK China Economic and Financial Dialogue: 17 June 2019', available at: assets.publishing.service.gov.uk/government/uploads/system/uploads/attachment_data/file/809590/EFD_Factsheet_FINAL__003_.pdf_1.pdf (accessed on 20 June 2022).
UK Parliament, 'Memorandum Submitted by the London Stock Exchange', Select Committee on Treasury Written Evidence (18 January 2005), available at: publications.parliament.uk/pa/cm200405/cmselect/cmtreasy/314/314we11.htm#n7 (accessed on 5 June 2022).
World Bank, 'Statement on Release of Investigation into Data Irregularities in Doing Business 2018 and 2020' (16 September 2021), available at: www.worldbank.org/en/news/statement/2021/09/16/statement-on-release-of-investigation-into-data-irregularities-in-doing-business-2018-and-2020 (accessed on 1 February 2023).
—— 'Doing Business: About Us', available at: archive.doingbusiness.org/en/about-us (accessed on 1 February 2023).
—— 'Protecting Minority Investors Methodology', available at: archive.doingbusiness.org/en/methodology (accessed on 1 February 2023).
—— 'Doing Business 2020' (2021), available at: www.doingbusiness.org (accessed on 1 February 2023).
World Federation of Exchanges, 'Statistics', available at: www.world-exchanges.org/our-work/statistics (accessed on 10 April 2022).

INDEX

Notes

1. In this index China denotes Mainland China, while Hong Kong or HK denotes the Special Administrative Region of Hong Kong
2. Page numbers in **bold** denote information in tables

www.ingramcontent.com/pod-product-compliance
Ingram Content Group UK Ltd.
Pitfield, Milton Keynes, MK11 3LW, UK
UKHW020249290926
15470UKWH00002B/825

9 781509 949281